THE T  7

THE THEOSOPHICAL SOCIETY
The History of a Spiritualist Movement

Jeffrey D. Lavoie

BrownWalker Press
Boca Raton

The Theosophical Society: The History of a Spiritualist Movement

BrownWalker Press
Boca Raton, Florida • USA
2012

ISBN-10: 1-61233-553-5 *(paper)*
ISBN-13: 978-1-61233-553-7 *(paper)*

ISBN-10: 1-61233-554-3 *(ebook)*
ISBN-13: 978-1-61233-554-4 *(ebook)*

www.brownwalker.com

Library of Congress Cataloging-in-Publication Data

Lavoie, Jeffrey D., 1981-
  The Theosophical Society : the history of a spiritualist movement /
Jeffrey D. Lavoie.
     p. cm.
  Includes bibliographical references and index.
  ISBN-13: 978-1-61233-553-7 (pbk. : alk. paper)
  ISBN-10: 1-61233-553-5 (pbk. : alk. paper)
   1. Theosophy--Relations--Spiritualism. 2. Spiritualism--Relations--
Theosophy. 3. Blavatsky, H. P. (Helena Petrovna), 1831-1891. I.
Title.

BF1275.T5L38 2012
299'.93409--dc23
                                                    2011043045

Acknowledgments

Various friends, colleagues, and academics have played an integral part in the preparation of this manuscript for publication. First, I would like to thank my professors at the University of Exeter- Nicholas Goodrick-Clarke and Hereward Tilton for their help in proofreading and commenting upon sections of this work (though in a much different format). Also, special thanks should be extended towards Paul K. Johnson, Joscelyn Godwin, and Anders Skjerli who examined different parts of this paper and offered their valuable suggestions and insight.

I am also very appreciative of Joe Fulton of the Theosophical Network who was willing to help me in obtaining all of the issues of the *Theosophist* quoted in this paper and additionally for his networking suggestions which have ensured that this project would become an academic contribution to the field of Theosophical studies.

Thanks must also be conveyed to James Santucci the editor of *Theosophical History* for his willingness to share rare booklets and occasional papers of which he allowed me access for this work.

Though a different type of inspiration, I would be remiss if I did not thank the great 'book of Judith scholar' Lawrence Wills at Episcopal Divinity School in Cambridge, MA for all of his valuable advice and guidance both within and outside the classroom, for his continued aid in my academic endeavors, and, of course, for the various lunches we enjoyed together in the Cronkhite Dining Room in Cambridge, MA. It was his inspiration and influence during my graduate studies that prompted me to pursue my current course of study at Exeter University.

Though I acknowledge the hard work and contributions of these above academics, it should be noted that *any errors or mistakes which will inevitably be found in this manuscript remain solely the responsibility of the author.*

A special thanks to the various staffs at all of the libraries I utilized during the writing of this work especially the Andover-Harvard Library and the Widener Library both at Harvard University for allowing me to access their resources for this particular project. Also, I am grateful to the staff at the reference section of the Boston Public Library in Copley Square as well as the American Antiquarian Society in Worcester, MA for their assistance in accessing the rare nineteenth century newspaper articles employed throughout.

Furthermore, on a personal level, I wish to thank my wonderful congregation at Calvary Baptist Church in Hanson, MA (especially my spiritual mentor Reverend Tim Shafer) who have stood by me and supported me in my academic endeavors while providing me with the resources to continue to pursue them.

And of course there are my loving parents Debbie and Dave Lavoie who have played such a critical part in both my personal and academic life and who have instilled in me a work ethic, morality and integrity; without them this book would not and could not be written- thank you for all of your encouragement. In a way, this book is the result of their continual sacrifices.

Furthermore, I must thank the source of my inspiration- my beautiful fiancée Laurie Barnard (Lavoie). Without whose constant support, patience, and understanding I could never have made it through the trials of life let alone academia!

Table of Contents

Part VI: Spiritualists Who Critiqued Theosophy

Part VII: Conclusion

Part I.
BACKGROUND

1.1 Preface

My first encounter with the Theosophical Society occurred while researching the religious roots of the Nazi movement for a World War II undergraduate class. It was through this experience that I read about one of the Theosophical Society's infamous co-founders who went on to become involved in many noteworthy tasks such as advocating for women's rights, performing the first recorded cremation in the history of the United States, and even helping an exploited country obtain a healthy sense of national pride (India). What I found to be even more captivating was that all of this had occurred during the Victorian era (1837–1901) and by a Russian woman who had been estranged from her husband. This woman turned out to be a creative, theatrical, and often times irascible Spiritualist named Helena Petrovna Blavatsky (1831–1891).

After my preliminary introduction to Blavatsky as an undergraduate student, I started acquainting myself with some of her major writings. The first book I examined was a curious publication titled *The Secret Doctrine* (1888) which I determined to be dense, circular, and non-sensical. Notwithstanding my initial reaction, I found this work to be full of strange ideas shrouded in the mystery of 'Eastern' terminology which made me all the more captivated by its admitted success and influence. After reading this perplexing work I resolved to learn everything that I could about the eccentric leader Madame Blavatsky and this mystical organization known as the Theosophical Society. Since then I have voraciously studied the history and philosophy of this movement. This led to graduate studies at Episcopal Divinity School in Cambridge, MA during which time I studied the roots of the modern feminist movement and examined historical methodologies while cross-registering in Eastern religion classes at Harvard Graduate School of Arts and Sciences. This was followed by doctoral studies in Western Esotericism at the University of Exeter under the supervision of both Professor Nicholas Goodrick-Clarke and Dr. Hereward Tilton. My doctoral thesis directly pertains to the topics of temporality (time), soteriology (salvation), and cosmology (origin) in the early Theosophical Society; however, through my academic endeavors I came to the realization that the Spiritualist movement of the nineteenth century held many similar elements to Blavatsky's later ideals purported in Theosophy even after the alleged 'Oriental shift' in her teachings. Despite Blavatsky's claim to have reformed the Spiritualist movement, it seemed evident that Blavatsky had not moved all that far away from mainstream Spiritualism. This realization mixed with the fact that many of the crucial figures associated with both of these movements have been ignored by modern history has led to the publication of this work.

1.2 Why Study Madame Blavatsky or the Theosophical Society?

Multiple studies and biographical accounts have been published on the life of Helena Blavatsky; all of these surveys have maintained differing perspectives on her contributions and accomplishments. Some accounts paint Blavatsky as a depraved opportunist preying on the ignorant and unfortunate; others still view Blavatsky as a highly evolved spiritual teacher, with a direct line to the world's hidden 'masters.' This particular work attempts a very different type of study. In a sense this work is not just about the life of Madame Blavatsky, Henry Olcott, or, even a general history of the Theosophical Society. Instead this study provides a comparative history of two 'distinct' nineteenth century religious movements and attempts to define the connection between them- the Theosophical Society and its intersection with the Spiritualist movement out of which it had emerged. Additionally, this study seeks to provide a deeper understanding of key individuals associated with this connection and a detailed analysis of Blavatsky's writings.

It is important to remember that the Theosophical Society was founded by a group of Spiritualists in the nineteenth century who were interested in the investigation of paranormal activity including spirit channeling, table levitation, and the appearance of spirits in human form (materializations).[1] There is a word (which will be employed throughout this study) that explains these various unexplainable psychic events mentioned above - 'phenomenon' (phenomena - plural). In this introductory statement it seems appropriate to define the word 'Spiritualism' and the beliefs associated with this term. Historically, there are all varying types of Spiritualist groups including Christian orthodox and progressive agnostic belief systems; however, all of these seem to agree on one overriding philosophical tenet- *that departed spirits of the recently deceased can communicate with the living through human beings known as mediums-* this belief is the main principle that unites all Spiritualists.

What many people do not realize is the enormous influence that Spiritualism exerted on Victorian culture. Numerous famous individuals were influenced by this movement including Arthur Conan Doyle, Mary Todd Lincoln, and Victor Hugo to name just a few. Though it is difficult to obtain accurate figures as to the number of Spiritualist practitioners in the nineteenth century, Michael Gomes, the Theosophical Historian noted the following numbers:

> ...in the United States between 9,000,000 and 10,000,000 Spiritualists in a population of some 44,000,000. The nine million figure was also reported by the Spiritualist authority, writer Andrew Jackson Davis. He arrived at his deduction not only by access to a 'superior condition' but from the fact that he ran his own bookstore and printing house on East Fourth Street in New York City. The Spiritualist weekly the Boston *Banner of Light*, challenged this figure in the March 7 issue, claiming that 'there are at least from ELEVEN TO THIRTEEN MILLIONS of Spiritualists in the United States.[2]

The late Janet Oppenheim in her monumental work *The Other World* suggested that the number of Spiritualists in Britain during the nineteenth century was difficult to calculate due to the elusiveness and the ever-shifting population of the time period. She conservatively estimated that there were somewhere between 'ten thousand and one hundred thousand spiritualists in the nineteenth century.'[3] Though the above figures are subject to debate, they seem to imply that one out of four people during this time period were somehow associated with the Spiritualist movement. Thus, the importance of this movement on Victorian history and modern religious movements cannot be denied.

It is further unfortunate that at this stage in modern history, the average person has probably never heard of the Theosophical Society which has gone on to shape 20th century culture through the influence of such pivotal figures as Mahatma Gandhi, L. Frank Baum (author of *The Wizard of Oz*), William Butler Yeats, and even the king of pop- Elvis Presley.[4] It has even been rumored that Albert Einstein consulted Blavatsky's *The Secret Doctrine* from time to time having a copy which he kept on his desk.[5] Even though this movement has dwindled in membership in recent years, it played an important role in the history and formation of the twentieth and twenty-first centuries. The conclusion seems evident- an understanding of these two past movements and their leaders remains critical towards ascertaining the religious and social climate of the present.

1.3 Spiritualism: A Nineteenth Century Religious Movement

Modern Spiritualism began in 1848 at the Fox household out in the city of Hydesville, NY. Strange and eerie noises ricocheted throughout the house on 31 March awaking the Fox family. Katy one of the Fox daughters then attempted to communicate with this apparition allegedly addressing the ghost 'Mr. Split-foot, do as I do.'[6] This was followed by a series of knocks which were believed to have been a communication from a spirit that was employing a type of Morse code to answer the questions it had been asked. Though other events prefigured this movement, this initial communication with the Fox sisters birthed a new religious belief system which was subsequently labeled Modern Spiritualism. Thus, at its very origination Spiritualism was directly connected to these psychical disturbances known as phenomena. This belief in the survival of the soul after death was eventually merged with Swedenborgian principles and provided the philosophy and the religious framework out of which the Theosophical Society would emerge. Some other different strains of philosophy that prefigured the Modern Spiritualist movement include Mesmerism and related 'sciences', mythography, the historical critique of Christianity, and the works of Andrew Jackson Davis. These belief structures provided the philosophical foundation on which Modern Spiritualism and eventually Theosophy would be built.

Most scholars recognize that when researching the Victorian cult known as the Theosophical Society that it should be divided into two chronological stages: the early Society which emerged out of Spiritualism from 1875-1878 and the later Theosophical Society which made an 'Oriental shift' having been relocated to India in 1879. Some researchers have labeled these two stages 'first' and 'second' claiming that these two periods remain philosophically distinct from one another; however, employing these categorizations implies that the 'second' Society was completely divergent from the views of the 'first' Society which does not seem to be supported by the evidence.

Despite the fact that the Theosophical Society underwent an obvious Oriental shift in 1879, from its inception the Society remained complicit to the basic belief of Spiritualism which held the possibility that the deceased spirit could somehow communicate with the living; this ideal was a central theme of the early Society and was maintained even in its post-Oriental years. Now an argument could be made for an epistemological shift in the Society from an existential and experiential leadership in its earlier years and its eventual adoption of a dictatorial style led by Blavatsky's 'mahatmas' in it post-Oriental stage; however, even this categorization appears much to cut and dry than the facts will permit. Given this consistent philosophical belief in the basic premise of Spiritualism, the designation 'first' and 'second' seems an inaccurate description as the Society maintained some similar doctrines including a Western Esoteric emphasis and its accessibility by Spiritualists throughout the years of 1876-1891. This belief will be defended throughout this work.

The main thesis of this book is two-fold: the first goal appears self-evident in the title *The Theosophical Society: The History of a Spiritualist Movement*. It is the belief of the author that despite all of the shifting claims made by Blavatsky and Olcott implying that the Theosophical Society was a separate organization distinct from Spiritualism that, in fact, its philosophies and belief systems remained compatible with Spiritualism up until the death of one of its most popular co-founders Helena Blavatsky in 1891 (though shifting slightly in the year 1888 the Society remained open and embracing to Spiritualists). The second purpose of this work is to provide updated biographical information for the important figures related to these two movements who have largely been ignored by modern scholarship. Whether the author is successful at presenting these biographies by connecting them to the thesis that the Theosophical Society was a reformed branch of Spiritualism can only be determined by each individual reader; however, at a minimum these pages contain a detailed history of two enchanting movements that went on to define the Victorian Era and mold modernity.

1.4 Theosophy: A Western Esoteric Spiritualist Movement

Despite its heavy interaction with Spiritualism, Theosophy has been categorized as a Western Esoteric movement. The term 'Western Esotericism' may be unfamiliar to some readers, but it is synonymous with another word which has an ominous connotation across the diverse circles of the Western world- the occult. The term 'occult' is typically associated with a wide range of different topics such as near death experiences, Wicca, Spiritualism, crystal gazing, tarot cards, yoga, kabbalah, hermeticism (a belief in the teachings of the *Hermeticum*), Freemasonry, and astrology to name only a few, but what does the word 'occult' actually mean? The word occult is derived from the Latin term *occultus* which signifies something that is hidden. Now, out of the list of subjects associated with occultism listed above, it should be noted than none of them would be considered hidden. In fact, throughout the last several hundred years numerous books have been published expounding upon all of these occult subjects; thus, the original definition of this term has been culturally changed to define something else. As 'occult' no longer denotes a hidden philosophy, a new word has been invented which describes the intellectual history of these 'occult' subjects and their involvement within the academic discipline of history now referred to as Western Esotericism.

The first word in this term, 'Western' signifies something that is relevant in the Western world. This region could be geographically defined as Europe and North America. The second word 'esotericism' is a vague term that comes from two Latin words- *eso* (inside) and *ter* (opposition). Thus, a literal definition of Western Esotericism means 'something that is opposed to Western (mainstream) teaching.' It seems indisputable that the dominant religious tradition in the Western world during the Victorian era was Christianity. Consequently, the original definition of Western Esotericism meant 'something that was not Western (i. e. Christian);' however, even this definition is incorrect as many esoteric groups have emerged out of Christian circles while other groups were meant to effectively function within Christianity.[7] Antoine Faivre the renowned pioneer of Western Esoteric scholarship suggested that 'esoteric currents could not, except by intellectual dishonesty, be defined as by nature marginal to the churches.'[8] Given the ambiguity of this term, Faivre established four main criteria to determine as to whether a religious belief could be classified as 'Western Esoteric.' Though these classifications are open to debate in the modern academic field of Western Esotericism, these guidelines are generally accepted as typical classifications for Western Esoteric beliefs. These include:

1) Correspondences- This implies that all of nature in all of its multiple parts (i.e. stars, planets, humans, animals, plants, minerals, states of mind, health, and disease) are linked through a series of correspondences or analogies.[9] This is where the saying which is commonly employed in occult circles 'as above, so below' originated from.

2) Living Nature- This characteristic is directly related to the concept of correspondences defined above. This phrase expresses the idea that nature 'must be read like a book.'[10] In other words the earth ('mother nature') also corresponds with the human condition. Thus, the use of particular herbs, stones, and other natural elements are employed to treat particular ailments. This idea also includes the use of talismans and birthstones. Hanegraaff notes that this belief 'furnishes the theoretical foundations for concrete implementation: various kinds of magical practice, "occult medicine", theosophical soteriologies based on the frame work of alchemy, and so on are based on it.'[11]

3) Imagination and mediations- This term implies an imagination that reveals mediations of all kinds such as rituals, symbolic images...intermediary spirits.'[12] A mediation could be an angel, chohan, demon, or any other supernatural or highly evolved being. This characteristic distinguishes occultism from mysticism as a mystic seeks a direct union with God without any intermediaries; whereas, the occultist focuses his attention on the intermediaries.[13]

4) Transmutation- mandates that the practitioner will experience an inner transformation. This transmutation (or transformation) comes after a realization of something profound or deeply spiritual.

Professor Goodrick-Clarke noted that 'Blavatsky's cosmology presents the prime characteristics of Western Esotericism as defined by Antoine Faivre's pioneering studies...These characteristics comprise (a) correspondences between all parts of the universe, the macrocosm and microcosm; (b) living nature as a complex, plural, hierarchical and animate whole; (c) imagination and mediations in the form of intermediary spirits, symbols, and mandalas; and (d) the experience of transmutation of the soul through purification and ascent.'[14] Thus, the characterization of the Theosophical Society as a Western Esoteric movement seems justifiable; however, this raises a tension that must be discussed upfront.

Antoine Faivre further explained that Spiritualism 'does not belong to the history of esotericism properly speaking, but would be closely associated with it because of its wide influence and because of the problems it raised.'[15] In other words, Spiritualism though exerting influence upon various Western Esoteric groups could not in itself be classified as a form of Western Esotericism because of its ambiguous definition. Because Spiritualism only required one common belief, it remained open to numerous interpretations and denominations. Case in point, the Theosophical Society originated as a Spiritualist movement and maintained a philosophy that seemed to continually align with Spiritualism; nonetheless, it evolved and adopted many characteristics and philosophies that would become typical of Western Esotericism- Theosophy was both a Western Esoteric and a Spiritualist movement. As Faivre noted there was some ambiguity in his definition and he also explained that the problems of Spiritualism led to the development of Western esotericism- this was certainly true of the Theosophical Society.

Looking back on history is a privilege of the present, yet the question remains, 'how would a contemporary of Helena Blavatsky have classified the relationship between the Theosophical Society and Spiritualism?' Though there is much disagreement on this issue, one Victorian newspaper reporter for the *Standard* claimed that Blavatsky was 'the principal exponent of a superior and more philosophical sort of Spiritualism; sometimes called Theosophy, and sometime Esoteric Buddhism.'[16] The belief that Theosophy was a philosophically advanced form of Spiritualism seems fitting. Also, after 1879 the Theosophical Society relocated to India and through this new environment was heavily influenced by Eastern texts and mythology. Henry Olcott the co-founder of the Society in his *Diary Leaves* referred to Blavatsky as a practitioner of 'Eastern Spiritualism' which also provided for the Eastern influence on the Western teachings of the Society especially apparent in such writings as *The Secret Doctrine* and *The Voice of Silence* while admitting the influence of Western Spiritualism.[17] The Theosophical Society's relocation to India in 1879 and the assimilation of the Society into Indian culture will be referred to throughout this writing as the 'Oriental shift.'

The term 'Oriental' is typically used to refer to countries in Asia; however, the term 'Orientalist' contains a slightly negative connotation though it more accurately describes the attitude of Blavatsky and Olcott upon entering India. Edward Said noted that 'in a quite constant way, Orientalism depends for its strategy on this flexible *positional* superiority, which puts the Westerner in a whole series of possible relationships with the Orient without ever losing him the relative upper hand;' this definition of 'Orientalism' is directly related to colonial imperialism and the belief of Western superiority in Eastern culture which remains an impending issue.

Regardless of this shift, the mere fact that Blavatsky was attempting to purify Spiritualism by providing an intellectually viable philosophy against materialism made her adopt many of the characteristics of Western Esotericism including a neo-Platonic world view which is at the core of Faivre's four characteristics of Western Esotericism. It should be clarified at the onset of this work that the purpose of this book is to examine and analyze the relationship between Spiritualism and the Theosophical Society, *not* to dispute over theoretical classifications.

1.5 Theosophy and Spiritualism: A Reformation

To Madame Blavatsky, Theosophy was a reformation of the Spiritualist movement. Throughout the course of this research, it has been determined that this reformation was more apparent than actual. Regardless of Blavatsky's claims that she had for the first time unveiled (or more accurately revealed) the 'ancient wisdom tradition' which was the foundational truth of all religions, her Theosophy actually affirmed many Spiritualist doctrines and continued to embrace these ideals long after the Society's relocation to India. Blavatsky continuously shifts back and forth between reconciling Theosophy with Spiritualism by listing their affinities while at other times attempting to clearly demarcate her organization from Spiritualism focusing upon their distinctions. Notwithstanding this wavering, one thing cannot be denied- that these two religious groups were intimately connected with one another both in history and philosophy. This book attempts to understand this connection and serves as the first step towards defining this ambiguous relationship. It is only fair to warn the reader upfront that there is no 'smoking gun' at the conclusion of this study that will put this work in perspective and clearly define this relationship; rather, it is only by chronologically examining the writings of key figures associated with both of these movements that the relationship between these two movements begins to be understood. Now many of these writings change and evolve over time and no one testimony (or quote) will prove or disprove this connection. Rather, it is only by comparing these writings to each other that the complexity of this relationship will begin to emerge. This relationship will provide the point of connection (or common ground) between the biographies of the various figures explored throughout this work.

It should further be noted that while many of Blavatsky's interactions and references to Spiritualism are mentioned throughout the pages of this book, nonetheless, some information had to be left out due to space constraints. Still, the author believes that the examples presented in this work provide a fair and balanced sampling of her views throughout the years. In order to arrive at a balanced conclusion, this study will examine the writings from some of the influential leaders of both of these unorthodox movements comparing and analyzing them for their relationship to each other. Examining each author's writings chronologically and noting the evolution of their thoughts through their works will assist the reader in ascertaining the kinetic social climate within these two Victorian religious movements. Again, whether the author succeeds at this task will be left up to the decision of the reader, but the author requests that readers embark upon this journey through Victorian history with an open mind towards truly understanding the richness and diversity of the events and personalities during the years 1875-1891 that contributed to the origination and promulgation of the Spiritualist movement known as the early Theosophical Society.

Notes

[1] This goal seemed apparent in the original Preamble of the 1875 Theosophical Society which asserted that the Founders hoped 'that by going deeper than modern science has hitherto done, into the esoteric philosophies of ancient times, they may be enabled to obtain, for themselves and other investigators, proof of the existence of an 'Unseen Universe,' the nature of its inhabitants, if such there be, and the laws which govern them and their relations with mankind.'

[2] Michael Gomes, *Dawning of the Theosophical Movement* (Wheaton, IL: The Theosophical Publishing House, 1987), pp. 19-20.

[3] Janet Oppenheim, *The Other World: Spiritualism and Psychical Research in England 1850-1914* (Cambridge: Cambridge University Press, 1985), pp. 49-50.

[4] Sylvia Cranston, *HPB: The Extraordinary Life and Influence of Helena Blavatsky, Founder of the Modern Theosophical Movement* (Santa Barbara, CA: Path Publishing House, 1993), pp. 511-512.

[5] Cranston, *HPB*, p. xx.

[6] Nancy Rubin Stuart, *The Reluctant Spiritualist: The Life of Maggie Fox* (Orlando, FL: Harcourt Books, 2005), pp. 5-6. Recently, some researches have suggested that this address to 'Mr. Splitfoot' was a later interpolation.

[7] There is a group referred to as Christian 'theosophists' (the lower case 't' differentiates this earlier philosophy from Blavatsky's nineteenth century 'Theosophy'-these two distinct movements should not be confused) which included Jacob Boehme (1575 – 1624), Robert Fludd (1574 – 1637), and Jan Baptist van Helmont (1579 – 1644); these figures could be considered 'esoteric' Christians.

[8] Antoine Faivre, *Access to Western Esotericism* (Albany: State University of New York, 1994), p. 6.

[9] Nicholas Goodrick-Clarke, *The Western Esoteric Traditions: A Historical Introduction* (New York: Oxford University Press, 2008), p. 8.

[10] Faivre, *Access to Western Esotericism*, p. 11.

[11] Wouter J. Hanegraaff, *New Age Religion and Western Culture: Esotericism in the Mirror of Secular Thought* (Albany, NY: State University of New York Press), p. 398.

[12] Faivre, *Access to Western Esotericism*, p. 12.

[13] Faivre, *Access to Western Esotericism*, p. 12.

[14] Nicholas Goodrick-Clarke, *Helena Blavatsky* (Berkeley, CA: North Atlantic Books, 2004), p. 141.

[15] Faivre, *Access to Western Esotericism*, p. 87.

[16] 'Supernatural Experiences of Madame Blavatsky,' *Standard* (19 November 1886), p. 2.

[17] Olcott, *Old Diary Leaves*, I, p. 15. Also, the term 'the Society' will be used in this book to refer to the Theosophical Society in cases where it seems grammatically awkward to employ the full name.

Part II.
THE THEOSOPHICAL SOCIETY

2.1 The Theosophical Society: An Historical Analysis

The Theosophical Society was founded in 1875 primarily (but not solely) by Colonel Olcott (1832-1907) and the capricious Helena Petrovna Blavatsky (1831–1891).[1] An attempt was made by these two individuals earlier that same year to institute a small Spiritualist organization known as 'The Miracle Club' for the purpose of investigating and propagating inquiries into psychic phenomena and mediums. The establishment of this club was announced in the *New York Daily Graphic* on 4 May 1875 and in the *Spiritualist Scientist* on 20 May of that same year though this group never seemed to take off due to a severe lack of leadership and direction.[2] This failure paved the way for the emergence of a similar yet different organization that would forever change the face of Spiritualism. On 7 September 1875 Blavatsky, Olcott, and about a dozen other colleagues had gathered to hear a lecture presented by George Felt on 'The Lost Canon of Proportion of the Egyptians.' At this meeting, Olcott suggested forming a society that would further the study of occultism (Western Esotericism).

On 13 September, in a private meeting it was decided that this society was to be called the Theosophical Society. The word 'Theosophy' (written with a capital 'T' to distinguish it from the theosophy of Jacob Boehme and other earlier practitioners of an unconnected belief system) was a combination of two Greek word 'theos' (God) and 'sophia' (wisdom). Though other names for the society were considered with the aid of a dictionary, among them 'Egyptological,' 'Hermetic,' and 'Rosicrucian' 'Theosophical' was finally chosen, as it was felt to express the esoteric truth they sought. A current edition of Webster's *American Dictionary* owned by Olcott gave a definition: Gk. 'wise in things of God.' Supposed intercourse with God and superior spirits, and consequent attainment of superhuman knowledge by physical processes, as by the theurgic operations of some ancient Platonists, or by the chemical processes of the German fire philosophers... a direct insight into the processes of the divine mind, and the interior relations of the divine nature.'[3]

At the core the Theosophical Society was formed for the express purpose of studying and understanding the 'Unseen Universe' and ascertaining the ancient 'occult' philosophies. It is imperative to observe at the beginning of this study that the very foundations of the Theosophical Society though rooted in Western Esotericism were defined for their relationship to Spiritualism. In the original Preamble issued with the legal by-laws in the November meeting it was stated that:

> It [The Theosophical Society] is formed neither as a Spiritualistic schism, nor to serve as the foe or friend of any sectarian or philosophic body... Its only axiom is the omnipotence of truth...The Spiritualists, who profess to be in constant relations with the departed, are unable to agree upon a system of philosophy. Thus the longing of the race for a practical demonstration of its future existence goes unsatisfied; the laws of intercommunication between the visible and the invisible worlds are not accurately defined; and the problem of the two eternities which bound this life remains unsolved, despite a multitude of churches and academies...

Thus, one of the early goals of the Theosophical Society was linked to establishing a clear philosophy for the Spiritualist movement. Based upon these original purposes set forth above, the Theosophical Society was viewed by many as another Spiritualist organization emerging out of this mainstream movement. Also of importance, most of the founders of this movement (including the two most well known- Helena Blavatsky and Colonel Henry Olcott) were both directly linked to the mainstream Spiritualist movement of the nineteenth century. This Society would go on to become one of the most popular occult movements of the twentieth century and even today continues to exert its influence on modern New Age and occult movements. Its initial popularity was largely due to its ability to attract the attention of multiple prestigious Spiritualists such as C. C. Massey, Emma Hardinge Britten, A. E. Newton and William Stainton Moses to name a few. Few would deny the direct connection between the Theosophical Society and Spiritualism at its inception. In order to ascertain the relationship between these two organizations an understanding of both individual belief structures must first be understood. At this point the Theosophical Society will be examined beginning with an evaluation of its two primary co-founders- Madame Blavatsky and Henry Olcott.

2.2 Helena Petrovna Blavatsky (1831- 1891):
A Feminist Genealogy

The main reason for the recounting of these biographical details concerning the life of Madame Blavatsky is to provide the reader with a basic chronological structure concerning the events that will be mentioned throughout this work. Many of these incidents will be expounded upon in later sections; however, at this point only a basic overview is required.

Helena Petrovna Blavatsky came from a long line of feminist thinkers.[4] Helena's maternal grandmother, Helena Pavlovna Dolgorukov (1789-1860), was an early example of an independent woman who was both intellectual and scholarly during a time when the world was dominated by men. Dolgorukov came from one of the 'most distinguished and aristocratic families in Russia' and was widely read in history, numismatics, archaeology, and natural science having published many works on botany.[5] Princess Helena Dolgorukov, who married Andrey Mihailovich de Fadayev (1789-1867), was a key influence on the young Helena Blavatsky during her formative years as she brought her up after the death of Helena's own mother, Helena Hahn. Indeed, Helena's mother, Helena Andreyevna von Hahn neé de Fadayev (1814-1842), was also a feminist in her own right, establishing herself as a successful novelist at a young age; her first work was published at the age of 23 in 1837, her three most famous works being *Utballa*, *The World's Judgment*, and *Theophania*.[6]

There are passages throughout Helena Hahn's writings that illustrated a feminist point of view. Specifically, Hahn tended to focus on the 'need for emotional emancipation of women.'[7] For example, *The World's Judgment* was written from a semi-autobiographical point of view. It contained the story of a woman who was a fiction writer and was unhappily married to a Russian officer. This story depicted the subservient life of a woman in nineteenth-century Russia whose dismal existence revolved around the whims of her husband's military career. Hahn's descriptive story-telling most probably influenced the young Helena Blavatsky who would, by contrast, refuse to submit to the lifestyle of the protagonists in her mother's stories. Instead, she would marry at a young age and quickly leave her husband in search of adventure. Although young Helena Blavatsky lost her mother when she was still young (*aet.* 11), the influence of her mother's feminist writings and convictions cannot be over emphasized.

Blavatsky's later attraction to Spiritualism as a movement illustrated her interest in feminist ideology and the continuation of her own maternal influences and the promotion of women's suffrage. Alex Owen in her study of Spiritualism in the nineteenth-century noted the high proportion of women involved in the movement, concluding that there was a strong link between Spiritualism and feminism in late Victorian England:

> Many women became involved in spiritualism via their participation in women's rights agitation and the anti-slavery crusades, and there was a strong feminist presence among American mediums and believers. Leading feminists also often became interested in spiritualism at some point during their careers, attracted by otherworldly promises of a new age which would see the development of women's potential.[8]

Thus, Spiritualism acted as one of the primary catalysts open to women to fight for social reform in the nineteenth-century. As it developed in the 1850s onwards, Spiritualism would be the natural place for Blavatsky who was largely influenced by the ideals of her mother and grandmother. These ideals included a desire to promote women's rights and to illustrate to society the oppression towards women that was prevalent during the nineteenth century. Aside from these feminist influences deriving from Blavatsky's maternal relatives, other aspects of her childhood should be considered here.

2.3 Blavatsky's Childhood Years

Helena Blavatsky was a creative child who possessed a vivid imagination that remained with her throughout her adult life. Blavatsky shared the same creative spirit as her mother and both were competent story tellers. This talent was exhibited in Blavatsky's early years by her ability to construct convincing alternate realities. Blavatsky's younger sister, Vera Petrovna Jelihowsky (1835-1896), told of the following events that occurred near the governor's villa:

> ...[the field was] evidently once upon a time the bottom of a sea or a great lake, as its soil yielded petrified relics of fishes, shells, and teeth of some unknown monsters. Most of these relics were broken and mangled by time, but one could often find whole stones of various sizes on which were imprinted figures of fishes and plants and animals of kinds wholly extinct which proved their undeniable antediluvian origin. The marvelous and sensational stories that we, children and schoolgirls, heard from Helen during that epoch were countless. I well remember when stretched at full

length on the ground, her chin reclining on her two palms, and her two elbows buried deep in the soft sand, she used to dream aloud and tell us of her visions, evidently clear, vivid, and as a palpable as life to her!...How vividly she described their past fights and battles on the spot where she lay, assuring us she saw it all; and how minutely she drew on the sand with her finger the fantastic forms of the long dead sea monsters, and made us almost see the very colors of the fauna and flora of those dead regions.[9]

The concept of fabricating stories connected with pre-historic animals was evidenced again by Blavatsky's sister. Jelihowsky further recalled that Blavatsky and she would often play in their grandmother's zoological collection, the old princess's museum of natural history housed in the governor's mansion. Jelihowsky noted that the young Blavatsky would often narrate 'to us the most inconceivable tales about herself; the most unheard of adventures of which she was the heroine, every night as she explained. Each of the stuffed animals in the museum had taken her in turn into its confidence, had divulged to her the history of its life in previous incarnations or existences.'[10] These tales were sufficiently credible that 'even grown-up persons found themselves interested involuntarily in her narratives.'[11] It should be understood that both of these above accounts were recounted by Jelihowsky the sister of Madame Blavatsky in an apparent attempt to mystify the early life of her sister; however, despite the questionable veracity concerning the details of these stories it seemed evident that Blavatsky was well known for her captivating tales and her inventive personality exhibited during her childhood years.

At an early age Blavatsky also possessed the ability to go into waking dreams or trances oftentimes referred to as a hypnotic writings[12] This was the method that Madame Blavatsky employed to write her later magnum opus *The Secret Doctrine* (1888). This same method was used by the protagonist in Blavatsky's fictional story 'A Bewitched Life':

> As I continued gazing...The space occupied by the empty rooms had changed into the interior of another smaller room...whose old, dark walls were covered from floor to ceiling with book shelves on which were many antiquated folios, as well as works of a more recent date. In the centre stood a large old-fashioned table, littered over with manuscripts and writing materials. Before it, quill-pen in hand, sat an old man; a grim-looking, skeleton-like personage, with a face so thin, so pale, yellow and emaciated, that

the light of the solitary little student's lamp was reflected in two shining spots on his high cheekbones, as though they were carved out of ivory…However it may be, the words uttered by the quill remained in my memory for days after. Nor had I any great difficulty in retaining them, for when I sat down to record the story, I found it, as usual, indelibly impressed on the astral tablets before my inner eye.[13]

Additionally, as a child Blavatsky developed an interest in Western esoteric literature through her multiple visits to her great-grandfather's library- Prince Pavel Dolgorukov. Dolgorukov was a noted Rosicrucian and Freemason who possessed an extensive collection of Western Esoteric titles.[14] Thus, potentially Blavatsky's familiarity with occult groups and ideas could have begun at an early age through her access to this library.

2.4 Blavatsky's Early Life

At the age of seventeen, the young Helena married Nicholas Blavatsky on 7 July 1849. Nicholas was around forty years old at the time though later in life Blavatsky claimed that he was in his seventies.[15] Blavatsky was known to exaggerate the truth and even fabricate stories if she thought it would be more entertaining to the listener. This trait was seen both in her fictional writings and more clearly by the well-documented account written by a follower turned critic, Vsevolod Solyvoff.[16] In fact, her ability to tell stories that captivated the imagination are found throughout her childhood and continued into her adult fictional tales such as those collected in the volumes *From the Caves and Jungles of Hindustan* (1892) and *Nightmare Tales* (1892) which were both written during 'leisure moments' between 1879-1880 for the pages of the Russian *Russki Vyestnik* and subsequently translated and published in English in 1892.[17] Enacting the feminist examples of her mother and grandmother in her youth, Helena deserted her husband in October 1849 and began a life full of world travel and adventures.

Concerning the events after her marriage, Nicholas Goodrick-Clarke has suggested the most likely summary of Blavatsky's travels:

The initial focus of her travels and quest lay in the Middle East. Initially she traveled to Turkey, Greece, and Egypt. At times she traveled with Albert Rawson, a young American explorer, author, and artist. In 1850, they studied with Paolos Metamon, a Copt magician in Cairo. In early 1851…Blavatsky went to London via

France ...her subsequent peregrinations through the United States (allegedly again with Rawson) and Latin America led her to India in 1852, but she failed to enter Tibet on this occasion. In 1854, she was again in the United States, and she traveled throughout India, Kashmir, Burma and parts of Tibet in 1856-1857. At Christmas in 1858 she returned to her family in Russia...[18]

2.5 Blavatsky: A Loving Mother?

According to the testimony of Blavatsky's first-cousin Sergei Yulyevich Witte (1849 -1915), around the year 1858 Blavatsky had rekindled a romantic affair with the opera singer Agardi Metrovich (though Witte's accounts were not always factual being based on rumors that he had heard from other family members).[19] This affair led to an enigmatic event in Blavatsky's personal history which remains obscured due to the prevailing Victorian code of morality that existed during this time period. Around the year 1862 a boy named Yuri was born into the world. The exact relationship of Blavatsky to Yuri remains unresolved; however, some biographers have suggested that Yuri was actually Blavatsky's biological son who had been her love-child- a result of her and Metrovich's fling. Others, more trusting of her integrity, believe Blavatsky's report that she had merely agreed to adopt this boy in order to help out a friend who had conceived this child with Baron Nicholas Meyendorff apparently out of wedlock. Marion Meade remains the most convincing advocate that Yuri was Blavatsky's own flesh and blood. In order to make this connection, Meade referred to two pieces of circumstantial evidence: 1) the report of Carl Erich Bechofer-Robert's *The Mysterious Madame* (1931) and 2) the fact that in her later letters sent to her family in Russia Blavatsky continuously references a troubled past which have never been clearly explained.[20]

Metrovich was described by Blavatsky in a letter written to Sinnett though this particular letter must be read discerningly understanding that its purpose was to entice Sinnett to ignore this event in compiling her biography. Sinnett was in the midst of writing Blavatsky's biography titled *Incidents in the Life of Madame Blavatsky* published in 1886 which was an attempt to vindicate Blavatsky from the Hodgson report circulated in 1885. Much of this biography had been derived from Blavatsky herself; however, Sinnett's history should not be discounted merely on these grounds or for the fact that he was a follower of Blavatsky. Sinnett's personal writings remain remarkably critical of Blavatsky and his wife Patty (Patience Edensor) kept meticulous records of the early Theosophical Society for the express purpose of reprinting them for future generations. Though most of Patty's diaries have been lost; nonetheless, Sinnett's historical recordings appear accurate though this biography certainly contains some discrepancies which were due to the original sources which he utilized in his writing.[21] This letter contained Blavatsky's explanation of her relationship with Metrovich:

> You say, 'Thus, for example we must bring in the whole of that Metrovich incident.' I say we must not….Well, I knew the man in 1850, over whose apparently dead corpse I stumbled over in Pera, at Constantinople, as I was returning home one night from Bougakdira to Missire's hotel…He was a Carbonaro, revolutionist of the worst kind, a fanatical rebel, a Hungarian, from Letrovitz, the name of which town he took as a nom de guerre. He was the natural son of the Duke of Lucea, as I believe, who brought him up. He hated priests, fought in all the rebellions, and escaped hanging by the Austrians, only because- well, it's something I need not be talking about. Then I found him again in Tiflis in 1861, again with his wife, who died after I had left in 1865 I believe; then my relatives knew him well and he was friends with my cousins Witte. Then, when I took the poor child to Bologna to see if I could save him I met him again in Italy and he did all he could for me, more than a brother. Then the child died; and as it had no papers, nor documents and I did not care to give my name in food to the kind gossips, it was he, Metrovich who undertook all the job, who buried the aristocratic Baron's child- under his, Metrovich's name saying 'he did not care,' in a small town of Southern Russia in 1867. After this, without notifying my relatives of my having returned to Russia to bring back the unfortunate little boy whom I did not succeed to bring back alive to the governess chosen for him by the Baron, I simply wrote to the child's father to notify him of this pleasant occurrence for him and returned to Italy with the same passport.[22]

Later, Blavatsky attempted to absolve herself from these scandalous claims of conceiving a child out of wedlock by proving that she had never been sexually active. Blavatsky was able to procure a certificate verified by the medical doctor Leon Oppenheim on 3 November 1885 which noted that Blavatsky had suffered from *anteflexio uteri* and had 'never borne a child, nor has she had any gynaecological illness.'[23] In modern biology, this condition is referred to as a 'tipped' or 'retroverted' uterus. It has recently been discovered that this issue does not affect a woman's ability to become pregnant and that pregnancy could actually be one of the causes of this condition. Note the following statement made in the sixth edition of *The Encyclopedia of Women's Health:*

> Often a tipped/retroverted uterus is congenital, but sometimes it occurs after pregnancy, owing to stretching of ligaments that normally keel it tilted forwards...it was formerly believed that a retroverted uterus hindered conception; today women with a retroverted uterus who have trouble becoming pregnant usually are told to try positions for intercourse other than the conventional 'missionary' positions...since in that position the cervix is not bathed in the pool of semen.[24]

Thus, this condition was not necessarily proof of Blavatsky's sexual abstinence as she had presumed. As this capability remained unknown in Victorian medicine, Dr. Oppenheim complied with Blavatsky's request to issue a second certificate in a more direct tone. This new certificate stated that 'I hereby certify that Mme Blavatsky has never been pregnant with child and so consequently can never have had a child Oppenheim'[25] Blavatsky had obtained this second certificate at the instigation of Olcott. Apparently this was a negative experience for Blavatsky who included with this certificate an attached letter written to Olcott (preserved in the Archives of the Theosophical Society) which stated:

> Here's your stupid new certificate with your dreams of *virgo intacta* [Latin term for virginity typically referring to an unbroken hymen] in a woman who had all her guts out, womb and all, by a fall from horseback. And yet the doctor looked, three times, and says what Professor Bodkin and Pirogoff said at Pskoff in 1862. I could never have had connection with any man without an inflammation, because I am lacking something and the place is filled up with some crooked cucumber.[26]

Curiously enough in her work *Performing Science and the Virtual*, Sue-Ellen Case suggested the implications of Blavatsky's above statement: 'Her description of the "crooked cucumber" that fills her vagina is a unique one, not covered under the medical description of *anteflexio*. It suggests an amazing feat of a woman penetrating herself through her own anatomy... She has so filled herself that no man can gain access. She is sexually/anatomically complete unto herself.'[27]

Three years later in her *Secret Doctrine* Blavatsky would elevate the position of hermaphrodites in her cosmology making them the progenitors of the human race. Blavatsky's later ability to suppress her sexual urges combined with her allegedly medical hermaphrodite condition seemed to validate her belief that she was an initiated messenger of the masters indicated through her identification with this earlier and more spiritual race.

Despite this startling conclusion it remained entirely plausible that Blavatsky's condition was the result of her having given birth to Yuri. It is interesting that the 'intact hymen' (*virgo intacta*) was not the diagnosis claimed by these doctors, but simply Blavatsky's problem was the tipping of the uterus (*anteflexio uteri*) which could have actually been caused by child birth; thus, allowing for the possibility that Blavatsky may have been pregnant at one time. Whatever may have been Blavatsky's relation to Yuri, he eventually passed away in 1867 at the age of five years old leaving behind only one definitive piece of evidence that would link this poor crippled child to Blavatsky. According to Mary Neff, in the archives at Adyar there is a passport dated 23 August 1862 with the following words written upon it: '…to the wife of Civil Counsellor Blavatsky, attaché of the Viceroy of the Caucasus and their infant ward Youry, to proceed to the provinces of Tauris, Cherson and Pskoff, for the term of one year.'[28] Though this would lead one to suspect that Yuri was the result of a passionate love affair between Blavatsky and Metrovich; nonetheless, the relationship between Yuri and Blavatsky must remain buried in the sands of history. It is currently believed that Agardi Metrovich died sometime around 1871 though the exact nature of his death remains a matter of controversy.

When Blavatsky finally arrived in New York City in 1873 she had no money to her name and her experiences with Metrovich and Yuri had left her emotionally distraught; however, her luck changed when she discovered the woman's tenement on 222 Madison Street in New York City which would connect her to the world of American Spiritualism.

2.6 Blavatsky and Colonel Henry Olcott

Blavatsky was a self-avowed Spiritualist despite her later insistence that she was never connected with this movement. This involvement in Spiritualism eventually led her to the Eddy farm in Chittenden, Vermont on 14 October 1874. William and Horatio Eddy lived in a small farmhouse along with their sister, Mary. These illiterate brothers claimed that full body materializations were occurring at their farmhouse nightly; this claim prompted the publishing of an article in the Spiritualist periodical *Banner of Light* grabbing the attention of the curious Colonel Henry Olcott (1832-1907).[29] Olcott obtained a commission from the *Daily Graphic* to write an article on the strange phenomena and headed out to the Eddy farm to begin personally investigating these bizarre occurrences. It was here at the Eddy brother's farmhouse that the 'Theosophical twins' were first acquainted. Blavatsky first came into contact with a future co-founder of the Theosophical Society, Henry Olcott impressing him to the point where he wrote the following description in his diary:

> [Blavatsky was wearing] a scarlet Garibaldian shirt...as in vivid contrast with the dull colours around. Her hair was then a thick blond mop, worn shorter than the shoulders, and it stood out from her head, silken-soft and crinkled to the roots, like the fleece of a Cotswold ewe. This and the red shirt were what struck my attention before I took in the picture of her features. It was a massive Calmuck face, contrasting in its suggestion of power, culture, and imperiousness, as strangely with the commonplace visages about the room as her red garment did with the grey and white tones of the walls and woodwork and the dull costumes of the rest of the guests.[30]

By contrast, Blavatsky saw the colonel as a means to entering the world stage. Here she had found an educated man (he was an attorney) who was trustworthy (he was a colonel in the army), and at the same time not overtly suspicious. Blavatsky possessed a temperament which was easily excitable into a fiery disposition that she often times unleashed on the well intentioned and unsuspecting Olcott; nonetheless, at this initial meeting Olcott had nothing but kind words to record about Blavatsky. The nature of their relationship seemed to be Platonic and remained strictly professional, as Olcott was a married man and Blavatsky had previously married an Armenian subject named Michael Bettanelly some years earlier in Philadelphia in 1875. This relationship with Bettanelly was tumultuous and appeared to last only a few months though the divorce was not official until 25 May 1878.[31] Blavatsky's divorce coincided with another tragic event for Blavatsky- the Philadelphia fiasco labeled by the *Banner of Light* Spiritualist magazine on 30 January 1875 though this event will be expounded upon in its respective section.[32]

Before Blavatsky arrived at the Eddy's farm in 1874 the 'spiritual manifestations' were simply the mundane European and American relatives of those attending the séance. After the arrival of Blavatsky at the Eddy farm the spirits appearing were transformed into exotic figures either closely related to Blavatsky's earlier life or from distant lands. There was the Georgian Michalko Guegidze, the late servant of Madame Witte, a close relative of Blavatsky; Abraham Alsbach who communicated with Blavatsky in German; Hassah Agha a Muslim from Tiflis known only to Blavatsky, a Kurd Warrior, a peasant girl, an African, and a turbaned Hindu appeared. The appearance of these new 'spirits' was directly due to Blavatsky's collusion. Olcott noted his opinion of Blavatsky and her unique 'mediumship' in his *People from the Other World*:

> I gradually discovered that this lady, whose brilliant accomplishments and eminent virtues of character, no less than her exalted social position, entitle her to the highest respect, is one of the most remarkable mediums in the world. At the same time, her mediumship is totally different from that of any other person I ever met; for, instead of being controlled by spirits to do their will, it is she who seems to control them to do her bidding.[33]

Using the term 'medium' to describe Blavatsky would be a continual label employed both in the Spiritualist press and by newspaper reporters throughout her lifetime. This term evidenced a connection between Blavatsky and Spiritualism during her years in the United States.

Blavatsky had left her home at 124 East Sixteenth Street in New York City and traveled to William and Horatio Eddy's farm at Chittenden, Vermont with the express purpose of meeting Olcott. He was in the midst of writing a series of articles for the *Daily Graphic* and seemed to be the ideal spokesman for Blavatsky's adventures in Spiritualism. Even in his later recollections as recorded in his *Old Diary Leaves*, Olcott noted the fact that Blavatsky had not been well known in Spiritualist circles before he had teamed up with her at the Eddy's farm. This fact seemed to be clearly confirmed by the following entry in his diary: 'We have it on her own authority, as quoted above, that she was sent from Paris to New York in the interest of Spiritualism, in the best sense of that word, and before we met she had attended séances and consorted with mediums, but never came under public notice.'[34]

On 13 November 1874 Blavatsky published a critical article of Dr. Beard's investigation of the Eddy's brother manifestation in the *Daily Graphic* and affirmed Olcott's earlier theories regarding the credibility of the phenomena. This article was avidly read by one Eldridge Gerry Brown the editor of the *Spiritual Scientist* and upon finishing it he promptly sent Blavatsky a sample of his own Spiritualist newspaper along with a letter thanking Blavatsky for her defense of these respected mediums.[35] This correspondence commenced a cordial relationship that provided Blavatsky with her first public platform to spread her thoughts on Spiritualism.

2.7 Blavatsky and the *Spiritual Scientist*

Notwithstanding this earlier correspondence, it wasn't until 29 April 1875 that Brown allowed his periodical to be used as the unofficial vehicle for Blavatsky by officially printing an article from 'the Brotherhood of Luxor.' This particular article was written pseudonymously by Colonel Olcott who admitted this in his diary; however, it clearly expressed the desires of Blavatsky which were to systematize the philosophy of American Spiritualism such as had been accomplished by Allen Kardec in France:

> The Spiritual Movement resembles every other in this respect: that its growth is the work of time, and its refinement and solidification the result of causes working from within outward....Until the present time these advanced thinkers have had no special organ for the interchange of opinions....In England the London Spiritualist, and in France the Revue Spirite, present to us examples of the kind of paper that should have been established in this country long ago- papers which devoted more space to the discussion of principles, the teaching of philosophy, and the display of conservative critical ability, than the mere publications of the thousand and one minor occurrences of private and public circles The best thoughts of our best minds have heretofore been confined to volumes whose price has, in most instances, placed to volumes whose price has, in most instances, placed them beyond the reach of the masses, who most needed to be familiar with them. To remedy this evil, to bring our authors into familiar intercourse with the great body of spiritualists, to create an organ upon which we may safely count to lead us in our fight with old superstitions and mouldy creeds a few earnest spiritualists have now united. Instead of undertaking the doubtful and costly experiment of starting a new paper, they have selected the Spiritual Scientist, of Boston, as the organ of this new movement.[36]

This article appeared within the midst of other columns contributed by such popular Victorian Spiritualists as Emma Hardinge Britten, F. J. Lippitt, and Gerald Massey. Brown went on to publish many of Blavatsky's letters beginning with an introductory article on 3 December 1874; in return for his service Brown received $1,000 of support from the future co-founders of Theosophy. An anonymous writer sent a letter to an unknown recipient (probably to William Stainton Moses a prominent Spiritualist and an early member of the Theosophical Society) that has recently been reprinted clarifying the nature of this relationship between Gerry Brown and Blavatsky:

> Among other to whom he [Brown] represented the difficulties of his position were Col. Olcott & Madame Blavatsky and they at once perceived and improved the opportunity by proposing to contribute to the mantanance [sic] of his paper provided he would admit to its columns such articles in favor of occultism as they chose to send him. With certain slight reservations he accepted their proposal and from that time for a certain period the Scientist became their vehicle for communication with the American Spiritualist public.[37]

This arrangement would not last for long and soon came to an unfortunate end. Apparently there was a falling out of sorts between Blavatsky and Brown around the end of 1876. This confrontation was evidenced in another letter written by Blavatsky:

> Several hundred dollars out of our pockets were spent on behalf of the Editor, and he was made to pass through a minor 'diksha' [initiation]. This proving of no avail-the Theosophical Society was established...the man might have become POWER, he preferred to remain an ASS. De gustibus non disputandum est [one must not dispute about tastes]...[38]

Gomes noted that 'until the publication of *Isis Unveiled* in 1877, H.P.B.'s philosophical expositions were mainly limited to the small audience of the *Spiritual Scientist*. By the time the public could get the book's second edition, read through its 1,200 pages, and form any conception of its author, she was ready to leave for India.'[39] He also pointed out that even at the beginning of her writing career, Blavatsky flavored her view of Spiritualism (in the *Scientist*) with Western Esotericism printing translations of Eliphas Levi and her infamous 'reply to a Few Question to HIRAF' in which she clearly associated her movement with Rosicrucianism, Paracelsus, alchemy, the Zohar, and the 'oriental cabala' (an idea prefigured in the *Anacalypsis* of Godfrey Higgins).[40] This 'oriental cabala' was the written philosophy of Truth that undergirded every world religion and was the basic religion of humanity before the fall of humanity. 'The practical, full, and only existing copy is carefully preserved at the headquarters of this Brotherhood in the East, and, I may safely vouch, will never come out of its possession.' This Western Esoteric shift (so obvious in these articles) would become assimilated into Blavatsky's Spiritualist ideology earning the title put forth in the introduction of this work- a Western Esoteric Spiritualism. The idea that the 'oriental kabbalah' was the source for all truth became eventually equivocated with her 'hidden wisdom tradition' which she maintained was the core of truth undergirding all religious movements. This true religion had remained concealed for centuries and the lot fell to Blavatsky to unveil it in *Isis Unveiled* and to explain it in *The Secret Doctrine*. Blavatsky suggested its origins as follows:

> The first Cabala in which a mortal man ever dared to explain the greatest mysteries of the universe, and show the keys to those masked doors in the ramparts of Nature through which no mortal can ever pass without rousing dread sentries never seen upon this side of her wall, was compiled by a certain Shimon Ben Yochai, who lived at the time of the second Temple's destruction. Only about thirty years after the death of this renowned Cabalist, his MSS. and written explanations, which had till then remained in his possession as a most precious secret, were used by his son Rabbi Eleazar and other learned men. Making a compilation of the whole, they so produced the famous work called Zohar (God's splendour). This book proved an inexhaustible mine for all the subsequent Cabalists their source of information and knowledge, and all more recent and genuine Cabalas were more or less carefully copied from the former. Before that, all the mysterious doctrines had come down in an unbroken line of merely oral traditions as far back as man could trace himself on earth. They were scrupulously and jealously guarded by the Wise Men of Chaldaea, India, Persia and Egypt, and passed from one initiate to another, in the same purity of form as when handed down to the first man by the angels, students of God's great Theosophic Seminary. For the first time since the world's creation, the secret doctrines, passing through Moses who was initiated in Egypt, underwent some slight alterations.[41]

Blavatsky ended this article by supplanting her idea of the 'oriental cabala' into biblical history giving it an heir of authority and historical precedence. Thus, Blavatsky was revealing the *prisca theologia*- the underlying philosophy behind very world religion which had been hidden in the East. She connected her conceptualization of her 'oriental cabala' (*prisca theologia*) to Spiritualism:

> As the prophet Mahomet, when he perceived that the mountain would not come to him, went himself towards the mountain so Modern Spiritualism made its unexpected appearance from the East, before a skeptical world, to terminate in a very near future the oblivion into which the ancient secret wisdom has fallen...Spiritualism is but a baby now, an unwelcome stranger, whom public opinion, like an unnatural foster-mother, tries to crush out of existence. But it is growing, and this same East may one day send some experienced, clever nurses to take care of it. The Rochester knockings, tiny as they were, awoke some vigilant friends, who, in their turn, aroused thousands and millions of jealous defenders for the true Cause. The most difficult part is done: the door stands ajar; it remains for such minds as Hiraf invites to help earnest truth-seekers to the key which will open the gates, and aid them to pass the threshold dividing this world from the next...It belongs to the exact knowledge of the Occultist to explain and alter much of what seems 'repulsive' in Spiritualism, to some of the too delicate Orthodox souls...I will close by startling, perhaps even Orthodox Spiritualists by re-affirming that all who have ever witnessed our modern materializations of genuine spirit-forms, have, unwittingly, become the initiated neophytes of the Ancient Mystery; for each and all of the have solved the problem of Death, have 'lifted the Veil of Isis.' [42]

Blavatsky would expound upon this idea in her work *Isis Unveiled* published in 1877. Thus, Blavatsky's Spiritualism was assimilated with her Western Esoteric ideology. Furthermore, Blavatsky attempted to connect Spiritualism to this ancient wisdom tradition by noting that Spiritualism was paving the way for this new 'Hermetic occultism' whose doctrines could be found in the 'oriental cabala', the hidden wisdom tradition, or better known as the 'secret doctrine' which had remained hidden in the East and which philosophy Blavatsky would attempt to disseminate through her major writings. Despite Blavatsky's theatrically brilliant marketing strategy this 'hermetic occultism' would remain relatively aligned with the basic tenets of Spiritualism though in a repackaged form.

2.8 Blavatsky's Spirit Guides and Masters

It is crucial before continuing the chronology of Blavatsky to understand her early conceptualization of invisible 'adepts' and 'masters'. According to her own admission she returned from her foreign travels to stay with her relatives in Russia between Christmas 1858 and 1860. During which time Helena encountered several invisible spirits/friends including a German artist,[43] a nice, kind fat old lady,[44] and a tall, very funny old man at Rougodevo,[45] the country house belonging to her sister Vera de Jelihowsky.[46] Later at New York, Blavatsky created another invisible friend, a spirit-guide whom she had adopted from contemporary Spiritualism called John King. Mr. King would play all types of pranks on Blavatsky which included continuously demanding and stealing money, forging people's handwritings, and playing practical jokes. He was especially known to write post scripts on letters sent out by Blavatsky. These notes were made in red and blue pencil a device that would later be used by the 'hidden Tibetan masters' as they communicated with outsiders.[47] In 1875, John King had left and was replaced by a new (albeit still invisible) occult Master Serapis Bey and Tuitit Bey, members of the Brotherhood of Luxor.[48]

As time carried on, Blavatsky continued her belief in invisible companions. She would later expound her conceptualization of John King into a belief in 'hidden masters' or 'adepts' that possessed a better understanding of the ancient wisdom tradition (*prisca theologia*) and had access to hidden knowledge. There remains some controversy over whether these masters were entirely fictitious, based upon historical individuals, or if they were Tibetan masters that Blavatsky had met in her travels.[49] The idea that these masters were based on actual historical figures in the life of Blavatsky has more recently been explored by Paul Johnson in his investigative work *The Masters Revealed: Madame Blavatsky and the Myth of the Great White Lodge* (1994), in which he summarizes the philosophy of influential figures on the life of Blavatsky; however, these spiritual 'master's' must remain forever beyond the reach of historians—because they were *not* historical individuals. This idea will be discussed more thoroughly later in this section.

In 1875, Blavatsky began writing her first major book *Isis Unveiled*, published in 1877 as a 1,300 page, double volume set that served as a manual for all things occult. It should be noted here that Blavatsky's writings are extremely circular with no central thesis. It has been demonstrated that *Isis Unveiled* was largely plagiarized from about one hundred different secondary sources even though nearly one thousand sources were cited as being primary.[50] Even in *Isis Unveiled* the beginning of Blavatsky's syncretism becomes apparent and her work towards comparative religion during this early time period was admirable. *Isis Unveiled* was published during a period when Eastern religions such as Buddhism and Hinduism were receiving more public and scholarly attention in the Western world.[51]

During the time that *Isis Unveiled* was published in 1877, Blavatsky continued her claims that many of the communicating spirits that were being channeled at séances across the Western world were not actually the spirits of the recently deceased as had previously been thought; rather, these 'spirits' were deceiving elementals which were the shells of former human beings who had passed beyond the ability to communicate. This 'theory of elementals' will be expounded upon in a later section; however, this rationalization was one of Blavatsky's more obvious attempts at reconceptualizing Spiritualism in order to make it a more philosophically advanced belief system.

Blavatsky was attempting to reform the Spiritualist movement which was being overrun by widespread accusations of fraud and trickery. As prophesied in her 'Reply to HIRAF article'- 'it belongs to the exact knowledge of the Occultist to explain and alter much of what seems 'repulsive' in Spiritualism, to some of the too delicate Orthodox souls' and Blavatsky made it her mission to demarcate her new 'hermetic occultism' from mainstream Spiritualism. Her theory of elementals attempted to explain the prevalence of deceitful mediums that conned people out of their hard earned money. The outcome of this doctrinal shift was noted by Blavatsky in the following letter dated 10 September 1875: 'The spiritualists are furious because we do not share many of their opinions and do not regard all their mediums' lies as Gospel truth.'[52] By advocating publicly for the reform of Spiritualism which would require a philosophical change in approach from its accepted practices, Blavatsky made herself a target to many contemporaneous Spiritualists. This reformation resulted in multiple repercussions especially through the corresponding Spiritualist William Emmette Coleman who would be one of the skeptics to charge Blavatsky with plagiarism.

From 1876-1878, Blavatsky moved in to an apartment on Eighth Avenue and Forty-Seventh Street in New York, affectionately known within her circle as the Lamasery. It was here that Blavatsky wrote *Isis Unveiled.* Additionally, while staying at the Lamasery, Blavatsky networked with an eclectic group of people ranging from eccentric

Spiritualists to Jewish rabbis.[53] A Connecticut reporter gave a detailed physical description of the Lamasery in the following article:

> we had a chance to observe the walls and furniture of this *New York Lamasery*. Directly in the centre stood a stuffed ape, with a white 'dickey' and necktie around his throat, manuscript in paw, and spectacles on nose. Could it be a mute satire on the clergy? Over the door was the stuffed head of a lioness, with open jaws and threatening aspect; the eyes glaring with an almost natural ferocity. A god in gold occupied the centre of the mantle-piece; Chinese and Japanese cabinets, fans, pipes, implements and rugs, low divans and couches, a large desk, a mechanical bird who sang as mechanically, albums, scrap-books, and the inevitable cigarette holders, papers and ash-pots, made the loose rich robe in which madame was appareled seem in perfect harmony with her surroundings.[54]

During this time period there were many notable visitors including prominent Spiritualists Charles Massey and William Stainton Moses.[55] Blavatsky's residence in the United States would, however, be curtailed. In May 1878 she received orders from the masters that she needed to go to India and start a Theosophical Society out there. This did not stop Blavatsky from becoming a citizen of the United States which she completed in July of 1878. Blavatsky and Olcott made preparations to leave for India in December 1879. This would be the last time Blavatsky would visit America.

2.9 Blavatsky and the Arya Samaj

In February 1879, the founders of the Theosophical Society set foot on Indian soil. Before their arrival into Bombay they had connected with the Vedic group known as Arya Samaj. On 2 June 1878, Blavatsky wrote an article for the New York magazine *Echo* explaining the new relationship between the group Arya Samaj and the Theosophical Society:

> The Aryas see an everlasting Principle, an impersonal Cause in the great 'Soul of the universe' rather than a personal Being, and accept the *Vedas* as the supreme authority, though not of divine origin…What more reasonable than the claim that such Scriptures, emanating from such authors, should contain, for those who are able to penetrate the meaning that lies half concealed under the dead letter, all the wisdom which it is allowed to men to acquire on earth? The Chiefs of the Arya Samaj discredit 'miracles,' discoun-

tenance superstition and all violation of natural law, and teach the purest form of Vedic Philosophy. Such are the allies of the Theosophical Society. They have said to us: 'Let us work together for the good of mankind,' and -- we will.[56]

The Arya Samaj was an offshoot of Raja Rammohun Roy's (1774–1833 CE) philosophies that replaced Roy's Christian tendency with a fundamentalist Vedic philosophy.[57] Roy was a noted Indian philosopher who acted as both a religious and social reformer. He advocated for gender equality while attempting to legitimize the religious practices of Hindu traditions to a Western audience. Roy possessed a working knowledge of Arabic, Persian, Hebrew, Greek, Latin Sanskrit, and his native tongue was Bengali. The Arya Samaj believed in God as the One unformed and unknowable deity, condemned any forms of idolatry, and maintained that infallibility and unity of the Vedas. The Theosophical Society gravitated to this group of religious reformers who viewed the Vedas as superior to any other Scripture. When Blavatsky and Olcott first arrived in India they were greeted by a group of about 300 natives welcoming them to their native land. They met in a wonderfully decorated hall and in honor of their arrival the Hindu drama *Sitaram* was acted out. At the end of these festivities Hurrychund Chitamon the president of the Bombay chapter of the Arya Samaj presented Blavatsky with a bill for all of the services rendered.[58] This was the beginning of the end of this relationship between these two groups. Also, at odds was the exclusivist attitude of the Arya Samaj in comparison to the eclectic theological position of the Theosophical Society. Finally, in 1879, Blavatsky and Olcott converted to Buddhism effectively ending the affiliation with Arya Samaj.

2.10 Blavatsky and Her Later Writings

When Blavatsky and Olcott first arrived in Bombay they attracted the attention of a newspaper editor named Alfred Percy Sinnett (1840-1921 CE). Sinnett is an intriguing character in his own right who first came to Theosophy from Spiritualism. Born in north London on 18 January 1840, he was the youngest son of five children. Sinnett's father made a living through journalism and literature, but he died relatively young aged about 45 in 1844 when Sinnett was only five years old. This left Sinnett's mother as the sole provider which she did by using her literary talents and 'indefatigable industry.'[59] Sinnett described his mother as a 'woman of quite exceptional literary talent and of unusual mental culture.'⁶⁰ As a result of his family's poverty, Sinnett attended the cheapest schools in the Camden and Kentish Town area where they resided. Eventually, through an exhibition procured by his aunt Sarah Fry, Sinnett attended the London University School in Gower Street. His schooling would not last long though due to his inability to grasp the Latin language. Sinnett's mother eventually withdrew him from the school and the young Alfred procured a job as a mechanical draughtsman.⁶¹

Sinnett entered the world of journalism, starting as an assistant sub-editor for *The Globe*, though after a short time he would be let go. Sinnett then began working as a freelance writer, writing articles in various publications such as the *Morning Chronicle, Birmingham Daly Gazette*, and the *Manchester Guardian*.⁶² He would become better known in journalistic circles, and in 1865 was invited to become the editor of the *Hong Kong Daily Press*. This senior three-year appointment in colonial journalism would be the turning point in his career. Back in London, on 6 April 1870, Sinnett married Patience 'Patty' Edensor. Patty had a remarkable dedication towards faithfully recording the events of both her and Alfred's life in various diaries that she kept. She managed to fill 31 volumes which Sinnett frequently cited throughout his autobiography. In 1872, Sinnett was offered the editorship of *The Pioneer*-- the leading English daily newspaper in India. As a leading organ of Anglo-Indian public opinion, *The Pioneer* provided the medium that would associate Sinnett with Blavatsky. Sinnett had earlier heard about her major book *Isis Unveiled* (1877) from Herbert Stack and upon hearing that its authoress was moving to India, he decided to write a note in his paper about Blavatsky and Olcott. Shortly afterwards Olcott contacted Sinnett initiating a steady correspondence between the Theosophists and himself.

Sinnett was fascinated with the theosophists and invited them to visit him and his wife at his summer home in Simla in 1880. Blavatsky and Olcott obliged and the result of this visit, including Blavatsky's psychical 'phenomena' and the apportment of objects and letters for Sinnett from the 'hidden masters' is captured in *The Occult World* (1881).⁶³ On its publication in London, Sinnett's book brought Theosophy and Helena Blavatsky's Eastern activities to a wider audience in Victorian England. *The Occult World* is a description of the various phenomena that Blavatsky had arranged while in the presence of the author.

Around the fall of 1880, Sinnett began to receive correspondences with some hidden, Tibetan masters.⁶⁴ These correspondences were delivered to Sinnett over the course of six years between 1881 and 1887 and became known as the Mahatma Letters. Most were delivered to him by Blavatsky in person; however, some came through the mail, others randomly fell from the ceiling, and still others were sent in even more peculiar ways. Most of these letters were written primarily in blue and red pencil, and contained the signatures of the Tibetan masters Morya and Koot Hoomi. Though these letters claimed to have been written by secret adepts, a report published by Richard Hodgson in the *Journal of the Society for Psychical Research* (1884/5) suggested that these letters were forgeries produced by Blavatsky.[65] Though Sinnett was not the sole recipient of these strange letters (some were delivered to A. O. Hume, Colonel Olcott, and Charles W. Leadbeater among others) in 1883 he published his own compilation of these letters in the work entitled *Esoteric Buddhism* that attempted to summarize the mysterious doctrines presented. Despite the question of their authorship, the publication of the Mahatma Letters (through the book *Esoteric Buddhism*) was monumental in influencing the future publication of *The Secret Doctrine* and the Theosophical Society as a whole.

In 1888, Blavatsky published her magnum opus *The Secret Doctrine* which she claimed was the essence of Hindu, Zoroastrian, Chaldean, Egyptian, Buddhism, Islam, Judaism and Christianity.[66] Its purpose was to reconcile all religions and strip everyone of its outward, human garments, and show the roots of each to be identical with that of every other great nature. Also, it attempted to 'prove the necessity of an absolute divine principle in nature.'[67] The syncretism behind this book was evidenced in these two statements. *The Secret Doctrine* took Western esoteric ideas and combined them with Eastern religious beliefs and terminology. Many Western esoteric ideas were explained in light of the *Vishnu Purana* and the concepts of Western esotericism and Hinduism were analyzed and compared. The truly remarkable aspect of *The Secret Doctrine* was in its syncretism not its originality. Blavatsky had succeeded in publishing a work that contained a full syncretism of most occult subjects and the major world religions. *The Secret Doctrine* would supply the basic tenets for the Theosophical Society and its offspring groups.

In 1889, *The Secret Doctrine* was followed by Blavatsky's publication of *The Key to Theosophy* which was more accessible than Blavatsky's earlier works and attempted to apply the basic tenets of Theosophy in a more practical manner (all of Blavatsky's later works will be explored in more depth in a later chapter). At the start of writing *The Key to Theosophy*, Blavatsky's health had deteriorated and eventually on 8 May 1891 Blavatsky died of influenza. Upon hearing about her demise, William Judge, the general secretary of the Theosophical Society in America at this time, made the following remarks:

> Up to her death she was working heart and soul for the cause for which she so ably preached. She can have no successor…in the spiritual sense nobody can succeed her…There was something about Madame Blavatsky that was not of this world. The good she has done is known to but few…They [the Theosophists] have done much charitable work among the poor and during the late severe winter did all they could for the distressed around them. The death of Madame Blavatsky will have no effect upon the movement here. We shall work as diligently as ever and try to carry out her teaching and wishes.[68]

The life of Helena Blavatsky continues to fascinate readers even in this modern age. Her works have gone on to influence such noted personalities as Mahatma Gandhi, Albert Einstein, and W. B. Yeats to name but a few. The Theosophical Society went on to multiply under the leadership of Annie Besant and chapters currently exist all across the world though its membership in the States has dwindled significantly in recent decades.[69] This work will now explicate the connection between Blavatsky and the Spiritualist movement of the nineteenth-century.

2.11 Blavatsky and Spiritualism

Blavatsky's earliest writings primarily concern her interaction with this intriguing movement. Furthermore, many of her letters during those earlier years attest to her Spiritualist affiliation and ideologies. Some of these letters will now be examined. The co-founder of the Theosophical Society, Colonel Olcott recorded some earlier letters written by Blavatsky; this first one noted her conversion to Spiritualism and was a summary of an article published in the *Daily Graphic* on 13 November 1874:

> In 1858, I returned to Paris and made the acquaintance of Daniel Home, the Spiritualist (He had married the Countess Kroble, a sister of the Countess Koucheleff Bezborrodke, a lady with whom I had been very intimate in my girlhood)…Home converted me to

Spiritualism…After this I went to Russian. I converted my father to Spiritualism.[70]

Despite this clear admission by Blavatsky's intimate friend and co-founder of the Theosophical Society, Michael Gomes noted a conflicting report and suggested that Daniel Dunglas Home (1833 – 1886) and Blavatsky had never met before. Gomes cited an article by Home published in March of 1884: 'The name of Madam B. was well known to me (but not as a medium) in the spring of 58' in Paris, but I never met with or ever saw her.' Gomes further noted that:

> in a bound copy of the *Spiritual Scientist* presented to the British National Association of Spiritualists in 1877, H. P. B. has annotated an interview with her from the 13 November 1874, New York *Daily Graphic*, reprinted on the front page of the Scientist for 19 November 1874. Underlining the words attributed to her, 'In 1858 I returned to Paris, and made the acquaintance of Daniel Home…Home converted me to Spiritualism,' she writes 'I never saw in my whole life neither D. D. Home or his wife; I never was in the same city with him for half an hour in my life…'[71] From 1851 to 1859 I was in California, Egypt, and India .In 1856-58 I was in Kashmere and elsewhere.[72]

In 1877 Blavatsky regretted giving this initial interview to the *Daily Graphic* and went through this article underlining and crossing sentences out claiming that 'these lies were circulated by American reporters' and that 'she had nothing to do with the publication of this article.' It seemed that Blavatsky had changed her opinion regarding the early events relating to her Spiritualist conversion; this could have been one of her later attempts at distancing her Theosophy from Spiritualism or she may have invented this conversion story by Home in order to connect her with the famous medium.[73]

In the body of his work *The Dawning of The Theosophical Movement*, Gomes observed an animosity that existed between Home and Blavatsky and noted that 'we do not know the reason for the enmity between H.P.B. and Home for they never met, but Home published a revealing letter from William Crookes to himself dated 21 January 1876, in his 1877 autobiography *Lights and Shadows of Spiritualism*.'[74] Next, Gomes recounted the content of Home's article: 'H. P. B was a common woman in 1857-8 in Paris; that she had a liaison there with Prince Emil de Sayn Wittgenstein,that in 1858 she gave birth to a deformed boy which died in Kieff in 1868.[75] Thus, it appeared that Home was antagonistic towards Blavatsky.

Gomes further admitted that Home possessed a motive for defaming Wittgenstein. Apparently Wittgenstein was present while Home was horsewhipped by an English officer for his role in defaming an English lady 'living abroad.'[76] In 1890, Blavatsky sued the New York newspaper that printed Home's article for libel. These charges were eventually cancelled upon Blavatsky's death on 8 May 1891; however, Gomes acknowledged that this New York paper issued a statement on 26 September 1892 saying that these statements 'are not sustained by evidence, and should not have been printed.'[77] On 1 March 1877, Olcott personally wrote a confrontational letter to Home in response to his article and in defense of Blavatsky noting that 'such behaviour is reserved for blackguards-and mediums.'[78]

Despite Olcott's exasperation at Home, in his 1895 history of the Theosophical Society titled *Old Diary Leaves* Olcott maintained the above quote that Blavatsky had been converted to Spiritualism by Daniel Home in 1858. It seemed possible that based on: 1) Home's fabrication that Blavatsky had a deformed child with prince Wittgenstein, 2) Olcott's admission in 1895 eight years after this scandal that Blavatsky had been converted to Spiritualism by Home, and 3) Gomes observation that enmity existed between these two figures, that all of these elements seem to suggest that there may have been some type of falling out between Blavatsky and Home. This seems to be a likely justification for an otherwise perplexing relationship. A second possibility which appears more critical of Blavatsky was that she had fabricated her experience with Home in order to give her own conversion story more authority.[79] After all, even as early as 1858 Home had become one of the most celebrated mediums of the Victorian Era.[80]

Despite whether one agrees with Olcott's testimony that Blavatsky was converted by Home (which was also printed in the New York *Daily Graphic* and the November 1874 edition of the *Scientist*) there seems little room to doubt the veracity of the statement that Blavatsky herself attested to, that she at one time converted to Spiritualism. This above letter was written by Blavatsky and reprinted by Olcott and is important because it evidenced her conversion by D. D. Home a reputed Spiritualist and further attested to her early enthusiasm exhibited in the successful conversion of her father. This zeal was further evidenced in some of the following letters.

13 December 1874

A second letter reprinted by her intimate friend Colonel Olcott clearly connected Blavatsky to Spiritualism during her earlier years:

> It is useless to deny that, throughout the early part of her American residence, she called herself a spiritualist and warmly defended Spiritualism and its mediums from their sciolistic and other bitter traducers. Her letters and articles in various American and English journals contain many evidences of her occupying that position. Among other examples, I will simply quote the following: [Letter of HP Blavatsky sent to *The Spiritualist* on 13 December 1874]:
> As it is, I have only done my duty; first, towards Spiritualism, that I have defended as well as I could from the attacks of imposture under the too transparent mask of science; then towards two helpless, slandered mediums...But I am obliged to confess that I really do not believe in having done any-good- to Spiritualism itself...It is with a profound sadness in my heart that I acknowledge this fact, for I begin to think there is no help for it. For over fifteen years have I fought my battle for the blessed truth; have travelled and preached it- though I never was born for a lecturer- from the snow-covered tops of the Caucasian Mountains, as well as from the sandy valleys of the Nile. I have proved the truth of it practically and persuasion. For the sake of Spiritualism I have left my home, an easy life amongst a civilized society, and have become a wanderer upon the face of the earth. I had already seen my hopes realized, beyond my most sanguine expectation, when my unlucky star brought me to America. Knowing this country to be the cradle of Modern Spiritualism, I came over here from France with feelings not unlike those of a Mohammedan approaching the birthplace of his Prophet....[81]

Blavatsky again acknowledged her association with Spiritualism in 1858 and her early connection with American Spiritualism and her dedication to this movement; however, it also exhibited her passion for this movement commencing in 1859.

30 January 1875

In a different letter written to F. J. Lippitt on 30 January 1875 Blavatsky admitted her frustration with the Spiritualist movement and the widespread allegations perpetrated against practitioners of her day: 'The time is close, my dear General, when Spiritualism must be cleansed of its erroneous misinterpretations, superstitions, and ignorant notions, all of which only make skeptics and unbelievers laugh at us.'[82] Furthermore, this letter is important because it allows the reader to see that Blavatsky viewed her Theosophy as a purified form of Spiritualism. Thus, she exhibited her emergence from and disappointment with mainstream Spiritualism. As noted in the previous letter, Blavatsky viewed the United States as the 'the cradle of Modern Spiritualism' equating her journey there as a religious pilgrimage, though she does admit that the present state of the movement was in disarray.

9 February 1875

In a similar letter written to Hiram Corson on 9 February 1875, Blavatsky expressed another thought related to Spiritualism: 'I came to this Country only on account of the Truth in Spiritualism, but I am afraid I will have to give it up. We shall never be able to draw the line of demarcation between the true and the false, as long as the so called pillars of Spiritualism will, notwithstanding their half rotten and unreliable condition, be supported and helped out to the last, by the too lenient backs of the cowardly Spiritualists.'[83] This letter articulated Blavatsky's frustration with the open philosophy of Spiritualism and its inability to control the kinds of manifestations mediums produced and the content of their spirit communications. In particular the mediums who had been influenced by reincarnation were giving vent to some really bizarre communications during this time period.

11 February 1875

Later that same month, Blavatsky wrote to A. N. Aksakoff the Russian Spiritualist and expressed the following thoughts:

> I wanted this, because I have already sacrificed myself for Spiritualism, and am ready at any moment to lay my head on the block, in defense of my faith and the truth; and in the court, before the Grand Jury, I would have shown who is innocent and who is guilty in this unparalleled swindle of Spiritualism, in this rascality, where no one sees what is truth and what is lies, and which is bringing despondency and confusion to the whole Spiritualistic world of America and Europe, and giving the skeptics the right to laugh at us.[84]

Here again Blavatsky's disappointment with deceitful practitioners of Spiritualism was evident as well as her dedication to promote this cause for the redemptive elements of truth that she believed could be found in this movement.

February 1875

In a different letter addressed to Aksakoff written that same month, Blavatsky again defended the cause of Spiritualism: 'For Spiritualism I am ready to work night and day as long as I have morsel of bread, and that only because it is hard to work when one is hungry...'[85] And in another letter written during that same time period (13 February 1875) Blavatsky identified herself as a Spiritualist to Lippitt: 'Spiritualism will never be able to crawl out from the clutches of suspicion and ostracism unless we Spiritualists help ourselves to extricate the genuine facts from under weeds of falsehood and lies that suffocate the former....'[86] Again the idea of reforming Spiritualism seemed to be at the forefront of Blavatsky's mind. At a minimum, it is clear to see that Blavatsky closely associated and identified with the Spiritualist movement in her early career.

16 February 1875

In another fascinating letter Blavatsky connected her Western Esoteric philosophy to Spiritualism. This is the first instance within her known writings where the term 'theosophy' was employed in defining a Western Esoteric ideology that was more pure than Spiritualism and was first found in the philosophies of astrology, Hermeticism, alchemy, kabbalah, and Neo-Platonism. Note the following pericope of a letter sent on 16 February 1875:

> I am here, in this country sent by my Lodge, on behalf of Truth in modern Spiritualism, and it is my most sacred duty to unveil what it is. And expose what it is not...When I became a Spiritualist, it was not through the agency of the ever lying, cheating mediums, miserable instruments of the undeveloped Spirits of the lower Sphere, the ancient Hades. My belief is based, on something older than the Rochester Knockings and spring out from the same source of information, that was used by Raymond Lully, Picus of Mirandola, Cornelius Agrippa, Robert Fludd Henry More etc etc all of whom have ever been searching for a system, that should disclose to them the 'deepest depths' of the Divine nature and show them the real tie which binds all things together. I found at last- and many years ago- the cravings of my mind satisfied by this *theosophy* taught by the Angels and communicated by them, that the protoplast might know it for the aid of the human destiny. The

Ain Soph of the Endless and the Boundless, with its ten Se-
phiroths or Emanations goes more towards opening your eyes
than all the hypothetic teachings of the leaders of Spiritualism....[87]

This letter illustrated the Western esoteric flavoring that Blavatsky
merged into her Spiritualist philosophy and mirrored her later hermetic article 'A Few Questions to HIRAF' which would be published in 15 and 22 July of this same year in which she would further
explore the connection between Western Esotericism and Spiritualism. Given Blavatsky's direct connection to Spiritualism during these
earlier days, it must be ascertained that the influence of this Victorian
religious movement on Blavatsky during her earlier years cannot be
over emphasized despite her later claims that she was never associated with this movement.

In her later attempts to demarcate the Theosophical Society from
Spiritualism (though Blavatsky continually shifted between reconciling and demarcating the relationship of these two organizations),
Blavatsky would deny having any connection with Spiritualism in her
rebuttal against Arthur Lillie written in the Spiritualist magazine *Light*
on 11 October 1884:

> I say again, I never was a Spiritualist. I have always known the real-
> ity of mediumistic phenomena, and defended that reality; that is
> all. If to have the whole long series of phenomena happen through
> one's organism, will, or any other agency, is to be a 'Spiritualist,'
> then was I one, perhaps, fifty years ago, i.e., I was a Spiritualist be-
> fore the truth of modern Spiritualism. As regards mediums, séanc-
> es, and the spiritualistic 'philosophy,' so-called—belief in the latter
> alone constituting a Spiritualist—then it may perhaps stagger your
> readers to learn that I had never known, nor even seen a medium,
> nor ever found myself in a séance room, before March, 1873,
> when I was passing through Paris on my way to America [accord-
> ing to Narad Mani's report it was during this time that Blavatsky
> had been introduced to the French Spiritist Lady Cathness; how-
> ever, as Joscelyn Godwin noted this report should not be taken at
> face value.].[88] And it was in August of the same year that I learned,
> for the first time in my life, what was the philosophy of the Spirit-
> ualists. Very true I had had a general and very vague idea of the
> teachings of Allan Kardec since 1860. But when I heard stated the
> claims of the American Spiritualists about the 'Summer Land,' etc.,
> I rejected the whole thing point blank. I might name several per-
> sons in America as my witnesses if the testimony of Colonel Ol-
> cott were not sufficient... In the beginning of 1872, on my arrival

> from India, I had tried to found a Spiritist Society at Cairo after the fashion of Allan Kardec (I knew of no other), to try for phenomena, as a preparative for occult science. I had two French pretended mediums, who treated us to bogus manifestations, and who revealed to me such mediumistic tricks as I could never have dreamed possible. I put an end to the séances immediately.[89]

Given the letters reprinted in this section, Blavatsky's claim to have never been a Spiritualist seemed to contradict many of her previous writings. Furthermore, Blavatsky's appeal to Olcott to validate that she was not a Spiritualist seemed futile as he noted plainly in his diary that 'it is useless to deny that, throughout the early part of her American residence, she called herself a spiritualist and warmly defended Spiritualism and its mediums from their sciolistic and other bitter traducers.'[90] As noted above, there would be an Eastern shift in the Theosophical Society after Blavatsky had departed for India in 1879; however, it is the premise of this work that this shift was much more apparent than actual. Even after this methodological 'shift' Blavatsky's philosophy seemed to continually make provision for Spiritualists including an acceptance of its main tenet and even other philosophical issues as well. Despite this inclusion, Blavatsky continuously shifts between a harmonization with Spiritualism to a demarcation away from this movement throughout her writings which she changes based on her mood and her audience. This continual shifting would push one Blavatsky critic Arthur Lillie to view Blavatsky as an opportunist who changed her philosophy in order to make money and to control her followers.[91] Whether or not finances and power were ultimate goal; nonetheless, this shifting remained apparent in many of her writings.

2.12 Blavatsky's Shifting Opinion of Spiritualism

Two letters deserve an examination which represent this continually shifting view regarding Spiritualism that Blavatsky maintained throughout her life. This first letter was written to John Bundy the editor of the *Religio-Philosophical Journal* on 26 January 1878 (several months following the publication of *Isis Unveiled*):

> I am a true, firm, if anything, too exalted spiritualist. Desiring as I do, to leave no stone unturned to force spiritualism and nobler truths upon the world of scientists in general and skeptics especially, I try to show the readers that I am neither credulous nor blind to the imperfections and short-comings of Spiritualism as it is

now. I work in my own way and try to do my best. Why believe me a deceiver and a schemer? I feel pained to see that I have no greater enemies in the world than spiritualists themselves, whose faith or rather philosophy I would see spread throughout the world and become the only and universal belief on earth. Please pitch into myself, cigarettes, entourage, fatness, Calmuck nose, etc., etc., as much as you like, and I will be the first to laugh but don't represent me as an enemy of true Spiritualism. Olcott is as sincere as myself in that. If he has several times protested against being called a spiritualist, I have as many times pitched into him for that. He may be a flapdoodle in his loose expressions, but he has always been a true spiritualist.[92]

It seemed apparent that as late as 26 January 1878 Blavatsky was still identifying herself as a Spiritualist; however, several months earlier in a different letter Blavatsky presented a completely opposing view towards 'Modern Spiritualism.' Note the content in the following communication written on 19 November 1877 to William Henry Burr (1819-1908) a painter and author from Washington, D.C who was curious about the teachings of Spiritualism:[93]

Let us settle, once and for all if you please, as to the word 'Spiritu-alist.' I am not one- not at least in the modern and American sense of the word. I am a Svabhavika, a Buddhist pantheist, it anything at all. I do not believe in a personal God, in a direct Creator, or a Supreme' [Being]; neither do I confess to a First cause, which im-plies the possibility of a Last one- and if so, then what comes next?...You are right in saying that you see no inconsistency in be-ing an Atheist and at the same time a Spiritualist. I am an Atheist and at the same time a Spiritualist. I am an Atheist in the Christian sense of the word, and yet I believe in the survival of the real inner man after the dissolution of his physical body...I emphatically de-ny that the spirits of the dead can show or manifest themselves objectively in any way or manner. But I do believe and know that these spirits have the power...to impress mortals on earth, to in-spire, and teach them, etc....I believe in some of the manifesta-tions produced by mediums, but hold that pretty nearly all such phenomena are the result of the freaks of the spirits of the medi-ums themselves, and are often helped by the 'elementary,' or dis-embodied men and women who, having parted forever from their immortal spirits, vegetate within the atmosphere of the earth, which alone attracts them, and use the organs of weak mediums to lead through them a fictitious life, and cheat annihilation for a short time yet.[94]

Blavatsky's undecided relationship with Spiritualism which she maintained throughout her life seems clearly presented in these two letters. Also, exemplified in this above letter were Blavatsky's views of eternal time (no first or last cause) were assimilated with the oriental ideal of annihilation (not a common element in Western Spiritualism as it opposed the 'law of progress') combined with her Western Esoteric form of Spiritualism. Despite these shifts and changes Blavatsky still believed that 'some of the manifestations produced by mediums' were genuine making her able to identify with the Spiritualist movement of the nineteenth century. At this point in the study, Blavatsky's contradictory nature should be apparent to the reader as this nature will remain a consistent flaw throughout her writings. Even in the above letter Blavatsky's mental dichotomy was exemplified in her belief that she was not a Spiritualist, yet maintained that some of the Spiritualist phenomena were genuine. Though Blavatsky did not always wish to identify as a Spiritualist; nonetheless, her doctrine remained compatible with Spiritualist teachings even through much of her later Oriental teachings. Blavatsky's continuously shifting and indecisive opinion towards Spiritualism would be a contributing factor towards the ambiguity associated with the relationship of these two movements. Another Theosophical doctrine that confused its relationship with Spiritualism was known as the 'theory of elementals' which will now be discussed.

2.13 Blavatsky and Her Theory of Elementals

Beginning in 1848 and into the early 1850s, Spiritualism was a new phenomenon in the United States that began rapidly gaining popularity and spreading throughout the country. As noted in the introduction, in the United States there were between nine and ten million people who identified themselves as Spiritualists in a population of some forty-four million. The experienced growth during this time period was soon countered by the subsequent exposure of multiple crooked mediums who were attempting to profit off of the grief of others. This widespread revelation prompted many practitioners to conclude that Spiritualism was nothing more than a theatrical performance and therefore any claims toward communications with the departed were merely the results of paltry parlor tricks performed to dupe the audience out of their money. Thus, as Blavatsky wrote in a letter to Hiram Corson in 15 March 1875 'Spiritualism as it is must be stoped (sic) in its progress and given another direction'- this direction would be towards a Western Esoteric flavoring and revolved around her 'theory of elementals.'

This publicization of exposures in the media seemed to be a result of the establishment of scientific organizations that combined the scientific method with the previous methods of paranormal investigation as exemplified by Henry Olcott in his work *People from the Other World* (1875- though Olcott was certainly not the most capable paranormal investigator of his time). These publicized exposures would have affected Blavatsky's willingness to identify herself as a Spiritualist, but more importantly these controversies would have prompted her reformation and institutionalization of the Spiritualist movement at large which she attempted to do through the early Theosophical Society. Blavatsky surmised what seemed to be a legitimate justification for this sudden surge of deceitful mediumistic practices- she attributed these practices as the workings of elemental spirits (also often times referred to as 'elementary spirits' as Blavatsky claimed that an elemental was the lowest form of an elementary spirit in *Isis Unveiled* though these terms are still often employed interchangeably throughout Theosophical literature).[95] Blavatsky's conceptualization of elementals underwent a strange evolution as their role shifted from *Isis Unveiled* to *The Secret Doctrine* published in 1888; originally, these spirit beings were never meant to become human beings; however, in *The Secret Doctrine* their role changed as they were now described as 'future human beings.'[96] Blavatsky's connection between elementals and the 'kabalists' who referred to these spirits as 'gnomes, sylphs, salamanders, and undines' evidenced her affinity with Eliphas Lévi (1810 – 1875) the French magician who maintained that:

> Elementary spirits are like children: they chiefly torment those who trouble about them, unless, indeed, they are controlled by high reason and great severity. We designate these spirits under the name of occult elements, and it is these who frequently occasion our bizarre or disturbing dreams, who produce the movements of the divining rod and rappings upon walls or furniture, but they can manifest no thought other than our own, and when we are not thinking they speak to us with all the incoherence of dreams... a man who is timid in the water will never reign over the undines; one who it afraid of fire will never command salamanders; so long as we are liable to giddiness we must leave the sylphs in peace, and forbear from irritating the gnomes.[97]

Thus, Blavatsky adhered to Lévi's definition that elementals were evil agents of unembodied spirits invoked at séances and possessed a malevolent and annoying disposition though still capable of producing physical phenomena.[98] Blavatsky's theory of elementals also reflected the earlier teachings of the once Theosophist Emma Hardinge Britten in her *Art Magic* (1876). Britten noted the nature of elementary spirits as follows:

> The Elementaries are neither wholly spiritual, nor entirely material in substance. The corporeity of their bodies is too dense to inhabit the spirit spheres, or consort with purely spiritual existences, yet not sufficiently palpable to become visible to material eyes, or the external senses of man. They inhabit strata of atmospheres infinitely more sublimated than gases, yet far less refined than pure Astral light...The disembodied Souls of men are the counterparts to man himself-the Elementaries to the world of matter, including the animal, vegetable and mineral kingdoms.[99]

Regardless of Blavatsky's sources, she presumed that the fraudulent mediums were deceitful because they channeled fraudulent spirits. This idea was elaborated in the article series based on Blavatsky's 'Mahatma letters' sent to A. O. Hume and printed in *The Theosophist* under the title 'Fragments of Occult Truth':

> Now probably Spiritualists will admit that our views would explain the vast mass of trash, frivolous non-sense and falsehood communicated through medium, as also the manner in which so many of these good and honest to begin with, gradually grow into immoral impostors.[100]

However, if a medium continuously invoked a deceitful spirit the natural outcome could be disastrous:

> only an adept can clearly and consciously place the spiritual Ego wholly under the domination of the Spirit. ...In truth, mediumship is a dangerous, too often a fatal capacity, and it we oppose Spiritualism, as we have ever consistently done, it is not because we question the reality of their phenomena, which, we know, can and do occur (despite the multitudes of fraudulent imitations) and which our adepts can reproduce at will without danger to themselves, but because of the irreparable spiritual injury (we say nothing of the mere physical sufferings) which the pursuit of Spiritualism inevitably entails on nine-tenths of the mediums employed....we have seen scores, nay rather hundreds of, so to say, good pure, honest young men and women....who through the gradual pernicious influence of these low, earth-bound natures have sunk, from bad

to worse, ending, often prematurely, lives that could lead but to spiritual ruin."[101]

Blavatsky elucidated this idea in her *Key to Theosophy* where the ailments of Spiritualism were evolved to include not just spiritual ruin but physical as well:

> Your best, your most powerful mediums, have all suffered in health of body and min. Think of the sad end of Charles Foster, who died in an asylum, a raving lunatic; of Slade, an epileptic; of Eglinton- the best medium now in England- subject to the same. Look back over the life of D.D. Home....[who]suffered for years from a terrible spinal disease, brought on by his intercourse with the 'spirits', and died a perfect wreck. Think again of the sad fate of poor Washington Irving Bishop. I knew him in New York when he was fourteen and was undeniably a medium. ..Finally, behold the veteran mediums, the founder and prime movers of modern spiritualism- the Fox sisters. After more than forty years of intercourse with the 'Angels', the latter have led them to become incurable sots, who are now denouncing, in public lectures, their own life-long work and philosophy as a fraud.[102]

These elementals could cause real physical and spiritual damage on a medium if they continuously invoked them; it was only safe for an adept to communicate with these mediums because they were not channeling spirits, rather they were traveling to the astral world and meeting them in their astral bodies.

The introduction of this concept of elementals in the early Theosophical Society remains unknown and seemed to have been developed by Olcott, Blavatsky, and/or Emma Hardinge Britten (though the belief in 'elementary spirits' was not original or unique to Theosophy). Despite this questionable origination it seemed to have been first capitalized upon by the early Theosophist- George Henry Felt the vice-president of the Theosophical Society. It was during his lecture on 'The Lost Canon of Proportion of the Egyptians' that Olcott originally had the inspiration to establish the Theosophical Society in September of 1875. Later, in Olcotts's first presidential address delivered on 17 November 1875 Olcott claimed that Felt possessed the knowledge and ability to prove the existence of these 'Elementary beings.' This startled Felt who in turn wrote a letter to the *London Spiritualist* claiming that Olcott had spoken a bit 'prematurely.'[103]

This incident was discussed by Blavatsky in a letter to Hiram Corson sent on 8 January 1876:

> For Felt, though he promised to all the Theosophists to clear the atmosphere chemically and show the unseen monsters around us, and though he has done so before a dozen witnesses at least, who traduced him and called him a sorcerer- I do not know whether or when he will make his promise good. But Olcott is such a sanguine fanatic, so sure of the other world, so certain spirits, pure, disembodied men and women, that he speaks of it very foolishly as it is was already demonstrated and done.[104]

Felt (who also affiliated with the Masons) was an integral figure in the early Theosophical Society known for his lectures though he only remained a member for a short period of time. The reason for his resignation was hinted at in Olcott's later recollection: 'Our first bitter disappointment was the failure of Mr. Felt to fulfill his promises. With difficulty I got him to give one or two more lectures, but he never showed us so much as the wag of the tail of a vanishing elemental.'[105] This disappointment was first exhibited at a 15 March Society meeting where the question was raised as to when it would be 'likely that the promised lectures and experiments by Mr. Felt would take place.' Felt replied 'that he had not yet had time to prepare his drawings, but that as soon as he could, he would get all things in readiness,' and continued to expound upon 'the Exhibition of Elementary spirits, the propositions he would prove, and what had already been accomplished by him.' The evening ended with a motion of thanks to Mr. Felt, and adjourned at 10:25 p. m...'[106]

On the evening of April 19, when the first lecture of the series was scheduled, Felt did not appear. Instead a 'communication' from him was read in which he stated that as he was required to reverse the order in which he had planned to deliver his lectures; he eventually declined to deliver any of them, and in which he also offered his resignation of the position of Vice-President of the Society.

James Santucci the editor of *Theosophical History* has written a biographical article on George Felt in which he summarized Felt's contribution to the Theosophical Society:

> Aside from his active participation from September to November 1875 and only occasional mention thereafter in the Minute Book of the Theosophical Society and scattered accounts and reminiscences, we might safely assume that Felt either lost interest in the

Society or was incapable of fulfilling his promise of demonstrating the existence of Elementals and Elementary (spirits), which would have raised occultism to an exact science. In any event, he completely removed himself from the Society in the latter part of 1876, and abandoned those who joined on the promise that he was on the verge of a great discovery. Indeed, a chapter in the Society was closed with his departure. Rene Guenon claimed that Felt had fulfilled his mission and that this mysterious disappearance suggested that he was in fact a member of the H.B. of L. (Hermetic Brotherhood of Luxor).[107]

Thus, Felt's short tenure as Vice President of the Theosophical Society ended in disappointment.

2.14 Blavatsky and Her Conceptualization of Spiritual Masters

Blavatsky's associations and philosophical ideologies were not the only elements shared with Spiritualism. Blavatsky's very conceptualization of her Tibetan Masters had its early roots in Spiritualism. Many Spiritualist mediums employed different 'spirit guides' to lead them through the spirit world. Oftentimes, mediums would adopt alternate personalities in their séances based upon the individual spirit guide that they were channeling. Many of these spirits were allegedly historical personages; thus, when channeling a historical figure such as William Shakespeare, the medium would take on the personality, speech, and behavior that was common for William Shakespeare. In fact the bard was a common figure making spectral appearances from the 18th to the 20th century revealing himself through a variety of phenomena including the most famous situation of his communication with Victor Hugo through a series of raps.[108] Thus, spirit guides could be famous figures of the past or unknown figures whose identification were too vague to verify.

Wouter Hanegraaff noted a further connection between the Victorian process of channeling spirit guides and the 18th century process of communicating with 'elevated beings' in such illuminist orders as 'Martinez da Pasqually's Elus-Cohens, Dom Antoine-Joseph Pernety's *Illumines d'Avignon*, Jean-Baptiste Willermoz's *Chevaliers Bienfaisants de la Cite Sainte*, and similar religious orders closely connected to or derived from them.'[109] Thus, the belief in spiritual masters that could communicate with mortals has a rich history that Blavatsky would utilize through her conceptualization of the Tibetan Masters. These Tibetan masters had a humble origination and first began through Blavatsky's conceptualization of the famous spirit guide-John King.

2.15 Blavatsky and John King

Blavatsky during her time in the States became attached to a spirit guide who she named 'John King'. King was an unidentifiable spirit guide who Brendan French expounded upon in his thesis which focused upon the subject of Blavatsky's 'masters':

> Central to the doctrines of Spiritualism was the existence of the 'spirit guide', the Hermesian entity responsible for transmitting *post mortem* communications. As Spiritualist séances proliferated, so too did the search for the most reliable and assiduous spirit guides. Of these, a number rose to prominence, even in some cases assuming dynastic proportions. Perhaps the most famous and ubiquitous of the early guides was the spirit known as John King. Having first appeared to the Davenport brothers in 1850 and the Koons soon thereafter, 'John King became a staple in the Spiritualist world, as did his 'daughter' Katie King; indeed, they were the most popular male and female spirit guides on either side of the Atlantic for many years. It is not insignificant that from reasonably humble (post-mortem) beginnings, John King was eventually to be represented in rather exalted fashion; in one instance he was shown to be the spirit of the buccaneer Henry Morgan (c.1635-1688), at another time he claimed to be the chief of a band of prelapsarian spirits.[110]

The concepts of Spirit guides and controls were a common theme in Victorian Spiritualism employed by a number of famous mediums including William Stainton Moses, Leonora Piper, and Emma Hardinge Britten to name only a few. Emma Harding Britten actually noted in her autobiography that Spirit guides were a fundamental aspect of nineteenth-century Spiritualism:

> In my subsequent experiences with thousands of mediums, in different countries, I can scarcely remember one who was not controlled, or at least assisted, by some special Spirit friend, whom the mediums regarded as 'Guides' or 'Controls'...The functions of these attendant, 'Guides' were still further explained to me by my own Spirit teachers as the fact that there were Medium Spirits in the higher world, just as there were medium mortals here on earth. In other words, certain Spirits only could effect a magnetic rapport with certain mortals called mediums.[111]

Thus, the very fact that Blavatsky associated with 'John King' evidenced her intimate connection to American Spiritualism.

'John King' had formed an unusual relationship with Blavatsky that has been predominantly ignored in modern Theosophical scholarship. One writer noted that John King was best defined as an 'undigested lump in Theosophical Literature' noting the lack of research that has been performed on ascertaining this mysterious spirit guide.[112] It seemed that this haunting figure was an externalized form of Blavatsky's psyche which seemed to emerge especially in the wake of traumatic events. Though this suggestion must remain speculative, it does seem that Blavatsky associated King with an externalized form of her 'intuition' as noted during the following tragedy alleged by Blavatsky and the demise of Metrovich on the *SS Eumonia* in 1871:

> I know John for 14 years. Not a day but he is with me; he made acquaintance with all Petersburg and half of Russia under the name of *Janka*, or 'Johny'; he travelled with me all over the world. Saved my life *three* times, at Mentana, in a shipwreck, and the last time near *Spezia* when our steamer was blown in the air, to atoms and out of 400 passengers remained but 16, in 1871, 21 of June.

Again though there is reason to suspect the veracity of this statement and Blavatsky's account of the death of Metrovich, it was curious that John King was attributed to Blavatsky and her unique survival skills especially in this situation. Another passage that connected John King to an externalized emotional state of loneliness was exhibited in the following quote recorded by Blavatsky's critic Solovyoff:

> Moreover the spirit John King is very fond of me, and I am fonder of him than anything on earth. He is my only friend, and if I am indebted to any one for the radical changes in my ideas of life, my efforts and so on, it is to him alone. He has transformed me, and I shall be indebted to him, when I 'go to the upper story,' for not having to dwell for centuries it may be in darkness and gloom. John and I are acquainted from old times, long before he began to materalise in London and take walks in the medium's house with a lamp in his hand.[113]

Thus, it seemed that an argument could be made that John King represented Blavatsky's early subconscious voice which she eventually brought into her practice of Spiritualism. Also, of importance was the belief that Blavatsky had been acquainted with and communicated with John King well before he began frequenting séance circles illustrating the superiority of her psychic abilities. Solyvoff noted the eventual evolution of John King as a servant to the Brotherhood of Luxor then eventually transforming into the Tibetan Masters Moray and Koot Hoomi: 'here are the first traces of the gradual transformation of John King into Mahatma Morya. The 'master' is not invented yet as it will only grow clear in the course of a couple of years in India, into whom the 'familiar spirit' is to be turned...However, what she says is quite enough for every reader of my narrative to recognise at once in this John King the first appearance on the stage of our old acquaintance, the famous Thibetan Mahatma Morya'[114] Previous to this event Solvyoff reprinted a letter that Blavatsky had written on 11 February 1875 expounding upon this strange relationship that existed between her and John King and noting Blavatsky's frustration with the Spiritualist movement:

> John King has sent Olcott to Havanna for a few days...I have quite ceased to get any letters from my aunts and sisters; they have evidently all forgotten me, and so much the better for them. I am now no credit to them, to tell the truth. I shall never go back to Russia. My father is dead, nobody wants me and I am altogether superfluous in the world. Here I am at least a human being; there I am-Blavatsky. I know that everybody respects me here, and I am needed for Spiritism. Now the spirits are my brothers and sisters, my father and mother. My John King alone is sufficient recompense for all; he is a host in himself to me....John King is a personality, a definite, living, spiritual personality. Whether devil or good spirit, he is at all events a spirit, and not the medium's prototype.[115]

Blavatsky identified with 'Spiritism' the French form of Spiritualism that she had practiced in her Societe Spirite while residing in Cairo. Given her association with this movement in 1871, it seemed only natural that she appeared most familiar with this French form of Spiritualism at this early stage in her life. The chronology of this letter was curious appearing immediately following an unsettling event for the Spiritualist movement-the exposure of the Holmes mediums. Jennie and Nelson Holmes were popular Spiritualist mediums who became well known for their abilities to materialize a spirit known as 'Katie King' the supposed daughter of 'John King'. These séances were attended by the acclaimed Robert Dale Owen (1801- 1877) a well known writer and a solid proponent of Spiritualism. For multiple months he had sat with the Holmes and even initiated a relationship with the physical phantasm Katie King. Owen from time to time would even present Katie with valuable presents including gold rings and bracelets. These items were believed to have been taken back with her into the spirit world from where she materialized; however, the Holmes were soon publically exposed as frauds in 1874 when it was shown that they had hired Eliza White to impersonate 'Katie King' at their séances. Jennie and Nelson Holmes were proven to be fraudulent mediums and were publicly denounced by Owen. This was a 'staggering blow' to Spiritualism as Olcott concluded in his *People from the Other World*.[116] In spite of this public exposure Blavatsky continued to defend these mediums with whom she had allegedly colluded; however, she clarified the nature of her relationship with the Holmeses in her Scrapbook:

> Yes. I am sorry to say that I had to identify myself during, that shameful exposure of the mediums Holmes with the Spiritualists. I had to save the situation, for I was sent from Paris on purpose to America to prove the phenomena and their reality and—show the fallacy of the Spiritualistic theories of 'Spirits.' But how could I do it best? I did not want people at large to know that I could produce the same thing at will. I had received ORDERS to the contrary, and yet, I had to keep alive the reality, the genuineness and possibility of such phenomena in the hearts of those who from Materialists had turned Spiritualists and now, owing to the exposure of several mediums fell back again, returned to their skepticism. This is why, selecting a few of the faithful, I went to the Holmeses and helped by M . . . and his power, brought out the face of John King and Katie King in the astral light, produced the phenomena of materialization and— allowed the Spiritualists at large to believe it was done thro' the mediumship of Mrs. Holmes.[117]

Blavatsky explained that the phenomena produced at the Holmes séances were indeed genuine; however, the true materializations were performed by herself with the help of her masters not by the mediumship of the Holmeses. This above excerpt also noted the role of 'John King' who was subservient to the master revealed here only as 'M.' Thus, John King began to evolve into his new role described previously by Solovyoff- he had become a messenger for a group of higher beings known simply as the Brotherhood of Luxor.

The further reconceptualization of John King as a messenger of the mysterious and elusive masters was further exhibited in the following letter written around this same time period. Incidentally, one author has marked this letter as evidence of Blavatsky's decisive turn away from Spiritualism:[118]

> From the Brotherhood of Luxor, Section the Vth to Henry Olcott. Brother Neophyte, we greet thee.
> He who seeks us finds *us*. Try. Rest thy mind - banish all foul doubt. We keep watch over our faithful soldiers. Sister Helen is a valiant, trustworthy servant. Open thy Spirit to conviction, have faith and she will lead thee to the Golden Gate of truth ... Brother 'John' [John King] hath brought three of our *Masters* to look at thee after the séance. Thy noble exertions on behalf of our cause now give us the right of letting thee know who they were:
> > *Serapis Bey* (Ellora Section)
> > *Polydorus Isurenus* (Section of Solomon)
> > *Robert More* (Section of Zoroaster)
> Sister Hellen (Helena Blavatsky) will explain thee the meaning of the Star and colors.
> > Activity and Silence as to the present.
> > By Order of the Grand
> > TUITIT BEY
> Observatory of Luxor.
> Tuesday Morning.
> Day of Mars.[119]

It is curious to note the gradual evolution of John King's role from a common spirit guide channeled in séances across the Western world to a servant for the mysterious Brotherhood of Luxor (a group of magi which met in the hollowed temples of the trodden Luxor and determined the spiritual destines of humanity) until his subsequent disappearance out of the Blavatsky's philosophy following her 'Oriental shift' and the discovery of her Tibetan Indian Mahatmas. The Tibetan master Morya would have no need of King and would make his will known to Blavatsky and especially to Olcott and Sinnett through the use of the 'Mahatma' letters. The following letter is written in code, but the initials likely correspond to the following names: T. B. for Tuitit Bey, J. K. for John King, and M. for Morya.

> An attempt in consequence of *orders* received from T*** B*** through p*** personating J. K. Ordered to begin telling the public

the *truth* about the phenomena & their mediums. And *now* my mar-
tyrdom will begin! I will have all the Spiritualists against me in addition to the Christians & the Skeptics! Thy Will, oh M∴ be
done!'[120]

This letter was delivered in May 1875 and pressed Blavatsky to immediately begin reforming Spiritualism through the founding of her
Miracle Club which actually never was officially established. This
announcement was made in the *Spiritual Scientist* and was found in
Blavatsky's Scrap Book for 1874-1875.

2.16 The Writing Habits of John King

One of the more common antics that John King played upon
Blavatsky was to write post scripts on her outgoing mail in either red
or blue colored markings; this habit would eventually become a
defining trait of the Mahatma letters as attested by C. Jinarājadāsa the
early Theosophical historian.[121] It appeared that Blavatsky could have
derived her preference to use blue and red writing as divine calling
cards of these invisible masters from a medium named Cozine as
explained in the following diary entry from the Theosophical
Society's co-founder- Henry Steel Olcott:

> ...on an evening of 1875, I sat at the house of the President of the
> Photographic Section of the American Institute, Mr. H. J. Newton,
> with a private medium named Cozine, to witness his slate-
> writings...the communications came upon the slate in bright blue
> and red colours...upon mentioning this to H.P.B. she said: 'I think
> I could do that; at any rate, I will try.' So I went out and bought a
> slate and brought it home; she took it...into a small, pitch-dark
> closet bed-room...after few minutes she reappeared with the slate
> in her hand...on the slate was writing in red and blue crayons, in
> handwritings not her own.'[122]

This concept was used by Blavatsky in a letter written to F. J.
Lippitt during her earlier days as a Spiritualist. In a reply letter written
on 23 June 1875 Lippitt described the hand-written, red and blue
pencil notes made by 'John King' on a letter that he had received
from Blavatsky.[123] John King even had his own peculiar style of
writing. As already observed, these notes were made in red and blue
pencil a device that would later be used by the brotherhood of Luxor
and finally by the Indian Mahatmas as they communicated with
outsiders. W. E. Coleman the Spiritualist critic of Blavatsky described

in his 'Critical Historical Review of The Theosophical Society' a situation where these colored pencils were discovered by some of Blavatsky's followers: 'While in Europe Mohini M. Chatterji and B. J. Padshah independently discovered fraud, and the three proceeded to sift the matter. They found bundles of blue and red pencils, with which the mahatma letters were written, and packs of Chinese envelopes, in which the missives were sent.'[124] Thus, these blue and red pencils became sanctified as the chosen communications of the Masters.

During Blavatsky's spiritualist phase, she channeled John King, and he became a cut-out for the Masters after she shifted from Spiritualism towards occultism. Between the months of March and August of 1875 Colonel Olcott started to receive various letters from an adept known as Master Serapis who was known for his simple exhortation-'try'.[125] Serapis wrote in Russian mannerisms (such as a dash above the letter 'm') that would later be employed by the mahatma Koot Hoomi.[126] Blavatsky defined the Brotherhood of Luxor as a mystical fraternity that had a Rosicrucian basis, and numbered many members.[127] The Brotherhood of Luxor identified with an Egyptian origination having taken the term Luxor which is the modern name for the ancient city of Thebes in Egypt. Furthermore, Blavatsky claimed to be an initiate of this brotherhood.[128] During Blavatsky's eastern years, this Egyptian brotherhood evolved into the Tibetan Masters. The Indian Mahatmas Koot Hoomi and Morya also preferred to write in blue and red pencils when communicating with others as exhibited in numerous examples in the Mahatma letters.[129] Thus, a connection between John King (pre-Oriental shift) and Blavatsky's Indian Mahatmas (post-Oriental shift) has been established. Now that an examination of Blavatsky's life and her connection to Spiritualism has been put forth, at this point another founding member of the Theosophical Society, Henry Olcott will be examined as well as his connection with Spiritualism.

2.17 Colonel Henry Steel Olcott: A Western Buddhist

Henry Steel Olcott (1832-1907) was born at Orange, New Jersey on 2 August 1832 to Henry Wyckoff and Emily Steel. The oldest of six siblings, Olcott possessed a rich family history eventually editing a book on his lineage tracing his roots back to the early Puritans and their journeys from England. Olcott had come to believe that he was a descendant of Bishop Dr. John Alcock, who in 1496 founded Jesus

College of Cambridge. In 1956 the book *The Olcotts and Their Kindred* was published by Mary L. B. Olcott who managed to trace the family tree back to the 1580s and had determined that the name 'Olcott' was a derivation of an older Norman term 'Olcotes'.[130] One of his most devoted friends throughout his life was his younger sister Isabelle Buloid (despite her adherence to orthodox Christian beliefs) who married William H. Mitchell in 1860.[131]

Olcott claimed that his first experience with Spiritualism occurred in 1844 when he witnessed the mesmeric powers of the youthful Andrew Jackson Davis who went on to become a major proponent of American Spiritualism.[132] This story seems entirely plausible given the general trustworthiness of Olcott for which he had been well known and understanding his close proximity to western New York during this time period. Olcott obviously possessed some noticeable intellect for at the age of fifteen he was enrolled at the University of New York. At the age of sixteen he was forced to drop-out due to a lack of finances and was sent out to start his own career.[133]

After being forced to withdraw from school, Olcott took up the profession as a farmer an occupation which forced him to depend upon his agricultural knowledge. He eventually traveled out to Amherst, Ohio where he was employed by his uncles. Then in 1848 the year that Olcott left home in search of his destiny, modern Spiritualism appeared at the Fox household in Rochester, NY. Olcott was introduced to Spiritualism through these maternal uncles: Edgar, Isaac, and George Steel Olcott; at the age of twenty Olcott converted to Spiritualism.[134] Olcott had been raised as a strict Presbyterian, yet despite this upbringing Henry started dabbling in Mesmerism which he believed contained elements of truth.[135] In a letter written to a dear friend Olcott described two Mesmerist healings he had performed as a young man- one healing gave him the ability to read thoughts and the second one he healed an 'inflammatory rheumatism.'[136] This background in Mesmeric healing will become important later in his adult life when he commenced a career as a healer in Ceylon. While in Ohio, Olcott engaged in regular séances and in 1852 he allegedly came into contact again with the spiritualist Andrew Jackson Davis who encouraged him to become a missionary reformer of Spiritualism.[137] In 1853, Olcott continued on to become one of the founding members of the New York Conference of Spiritualists.[138]

Through his agrarian experience, Olcott acquired a unique knowledge of both sorgho and an African sugar plant called imphee. His expertise was much needed and in 1856 he lectured before the legislatures in Ohio, Massachusetts, and New York. These lectures were eventually adapted into a book which was published in 1857 titled *Sorgho and Imphee, The Chinese and African Sugar Canes: A Treatise on Origins, Varieties, and Culture.* This particular work become quite popular and was placed in libraries across Illinois continuing on to be reprinted in seven editions. Olcott's second work was published in 1858 and was called *Yale Agricultural Lectures* which was published while he was only 26 years old.[139] The great financial success that Olcott experienced in the farming industry went into supporting his agricultural science school- the Westchester Farm School in New York. This school was established in 1856 and was based on 'the Swiss model'; however, this facility soon closed from its lack of financial support.[140] All of Olcott's capital was lost in this business venture and he was left with nothing. Some of Olcott's other life achievements around this time period which are not widely published included an offer from the government to embark on a fully funded botanical mission to Caffraria, a prestigious position as the Chief Commissioner of Agriculture, and a professorship in agriculture at the University of Athens in Greece. Olcott was at one time employed as the Agricultural Editor of Horace Greely's the *Tribune* and was an American Correspondent of the *Mark Lane Express* an agricultural journal. Through his vast knowledge of horticulture, Olcott went on to be awarded two Medals of Honour by the United States National Agricultural Society and received a silver goblet by the American Institute.[141]

By the 1850s, Olcott had converted to Spiritualism and took an interest in the social reform issues of the nineteenth century.[142] Between 1853 and 1856, Olcott published several articles in the *Spiritual Telegraph* under his pen name 'Amherst'. Stephen Prothero whose doctoral thesis dealt with the influence of Olcott in India noted the following concerning his early involvement with Spiritualism:

> In 'The Spiritualist's Faith,' his most systematic piece, Olcott presented a grand historical and moral apologia for the movement. He began by postulating an evolutionary cosmos in which all things progress 'from lowest to highest, from bad to good, from small to great...upward, onward, to something more perfect, more Divine!' He then arranged all religious traditions in accordance with this evolutionary and hierarchical imperative. His *Heilsgeschichte* began with fetishism ('steeped in barbarism, low and degraded in the scale of human being'), moved on to Islam (preferable to fetishism but based nonetheless on 'gratification of lust' and 'thirst

for dominion'), and culminated with spiritualism (rooted in 'reasoning, hopefulness, mirth, benevolence, spirituality, reverence and universal tolerance').[143]

Just before he joined the Union Army in 1861, Olcott married Mary Eplee Morgan, the daughter of an Episcopal priest from New Rochelle, NY. Together they had four children, two of which died as youths. Olcott allegedly enlisted in the northern Union Army at the onset of the Civil War where he served under the famous general Ambrose Everett Burnside in his successful North Carolina campaign.[144] Following his discharge from the service and while in his mid-thirties, Olcott studied law and was eventually admitted into the New York State Bar in 1868. Additionally, Olcott became involved as an 'antislavery advocate, civil service reformer, government investigator of Lincoln's assassination, insurance lawyer, and chaste reviewer of raucous burlesque productions. In the process, he earned some notoriety as a social reformer as well as admission into the Lotos Club, a prestigious men's social organization catering to Manhattan's artistic and literary elite.'[145]

In 1874, Olcott read an article in the *Banner of Light* a popular Spiritualist magazine, about the Eddy Brothers who were manifesting full body materializations at their farmhouse in Vermont. Olcott used this story as an opportunity to explore the world of Spiritualism and gaining permission and funding from the *Daily Graphic* to print a story on these events, he travelled to Chittenden, Vermont in order to investigate these claims. This journey would forever change his life because it would be during this investigation that Olcott would be introduced to the Russian immigrant Helena Petrovna Blavatsky. The articles that Olcott published in *Daily Graphic* were subsequently collected and printed in 1875 under the title *People from the Other World* which was written from an investigative 'layman' point of view.[146]

It seemed that after meeting Blavatsky, Olcott's marriage quickly dissolved seemingly due to his own neglect. On 28 December 1874 Mary Olcott filed for divorce claiming that Henry had 'committed adultry (sic) on the second day of May one thousand eight hundred and seventy three at a house of prostitution in the City of New York.'[147] In April 1875, Olcott had effectively bought the publishing rights in the *Spiritualist Scientist* which he used to promulgate Blavatsky's reformative message which noted the moral degradation of many Spiritualist mediums and called for the establishment of philosophical ideals and parameters. Again, the basic tenet of Spiritualism was the belief that departed spirits could communicate with the living; this left room for multiple disagreements among its practitioners. Blavatsky initiated Olcott into her slightly modified philosophy of Western Esoteric Spiritualism which eventually became centered around the belief in 'adepts', 'masters', and ultimately established the belief that elementary spirits were the cause of most séance phenomena. Though this idea seemed to have been developed by Blavatsky, Olcott would be the first founder to go on record speaking about the nature of elementals which he wrote in his famous article titled 'The Immortal Way' published on 23 August 1875 in the *New York Tribune*. Though this doctrine would be used as a dividing characteristic between Theosophy and Spiritualism, its demarcation was much more apparent than actual. Throughout her life Blavatsky recognized that some of the Spiritualist phenomena were genuinely the work of departed spirits, thus fulfilling the one requirement that Spiritualists had required- the belief that departed spirits could contact the living.

As previously noted, the doctrine of elementals would explain the lack of morality among some contemporary Spiritualists. This explained why some mediums lived uninhibited sexual lives practicing free love while others recreationally used drugs and alcohol, and still others depended upon trickery and confederates in order to perform their séances. Thus, the doctrine of elementals attempted to explain the notorious fraudulency that was becoming associated with Spiritualism as emphasized by the secular media. Though this lecture brought scathing reviews from many noted Spiritualists including Mary Fenn Davis (the wife of Andrew Jackson) who wrote sarcastically to Olcott in a published booklet, it also managed to attract the attention of one noted Spiritualist Emma Hardinge Britten and prompted her to write a letter reintroducing herself to Olcott on 2 September 1875. Gomes noted that he had seen Olcott's copy of this letter and handwritten on the bottom 'was a renewal of acquaintance with Mrs. Britten after a break of twenty years.'[48] Around this same time Britten was seeking to make her entrance back into the ranks of Spiritualism which she had left in 1873 in hopes of establishing a successful galvanic medicine practice. Britten would provide competent and outspoken partner for Blavatsky to propagate her 'Theosophy' (see section on 'Emma Hardinge Britten' for a fuller explanation of the relationship between these two fascinating figures).

On 26 September 1875 Olcott and Blavatsky, along with roughly a dozen other founding members, established the Theosophical Society for the express purpose 'for the study and elucidation of Occultism the Cabbala, etc.' That same year on 17 November three by-laws were added to this organization, the first naming the title of the society as the Theosophical Society, the second explaining that 'the objects of the society are, to collect and diffuse a knowledge of the laws which govern the universe, and the third clarifying that membership should be divided into active, honorary, and corresponding members.'[149] Also on that day, Olcott delivered his first presidential address which reflected the heavy influence of Blavatsky's obsession with esoteric saint including Albertus Magnus, Roger Bacon, Cagliostro, Pico della Mirandola, Robert Fludd, Paracelsus, Cornelius Agrippa and Henry More as well as the ancient Chaldeans, Kabalists, Egyptians, hermeticists, Alchemists, and Rosicrucians.[150] Thus, this identification evidenced that the early Theosophical Society could be considered a Western Esoteric branch of Spiritualism.

Olcott later described the state of the Theosophical Society from 1876 to 1878 and observed that during this time period the organization was largely inactive- its by-laws had become 'a dead letter,' and the Society nearly stopped meeting all together. This was due largely to George Felt and his failed attempts at producing an elemental (examined earlier):

> The chance of giving verifiable confirmation of occultism had led Olcott to suggest the founding of the Theosophical Society, and he closed his Nov. 17 speech with a reference to Felt's promise 'by simple chemical appliances,' to make visible the creatures of the elements. 'What will the Spiritualists say, when through the column of saturated vapor flit the dreadful shapes of beings whom, in their blindness, they have in a thousand cases revered and babbled to as the returning shades of their relatives and friends?' (p. 44)…He was soon to find out for Felt reneged on his promise. It was precisely on Felt's failure to display the creatures Olcott held responsible for mediumistic phenomena that the Spiritualists rebuked the Theosophists.[151]

The Spiritualists who had been such an integral part in the formation of the early Society had all withdrawn their membership and the Society did not renew their rental agreement with the Mott Memorial Hall, in Madison Avenue New York. More importantly Olcott noted that: 'the fees formerly extracted upon entrance of members were abolished.'[152] Olcott hinted that the new 'Oriental shift' of the Theosophical Society would be largely based on the belief in ascended masters or adepts:

Our Headquarters' life was ideal throughout those closing years. United in devotion to a common cause, in daily intercourse with our Masters, absorbed in altruistic thoughts, dreams and deeds, we two existed in that roaring Metropolis as untouched by its selfish rivalries and ignoble ambitions as though we occupied a cabin by the seaside, or a cave in the primeval forest. I am not exaggerating when I say that a more unworldly tone would not be found in any other home in New York.[153]

Earlier in 1878, Olcott had published a tract in the *Indian Spectator*, defending Buddhism to the Theosophical Society and other interested readers. In 1879 at the instigation of a hidden brotherhood of adepts, both Blavatsky and Olcott agreed to move the Theosophical Society's headquarters to India. After which time period Olcott traveled to Ceylon where he described this elaborate reception:

A white cloth was spread for us from the jetty steps to the road where carriages were ready, and a thousand flags were frantically waved in welcome. The multitude hemmed in our carriages... The roads were blocked with people the whole distance, and our progress was very slow. At the house three Chief Priests received and blessed us at the threshold...Then we had a levee and innumerable introductions; the common people crowding every approach, filling every door and gazing through every window.[154]

On 25 May 1880, both Olcott and Blavatsky converted to Buddhism and recited in their imperfect knowledge of Pali the Three Refuges and the five Precepts of Theravada Buddhism.

2.18 Olcott's First Ceylon Tour

After this formal conversion to Buddhism, Olcott took the Christian educational pedagogy of which he was familiar through his Presbyterian upbringing, and applied this methodology to Buddhism. Olcott formed 'Buddhist secondary schools and Sunday schools affiliated with the BTS (Buddhist Theosophical Society), thus initiating what would become a long and successful campaign for Western-style Buddhist education in Ceylon.'[155] This initial tour was concluded with a last minute debate spurned by the Christian missionaries. This confrontation was initiated by the missionaries who invited Olcott to debate the Christian religion at the Society for the Propagation of the Gospel (S. P. G.) Missional School. It seemed that the missionaries did not intend for Olcott to indulge their request because when the Theosophists showed up they could not agree to nominate a chairman who could be approved by both the Theosophists and Christians. Olcott explained that despite these problematic elements, he felt inspired to read a paper which he had previously prepared on the trinity. After reading this paper he left without rebuttal though this action did prompt a mob to gather and clamorously shout slurs at the Theosophists. Olcott noted that some gunshots were fired in the distance which he attributed as protest from those natives loyal to the Christian missionaries who had expected Olcott to simply decline their initial invitation.[156] This debate must have caused quite a stir and seemed to provide validation to the indigenous religious practices of the Indians confirming that their religions were not inferior to Western Christianity as the missionaries had been teaching. Given this result it should come as no surprise that the Theosophical Society soon became connected to various Indian nationalist movements.[157]

2.19 Olcott's Second Ceylon Tour

Olcott's second tour of Ceylon began in April of 1881. During this visit Olcott ran into Edwin Arnold (1832 – 1904) and his family. Arnold, an Oxford graduate, was the author of the poem *The Light of Asia* (1879) a work that positively introduced Buddhism to the Western world during a time when few people knew or cared about Eastern religions.[158] It was during this second tour that Olcott and Blavatsky encountered the peculiar Chief Calvary Officer of the Maharaja of Bhaunagar- Mirza Murad Ali Beg on 20 January 1881. Mirza Murad Ali Beg was the name chosen by the Anglo Godolphin Mitford after his conversion to Islam.[159] Mitford who also happened to be the author of the occult work titled *The Elixir of Life* was a European who had descended from the successful Mitford family. Mitford managed to publish several articles in the *Theosophist* including a two part series on the history of civilization, racial evolution, and the origin of humanity in the northern section of the Himalayas.[160] Despite his literary skills, Mitford maintained a faint grasp on reality. Olcott gave some alarming details concerning Mitford's interaction with the Theosophical Society:

> [Mitford] had dabbled in black magic among other things, and told me that all the sufferings he had passed through within the preceding few years were directly traceable to the malign persecutions of certain evil powers which he had summoned to help him get into

his power a virtuous lady whom he coveted…Certainly he was a distressful person to be with. Nervous, excitable, fixed on nothing, the salve of his caprices, seeing the higher possibilities of man's nature, yet unable to reach them, he came to us as to a refuge…from the time that he came to us he seemed to be engaged in a strong mental and moral conflict within himself. He complained of being dragged hither and thither, first by good, then by bad influences. He had a fine mind, and had done a good deal of reading; he wanted to join our Society, but, as I had no confidence in his moral stamina, I refused him. H.P. B., however, offering to become responsible for him, I relented and let her take him in. He repaid her nicely, some months later, by snatching a sword from a sepoy at Wadhwan Station, and trying to kill her, crying out that she and her Mahatmas were all devils! In short, he went mad.[161]

After this event Olcott returned to Ceylon and started fundraising for his National Education Fund 'to promote the education of Buddhist boys and girls.'[162] Then on 25 February 1881 Blavatsky and Olcott agreed to 'reconstruct the T. S. on a different basis, putting the Brotherhood idea forward more prominently, and keeping the occultism more in the background, in short, to have a secret section for it.[163] The Theosophical Society made a decisive shift towards promoting unity and adopted this ideal for which they are still most famously known. On this same tour, Olcott reached Point de Galle and began composing his *Buddhist Catechism* 'on the lines of the similar elementary hand-books so effectively used among Western Christian sects, working at it at odd times, as I could find leisure. To fit myself for it I had read 10,000 pages of Buddhist books, of course in English and French translation.' He finished his draft on the 5th of May in 1881.[164] This work would prefigure Blavatsky's *Key to Theosophy* being written in an accessible, conversational, question and answer style format.

Olcott lectured in Marriage Hall (so called because members of the Royal Family of Baroda were married there) and addressed such affluent members of Indian society as the Gaikwar and his prime minister, and 'all the nobles and English-knowing officials of the States, together with the British resident and staff.'[165] This lecture was followed by some phenomena performed by Blavatsky including reading the contents of a telegram sealed inside an envelope, the ringing of bells, and the production of table rappings.[166] From Baroda, Blavatsky and Olcott ended up in Wadhwan and then continued on to Bombay.

2.20 Third Ceylon Tour

In July of 1882, Olcott returned to Colombo for his third Ceylon Tour to further advance his Educational Propaganda campaign. He soon became discouraged with the present state of the Buddhist Theosophical Society as he discovered that only a mere 100 of the pledged 13,000 rupees had actually been collected. He then began educating the Buddhists on the dire necessity of financially supporting ones spiritual institution and teachers which he did by converting the Christian conceptualization of tithing 10% into its Buddhist equivalent.[167]

While celebrating the anniversary of the Theosophical Society in Colombo, Olcott noticed a drawing of a white hand clasped together with black one with the word 'brotherhood' written underneath it. On the other side of this drawing was the phrase: 'The Past you cannot recall. The Present is yours- the Future will be what you make it.'[168] Olcott continued his travels to Galle and then to Dondera on the southern point of the island. About this time Olcott had turned 50 years of age when an unusual incident of note occurred on the 19th of August. One day Olcott was confronted by a half-paralyzed man. This man said to Olcott 'Here's your chance for the holy well.' Olcott, drawing on his earlier experience of Mesmeric healing, now felt a sudden surge of sympathy which prompted him to make some passes over the invalid's arm. He then told this crippled man that he might feel better for this encounter. The man went on his way; however, later that evening while chatting with some of his colleagues from Gall this man returned and interrupted Olcott's conversation. This man explained that after his encounter with Olcott his health had started to improve, compelling him to return in order to personally thank Olcott for his service.

For the next couple of days Olcott treated this man again and again and by the fourth day this disabled man was able to 'whirl his bad arm around his head, open and shut his hand, and clutch handle objects as well as ever.'[169] Soon this invalid was able to sign his name to attest to this incredible transformation. Olcott had also treated this man's leg which within a short time healed magnificently allowing this man to run freely. News of this healing spread across the town and district. Immediately, Olcott's services became in great demand as people flooded to this miracle worker. Olcott then commenced upon a charismatic healing practice working all hours of the morning and late into the night laying his hands on the sick.[170]

This third tour definitively linked Olcott with the pre-Spiritualist philosophy known as mesmerism. Olcott performed multiple healings and gave numerous lectures on this subject during this Indian tour. Olcott continuously employed mesmeric practices including mesmerizing the rings and pipes of various crowd members, vessels of water,[171] and even a tree at the Tinnevelly Railway station.[172] Olcott's reputation spread throughout South Asia as a mesmeric healer and he went on to cure people of such ailments as back and limb pains, deafness, and epilepsy to name but a few.[173] Stephen Prothero commented on this event:

> [Olcott now possessed] a gift on a par with Blavatsky's conjuring abilities, scores of patients lined up outside the Theosophical Society headquarters in Adyar (a suburb of Madras), and on an 1882 tour of Bengal Olcott supposedly treated 2,812 patients. Soon, however, the seemingly insatiable needs of his followers overwhelmed Olcott. His popularity became a burden and when, toward the end of 1883, the Theosophical Masters (adepts with whom Blavatsky is supposed to have communicated telepathically) handed down an order to stop the healings, Olcott happily complied.[174]

2.21 Arrival in England

On April 1884, Olcott arrived in London where Vsevolod Solovyoff (1849–1903) recorded meeting him:

> He wore spectacles, somewhat concealing thereby the one defect of his appearance, which none the less was a real 'spoonful of tar in a barrel of honey.' The fact is one of his eyes was extremely disobedient, and from time to time used to turn in all directions, sometimes with startling and most disagreeable rapidity. As long as the disobedient eye remained still, you had before you a handsome- agreeable and kindly, but not particularly clever man, who won you by his appearance and inspired you with confidence. Then suddenly something twitched, the eye got loose and began to stray suspiciously and knavishly, and confidence vanished in a moment....He spoke French very tolerably.[175]

In December of 1885 the findings of Richard Hodgson's devastating report for the Society of Psychical Research had been widely circulated in Spiritualist circles claiming that Blavatsky's psychic powers were the result of fraudulent practices. Despite the clear negativity that this report cast upon Blavatsky and her phenomena; nonetheless, Olcott's outstanding character and integrity were commended even if it was implied that he lacked 'perspicacity':

> The testimony of Colonel Olcott himself I found to be fundamentally at variance with fact in so many important points that it became impossible for me to place the slightest value upon the evidence he had offered, But in saying this I do not mean to suggest any doubt as to Colonel Olcott's honesty and purpose...[176]

Olcott's character was reinforced again by the investigating committee reporting to the Society of Psychical Research, though again this confirmation came at the cost of his intellect:

> There is only one special point on which the Committee think themselves bound to state explicitly a modification of their original view. They said in effect in their First Report that if certain phenomena were not genuine it was very difficult to suppose that Colonel Olcott was not implicated in the fraud. But after considering the evidence that Mr. Hodgson has laid before them as to Colonel Olcott's extraordinary credulity, and inaccuracy in observation and inference, they desire to disclaim any intention of imputing willful deception to that gentleman.[177]

From 1886-1888, Olcott worked on several projects including translating into English a 305-page work by Adolphe d'Assier published under the title of *Posthumous Humanity, a Story of Phantoms* and the founding of the great Adyar library (which still exists as of this writing only in a different location). The year 1888 was an especially difficult time for Olcott who suffered from bad health including persistent boils and a sore leg likely caused by gout.[178] These infirmaries forced Olcott to begin winding down his speaking schedule even as Blavatsky's wrath was simmering in London at her disgruntlement with the current leadership in Adyar, Madras. Kirby Van Mater described this situation in the following article:

> During these years of Mme. Blavatsky's retirement from direct participation in theosophical affairs (1885-87), the Society had drifted away from the influence of the Adepts. This is apparent from a conversation she had with one of her teachers where he remarked that Colonel Olcott in spite of his great labors had during this time allowed the T.S. to liberate itself from their influence, and that it would not long survive his death (cf. *Letters from the Masters of the Wisdom*, First Series, Letter 47, 5th edition). Though the

date of this discussion is not given, it can be placed approximately in the closing months of 1887 or early 1888. From this time onward till her death in 1891, H. P. Blavatsky played an increasingly significant role in the Society's administration so as to reestablish and maintain the work along the original lines. This caused some unhappiness and misunderstanding between herself and Colonel Olcott. Eventually, in 1890, much distressed over circumstances, he stated that he would resign as president at the next convention in December. However, at the final moment he announced a change of mind and retained his position in the Society, though his views and lack of confidence in H.P.B.'s methods of work remained unchanged...Olcott arrived in London in late August 1888, to find H. P. Blavatsky not well and with much to do. A few weeks later on October 3rd he wrote Judge that he was busy helping her with *The Secret Doctrine* and *Lucifer* and in settling affairs in Paris — that he was acting 'on the lines' of the letter he received from K.H. on board the *Shannon*.[179]

In 1891, Blavatsky went on to publish both *The Key to Theosophy* and the *Voice of Silence* making the concepts of Theosophy more accessible to the general public. On 23 September 1891 Olcott returned to New York. It was here that he was reunited with the Steel brothers-Isaac, George and Edgar his beloved uncles that had employed him and introduced him to Spiritualism many years previous.[180] From New York, Olcott traveled to San Francisco then to Japan and finally back to India again in December of 1891.[181] On 16 January 1892, Olcott began writing his autobiography describing his vast experiences and his pivotal role within the early Theosophical Society. He managed to compose 'a series of historical reminiscences of the T.S. and H.P.B. under the title of 'Old Diary Leaves.'[182] On 14 June 1894, Olcott returned to England and in 1899 the Theosophical Society suffered a fragmentation through a divisive issue concerning one of its influential members William Quan Judge (1851–1896). A full explanation of the events surrounding this division is unnecessary for this study; however, it is sufficient to note that this split concerned the legitimacy of communications with the mahatmas (masters) and led to the establishment of Judge's faction referred to as the Theosophical Society International Offices, Pasadena CA as demarcated from the continued organization of the Theosophical Society-Adyar under Henry Olcott and his successor Annie Besant (1847–1933). In his *Old Diary Leaves*, Olcott chronologically, year by year, detailed the events of the early Theosophical Society. Despite his honesty as previously applauded by Hodgson, one must read this faithful diary with a critical eye understanding his credulity and that he had often been manipulated by those around him especially Blavatsky.

In 1898, Olcott opened a suburban school naming it the H.P.B. Memorial School in honour of Madame Blavatsky and her work. The following year he invested in a third school which he named after another member of the early Theosophical Society 'The Damodar Free School'; Olcott would go on to open up two more schools over the next couple of years.[183] Also of interest, Taranath Tarka Vachaspati the author of a well-known Sansrkit dictionary gave Olcott the honour of adopting him into his gothra (family tree). This was Olcott's official acceptance and recognition into the Indian culture that he had served for many years. After accepting this honour he began adapting to the native culture through his dress by wearing clothing such as a 'wide, loose, native-style cotton trousers, and the long, collarless shirt known as a kurtha, while on his feet he mostly wore chappals (sandals) with a black round cap on his head.'[184]

In 1902, while Olcott was in his seventies he began suffering from rheumatic issues which affected his feet, arms, and legs. This incapacitated him sentencing him to a painful existence on crutches. Even this bout with pain could not keep Olcott down, and within a short period of time he was back to his old routine enjoying such activities as playing tennis, writing, lecturing and travelling.[185] Then in 1906 a situation was revealed concerning Charles Leadbeater (1854 – 1934) and his inappropriate behaviour with young boys that placed Leadbeater outside the Theosophical circles until the inauguration of Annie Besant. This situation is more complex than it may initially appear and as these complexities have little bearing on Theosophy's connection to Spiritualism in the nineteenth century there seems little need to mention them in this present volume. Olcott commenced his aspirations of travelling the world eventually ending up in Paris and then on to Holland where he spent his 74th birthday in Amsterdam crippled by his gout when a feeling of sickness overcame him.

In August, Olcott left Holland for Liverpool and ended up in Boston where a fellow Society member allowed him to use his apartment rent free. While in the metropolitan area, Olcott visited the Boston Public Library where he was able to search their catalogue and discovered that they possessed two of his own written works- his Yale Agricultural Lecture which he had published many years ago in and his Theosophical Society Inaugural Address of 17 November 1875. From Boston he travelled to Toledo, then to Chicago for the Con-

vention where, where he continued to defend his long time friend
Charles Leadbeater against the scandalous allegations of pederasty
which he hade been accused. Olcott finally arrived back into New
York though at this period in his life he existed on primarily a liquid
diet. Then finally on 3 October 1906 Olcott passed away from this
world, leaving behind his Theosophical Society for which he had
laboured most of his adult life. This Society would continue to grow
under the leadership of Annie Besant and would go on to exert
influence through the guise and genius of it future members. In his
obituary in *The Times* on 20 February 1907 some of Olcott's philanthropic accomplishments were noted:

> Colonel Olcott was so successful in urging educational advance-
> ment upon the Buddhists of Ceylon that he lived to see three col-
> leges and 250 schools with some 30,000 pupils established, largely
> as a result of his labours. His 'Buddhist Catechism' has been trans-
> lated into 23 languages. He closely identified himself with Eastern
> philosophic thought, and in recognition of his services for the re-
> vival of Hindu philosophy one of the leading pandits conferred on
> him the sacred thread of Brahmin caste, and adopted him into his
> gotra- a distinction achieved by no other white man. The Theo-
> sophical Society operates in 42 countries, and a large portion of its
> 600 branches are in India, where its headquarters were established
> when Colonel Olcott moved thither.[186]

2.22 Olcott's Unusual Form of Buddhism

Stephen Prothero noted his own analysis of Olcott's form of Buddhism (which would also be confirmed by other critics of the Theosophical Society including Arthur Lillie in his *Koot Hoomi Unveiled*
1884 who had spent many years serving in the British forces in India): 'The faith Olcott now confessed was an odd sort of Buddhism.
Long before Olcott departed for India with the express intent of
sitting as a disciple at the feet of monks and gurus, he had constructed for himself a relatively fixed image of 'Buddhism.' Prothero noted
that this image bore as much resemblance to Blavatsky's Theosophy
and liberal Protestantism as it did to the Buddhism of Theravada
monks.'[187]

> Like Olcott, pioneering Buddhologists such as Rhys Davids
> (whom Olcott eagerly read) tended to reduce the Buddhist tradi-
> tion to what the Buddha did and what the Buddhist scriptures said.
> This tendency permitted them to praise the ancient wisdom of the

East and to condemn its modern manifestations to view Asian religious traditions much like Calvin viewed the human race: as fall-
en from some Edenic past. It was Olcott's uncritical and unconscious appropriation of this aspect of academic Orientalism that
led him to the rather absurd conclusion that Ceylons Buddhists
knew little, if anything, about real Buddhism...He decided to
compile for use in his Buddhist schools a catechism of basic Buddhist principles, on the lines of the similar elementary handbooks
so effectively used among Western Christian sects, both Protestant
and Catholic, Olcott's *The Buddhist Catechism,* which would eventually go through more than forty editions and be translated into
over twenty languages, is in many ways the defining document of
his Buddhism. It first appeared, in both English and Sinhalese, on
July 24, 1881. Hugely influential, it is still used today in Sri Lankan
schools... Olcott's ostensibly non-Christian Buddhism sounded
like liberal Protestantism. More than an antidote to Christianity,
Olcotts *Catechism* was a homeopathic cure, treating the scourge of
Christianity with a dose of the same. His critique of Christianity
shared many elements with liberal Protestants critique of Christian
orthodoxy, including a distrust of miracles, an emphasis on reason
and experience, a tendency toward self-reliance, and a disdain for
hell. Like their Jesus, his Buddha was a quintessential Christian
gentleman: sweet and convincing, the very personification of self-
culture and universal love.[188]

Given Olcott's eclectic form of Buddhism, which largely appeared
to be a Westerner's preconceived view of Eastern religious beliefs it
seemed that Olcott was combining his Western view of Eastern
Buddhism with his Western Esoteric form of Spiritualism. Thus,
Olcott attempted to Westernize this Eastern movement (which
seemed obvious from the Western methodologies he employed to
propagate Buddhism) by combining elements of Buddhism and his
Western Esoteric Spiritualism into one incredible religion-
Theosophy. This goal seemed evident as explained in the opening
of Olcott's *Old Diary Leaves* where he explained that 'the whole
thing is here made plain: the Spiritualism she [Blavatsky] was sent to
America to profess and ultimately bring to replace the cruder Western mediumism, was Eastern Spiritualism, or Brahma Vidya [un-
derstanding reality].'[189] The term 'Eastern Spiritualism' seems to be a
fitting designation for the philosophy of early Theosophy as it com-
bines the two main belief structures Olcott and Blavatsky had assimilated together- a Western Esoteric flavor of Spiritualism and
Eastern philosophy.

Another point that is critical towards understanding the relationship between Theosophy and Spiritualism in the nineteenth century was noted by the eastern guru, Swami Vivekananda. Vivekananda after having been offended by Olcott's lack of support for his branch of Hinduism critiqued the Theosophical Society with a similar argument that the thesis of this book has set out to prove- that Theosophy remained a modified form of Spiritualism. Vivekananda's accusation was as follows: He claimed that Olcott had attempted to assimilate Hinduism and Buddhism into one Spiritualist belief structure. Though Vivekananda recognized that Theosophy had performed many good deeds throughout India he still believed that Theosophy was an 'Indian grafting of American Spiritualism- with only a few Sanskrit words taking the place of spiritualistic jargon- Mahatma missiles taking the places of ghostly raps and taps, and Mahatmic inspiration that of obsession by ghosts.'[190] Hindus, he added angrily, 'do not stand in need of dead ghosts of Russians and Americans.' They have 'no need or desire to import religions from the West.'[191] This combination of Buddhism and Spiritualism seems to be clearly evident in Blavatsky's monumental work published in 1888 titled *The Secret Doctrine* which will be explored in a later section. Thus, it seemed that even Olcott's (and therefore the Theosophical Society's) *contemporaneous critics believed that the Theosophical Society maintained a deep connection with Spiritualism both practically and philosophically.* Now that Olcott's biographical information has been examined it is fitting to explore the relationship that Olcott maintained with several key individuals who were influential members of nineteenth century Spiritualism.

A Three –Way Friendship:
Spiritualism and the Connection between Henry Olcott, William Stainton Moses, and Charles Carleton Massey

2.23 Charles Carleton Massey (1838–1905)
Olcott shared a special friendship with one of the founding members of the Theosophical Society- a Spiritualist named Charles Carleton Massey (1838-1905). It seemed that these two individuals met while Olcott was on a business trip to England in 1870 though it wasn't until Massey visited New York in 1875 that their friendship really seemed to develop.[192] After Massey's move to the States, he and Olcott visited Henry Slade, the slate-writing medium, then Massey traveled alone to experience the Eddy Brothers séances in Chittenden,

VT.[193] Olcott observed that he and Massey had visited 'several mediums' together and that before leaving America, Massey had 'attended the meeting of the new Theosophical Society on 13 October and was elected a Fellow. Returning to England, he became the first President of the London Branch of the Theosophical Society [27 June 1878], wrote about his experience in *The Spiritualist*, and shared his private thoughts with Stainton Moses. For a few years, Massey united English spiritualism with the new movement from America, while reserving an inner spiritual life on Behmenist Christian principles.'[194]

In 1883 Massey was succeeded in the London Branch by Anna Kingsford who would take over leadership from January to June of 1883 and Kingsford was eventually succeeded by the anglo-Indian Alfred Percy Sinnett. Possessing the original minute book which he quoted in his work *Early Days of Theosophy*, Sinnett provided a detailed description of the founding of the London chapter as it was the first Theosophical branch which was established outside of the United States. Sinnett further explained that Massey was chosen by ballot as the branch president and his elected secretary was Miss Emily Kislingbury.[195] Kislingbury was the author of an influential work attempting to reconcile Theosophy with Spiritualism in an ingeniously titled article 'Spiritualism in its Relation to Theosophy' published in 1892. In this tract, Kislingbury noted her opinion that 'there is much in common between Spiritualists and Theosophists, and I don't see why there should be now any antagonism between them.'[196] It should be observed that Kislingbury was very well acquainted with the basic tenets of Theosophy having prepared the index for Volume two of *Isis Unveiled*.[197] Kislingbury further noted that the London Lodge of the Theosophical Society was initially comprised of Spiritualists:

> In England, four out of five of the original group were members of the British National Association of Spiritualists, as well as the first two presidents, Mr. C. C. Massey and Dr. George Wyld. During the first year of its existence, the English Theosophical Society continued to be recruited almost entirely, if not solely, from the Spiritualist ranks (Mrs. Edwin Ellis, Madame de Steiger, Miss Arundale are names which occur to me at this moment).[198]

Spiritualists and Theosophists did not adhere to any clearly defined doctrinal beliefs; therefore, the relationship between these two movements was largely experiential and different for each individual.

Both Massey and Kislingbury were mentioned in a letter which Blavatsky had written to Hurrychund Chintamon on 22 May 1878 which
was labeled 'personal and confidential.' The main subject of this letter was a request for Chintamon's help in order to trick these two
faithful Spiritualists into believing in the phenomena of the Society:

> Another [devoted Theosophist] is Charles Carleton Massey (Athe-
> naeum Club) son of an M.P. who was formerly Minister of Indian
> Finance. C.C.M. is what you may call a *congenital mystic* and I feel
> perfectly sure, that if Pundit Dyanand will write to him any request
> he will joyfully comply. English Spiritual[sm] is the great opposing
> force to Theosophy as you may have noticed in the papers sent
> you (*Spiritualist*) C. C. Massey has for three years bravely defended
> theosophy, our Society, and selves. But what can we do? He hun-
> gers after truth, and the sight of a *fakirs* phenomenon (however
> fanatical and idolatrous) would make him do anything in the
> world. Another brave loyal heart is Miss Emily Kislingbury, secre-
> tary, guiding spirit in fact soul of the B.N.A. of Sp[ts] She has cour-
> age enough to make herself a heroine, and her motives and charac-
> ter are as pure as gold. But, like most women her emotional nature
> calls for a proof to lean upon; and for lack of that (since we all re-
> pudiate mediumship) she feels as though she would turn to the Xn
> church for support…We want you to secure her from her weaker
> self. Write to her in the name of the Arya Somaj and to C. C. Mas-
> sey (I send you both addresses) and in the name of TRUTH save
> them both! A direct letter from India would fire the zeal of both,
> for it is what they have been waiting and hoping for three years.
> They regard India as the land of mystery, wisdom and *Spiritual
> Power.* My devotion, love and enthusiasm for India has fired them
> both (for last year they have come both- C. C. Massey and Emily
> Kislingbury-accross (sic) the ocean to see me and lived with me)
> but unfortunately I am but a white-faced IDIOT not a Hindu,
> what *can* I do more! In the name of truth then and the great Un-
> seen, Power, help me to rescue both these enthusiasts either from
> Christianity-worse than that- Catholicism, into which both are div-
> ing rapidly and give them work to do- real hard work, for both are
> of the stuff that helps making MARTYRS…The more mystery
> you can throw about the communication the better and deeper
> impression it will make. If it would not be deemed impertinent in
> me to suggest a form of a letter I would propose the follow-
> ing…Do not think we are resorting to childish method. Believe
> me, we know what is best for these EX-Spiritualists—these half-
> born theosophists.'…[199]

Blavatsky then proceeded to dictate word-for-word the contents of each of these letters which she wanted to be written in Chintamon's handwriting. These letters were to be mailed to both Massey and Kislingbury giving the impression that they had been sent by an official of the Arya Samaj who had mysteriously known of their inner doubts when in reality it was all a result of Blavatsky's manipulation; thus, evidencing that Blavatsky used letters as a method of control in the early Theosophical Society. Blavatsky was attempting to deceive these two half hearted Theosophists to become fully acceptant of the Theosophical phenomena and she believed these letters would be the answer.

Based on this above letter it appeared that Blavatsky had originally viewed Hurrychund Chintamon (the leader of the Bombay chapter of the Arya Samaj) as a wise master and adept, though this belief was short lived. Chintamon was the one who had received Olcott and Blavatsky at their initial visit to India and had asked for reimbursement from them to throw the elaborate greeting party mentioned earlier. Chintamon also assured the Theosophists that their organizations were in total alignment with one another even though the Arya Samaj was a fundamentalist Hindu group that stressed the infallibility of the Vedas. Furthermore, Chintamon was known to 'cheat and swindle and was eventually expelled from both the Arya Samaj and the Theosophical Society for his detestable behavior.[200] Upon his expulsion Chintamon found himself siding with the Western opponents of the Society- a list that included William Stainton Moses, William Oxley, Emma Hardinge Britten, Thomas Lake Harris, and others.[201]

Chintamon went to London and while there he met up with C. C. Massey towards the end of 1882. Chintamon told the president of the British Theosophical Society (Massey) all about the letters he had received from Blavatsky attempting to dupe him and insisted that the masters were nothing more than elaborate hoaxes designed to attract followers to Blavatsky.[202] It seemed that Chintamon had shown Massey a letter urging him to plant an infamous 'Mahatma letter' in one of Massey's pockets while he was unaware,' similar to the letter detailed above.[203] Upon viewing a copy of this letter and hearing about these deceitful actions, Massey decided to resign his membership and presidency with the London Lodge of the Theosophical Society (Richard B. Westbrook left over a similar fraudulent phenomenon). On 22 July 1884 Massey wrote the following letter and sent it to *Light* magazine announcing his official resignation from the Theosophical

Society though he still acknowledged his friendship with and his high esteem of Olcott:

> I have only to add that while preserving all the interests, and much of the belief which attracted me to the Theosophical Socie-ty, and which have kept me in it up to now, notwithstanding many and growing embarrassments, I do not think that the publication of the conclusions above expressed is consistent with loyal Fellow-ship. The constitution, no doubt, of the Society is broad enough to include minds more sceptical than my own in regard to the alleged sources of its vitality and influence. But let any one try to realise this nominal freedom, and he will find himself, not only in an un-congenial element, but in an attitude of controversy with his os-tensible leaders, with the motive forces of the Society. That is not consistent with the sympathetic subordination or co-operation which is essential to union. If anything could keep me in a position embarrassing or insincere, it would be the noble life and character of the president, my friend, Colonel Olcott. But personal consid-erations must give way at length; and accordingly, with unabated regard and respect for many from whom it is painful to separate, I am forwarding my resignation of Fellowship to the proper quar-ters.[204]

The purpose of reprinting this article is to prove that Massey who was a self-avowed Spiritualist and Theosophist in 1882 did not leave the Theosophical Society solely over philosophical or ideological disputes; rather, Massey left this organization because he had felt deceived by one of its founders – Madame Blavatsky. Massey later joined the Society of Psychical Research and cooperated with one of its members Richard Hodgson aiding him in the compilation of his famous report published in December 1885 that would cast Blavat-sky as a fraud. The investigating committee of the Society for Psy-chical Research noted that 'Mr. C. C. Massey had brought before them [Hodgson and his hand writing experts] evidence which con-vinced both him and them that Madame Blavatsky had, in 1879. Ar-ranged with a medium, then in London, to cause a "Mahatma" letter to reach him in an apparently "mysterious" way.'[205]

Despite this betrayal, Massey did not hold any ill will towards the honest and well intentioned Olcott. In fact, when writing his diary in 1895 Olcott considered Massey an intimate friend and continued to speak highly of his relationship with Massey noting that they shared a 'brotherly friendship' that lasted many years. This relationship was a three way friendship that included one other individual. Olcott claimed that he had first introduced Massey to William Stainton Moses one of the primary leaders of Spiritualism 'and thus began that intimacy between us three which has only been interrupted by the death of 'M.A. Oxon' [Moses].²⁰⁶ He referred to both Massey and Stainton Moses as 'life-long friends.' This relationship is confirmed through the various correspondences sent between these three men.²⁰⁷

2.24 William Stainton Moses (1839–1892)

During his career as a Spiritualist, Olcott had befriended the popular Christian Spiritualist William Stainton Moses (1839–1892). Moses was a prominent Spiritualist who became actively involved with a number of organizations including the British National Associations of Spiritualists in 1873, the London Spiritualist Alliance in 1884, the Psychological Society of Great Britain in 1875, the Society for Psychical Research in 1882 and was both a member of the English Rosicrucians and a Freemason.²⁰⁸ Additionally he published multiple articles in numerous Spiritualist magazines under the pseudonym 'M. A. Oxon' and graduated from Exeter College of Oxford University. In 1882 Moses helped to launch the Ghost Club, a monthly dining club whose members had to provide 'an original Ghost story, or some psychological experience of interest or instruction, once during the years.'²⁰⁹ Moses went on to take over the editorship of a popular British Spiritualist publication *Light* which gave him a platform to voice his views and opinions. Another fascinating attribute of Moses was that he was an ordained priest in the Anglican Church, though in later years he gave up his affiliation with the Church of England, but continued to utilize the title 'Reverend' in his signature.

In 1872 Moses developed his own psychic powers as a medium and became popularly known for the publication of his automatic writings which he published under the titles of *Spirit Identity* (1879) and *Spirit Teachings* (1883) which went on to become extremely influential in the Spiritualist movement even earning the reputation as the 'Bible' of British Spiritualism. In his book *Modern Mystics*, Arthur Lillie spoke favorably of Moses, despite his disdain for the Theosophical Society of which Moses was a member. In fact, Lillie used Moses as proof that the Theosophical Society's primary object was to act as a Spiritualist movement. Lillie asked the question 'How, then, did M. Stainton Moses become a member of the Theosophical Society? For the simple reason that it was announced to be a spiritualistic Society.'²¹⁰ Despite Lillie's underlying agenda, it seemed to be a fair question to inquire as to how Moses became involved with Theosophy.

It seemed most probable that Moses had become aware of Blavatsky through reading an article in the *Spiritualist* written by James Martin (J. M.) Peebles a noted Spiritualist and a member of the Society of Psychical Research (SPR) titled 'A Séance on the Great Pyramid' published on 13 February 1874. In later issues following Peebles article, the *Spiritualist* printed some of Blavatsky's earliest writings including a defense of the Eddy's brother séances and a pericope noting Olcott's intention to publish *People from the Other World.*[211] Upon reading about Olcott's pending publication, Moses 'wrote to his friend Epes Sargent in Boston, offering to introduce Olcott's book (*People of the Other World*, published April 1875) to English Spiritualists.'[212] As a result he heard from Olcott himself on 10 April 1875. Thus, a correspondence had commenced between these two individuals that would blossom into an intimate relationship. In 1891, Olcott warmly recollected the nature of his relationship with Moses saying that 'no two men could have been more drawn to each other than he and I our friendship, begun through correspondence while I was still at New York, had continued unshaken throughout all changes and frictions between our respective parties, the Spiritualists and Theosophists.'[213]

Moses' initial reasons for joining the Theosophical Society were revealed in some correspondences to Major F. G. Irwin (a major figure in English occult circles) written between 1877 and 1881. It seemed that Moses' desire was to become part of a secret organization that held its members in strict confidentiality. Moses had previously joined Freemasonry believing that this organization's polity held these ideals of secrecy; however, he soon came to the realization that their religious eclecticism prevented them from maintaining this type of secrecy. Moses then turned to the Theosophical Society which on 19 January 1877 decided to become a secret organization that 'in future this Society adopt the principles of secrecy, in connection with its proceedings and transactions, and that committee be appointed to draw up and report upon the details necessary to the effect of such change.'[214] This arrangement was passed on 16 February and seemed to be the result of a temporary resignation by the Spiritualist and social radicalist Charles Sotheran on 5 January 1876. Blavatsky noted this reason in an annotation made in her early Scrapbook noting that due to Sothern's resignation the dealings of the Society had to be kept in confidentiality as Sotheran 'began to revile our experiments & denounce us to the Spiritualists & impeded the Society's progress & it was found necessary to make it secret."[215]

So it was that Moses believed the Theosophical Society was that secret organization which he had been searching for, but to his disappointment this secrecy would not last. On 21 December 1878 Moses wrote to Irwin stating: 'I hear Olcott is coming to London in January. But it has been so rumoured before. However Massey told me that he and Madame B. are going to India & that O. called here en route. I shall be glad to see him & tell him I have no faith in his Society. The English Branch is worse. I do not belong to it, & have resigned my Fellowship in the NY Order. This however they refuse to accept...'[216] Thus, Moses frustration with the organization of the Theosophical Society was apparent though philosophically it did not seem divergent from Spiritualism. In an article written for the *Theosophist* in May of 1880 Moses explained his justifications for reconciling Spiritualism and Theosophy:

> And some, less insane and stupid, seem to postulate an antagonism between Spiritualism an Theosophy, as though a man could not cultivate the highest powers of his own spirit, and yet lend an ear to what is going on outside of him: as if a Theosophist must be self-centred, and self-contained, and selfish together. Of course, views of this kind are crude and foolish, and the mere statement of them shows this at once. I should think them worth refuting, were it not that some such antagonism between Spiritualism and Theosophy, and some misunderstanding of what Spiritualism is, unfortunately prevails even amongst the instructed writers who grace your columns. Spiritualism is by no means the silly and wicked thing that some consider it. Spiritualism in my vocabulary includes much that is contained in your definition of Theosophy. I have no sort of objection to the term; I will adopt it with pleasure, and avow myself Spiritualist and Theosophist too...The perfect Theosophist would be a Spiritualist and he would be but a sorry Spiritualist who was not, in some sense, a Theosophist as well.[217]

In 1880, Moses was not adversarial to Theosophy, but saw this organization as a complimenting agency towards Spiritualism. In other words, all Theosophists were in definition Spiritualists, and all Spiritualists, if they were honest would consider themselves Theosophists. To Moses, there was no contradiction in these two statements.

As noted in the quote above, Moses was an ardent Spiritualist and was especially famous for his production of automatic writings especially through the channeling of one Spirit guide in particular known simply as 'Imperator'. In 1876, Olcott wrote to Moses and believed that Imperator + was not really a spirit master as Moses believed but instead that this 'spirit guide' and his whole 'band' were really highly evolved adepts that lived in the same camp as the ones that Blavatsky communicated with. Despite Moses' refusal to see Imperator + as an adept, Olcott continued to believe that both Blavatsky and Moses had tapped into the same power source.[218] The belief that Moses was really led by an 'adept' even though he was not aware of this was curious because Spiritualists claimed an opposing argument against Blavatsky claiming her adepts were really 'spirit guides' unbeknownst to her.[219]

In his fascinating study *The Theosophical Enlightenment*, Joscelyn Godwin noted that there were some remarkable similarities between the controls of Stainton Moses and Blavatsky's early reply to HIRAF published in the *Spiritual Scientist*.[220] He noted the correspondences as follows:

> This planet is a place of transition where we prepare for eternity [112]
> There is eternal progress for every living being [112]
> Elementary spirits are often mistaken for those of the dead [112]
> Reincarnation is a modern misunderstanding [112]
> Oriental philosophy denies the existence of Satan [111]
> The Jewish religion is derived from the pagan Mysteries [118]
> Ancient Cabalists knew as much as modern scientists [115]
> Egyptian initiation took away the fear of death [115]
> The Scripture are full of secret meanings [114-115]
> With the Hydesville rappings, the door is ajar [117]
> Now occultism needs to explain and alter much of spiritualism [117]

(the page numbers in brackets above correspond with *volume one* of Blavatsky's *Collected Writings* as compiled by Boris de Zirkoff).[221]

This similarity certainly appears plausible given the close relationship between these two individuals and their similar belief systems during these early days of the Society. Despite these similarities, Moses would eventually leave the Theosophical Society following the Kiddle incident in 1884 which will be explained in more depth in a later section.[222]

In 1892, Olcott was charged with the task of writing the obituary for his dearly departed friend Moses the acknowledged leader of the

Spiritualists for the *Theosophist*. During Moses' final days Olcott tried to convince him to travel to India and begin working on a combined book together - 'a favorite project that he and Massey and I had discussed for years,' but Moses declined. Olcott wrote very highly of Moses and his relationship to the Theosophical Society; however, he also noted a peculiar event that will be mentioned through the course of this study. Apparently, in 1888 Moses had struck a truce with Blavatsky and both sides agreed to become more congenial to the other. Olcott recorded this arrangement in his diary and in Moses' obituary:

> His views were broad and catholic upon those subjects (literature and physical science), and, but for the bigotry of the majority of Spiritualists, he and I would have gone far towards our establishing friendly relations between our two parties that in reason should subsist. [we both knew that it was a suicidal policy for two bodies to be wrangling and mutually hating, when a common foe- Materialistic Agnosticism- was undermining the foundations of spiritual belief- our mutual belief- and hence of religious conviction].
>
> [In 1888 he proposed to me that] In an earlier chapter I have mentioned the proposal he made me in 1888 that if I would manage to keep H.P.B. in a gentle mood towards Spiritualists, he would use his best influence with the latter to come to a more brotherly understanding with the Theosophists [I did my part easily; H.P.B. agreeing to spike her cannon for the term of the experiment...]. We agreed to make the trial, and HPB fell in with my wishes; he, on his part, began writings benevolently about us in *Light*. We used to see each other often that season n London and compare notes...He read me extracts from some of the letters, printed some in *Light*, and at last told me, sadly, that he should have to give it up, or he should lose all his influence with his party. It was the knowledge of this fact, corroborated amply by the brutal treatment she had personally received from leading Spiritualists that helped to make H.P.B.'s later criticisms upon modern Spiritualism so bitter.[225]

The proposal mentioned above was said to have occurred during the same year *The Secret Doctrine* was published which did not allow for any belief in the core doctrine of Spiritualism (communications with the dead). It seemed that in The *Key to Theosophy* Blavatsky agreed to allow Spiritualism a place in her Theosophical Society though it would only be in rare cases that communication would be possible; nonetheless, the possibility of communication was still there. Though the idea that this provision allowed in the *Key to Theosophy* for Spiritualism was a direct result of this truce must remain speculative; however, there does appear to be shift from *The Secret Doctrine*'s denial of communication with the dead and the *Key to Theosophy*'s acceptance of this practice in extremely rare circumstances. For Blavatsky, this 'team-up' would allow her to again target the ranks of Spiritualism for potential due paying members, but also allot her the ability of reconciliation with Western Spiritualism-a movement that had previously shamed her out in both the Kiddle incident and the Hodgson report.

2.25 M. A. Oxon and Spiritualism

Olcott's correspondences with Moses are important in ascertaining the role of Spiritualism in the life of Olcott. In a series of undated letters written to Moses between the years 1875-1876, Olcott elucidated upon the ideals of the Theosophical Society and their bearing on Spiritualism; he attempted to convince Moses of what he has come to believe- that Blavatsky possesses supernatural abilities. These lengthy quotes are intended to give the reader a picture of Olcott's early belief structure and to note the influence of his new acquaintance Blavatsky. The first letter illustrated Olcott's assimilation of Blavatsky's philosophy of elementary spirits within his Spiritualist belief structure:

> The main points of their [Occultist's] philosophy relate: (1) To the nature and attributes of the First Cause --- the En-Soph; (2) to the evolution of spirit and matter --- their progressive changes, combinations, relations, attributes or properties, and destiny; (3) to the evolution of intelligence, moral faculties, and spiritual capabilities, and their embodiment in the elementary spirits, in man, in angels, seraphs, and other entities. In this department are included, of course, all that relates to the domination of the human spirit over the lower races of spirits and the forces of nature, in the microcosm; and also to our gradual evolution and progression from lower to higher conditions, from the bottom to the top of the ladder that reaches from earth to Heaven, from base matter to pure spirit, from us to God.
>
> The bearing of this philosophy upon the question of Spiritualism is most important. It shows us, what I for one at least never suspected, that there are such things as elementary spirits, which we may define simply as beings possessed of intelligence and craft, but not of immortal souls; that these beings are able to and do produce a majority of the physical phenomena of mediumship; that each of us was, once upon a time, an elementary, and each of

those we left behind is sure to become, like us, immortal men by having the breath of the En-Soph breathed into him at birth; and that by reason of our share of that Immortal Breath, that portion of the Deity possessing all the attributes of Himself, in degree, we may subjugate these elementaries and make them do our will...Yes, as you say, Spiritualism *is* 'only one part of a vast subject,' and I leave it to your high intelligence and clear intuition to answer your own question whether 'the profit equals the risk' of pursuing the study.[224]

In the course of these letters Olcott exhibits a gradual acceptance of Blavatsky's ideas and was trying to entice Moses to accept them as well. In another letter written to Moses, Olcott discussed the relationship between Theosophy and Spiritualism, the superiority of adepts, as well as Olcott's belief that nine tenth of channelled spirits are really deceitful elementals masquerading as the departed:

Again, depend upon it that nine-tenths of spiritual communications --- oral, trance, and written --- are not from ascended spirits, but from the elementaries whom Madame Blavatsky described in the 'Scientist' so well. I totally disbelieve in the current theory of 'guides,' 'controls,' and 'bands,' as well as in the identity of most of the 'spirits,' who not only claim to be the former denizens of this sphere, but by their Protean powers can assume their shapes and clothe themselves with their magnetic effulgence... Depend upon it, that those who are true adepts of the Orient write no letters, make no boasts, and display their powers only under very exceptional circumstances. *You* will encounter them --- I know it; for to you the Brotherhood looks to lead the English public towards the light, as they do to me in this country to perform the same office. Read, mark, and digest. You will soon hear the truth.[225]

Olcott's goal of convincing Moses about the credibility and sagaciousness of Blavatsky was further evidenced in the following letter. It should be noted that most of these letters were circular and appear to have also been shared with C. C. Massey:

I sincerely hope that Madame Blavatsky and her letters will not give you chronic dyspepsia, since you say that you are 'digesting' the latter. They must be tough indeed if they tax your gastric juice. Wait until we have time to finish her book, and you will find Occultism done into 'plain English... For thirty years I have groped in darkness; now a guide leads me by the hand towards the quarter where morning breaks. That guide is the woman whom you have heard calumniated, whom you half suspect of criminality. She is my sister. She has shown me the documentary record of her past life. I know it all, from girlhood until now. I have seen the letters from her kinsfold --- some of her orders from the Brotherhood --- the letters from persons of high social position, for whose offences she has silently borne calumny and reproach. They confess her beneficience and fidelity, and 'their' own unworthiness. I tell you, my brother 'Oxon,' that this woman is a heroine; and that is about all I can tell you. What she has shown me, as to a tried and trusty brother, is not mine to repeat. If my word is of weight --- if I have proven by my conduct the right to have it respected by honest people --- that must suffice. She is blameless of evil conduct, and she is worthy of your full confidence and respect. If you will tell me just what stories you have heard about her, instead of giving me hints which only perplex without enabling me to answer, I will let you know all that is necessary to set her right in your eyes and Massey's… but still you ask, 'Does anybody know anything about it except Madame Blavatsky?' How the deuce can you be satisfied? It's impossible, 'Oxon,' until you see things for yourself. So wait patiently, and talk to the Brother whom you think one of your 'Band.' Get the Elementaries down and sit on them; that's half the battle. The other half is in learning to exercise your will-power.[226]

Here yet again Olcott's persuasion of Moses to believe in Blavatsky's elementals seemed obvious. He went on to appeal to his own intellect and trustworthiness of which he was well known:

Mind you, I'm forty-three, not twenty-three --- and so neither a callow enthusiast nor a credulous simpleton. Why, during the four years of our war, I examined some fifteen hundred witnesses (I and my few subordinates, I revising their work always) a year, and Secretary Stanton entrusted me --- as he said --- with as much power and discretion as he himself enjoyed. He constantly issued orders, ordered trials, changed officers, established regulations upon my simple report and recommendation. Do you think I am to be made a dupe by a woman about a matter of scientific and philosophical truth? Do you suppose I don't know this woman --- whom I have known as intimately as a brother a sister for over a year, so as to be able to discover if she is a strumpet, a liar, or a cheat?

In a subsequent letter coming from this same series, Olcott begged Moses to try to push his spirit guide to convince Blavatsky to change her mind regarding her travel plans to India as he believed this will not be good for her mental health:

> I wish you would ask Imperator, with my compliments, if he can't do *something*, in the psychological way, to prevent Madame Blavatsky from going to India. I am very anxious upon this point. I can do nothing myself. She is a changed woman these past few weeks. She is moody, reserved, and apparently desperate. The calumnies circulated in Europe and here have cut her so deeply; she feels such a disgust with our world; she so longs for her sacred Ganges, and the society of her Brethren, that I am afraid we will lose her. It may be a small matter to Spiritualists, but it is a great one for us three. She will give me no answers to my questions as she used to, when these phenomena occur --- as they do now almost daily. I have seen some new and very interesting.

This request would be ineffective for on 16 February 1879 Olcott and Blavatsky departed from New York at the request of her 'adepts' and landed in Bombay on February 1879. It was during this time period that a great shift occurred in the Theosophical Society and the organization began to take on a much more Eastern flavor. This is what will be referred to throughout this study as the 'Oriental shift.' Before this occurred, the Society utilized Spiritualist terminology and illustrations in order to promulgate a Western Esoteric form of Spiritualism- holding to a very experiential form of polity; whereas, after this 'Oriental shift' the Society would assimilate Eastern terminology and philosophy focusing upon the idea of brotherhood and advocating a 'follow the leader' type of polity led by the masters through their letters and initiates. Despite this epistemological change, Blavatsky, especially in *The Secret Doctrine* and her subsequent writings, went on to assimilate many Eastern concepts into her philosophy, nonetheless, her Society remained opened to Spiritualists and aligned with the basic belief of Spiritualism. Even her desire to emerge out of Spiritualism and focus on 'universal brotherhood' a trait for which Theosophy is still well known was prefigured in the 'Harmonial philosophy' of Andrew Jackson Davis. Now that an understanding of the early Theosophical History has been explained and key figures explored, the alignment of Blavatsky's later ideas and Spiritualism will be cross-examined in the following section on the key figures of Spiritualism.

Notes

[1] The Theosophical Society was established in New York by a group of about two dozen founders, but after Olcott and Blavatsky went to India they referred to themselves alone as 'the Founders' and the usage became generally adopted in the Society as the rest of the original founders gradually resigned.

[2] Stephen Prothero, *The White Buddhist: The Asian Odyssey of Henry Steel Olcott* (Indiana: Indiana University Press, 1996), p. 49.

[3] Michael Gomes, *Dawning of the Theosophical Movement* (Wheaton, IL: The Theosophical Publishing House, 1987), p. 87.

[4] The term feminist here refers to one who advocates for the social, political, and economical equality of women with men.

[5] *A History of Russian Women's Writings 1820-1992*, edited and translated by Catriona Kelly (Oxford: Clarendon Press, 1994), p. 110.

[6] This is according to a list published in 1906 that was edited by Dudley Warner, *Library of the World's Best Literature, Ancient and Modern: Volume XXIX* (New York: J. A. Hill & Company, 1906), p. 243.

[7] *Russian Women, 1698-1917: An Anthology of Sources*, compiled by Robin Bisha, Jehanne M. Gheith, Christine Holden, and William G. Wagner (Indianapolis: Indiana University Press, 2002), p. 210.

[8] Alex Owen, *The Darkened Room: Women, Power and Spiritualism in Late Victorian England* (Philadelphia: University of Pennsylvania Press, 1990), p. 31.

[9] A.P. Sinnett, *Incidents in the Life of Madame Blavatsky: Compiled from Information Supplied by Her Relatives and Friends* (London: The Theosophical Publishing Society, 1913), p. 27.

[10] Sinnett, *Incidents in the Life of Madame Blavatsky*, p. 28.

[11] Sinnett, *Incidents in the Life of Madame Blavatsky*, p. 28.

[12] Sinnett, *Incidents in the Life of Madame Blavatsky*, pp. 72-73.

[13] H. P. Blavatsky, 'A Bewitched Life' in *Nightmare Tales* (London: Theosophical Publishing Society, 1892), pp. 10-11.

[14] Nicholas Goodrick-Clarke, *The Western Esoteric Traditions: A Historical Introduction* (New York: Oxford University Press, 2008), 216. For a list of Renaissance authors HPB later recalled see 'HPB to Prince A. M. Dondoukoff-Korsakoff,' letter dated 1 March 1882, in *H. P. B. Speaks*, edited by C. Jinarajadasa, 2 vols (Adyar: Theosophical Publishing House, 1950-51), II, 50-71 (pp. 62-63).

[15] Iverson L. Harris, 'Incidents in the Life-History of Helen Petrovna Blavatsky' in *The Theosophical Path*, ed. Katherine Tingley, 20:1 (January 1921), p. 13. There is some significance to the ages seventeen and seventy. In Helena Hahn's story entitled *Society's Judgment*, there is a male character who appeared to be seventy (though the reader is told that he is really just under forty years of age) and he is cared for by his seventeen year old niece. It seemed ironic that Blavatsky employed this same age exaggeration for her husband Nicholas. Helena Gan, 'Society's Judgment' in *Russian Women's*

Shorter Fiction: An Anthology 1835-1860 trans. Joseph Andrews (Oxford: Clarendon Press, 1996), p. 57. and Sinnett, *Incidents in the Life of Madame Blavatsky*, p. 53.

[16] 'Helen Blavatsky was a cheerful witty companion, with an inexhaustible store of rough but real humour, of narratives, interesting, though alas! By no means always founded on strict truth, and of anecdotes...' See Vsevolod Solovyoff, *A Modern Priestess of Isis*, trans. Walter Leaf (New York: Longmans, Green, and Co., 1895), p. 5.

[17] H. P. Blavatsky, *From the Caves and Jungles of Hindustan* (London: The Theosophical Publishing Society, 1908), p. iii.

[18] Goodrick-Clarke, *The Western Esoteric Traditions*, p. 213. Also, see Patrick John Deveney, 'The Travels of H. P. Blavatsky and the Chronology of Albert Leigh Rawson: An Unsatisfying Investigation into H.P.B.'s Whereabouts in the early 1850s', *Theosophical History* 10: 4 (October 2004), pp. 8-31.

[19] *The Memoirs of Count Witte: A Portrait of the Twilight Years of Tsarism by the Man Who Built Modern Russia*, trans. Sidney Harcave (New York: M. E. Sharp. Inc., 1990), p. 9. There is some evidence which presumed that Blavatsky had married Metrovich. Dr. Elliott Coues recorded a letter in the 20 July 1890 issue of *The New York Sun*, sent by the later Theosophical detractor- Emma Coulomb in 1885 to Col. John C. Bundy of Chicago noting that 'Mme. Blavatsky is not Mme. Blavatsky. She is Mme. Metrovitch. I have known her husband in Egypt. I have kept this always to myself, but now that she has tried to injure me in any way she could, I am not bound to be secret any more.' Elliott Coues, 'Blavatsky Unveiled! The Tarta Termagant Tamed by a Smithsonian Scientist', *New York Sun* (20 July 1890), 17.

[20] Marion Meade, *Madame Blavatsky: The Woman Behind the Myth* (New York: G. P. Putnam's Sons, 1980), pp. 76-93.

[21] For instance, there is a story in the opening of Sinnett's *Incidents in the Life* in which Vera Jelihowsky explained the events surrounding Blavatsky's baptism including a horrific fire at the church where 'several persons-chiefly the old priest- were severely burnt.' This tale seems to be a fabrication allegorizing the fact that Blavatsky had certain spiritual forces working upon her life immediately upon her birth. Though the veracity of this statement remains unknown these stories must be read critically. Sinnett, *Incidents in the Life of Madame Blavatsky*, p. 19.

[22] Letter LX in *The Letters of H. P. Blavatsky: 1861–1879* (Wheaton, IL: The Theosophical Publishing House, 2003), p. 144.

[23] Henry Steel Olcott, *Old Diary Leaves: The True Story of the Theosophical Society*, 6 vols (New York: GP Putnam's Sons, 1895), III, p. 319.

[24] Christine Ammer, *The Encyclopedia of Women's Health*, 6th ed. (New York: Infobase Publishing, 2009), p. 374. Now pure speculation allows one to understand that even if this was a congenital condition Blavatsky could still have been impregnated. Blavatsky exhibited a need to control her environment which could have also applied to her sex life; it seems possible that

during sex Blavatsky could have preferred the top position so that she could control the rhythm and depth of penetration. Though this idea can only be speculated; nonetheless, in Blavatsky's *The Secret Doctrine* sex appeared as a negative concept (Blavatsky, *The Secret Doctrine*, II, pp. 30, 296, 415). Thus, a position that allowed skin contact and the ability to look into one's partner's eyes could seem shameful to Blavatsky. Despite this possibility it seems much more plausible that this condition was the result of her pregnancy with Yuri.

[25] *Personal Memoirs of H. P. Blavatsky*, comp. Mary K. Neff (London: Rider & Co.,1937), p. 187.

[26] Neff, *Memoirs of H. P. Blavatsky*, pp. 187-188.

[27] Sue-Ellen Case, *Performing Science and the Virtual* (New York: Routledge, 2007), p. 65.

[28] Neff, *Personal Memoirs of H. P. Blavatsky*, p. 184.

[29] This account came from the trustworthy (though at times naïve) Henry Olcott who defended his account noting that 'I have not relied upon the diaries of verbal statements of the Eddy themselves in making these strictures, but solely upon the testimony of the editorial descriptions of the whole press.' Olcott, *People from the Other World*, p. 36. For remarks concerning the integrity of Olcott see section 2.21.

[30] Olcott, *Old Diary Leaves*, I, p. 4.

[31] Helmuth von Glasenapp, *Image of India* (New Delhi: Indian Council for Cultural Relations, 1973), p. 173.

[32] H. P. Blavatsky, 'The Philadelphia "Fiasco", or, Who is Who?', *Banner of Light*, 36 (30 January 1875), 3-5.

[33] Olcott, *People from the Other World*, p. 453.

[34] Olcott, *Old Diary Leaves*, I, p. 25.

[35] Nicholas Goodrick-Clarke, *Helena Blavatsky* (Berkeley, CA: North Atlantic Books, 2004), p. 29. This letter is reprinted in 'Elbridge Gerry Brown', in *H. P. Blavatsky: Collected Writings: 1874-1878*, comp. Boris De Zirkoff, 15 vols (Pasadena: CA: Theosophical Publishing House, 1966), I, pp. 45-46.

[36] 'Important to Spiritualists', *Spiritual Scientist*, 2:8 (29 April 1875), 85.; Olcott, *Old Diary Leaves*, I, pp. 75-77.

[37] Joscelyn Godwin, 'The Haunting of E. Gerry Brown: A Contemporary Document', *Theosophical History*, 4:4-5 (October 1992-January 1993), 115-120 (p. 118).

[38] Neff, *Personal Memoirs of H. P. Blavatsky*, p. 227.

[39] Michael Gomes, 'Studies in Early American Theosophical History: Colonel Olcott and the American Press- 1875', *The Canadian Theosophist*, 70:6 (Jan. - Feb. 1990), 125-130 (p. 125).

[40] Michael Gomes, 'Studies in Early American Theosophical History: Elbridge Gerry Brown and the Boston "Spiritual Scientist"', *The Canadian Theosophist*, 69:6 (Jan. - Feb. 1989), 122-130 (pp. 129-130).

[41] H. P. Blavatsky, 'A Few Questions to "HIRAF"', *Spiritual Scientist*, 2:19 (15 July 1875), 217-218, 224 (p. 224).

[42] H. P. Blavatsky 'A Few Questions to "HIRAF"', *Spiritual Scientist*, 2:20 (22 July 1875), 236-237 (p. 237).

[43] Sinnett, *Incidents in the Life of Madame Blavatsky*, p. 92.

[44] Sinnett, *Incidents in the Life of Madame Blavatsky*, p. 93.

[45] Sinnett, *Incidents in the Life of Madame Blavatsky*, p. 94.

[46] Sinnett, *Incidents in the Life of Madame Blavatsky*, p. 99.

[47] Gertrude Marvin Williams, *Madame Blavatsky Priestess of the Occult* (New York: Lancer Books, Inc., 1946), pp. 181-184.

[48] Nicholas Goodrick-Clarke, *Helena Blavatsky*, p. 7. Michael Gomes observes that one of the primary members of this brotherhood was Serapis Bey who hailed from Elora, India. Gomes, *Dawning of the Theosophical Movement*, pp. 71-72. For more information on John King, Serapis and Tuitit Bey, etc. refer to Nicholas Goodrick-Clarke, 'The Coming of the Masters: The Evolutionary Reformulation of Spiritual Intermediaries in Modern Theosophy', in *Constructing Tradition: Means and Myths of Transmission in Western Esotericism*, ed. Andreas Kilcher (Leiden: Brill, 2010).

[49] For some possibilities of this historical view see K. Paul Johnson, *The Masters Revealed: Madame Blavatsky and the Myth of the Great White Lodge* (Albany: State University of New York Press, 1994).

[50] See the section on Blavatsky's Critics: William Coleman. William Emmette Coleman, 'The Source of Madame Blavatsky's Writings', in *A Modern Priestess of Isis* (New York: Longmans, Green, and Co., 1895), pp. 353-366.

[51] On Orientalism and its influence on Theosophy, see Nicholas Goodrick-Clarke, 'The Theosophical Society, Orientalism, and the "Mystic East": Western Esotericism and Eastern Religion in Theosophy', *Theosophical History* 13: 3 (July 2007), 3-28 (pp. 11-14). In the late 18th- early 19th century, knowledge of India was brought to the Western world largely from the publication of *Asiatic Researches*. This magazine was started by a group of scholars (led by Sir William Jones) who were mostly members of the East India Trading Company as a means of enquiring 'into the history and antiquities, art, sciences and literature of Asia.' See Rajendralala Mitra, *Cetenary Review of Asiatic Society of Bengal from 1784-1883* (Calcutta: Asiatic Society, 1884), p. 4. Many of the comparisons and observations made throughout the early days of this publication were from devout Christian scholars. Often times the biases of these men degraded the texts and people they were studying. Blavatsky took the complete opposite approach to history in *Isis Unveiled*. Instead of showing the inferiority of the Hindu texts compared to the Bible, Blavatsky tried to show that the Indian religions were more ancient and, therefore, more original than the authors of the Hebrew cosmogony.

[52] Solvyoff, *Modern Priestess of Isis*, p. 254.

[53] Sylvia Cranston, *HPB: The Extraordinary Life and Influence of Helena Blavatsky, Founder of the Modern Theosophical Movement*, Santa Barbara, CA: Path Publishing House, 1993), p. 169.

[54] H. P. Blavatsky, 'The Theosophical Society: The Lamasery at New York', *Hartford Daily Times* (2 December 1878), p. 1.

[55] For a more detailed biography of Stainton Moses see Joscelyn Godwin, *The Theosophical Enlightenment*, (Albany: State University of New York Press, 1994), pp. 293-300; for Charles Massey see Godwin, *Theosophical Enlightenment*, 245-246, 295-300; and for William Q. Judge see Kirby Mater, 'William Quan Judge: A Biographical Sketch' in *Sunrise Magazine* April/May (Pasadena: Theosophical University Press, 1996).

[56] H. P. Blavatsky, 'The Arya Samaj: Alliance of Theosophy with a Vedic Society in the Far Orient', *New York Echo* (2 June 1878) reprinted in *H. P. Blavatsky Collected Writings: 1874-1878*, comp. Boris De Zirkoff, 15 vols. (Wheaton, IL: Theosophical Publishing House, 1966), I, p. 383.

[57] For Roy's writing on gender equality see *Abstract of the Arguments Regarding the Burning of Widows Considered as a Religious Rite* (1830).

[58] John Symonds, *The Lady with the Magic Eyes: Madame Blavatsky- Medium and Magician* (New York: Thomas Yoseloff Publisher, 1960), p. 113.

[59] *Autobiography of Alfred Percy Sinnett* (London: Theosophical History Centre, 1986), p. 4.

[60] *Autobiography of Alfred Percy Sinnett*, p. 10.

[61] *Autobiography of Alfred Percy Sinnett*, pp. 4-5.

[62] *Autobiography of Alfred Percy Sinnett*, p. 10.

[63] *The Occult World* was dedicated to 'Koot Hoomi- whose gracious friendship has given the present writer his title to claim the attention of the European world, this little volume, with permission sought and obtained, is affectionately dedicated.' The *St. James Gazette* noted that the name Koot Hoomi was made up of syllables from the names of two prominent Theosophical Society members probably Henry Olcott and A.O. Hume- (ol)Cott Hume. Arthur Lillie, *Koot Hoomi Unveiled; or, Tibetan "Buddhists" versus the Buddhists of Tibet* (London: The Psychological Press Association, 1884), p. 14.

[64] For the progression in the definition of the 'Masters' and their successive Hinduization, then Tibetanization, see Nicholas Goodrick-Clarke, 'The Coming of the Masters', pp. 128-132.

[65] There is still some opposition to this conclusion. See Vernon Harrison, *H.P. Blavatsky and the SPR: an examination of the Hodgson Report of 1885*, (Pasadena, CA: Theosophical University Press, 1997). and Michael Gomes, 'Response to Kerri Barry's Genius, Fraud, or Phenomenon?', *Theosophical History: A Quarterly Journal of Research*, 13 (2007), 3-9.

[66] H. P. Blavatsky, *The Secret Doctrine: The Synthesis of Science, Religion and Philosophy*, 2 vols, (Adyar: The Theosophical Publishing Company, 1888), I, p. viii.

[67] Blavatsky, *The Secret Doctrine*, I, p. xx.

[68] 'Madame Blavatsky Dead', *New-York Daily Tribune*, (9 May 1891), p. 7.

[69] 'From a high of 8520 members in 1927, and a post-war high of 6,119 in 1972, official American membership declined to 3,546 in 2010.' Robert Ellwood, 'Theosophy After the Baby Boomers', in *Quest Magazine*, 99:1 (Winter 2011), 30-31, 39 (p. 30).

[70] Olcott, *Old Diary Leaves*, I, p. 70. The parenthesis noted include what Olcott did not record in his diary from this article as it appeared in the *Daily Graphic*.

[71] Gomes, *The Dawning of The Theosophical Movement*, p. 217.

[72] Michael Gomes, 'From The Archives', *Theosophical History*, 9:4 (October 2003), 21-26 (p. 26).

[73] Gomes, 'From The Archives', p. 26.

[74] Gomes, *The Dawning of The Theosophical Movement*, p. 95.

[75] Gomes, *The Dawning of The Theosophical Movement*, p. 96.

[76] Gomes, *The Dawning of The Theosophical Movement*, p. 96.

[77] Gomes, *The Dawning of The Theosophical Movement*, p. 96.

[78] Gomes, *The Dawning of The Theosophical Movement*, p. 96.

[79] There seems to be some historical precedence to this idea that Blavatsky had used Home's name in order to bolster her own authority among contemporary mediums. In a letter written in January 1872 to the Spiritualist newspaper *Medium and Daybreak* Blavatsky wrote seeking a subscription, but went on to write a strange note: 'If you should chance to see Mr. D. Home medium, please tell him that a friend of his late wife 'Sacha'- a St. Petersburg friend of past years- sends him her best compliments.' 'Sacha' was Home's first wife Alexandrina de Kroll who had died of tuberculosis in 1862. It seemed that Blavatsky was 'name dropping' to the staff at the *Medium and Daybreak* in attempting to connect herself with this famous medium (perhaps for a reduced rate). Letter No. IV in *Letters of H. P. Blavatsky*, p. 19.

[80] Peter Lamont, *The First Psychic: The Peculiar Mystery of a Notorious Victorian Wizard* (New York: Little, Brown, and Company, 2005), p. 318.

[81] Olcott, *Old Diary Leaves*, I, p. 13.

[82] Letter XIV in *The Letters of H. P. Blavatsky: 1861 – 1879* (Wheaton, IL: The Theosophical Publishing House, 2003), p. 59.

[83] Letter XV in *Letters of H. P. Blavatsky*, p. 68.

[84] Letter XVII in *Letters of H. P. Blavatsky*, pp. 70-71.

[85] Letter XVIII in *Letters of H. P. Blavatsky*, p. 73.

[86] Letter XX in *Letters of H. P. Blavatsky*, p. 75.

[87] Letter XXI in *Letters of H. P. Blavatsky*, p. 86.

[88] Joscelyn Godwin, *Lady Caithness and Her Connection with Theosophy*, AAR Seminar on Theosophy, Unrevised Draft (6 October 1995), p. 5.

[89] H.P. Blavatsky, 'Mr. Arthur Lillie', *Light*, 4:197 (11 October 1884), 418-419 (p. 418).

[90] Olcott, *Old Diary Leaves*, I, p. 13.

[91] Arthur Lillie, *Madame Blavatsky and Her Theosophy* (London: Swan Sonnenschein & Co., 1895), p. 183.

[92c] The extract given here, from a letter to him dated Jan. 26, 1878, runs counter to what H.P.B. has already written on the subject, but I include it for the sake of completeness. It was quoted by William Emmette Coleman in a series on the early history of the T.S., "Spiritualism and the Wisdom Religion" (*The Carrier Dove*, San Francisco, Nov. 1891, p. 298)...' Michael Gomes, 'Studies in Early American Theosophical History: H.P.B.'s American Correspondence', *The Canadian Theosophist*, 71:5 (Nov. – Dec. 1990), 102- 107 (pp. 103, 107).

[93] Godwin, *Theosophical Enlightenment*, p. 414.

[94] Gomes, *Dawning of the Theosophical Movement*, pp. 179-181.

[95] H. P. Blavatsky, *Isis Unveiled: A Master Key to the Mysteries of Ancient and Modern Science and Theology*, 2 vols (New York: J. W. Bouton, 1877), I, pp. 310-311.

[96] In Blavatsky first major writing of *Isis Unveiled* in 1877 Elementals could never become human beings: 'Elemental Spirits- The creatures evolved in the four kingdoms...called by the kabalists gnomes, sylphs, salamanders, and undines...Such beings never become men. Blavatsky, *Isis Unveiled*, I, pp. xxix, 311. Compare this characteristic to her *The Secret Doctrine* published in 1888:

> In this Round- with the exception of the highest mammals after man, the anthropoids destined to die out in this our race, when their monads will be liberated and pass into the astral human forms (or the highest elementals of the Sixth and the Seventh Races, and then into lowest human forms in the fifth Round-no units of either of the kingdoms are animated any longer by monads destined to become human in their next stage, but only by the lower Elementals of their respective realms... In sober truth, as just shown, every 'Spirit'; so-called is either a disembodied of a future man. As from the highest Archangel (Dhyan Chohans) down to the last conscious Builder (the inferior class of Spiritual Entities), all such as men, having lived aeons ago, in other Manvantaras, on this or other Spheres; so the inferior, semi-intelligent and non-intelligent Elementals- are all future men. Blavatsky, *The Secret Doctrine*, I, pp. 184, 277.

[97] Elipha Lévi, *Transcendental Magic: A Complete Translation of 'Dogme et Rituel de la Haute Magie' with a Biographical Preface*, trans. by A. E. Waite (London: George Redway, 1896), pp. 215-216.

[98] Blavatsky, *Isis Unveiled*, I, pp. xxix, 71.

[99] Emma Hardinge Britten, *Art Magic, or, Mundane, Sub-Mundane and Super-Mundane Spiritism* (Chicago: Progressive Thinker Publishing House, 1909), p. 257.

[100] A. O. Hume, 'Fragments of Occult Truth', *The Theosophist*, 3:1 (October 1881), 17-22 (p. 20).

[101] Hume, 'Fragments of Occult Truth', p. 21.

[102] H. P. Blavatsky, *The Key to Theosophy: Being a Clear Exposition, in the Form of Question And Answer of the Ethics, Science, and Philosophy* (London: The Theosophical Publishing Company, 1889), pp. 195-196.

[103] Olcott, *Old Diary Leaves*, I, pp. 126-131.

[104] Letter CXIV, *Letters of H.P. Blavatsky*, p. 233.

[105] Henry Steel Olcott, 'The First Leaf of T. S. History', *The Theosophist*, 12:2 (November 1890), 65-70 (p. 68).

[106] Michael Gomes, 'Studies in Early American Theosophical History: The Ante and Post-Natal History of the Theosophical Society', *Canadian Theosophist*, 4:70 (Sept. – Oct. 1989), 77-82 (p. 77).

[107] James Santucci, 'George Henry Felt: The Life Unknown', *Theosophical History*, 6:7 (July 1997), 243-162 (p. 245).

[108] Helen Sword, *Ghostwriting Modernism* (Ithaca, NY: Cornell University Press, 2002), p. 51.

[109] Wouter Hanegraaff, *New Age Religion and Western Culture: Esotericism in the Mirror of Secular Thought* (Albany: State University of New York Press), p. 436.

[110] Brendan James French, *The Theosophical Masters: An Investigation into the Conceptual Domains of H. P. Blavatsky and C. W. Leadbeater*, 2 vols (unpublished doctoral thesis, University of Sydney, August 2000), I, pp. 86-87.

[111] Emma Hardinge Britten, *Autobiographical Sketch of the Life and Spiritual Experiences of Emma Hardinge Britten, Trance Clairvoyant and Inspirational Spirit Medium* (Manchester and London: John Heywood, 1900), p. 42.

[112] H. J. Spierenburg, 'Dr. Rudolf Steiner on Helen Petrovna Blavatsky', *Theosophical History*, trans. J. H. Molijn, 1:7 (July 1986), 159-174 (p. 168).

[113] Solovyoff, *A Modern Priestess of Isis*, p. 247.

[114] Solovyoff, *A Modern Priestess of Isis*, pp. 247, 244.

[115] Solovyoff, *A Modern Priestess of Isis*, p. 243.

[116] Henry Steel Olcott, *People From The Other World* (Hartford: American Publishing Company, 1875), p. 436.

[117] H. P. Blavatsky, *Scrapbook*, Vol. I between pages 20 and 21 in Blavatsky, 'Important Note', *Collected Writings: 1874-1878*, comp. Boris De Zirkoff, 15 vols. (Pasadena: CA: Theosophical Publishing House, 1966), I, p. 73.

[118] Bruce Campbell, *Ancient Wisdom Revealed: A History of the Theosophical Movement* (Berkeley, CA: University of California Press, 1980), p. 24.

[119] Curuppumullage Jinarājadāsa, *The Golden Book of the Theosophical Society: A Brief History of the Society's Growth from 1875-1955* (Adyar, Madras: Theosophical Publishing House, 1925), pp. 13-14.

[120] Olcott, *Old Diary Leaves*, I, p. 25.

[121] Curuppumullage Jinarājadāsa, *Did Madame Blavatsky Forge the Mahatma Letters* (New York: Macoy's, 1934), pp. 6, 18, 22, 24, 26, 32, 42.

[122] Olcott, *Old Diary Leaves*, I, p. 362.

[123] *The Letters of HP Blavatsky*, pp. 185-186.

[124] Arthur Lillie, 'Critical Historical Review of The Theosophical Society', *The Religio-Philosophical Journal*, (6 September 1893), 264-266. < http://www.blavatskyarchives.com/cole1893.htm> (accessed on 23 August 2011) [para. 19 of 27]

[125] Annie Besant, 'The Egyptian Brotherhood and H.S. Olcott 1875', *Theosophist Magazine*, 54 (August, 1932), 479-493 (p. 481).

[126] C. E. Bechhofer Roberts, *The Mysterious Madame: Helena Petrovna Blavatsky: The Life and Work of the Founder of the Theosophical Society, with a Note on Her Successor, Annie Besant* (New York: Brewer and Warren, 1931), p. 17. The use of the word 'try' evidences the influence of P. B. Randolph on Blavatsky.

[127] *The Hermetic Brotherhood of Luxor: Initiatics and Historical Documents of an Order of Practical Occultism.* Joscelyn Godwin, Christian Chanel, John Deveney (York Beach, ME: Samuel Weiser, Inc., 1995), p. 292.

[128] See *The Hermetic Brotherhood of Luxor*, p. 53.

[129] *The Mahatma Letters: to A. P. Sinnett*, comp. A. Trevor Barker, (Theosophical University Press, 1975), pp. xliii-xlv.

[130] Howard Murphet, *Yankee Beacon of Buddhist Light: The Life of Col. Henry S. Olcott* (Wheaton: Quest Books, 1988), p. 1. Despite the fact that this source is a hagiographic account of Olcott's life; nonetheless, it presents relevant biographical data.

[131] Sven Eek, *Damodar And the Pioneers of the Theosophical Movement* (Adyar: The Theosophical Publishing House, 1965), p. 640.

[132] Henry Steel Olcott, 'Opening Remarks: Sorcery in Science', *The Theosophist* 11:128 (1890 May), 442-451 (p. 442).

[133] Murphet, *Yankee Beacon of Buddhist Light*, p. 2.

[134] Prothero, *The White Buddhist*, pp. 22-23.

[135] Murphet, *Yankee Beacon of Buddhist Light*, p. 6.

[136] Prothero, *The White Buddhist*, p. 23.

[137] Prothero, *The White Buddhist*, p. 23.

[138] Prothero, *The White Buddhist*, p. 24.

[139] Murphet, *Yankee Beacon of Buddhist Light*, p. 7.

[140] H. P. Blavatsky, 'A Word with Our Friends', *Supplement To The Theosophist*, 2:4 (January 1881), 1-4 (p. 1).

[141] Blavatsky, 'A Word with Our Friends', p. 1.

[142] Stephen Prothero, 'From Spiritualism to Theosophy: "Uplifting" a Democratic Tradition', *Religion and American Culture: A Journal of Interpretation*, 3:2 (Summer 1993), 197-216 (p. 201). Murphet, *Yankee Beacon of Buddhist Light*, pp. 5-6.

[143] Prothero, 'From Spiritualism to Theosophy', p. 200.

[144] Murphet, *Yankee Beacon of Buddhist Light*, p. 13.

[145] Prothero, 'From Spiritualism to Theosophy', p. 201.

[146] Olcott, *People from the Other World*, p. viii.

[147] New York County Court House, Index #1874-719. reprinted in Prothero, *The White Buddhist*, p. 197.

[148] Gomes, *Dawning of the Theosophical Movement*, pp. 84, 214.

[149] Jinarājadāsa, *Golden Book of the Theosophical Society*, p. 23.

[150] Prothero, *The White Buddhist*, pp. 50-51.

[151] Michael Gomes, 'Studies in Early American Theosophical History: The Ante- and Post-Natal History of the Theosophical Society', *The Canadian Theosophist*, 70:4 (Sept. – Oct. 1989), 77-82 (p. 77).

[152] Olcott, *Old Diary Leaves*, I, pp. 330-331.

[153] Olcott, *Old Diary Leaves*, I, p. 331.

[154] Olcott, *Old Diary Leaves*, II, p. 158.

[155] Prothero, *The White Buddhist*, p. 97.

[156] Olcott, *Old Diary Leaves*, II, pp. 192-194.

[157] For details concerning this relationship reference Carl T. Jackson, 'Theosophy', in *Oriental Religions and American Thought: Nineteenth-Century Explorations* (Westport, CT: Greenwood Press, 1981), 157-177.

[158] Olcott further noted the influence of Arnould that 'In her [Blavatsky's last Will, H. P. Blavatsky expressed the wish that yearly, on the anniversary of her death, some of her friends 'should assemble at the Headquarters of the Theosophical Society and read a chapter of The Light of Asia.' Olcott, *Old Diary Leaves*, IV, p. 453.

[159] K. Paul Johnson, *Initiates of Theosophical Masters* (Albany: State University of New York Press, 1995), p. 39.

[160] Mirza Moorad Alee Beg, 'The Mother-Land of Nations', *The Theosophist*, 2:11 (August 1881), 234 -236. and Mirza Moorad Alee Beg, 'The Mother-Land of Nations', *The Theosophist*, 2:12 (September 1881), 254 -256.

[161] Olcott, *Old Diary Leaves*, II, pp. 289-291.

[162] Olcott, *Old Diary Leaves*, II, p. 293.

[163] Olcott, *Old Diary Leaves*, II, pp. 294-295.

[164] Olcott, *Old Diary Leaves*, II, p. 299.

[165] Olcott, *Old Diary Leaves*, II, p. 368.

[166] Olcott, *Old Diary Leaves*, II, p. 369.

[167] Olcott, *Old Diary Leaves*, II, p. 370.

[168] Olcott, *Old Diary Leaves*, II, p. 371.

[169] Olcott, *Old Diary Leaves*, II, p. 375.

[170] Olcott, *Old Diary Leaves*, II, pp. 374-376.

[171] 'Colonel Olcott at Bankura', *Supplement to the Theosophist*, 4:9 (June 1883), 4.

[172] S. Ramaswamier, 'The President-Founder's Reception at Tinnevelly', *Supplement to the Theosophist*, 4:11 (August 1883), p. 5.

[173] Surji Kumar Bysack, 'Cures Effected by the Colonel Olcott in Calcutta by Mesmeric Passes', *Supplement to The Theosophist*, 4:7 (April 1883), pp. 4-5.; *Supplement to The Theosophist*, 4:8 (May 1883), pp, 1-4.; *Supplement to the Theosophist*, 4:9 (June 1883), pp. 4-5.; 'Colonel Olcott's Lecture on "Dr. Esdaile and Mesmeris in Calcutta Thirty-six Years Ago"', *Supplement to the Theosophist* 4:10 (July 1883), p. 7-8, 12.

[174] Prothero, *The White Buddhist*, p. 109.

[175] Solovyoff, *A Modern Priestess of Isis*, pp. 36-37.

[176] Richard Hodgson, 'Mr. Hodgson's Report', *Proceedings of the Society for Psychical Research: Volume III* (London, Trubner and Co., 1885), pp. 210, 216-217. Later while writing regarding the Hodgson report to her follower A. P. Sinnett, Blavatsky seemed most outraged with this opinion of Olcott: 'Surely no sane man with sound reasoning…shall ever dare to write himself down such as ass as to say that while I am a full blown fraud and all my phenomena tricks, that the Colonel is to be charged simply with 'credulity and inaccuracy in observation and inference' !! *Letters of H.P. Blavatsky to A. P. Sinnett*, p. 109.

[177] 'Statement of the Committee', *Proceedings of the Society for Psychical Research: Volume III* (London, Trubner and Co., 1885), p. 205.

[178] Murphet, *Yankee Beacon of Buddhist Light*, p. 229.

[179] Kirby Van Mater, *Historical Perspective* (Theosophical University Press, 1979) <http://www.theosociety.org/pasadena/hpb-am/hpb-amh.htm> [accessed on 6 July 2011] (para. 25 of 50)

[180] Murphet, *Yankee Beacon of Buddhist Light*, p. 250.

[181] Murphet, *Yankee Beacon of Buddhist Light*, pp. 250-251.

[182] Olcott, *Old Diary Leaves*, IV, p. 457.

[183] Murphet, *Yankee Beacon of Buddhist Light*, p. 279.

[184] Murphet, *Yankee Beacon of Buddhist Light*, p. 282.

[185] Murphet, *Yankee Beacon of Buddhist Light*, p. 288.

[186] 'Obituary: Colonel Henry Steel Olcott', *The Times* (20 February 1907), p. 11, Issue 38261, col. C.

[187] Prothero, *The White Buddhist*, p. 66.

[188] Prothero, *The White Buddhist*, pp. 100-101, 104.

[189] Olcott, *Old Diary Leaves*, I, p. 15.

[190] Swami Vivekananda, 'Stray Remarks on Theosophy', *The Complete Works of Swami Vivekananda* (Calcutta: Advaita Ashrama, 1955), IV, p. 318.

[191] See also Swami Vivekananda, 'My Plan of Campaign', *The Complete Works of Swami Vivekananda* (Calcutta: Advaita Ashrama, 1955), III, 207-227 (pp. 208-209). and Olcott, *Old Diary Leaves*, VI, pp. 128-129, 136-137,; 'Death of Swami Vivekananda', *Theosophist*, 23:11 (August 1902), 696-697.

[192] Godwin, *Theosophical Enlightenment*, p. 296.

[193] This experience was described by Massey himself in his SPR report. C. C. Massey, 'The Possibilities of Mal-Observation in Relation to Evidence for the Phenomena of Spiritualism', in *Proceedings of the Society for Psychical Research, Volume 4:1886-87* (London: Trubner and Co., 1887), 75-110.

[194] Godwin, *Theosophical Enlightenment*, p. 296. See also A.P. Sinnett, *Early Days of Theosophy in Europe* (London: Theosophical Publishing House, 1922), pp. 9-10.

[195] See Sinnet, *Early Days of Theosophy*, p. 11. and Olcott, *Old Diary Leaves*, I, p. 475.

[196] Emily Kislingbury, 'Spiritualism in Its Relation to Theosophy', in *Theosophical Siftings V: 1892-1893* (London: The Theosophical Publishing Society, 1892), p. 4. Kislingbury's membership seems to have been a matter of controversy. In a letter reprinted by Constance Wachtmeister, Kislingbury noted that she went to Wurzburg to visit Blavatsky and noted 'H.P.B had her invisible helpers as she sat writing in the room sacred to her work. As I was not at that time a member of the T.S., though I had known H.P.B.almost since its foundation. Little was said either to me or before me of the methods used.' Constance Wachtmeister, *Reminiscences of H. P. Blavatsky and The Secret Doctrine* (London: Theosophical Publishing Society, 1893), p. 37.

[197] *The Letters of H. P. Blavatsky*, p. 576.

[198] Emily Kislingbury, 'Spiritualism in Its Relation to Theosophy', p. 6.

[199] Letter CXVIII in *The Letters of H. P. Blavatsky*, pp. 435-437.

[200] K. Paul Johnson, *The Masters Revealed: Madame Blavatsky and the Myth of the Great White Lodge*, (Albany: State University of New York, 1994), pp. 109-110.

[201] *The Hermetic Brotherhood of Luxor*, p. 36.

[202] Meade, *Madame Blavatsky*, p. 254. and Williams, *Madame Blavatsky Priestess of the Occult*, pp. 206-207.

[203] 'Details of the Evidence Referred to on Page 207', *Proceedings of the Society for Psychical Research* (London, Trubner and Co.,1885), III, pp. 397-400.

[204] C. C. Massey, 'The Explanation of the Kiddle Incident in The Fourth Edition of the Occult World', *Light*, 4:186 (26 July 1884), 307-309 (p. 309).

[205] 'On Phenomena Connected with Theosophy', *Proceedings of the Society for Psychical Research* (London, Trubner and Co.,1885), III, p. 207.

[206] Olcott, *Old Diary Leaves*, I, p. 61.

[207] Joscelyn Godwin confirmed this relationship and reprinted several of these letters in Joscelyn Godwin, 'Communications Colonel Olcott Meets the Brothers: An Unpublished Letter', *Theosophical History* 5:1 (January 1994), 5-10; Joscelyn Godwin, 'From the Archives: H. P. Blavatsky to 'M.A. Oxon': An Unpublished Letter', *Theosophical History*, 4:6-7 (April-July 1993), 172-177; Olcott, *Old Diary Leaves*, I, pp. 299-300, 476. Theodore Besterman, *Mrs. Annie Besant: A Modern Prophet* (London: Kegan Paul, 1934), pp. 149-150. and in *Light*, 12 (23 July 1892), p. 356.; (9 July 1892), pp. 330-32.; (23 July 1892), pp. 354-57.

[208] Godwin, *Theosophical Enlightenment*, p. 294.

[209] Oppenheim, *The Other World*, p. 77.

[210] Arthur Lillie, *Modern Mystics and Modern Magic: Containing a Full Biography of the Rev. William Stainton Moses* (London: Swan Sonnenschein & Co., 1894), p. 115.

[211] Joscelyn Godwin, 'From the Archives: H. P. Blavatsky to 'M.A. Oxon': An Unpublished Letter', *Theosophical History*, 4:6-7 (April-July 1993), 172-177 (p. 172).

[212] Godwin, 'From the Archives: H. P. Blavatsky to M.A. Oxon', p. 172.

[213] Olcott, *Old Diary Leaves*, IV, p. 406.
[214] Gomes, *Dawning of the Theosophical Movement*, p. 92.
[215] Blavatsky, *Collected Writings: 1874 -1878*, I, p. 194.
[216] John Hamill, 'Additional Light on William Stainton Moses and the Theosophical Society', *Theosophical History*, 7:7 (July 1999), 252- 255 (p. 254).
[217] W. Stainton Moses, 'Spiritualism and Theosophy', *The Theosophist* 1:8 (May 1880), 198-199.
[218] Olcott, *Old Diary Leaves*, I, p. 320.
[219] A. P. Sinnett, 'The Brothers of Theosophy', *Light*, 3:155 (22 December 1883), 557-559 (p. 558).
[220] H. P. Blavatsky, 'A Few Questions to 'HIRAF'', *Spiritual Scientist*, 2:19 (July 1875), 217-218.; H. P. Blavatsky, 'A Few Questions to 'HIRAF'', *Spiritual Scientist*, 2:20 (July 1875), 236-237.
[221] Godwin, *Theosophical Enlightenment*, p. 296.
[222] Lillie, *Modern Mystics*, p. 117.
[223] Olcott, *Old Diary Leaves*, IV, pp. 497-498. Words in parenthesis were added to give the reader a better understanding of the context of this passage; the sentences in brackets were taken from the earlier article that Olcott referred to in his *Old Diary Leaves* found in Henry Steel Olcott, 'William Stainton Moses', *The Theosophist*, 14:2 (November 1892), 109-111 (p. 109).
[224] Letter from Henry Olcott No. 5 reprinted from *Light* (London), 9 July1892, pp. 330-32; and 23 July 1892, pp. 354-57. printed in William Stainton Moses, *Early Story of TS*, The Theosophical Society in America (9 and 23 July 1892) <http://www.theosophical.org/component/content/article/65-olcott/1852> [accessed 22 August 2011] (para.32-33 of 66)
[225] Letter from Henry Olcott No. 5 printed in William Stainton Moses, *Early Story of TS*, The Theosophical Society in America (9 and 23 July 1892) <http://www.theosophical.org/component/content/article/65-olcott/1852> [accessed 22 August 2011] (para.50 of 66)
[226] Letter from Henry Olcott No. 6 printed in William Stainton Moses, *Early Story of TS*, The Theosophical Society in America (9 and 23 July 1892) <http://www.theosophical.org/component/content/article/65-olcott/1852> [accessed 22 August 2011] (para.54 -56 of 66)

Part III.
SPIRITUALISM

3.1 The History of Spiritualism

As previously explained, the term 'Spiritualism' was a title applied to a group of people who held to one loose philosophical tenet- the belief that the spirits of the recently departed could communicate with the living through the use of certain means and individuals referred to as mediums. Though this was the unifying doctrine of Spiritualism, aside from this one core belief there were many diverse offshoots and differing ideological groups spanning from traditional Christian to progressive agnostic belief structures throughout the nineteenth century.

Nicholas Goodrick-Clarke noted the widespread acceptance of Spiritualism during the Victorian Era (1837-1901) in the US and observed that 'several authorities gave high estimates of the number of spiritualists in the United States, between 9 and 10 million in a population of some 44 million.'[1] This religion was further bolstered by the conversion of the noted scientist Alfred Wallace who held prestige within the intellectual community as a co-founder of natural selection alongside the more popular Charles Darwin. Thus, one cannot underestimate the influence of Spiritualism which provided an unorthodox religious movement out of which would spring many of the occultist and magical circles of the nineteenth century.[2]

3.2 The Fox Sisters

Despite the fact that necromancy had been around since ancient Sumer and was found in the biblical story of Saul's consulting a ventriloquist at Endor in 1 Samuel 28, a new religion known as American Spiritualism was birthed on 31 March 1848 at a residence in Hydesville, New York in the home of the Fox sisters (the term 'American Spiritualism' refers to the practice of 'modern Spiritualism' in the United States). Modern Spiritualism began with strange noises and eerie sounds that woke the unsuspecting Mrs. Fox up late one fateful evening. The family deduced that the cause of these disturbances was a supernatural being. This event was allegedly followed by Katy's addressing of this ghost: 'Mr. Split foot, do as I do' and then she began to snap her fingers. The strange sounds simulated the rapping noise and eventually these noises began to follow a sequence when inquired.[3] Thus, this communication with a departed spirit signified the birth of Modern Spiritualism and triggered a worldwide movement. In lieu of the fact that Spiritualism began with two girls who were unlearned in Swedenborg's philosophies and Mesmerism, Spiritualism eventually became rooted in these ideologies as will be explored throughout this section. Thus, it is important to note that the origin of Modern Spiritualism began with the Fox sisters though it would soon spread across the Atlantic Ocean and into other Western Countries including England and France.

3.3 The Davenport Brothers

The Davenport brothers were pioneers of the early Spiritualist movement for their cabinet séances, physical mediumship, and international touring. By the end of their career which spanned the Victorian age from 1855 until 1877 they had become internationally renowned having performed sittings in the United States, Canada, England, France, Russia, England, and as far as Australia. These boys elicited much attention and as a result numerous pamphlets, articles, and books have been written on account of their alleged clairvoyant abilities. In order to ascertain their influence on the early Spiritualist movement understanding some biographical information seems essential. Both Ira Erastus and William Henry Davenport were born in Buffalo, New York the former in 17 September 1839 and the latter in 1 February 1842. These two boys bore a striking resemblance to each other both were handsome with small builds. Also both were educated in the typical fashion, and had one younger sibling a sister named Elizabeth Louisa who was born on 23 December 1844.[4]

The Davenport brothers experienced a rather mundane childhood with few events that would foreshadow their later profound psychic abilities. Then something unprecedented occurred in 1846. Suddenly, an outpouring of 'raps, thumps, loud sudden inexplicable noises, snaps, cracking noises' all began to ring out uncontrollably at the Davenport estate. This disturbance continued until the Rochester Knockings of 1848 when public attention and media coverage focused upon the Fox sisters. When the Davenports realized that these sounds could actually be the communications of departed spirits seeking communication, they decided to attempt to contact these spirits directly employing methods similar to those that the Fox sisters had implemented. The results would forever shape American Spiritualism.

T. L. Nichols a licensed medical doctor wrote a favorable biography of the Davenport boys noting two prevailing thoughts that circulated about their abilities. First, ideas existed that these youths were nothing more than illusionists similar to Harry Houdini whose stage magic consisted of illusions aided with the help of machinery and confederates. A second widely held opinion was that these manifestations were an example of genuine psychic phenomena and provided proof that communication with departed spirits was possible.[5]

The Davenport brother's first séance was performed on 13 February 1855.[6] News of their abilities had become widely circulated through the effort of their father Ira senior and the Davenport boys became an immediate success, able to fill their house and yard with intrigued attendees. Ira and William commenced their youthful careers as Spiritualist mediums by channeling various spirits and, in doing so, established a methodology that would become the norm for multiple Spiritualists across the Western world. These norms included: receiving temporary bouts of strength, automatic writing, levitating, the mysterious moving of objects on their own, the appearing of apparitions, pencils writing without human aid, the playing of musical instruments, and, of course, communicating with spirits. At the onset of these communications the Davenport boys experimented with pistols which they inexplicably discharged using heir psychic abilities and employing the assistance of strange spirit hands. Visitors were said to bring their own pistols and lay them upon the table for the spirits to use. As time went on suspicions arose, and the brothers (attempting to prove that their phenomena were not the results of their own personal collusion) subjected themselves to multiple test conditions.[7] The brothers even began the practice of filling their hands with flour to prove that these spectacles were not a result of their own hands, but, rather, the departed spirits exerting their power through their spirit hands. The brothers even agreed to participate in certain scientific experiments including being sewn up in bags, enclosed in wooden tubs, and other unusual test conditions.[8]

The Davenport brothers became especially known for their psychic ability of producing phenomena involving musical instruments that would play themselves including the violin, tambourine, trumpet, and guitar.[9] The boys also appeared to be the first mediums to communicate with 'John King' the elusive and infamous spirit of early American Spiritualism. As noted in the previous section, John King would play an integral role in the life of Madame Blavatsky and would become the prototype of her later Tibetan masters. Thus, the

Davenport Boys created the elements that Blavatsky would utilize in establishing her Theosophical Society. John King was an important figure in the lives of the Davenport brothers as well informing them of their duty to the world:

> After a variety of physical effects had been produced, 'King; vocally told Davenport that himself and boys had a great duty to perform, and that the time had nearly come to begin it; that he must take them before the world to help demonstrate the great fact of man's post mortem existence; that the media were powerful, and the operators ready to do their part.[10]

The boys were chosen to commence a supernatural mission to prove the empirical nature of Spiritualism. The Davenport brothers also appeared to be the first mediums to incorporate a 'cabinet' into their séances; this would soon become a common element associated with nineteenth-century Spiritualism as observed through its later use by the Eddy brothers and numerous other Victorian mediums.

3.4 Criticisms and Skeptics

Despite the popularity of their séances, the brothers also shared a number of critics. One such critic was George Smith Buck (1836-1904) the famous illusionist who went by the stage name 'Herr Dobler' and performed similar 'phenomena' in his stage act. Buck was a popular magician and went on to perform in front of two extremely gifted Victorian authors- Charles Dickens (1812-1870) and the Oxford mathematician Charles Dodgson who was more famously known as Lewis Caroll (1832-1898) the author of *Alice in Wonderland*.[11] Dobler provided an extensive summary of the cabinet in his 1889 work which he published with the purpose of exposing the Davenport Brothers as frauds. He noted the following:

> Here were two men, who, after being securely fastened with ropes, and brought into a dark room or Cabinet, could, by the mere force of their power, cause musical instruments to play, to fly about, and a hundred other fantastic things to take place. Every test being used to detect any physical deception on their part, and every proof being given that they, bodily, had nothing to do with it....[12]After having paid your admission fee of 7/6, 5/, 2/6, according to the class of seat you intended to occupy, the first object that would meet your eye, standing on the platform- from which it was raised by tressels- would be a rather ponderous but simple

piece of furniture, in shape like a large cupboard, and of about the following dimensions:- Height, 6 feet; length, 7 feet; and depth, 2 feet. Three doors were placed in the front, the centre one having a diamond-shaped aperture, with a piece of black cloth hung inside as a covering. The cupboard was provided with three seats, one at each extremity, for the performers who sat facing each other, and an extra seat in the centre. This was the cabinet in which the manifestations were to take place. In all spiritual séances, darkness is supposed to be absolutely necessary, and the Cabinet was an invention which allowed the Davenports to perform before a large audience without imposing upon the latter necessity of sitting a long time in the dark, the Cabinet being made in such a manner that closing the doors secluded every particle of light, all that was required was simply the light of the room to be subdued to some extent.[13]

The description of the séance described in the above quote allows the reader a glimpse of the devices that these brothers employed. Buck continued on to describe this spectacle noting that this 'phenomena' was succeeded by a convincing speech made by Mr. Ferguson concerning the spiritual world 'and such were the strength of his arguments, that many were convinced even before the manifestations were given.'[14] Volunteers were then chosen from the audience in order to bind the hands of the Davenport brothers so that they could not be accused of causing the incredible phenomena about to be produced. After the boys had been adequately bound, Ferguson placed some musical instruments such as a guitar, two tambourines, two bells, a violin, and a trumpet into the cabinet with them. The doors were then closed and in a short amount of time the instruments would make slight noises; then the trumpet would fall a sign that the mediums were being released from their bonds. Then the doors were opened by the lecturer, where it was discovered that the Davenport boys were tied to their seats- their hands pulled through double knots, even more secured then when they had initially entered the cabinet. This would amaze the crowd as there was no obvious way that the boys could have tied themselves up in this manner. The cabinet was then shut again and then a ruckus of loud noise was heard coming from the cabinet. Again the cabinet doors were opened only to reveal that the brothers remained tied up- this truly appeared to be a remarkable feat.

For the next act, a volunteer was handpicked from the audience and given the privilege of being tied up and placed in the cabinet with the two mediums to determine whether the music was truly caused by departed spirits. Their experience always seemed to be the same; the door would close a dozen hands could be seen ringing the bells, playing the tambourines, and then a tambourine was placed on the spectator's head just in time for the door to open again and reveal to the audience what had occurred. The finale consisted of a similar spectacle only this time flour was poured into the hands of both boys assuring that they could not be using their own hands to produce these instrumental sounds. The door was closed and again the music would mysteriously play only this time when the doors opened the ropes would be perfectly coiled on the floor, and the boys would stand and hold out the palms of their hands revealing the flour proving that they had somehow become the 'passive instruments of some supernatural agency.'[15]

Despite the impressive depth of this illusion, Buck went on to debunk the supposed supernatural feats achieved the by these mediums. He commenced by noting that it was 'far more difficult for an inexperienced person to secure another with ropes than it would be for that person to release himself after having been tied.' Another advantage that the Davenport brothers enjoyed was the fact that there were two of them in the cabinet at the same time which proved useful if one of the brothers required assistance undoing his knots. Buck then continued to explain the art of tying knots and noted that with a little training these boys could have easily have tied themselves to give the illusion that they had been bound tightly when in reality they were not. Then there was the issue of the spectator coming into the cabinet with them. This spectator had been tied up as well, and when the doors closed all that was necessary for the boys to do was to take a hand from behind their backs, and touching their visitor on the face and other parts with their open fingers, make him believe that each finger was a separate hand. While one brother was performing the spirit hands this freed the other brother up to bang on the instruments. As for the flour in the hands, Buck noted that when flour is placed in the palm of the hand with very little practice the three fingers may be placed so as to entirely confine it, leaving the thumb and forefinger quite at liberty. This was the method adopted by the Davenports, 'as, no matter how difficult, they were bound to leave not a single clue.'[16] Thus, Buck presented a rational alternative that counteracted the Davenport phenomena.

Another vocal critic was Thomas Carr who noted some crucial 'facts' about the Davenport brothers. Though Carr's points seem legitimate, he in no way caught the boys in the flagrant act of dishonesty; nonetheless, most of his observations remain circumstantial. Carr noted firstly that the boys were of low moral character which he claimed was 'admitted by their best friends.'[17]

Secondly, the brothers were previously arrested on charges of swindling and were warned not to 'obtain money on false pretences.'[18] This 'criminal record' was attested to by Dr. Luke P. Rand who wrote a booklet in 1859 describing the brother's arrests in Mexico, Phoenix, and New York. Rand vividly recollected an experience he had shared with the Davenport mediums in July 1859 and their embarrassing arrest and incarceration at a jail in Oswego, New York noting their subsequent escape after being incarcerated for twenty-nine days. What appeared intriguing about Rand's ramblings was that he claimed while imprisoned in the Oswego Jail that they had an unexpected visitor whose connection with the Theosophical Society will be discussed in a later section. This visitor was none other than the esteemed Spiritualist and original member of the Theosophical Society Emma Hardinge Britten.[19]

The third issue that Carr raised against the Davenports concerned their ropes. The boys refused to be bound with any rope that was not their own and were strands of no more than 10 feet in length. When the Davenport brothers emerged out of the closet, the author noticed their hands and seemed confident that the boy's hands were the ones he had witnessed during the séance. Also, at the conclusion of each performance their manager J. B. Ferguson (a former clergyman from Nashville, Tennessee) rushed with all his speed to the doors and by so doing was a 'perpetual annoyance.'[20]

When asked why Ferguson would need to rush in at the close of each séance he simply explained that all questions would be resolved at a later point. Carr noted that Ferguson never did explain his justifications for running into the cabinet and Carr deduced that it was likely done to cover up some unknown deception. Carr's fourth accusation involved the conclusion of the séance. After the finale, while the boys were being bound, he could distinctly hear the sound of the rope as it came whizzing against his legs, and when they spoke which they often did in answer to inquiries, their voice beckoned great physical exertion. Carr noted that 'this is very important, in the dark ears must take the place of eyes...'[21] Finally, Carr cited the darkness as a primary obstacle towards believing in the integrity of the Davenport brothers and their phenomena. Carr could not understand why the boys insisted on only performing under the cover of darkness if their phenomena were indeed legitimate.

In concluding, Carr observed that illusions much more impressive than the Davenport parlor tricks were shown to be the result of sleights of hand, asserting that the messrs Ferguson, Fay and the Brothers Davenport, were 'impious impostors, low bred charlatans, trifling with the dearest feelings of human hearts, sporting with the memories of the peaceful dead, deserving the bitterest contempt of every thinking man.'[22]

Frank Podmore the critical, psychic investigator mentioned the Davenport Brothers in his work *Modern Spiritualism*. Podmore noted a particular instance following a successful tour of London that occurred in Liverpool, England in February 1865. He noted that volunteers were selected from the audience on the first night to tie the boy's arms using their typical ropes. Well these specific spectators knew how to tie a unique knot referred to as the Tom Fool's knot. Podmore observed that 'this knot they applied to the wrists of the Davenport Brothers. Each protested that the knot was unfairly tight, and injured the circulation. A doctor summoned to the platform gave it as his opinion that no injury to the circulation was to be apprehended, and that, in view of the smallness of the mediums' hands, the knot was not unnecessarily tight. The Davenports refused to proceed with their performance under such conditions, and Ferguson was ordered to cut the knots.[23] This was not the first exposure of their phenomena nor was it their last.

Finally, in a 1910 copy of *The Strand* magazine the famous illusionist John Maskelyne stated that in 1865 while attending a séance performed by the Davenport brothers a small ray of light had illuminated the box as the center door opened. This light had allowed him to view the method by which the brothers produced their alleged phenomena. He informed the audience of his discovery but he was challenged by Spiritualists for him to prove it. Maskelyne did just that and started to produce in the same hall no less than 'every item of the Davenport séances down to the smallest detail.'[24]

Validating the testimony of Luke Rand in her *History of Modern American Spiritualism* and revealing a connection between these mediums, Emma Hardinge Britten wrote fondly of the passing of 'Willie' Davenport the younger brother and his contribution to the Spiritualist movement.[25] She noted that he met his demise in Sydney, New South Wales and described his unusual tomb stone:

Ira had much difficulty to obtain leave to erect a monument to his dear companion's memory, because he determined to have upon it a sculpture device representing the time-honoured cabinet and other paraphernalia which recalled poor Willie's earthly work and frequent martyrdoms. Ira succeeded at last, but he might have spared himself the context. The young man's monument is already set up in the ineffaceable lines which Spiritualism has made on public opinion. She then quotes an obituary found in the Spiritual journals.[26]

After the death of his younger brother in 1877, Ira befriended the great Illusionist Harry Houdini to whom he sent a letter expressing his indifference with Spiritualism a movement that he had been persecuted for enabling his entire life:

We never in public affirmed our belief in Spiritualism that we regarded as no business of the public; nor did we offer our entertainment as the result of sleight-of-hand, or on the other hand as Spiritualism. We let our friends and foes settle that as best they could between themselves, but unfortunately we were often the victims of their disagreements.[27]

3.5 The Davenport Brothers and Blavatsky

The Davenport Boys have already been connected with a prominent member of the early Theosophical Society- Emma Hardinge Britten; however, their relationship to Blavatsky must now be explained. It seemed that Blavatsky was familiar with the Davenport Boys and their phenomena as noted in her first major writing *Isis Unveiled* where she described their imprisonment in the Oswega jail.[28] In her later work, *The Key to Theosophy* Blavatsky explained that such manifestations similar to the 'Davenport; - like manifestations' occurred through the 'astral body.[29] She also alluded to the Davenport Boys in the 1882 March issue of the *Theosophist* and noted their dexterity.[30] It seems obvious that Blavatsky had become aware of the Davenport Boys though no formal meeting between the brothers and herself has ever been recorded; however, given the brothers close proximity to Blavatsky in New York and their famed world travels it does not seem unlikely that these gifted mediums would have crossed paths at some point. Again, though no formal relationship between these mediums existed they did manage to share some similar elements. The first element was already mentioned above- both the brothers and Blavatsky believed they could communicate with the spirit guide known as John King. In fact, Blavatsky believed that she was the first person to ever channel John King, though he eventually became a famous spirit-guide who had been channeled in households across the Western World. It seems significant that King originated with the Davenport Brothers and was used as a prototype for Blavatsky in creating her philosophy of masters and adepts.

Another similarity between Blavatsky and the Davenport mediums is found in the story of the 'mysterious manuscript' described in the 1869 book by Paschal Beverly Randolph titled *The Davenport Brothers:*[31]

> [all of a sudden] like unto the rattling of a stiff sheet of paper on or near the ceiling, and directly over the table, and, in an instant thereafter, a sheet of paper, uncrumpled in the least degree, fell upon the table; and, when lights were called, these sheets were found to be neatly and closely written all over, in a hand-writing whose beauty and evenness approximated copper-plate engraving in excellence and precision of execution; and this writings proved to be beautiful, eloquent, and profound essays, in brief, upon various important themes and topics. Some were on science, others upon art, literature, philosophy, medicine, ethics, aesthetics, electro-dynamics, sculpture, geology, anthropology, paleontology, biology, and a score of others equally profound and interesting, and all alike exhibiting evidences of deep and varied research; and many of them are still in possession of persons in all parts of the country…[32]

This process will become important when examining the writing of the Mahatma Letters which were said to have been 'precipitated' by highly-evolved, yet invisible spiritual masters. Thus, the Davenports created another element that Blavatsky would employ in the dissemination of her teachings through her Mahatma letters which were sent mainly between the years 1881-1883 after the Oriental shift in the Society. Now that some of the basic elements of American Spiritualism have been explained, focus will now be shifted on two of the major Spiritualists in the nineteenth century. Both of these two individual mediums were heavily influenced by the teachings of Swedenborg. Robert S. Elwood observed that 'spiritualism is Swedenborgian ideology mixed with an experimentation with transic states inspired by mesmerism.'[33] This Swedenborgian influence will be evidenced both in the life of Andrew Jackson Davis and Allan Kardec explored in the following sections below.

3.6 Andrew Jackson Davis

Andrew Jackson Davis, or the 'Poughkeepsie Seer' as he was more commonly known, would go on to become a pivotal figure in American Spiritualism. Davis attracted a large following of spiritual seekers across the country, but it all began with a humble beginning in Blooming Grove, New York. Andrew Jackson Davis was born on 11 August 1826 and was named after the soon-to-be-elected United States president Andrew Jackson at the request of his drunken uncle Thomas Maffet.[34] As Davis grew he obtained a job working for W.W. Woodworth a local attorney who gradually moved from a private counselor-at-law to becoming elected into the National Congress. While in the employ of Woodworth, Davis decided to attend an Episcopal Church with the entire Woodworth family. Davis told of a particular situation when he was confronted by an Episcopalian Sunday school teacher. This teacher asked him the question: 'Who redeemed you?' To which the young Davis recollected: 'The meaning of the word 'redeemed' dwelt rather vaguely in my brain, and caused me for a moment to forget the printed answer; but, quickly gathering my thoughts into form, I replied- 'Christ,' How glad I was that she did not question me as to the precise time when my redemption happened! If she had, I felt sure that my memory would have failed me.'[35]

Davis went on for a short while to attend his family's Reformed Dutch Church where he became acquainted with the doctrines of Calvinism. The basic doctrines of John Calvin (1509-1564) were eventually systematized during the Synod of Dort held in 1618 and have since been summarized through the simple acronym TULIP.[36] The 'T' in this acronym stood for 'total depravity' which meant that humanity was inherently evil and wicked; the 'U' represented the doctrine of 'unconditional election' and meant that God chose those who would be saved based on no previous conditions; the 'L' signified 'limited atonement' which referred to the conceptualization that Jesus would only die for those whom God had chosen; and 'I' meant 'irresistible grace' which expressed that once God had chosen a person, that individual could not 'resist' this decision diminishing any notion of human free will; and, lastly, 'P' which referred to the 'perseverance of the saints' and implied that if God had picked an individual, that this person would then continuously (persevere) keep coming back to God throughout his life. These doctrines once made familiar to Davis instilled in him a great sense of 'anxiety' and 'confusion.' Early on Davis began to question this fatalistic belief structure realizing that a paradox existed between a God of love that would create people just to send them to eternal torment.[37]

This grappling with Calvinistic doctrine pushed Davis out of the Dutch Reformed church and influenced his later adaptation of Swedenborgian theories of the afterlife. The heavy influence of Swedenborg philosophy on Davis has prompted one Western Esoteric scholar to note that Davis' worldview was essentially 'Swedenborgianism in 19th-century garb.'[38] It seemed natural that Davis would adapt Swedenborg's theology given his disdain for Calvinism which Swedenborg noted was 'the head of Gorgon or Medusa engraved upon the shield of Pallas' and furthermore asked:

> But what could have been devised more pernicious, or what could have been believed concerning God more cruel that that some of the human race were predestined to damnation? For it would be a cruel faith, that the Lord, who is Love itself and Mercy itself, wills that a multitude of men should be born for hell...Since I thought that such a frantic thing could never have been decreed, still less declared and published to the world by an Christian.[39]

At a young age Davis lost his dear sister Julia Ann which had supposedly been prophesied by Davis' deeply-religious and illiterate mother through a vision concerning a white lamb. Though this was a tragic experience for the Davis family, it helped to inaugurate Davis' spiritual illumination. At age eleven, Davis started his vigils of his sonambulic faculty which he would hide from his father despite the fact that they kept him up all hours of the night.[40] In 1843 through his association with Ira Armstrong the shoe merchant, Davis attended a revival at a Methodist church. While there a skinny shoe maker pressed Davis inquiring if he could call him his Christian brother. This man then employed an unusual metaphor to express his desire for Davis to repent- the man claimed that his bowels yearned for him. Davis not knowing what this strange phraseology meant suggested that this man should ingest some 'catnep-tea' to help with this intestinal problem. Hearing this reply, the man left angrily leaving Davis to note that: 'the abruptness of his retirement from my side, and the half-angry expression of his countenance, made the whole talk about being 'my brother in Christ' seem extremely foolish and absurd, if not absolutely hypocritical and wicked.'[41]

Davis told of a different confrontation with the 'itinerant revival minister' at the store where he was employed.[42] The minister probed

Davis and asked him if he felt regretful for his sins. Davis responded, 'No, sir I don't feel that I'm very wicked: only sorry for something, which I won't ever do again.' A conversation then ensued to
which the preacher ended 'I fear the day of grave is past! I fear you
will be lost forever![43] This comment caused Davis to examine his
young life from a paradoxical Calvinistic perspective. If Davis had
never been elected by God, he would still suffer eternal damnation
no matter how noble or virtuous his actions may be. Davis concluded: 'If I live a pure and blameless life, damnation will be my destiny;
and if I should be desperately wicked, it could in the end make no
difference; for it if be true, as this man says, that the day of grace is
past, I am eternally lost- lost in hell- where, as mother told me,
'there's nothin' but a-weepin' an; a wailin' an; a-gnashin' of teeth!'[44]

Later that same year Davis recalled his fear of death and damnation:

> Indeed, so horrid and gloomy were my contemplations one night,
> in view of the possibility of dying, and going to a pit of inextin-
> guishable fire, that I leaped from my bed, dressed myself, and was
> about to ask permission to sit by the kitchen-stove till morning,
> when I heard the voice- soothing and loving like my mother's re-
> peating in minor tones: Be calm! Jackson. The pastor is wrong-
> you shall see![45]

This prospect of eternal damnation and punishment for sins
would heavily influence Davis' conceptualization of wickedness and
evil. Then one day Davis discovered his unique abilities. Dr. J. S.
Grimes a professor of Jurisprudence in the Castleton Medical College and a noted Mesmerist had come to town and requested that
Davis sit for him. Davis entered this sitting with 'a vague, apprehen-
sive faith in the Bible doctrine of eternal misery; a tendency to spon-
taneous somnambulism; an ear for imaginary voices...'.[46] During this
session Davis experienced extreme mental anguish though when he
emerged he felt incredibly wonderful. He was then told that unbeknownst to him that during this session he had acted as a clairvoyant
alerting people to their hidden diseases and proving his gift by reading the watches of spectators even though he could not physically
see them. Davis emerged from this session believing that he possessed the gift of clairvoyance and felt a 'calling from the pinnacle of
an unknown mountain.'[47]

In January of 1844, Davis recounted another visionary revelation
where he experienced a feeling of being 'born again' which he associ-

ated with Mesmerism. He vividly portrayed this spiritual vision that he endured under the magnetism of Dr. Grimes: The room illuminated...each body was glowing with many colors brilliant and magnetical. Each figure emanated a light atmosphere that extended up the arms and pervaded the entire body. Their nails had one sphere of light surrounding them, the hair another, the ears another, and the eyes still another...the head was luminous; these emanations spread out into the air. Davis could see inside people...into their organs in colors and emanations. Their hearts gave out a distinct flame and the light from their brains was luminous with prismatic colors.[48] This visionary experience became widened as Davis was given the ability to see the individual atoms that composed a given object. Also, he now possessed the ability to see through any object that he pleased. Davis then described an unusual awareness of correspondences between metals and organs from within the human body; he could see thousands of miles away from the room in which he was observing; this was followed by a strange out-of-body experience where he was allowed the unique opportunity to see everything that most people couldn't see until after their own death.[49] This could be considered an early form of astral projection a device explained by Blavatsky under the heading 'The Flight of the Astral Body' printed in *Isis Unveiled*, II, 597 and an aim of the first Theosophical Society (see section on 'Emma Hardinge Britten').

Davis' visionary experiences quickly became a highly sought after attraction. On 6 March 1844 Davis experienced an extraordinary vision that the world was comprised of white sheep. This trance was prefigured in his mother's vision concerning his sister's death. Davis ascertained that these sheep though misdirected had spiritual sympathies. Contained in this vision was a great shepherd described as the Universal Father who communicated telepathically with Davis and explained that these sheep were trapped in ignorance and confusion and required some gentle discipline. To this Davis acceded. The shepherd explained that this confusion had resulted from a misunderstanding of theology and was due to conflicts between truth and error, reason and theology, reality and imagination and most importantly the 'intense anxiety of each person who desires, but cannot believe in, immortal life.'[50] Thus, this vision could be seen as anthropomorphism of Davis' disdain for Calvinistic theology.

The next part of this vision seemed especially valuable in a comparative examination of Davis' philosophy with Helena Blavatsky's teachings. There are three attributes that Blavatsky would later em-

ploy in her own writings that are paralleled in this next visionary experience recorded in Davis' 1857 autobiography- they are numbered
in their respective places. Davis recounted another experience that
overtook him while meditating. A man of a diminutive yet beautiful
stature approached him.[51] This man was greatly advanced in years
and his clothing resembled that of an unspecified friend. His hair was
silvery white and his face was expressive. 1) Most importantly 'he
was a spiritual being''[52] [This conceptualization of a spiritually ascended being interacting with humanity will become a crucial element in Blavatsky's later Theosophy].[53]

In his hand he held a clear white scroll that sparkled with a gilding
of high quality. This spirit-man then proceeded to elevate the scroll
to his lips and kissed it before handing it to the stupefied Davis to
read. Davis opened this divine communication with great delicacy
and precision and peered inside. He recounted that 2) 'it contained
writing in characters which I had never before seen; but I could
translate them without hesitation. The language was clear and comprehensive''[54] [This same process of divine translation and mysterious
manuscripts will be utilized by Blavatsky in both her *The Secret Doctrine* and *The Voice of Silence* which was written after her relocation to
Madras, India].

It read, 'as they were, so they are; as they are, so they will be!' Davis signed his name at the bottom of this manuscript understanding
the interpretation to convey that the world would one day be united
in happiness from 'misdirection and suffering; ignorance and depravity;[55] from pride and sectarian intolerance.' The temporality of this
vision seemed skewed; however, not long after Davis was again visited by this strange spirit-man and they conversed at great length
about love and wisdom. 3) Then Davis perceived the natural laws
pertaining to the vegetable kingdom, the animal kingdom, and the
perfection of humanity [Blavatsky's 'law of progression' and her idea
that humanity would eventually evolve into god-like beings through
the various rounds as a mineral, vegetable, animal, and human
seemed prefigured in Davis' early philosophy; however, this evolution seemed to be a common trait in American Spiritualism].

In the fashion of Pythagoras, Davis was told by this spirit guide
that the entire world could be reduced to the number three. 4) Thus,
there existed a triune power in every compound in this universe-
three essential parts to every established organization- which was
absolutely necessary to all things, in order that they may be perfectly
organized[56] [This preoccupation with the number three is reminis-

cent of Blavatsky's eventual focus on the number seven (septenary constitution) which she argued was the key towards understanding this round of humanity].

Davis continued 'accordingly I founded a system upon these principles and considerations, which may be called a 'medical system of the trinity. In this system I maintain the proposition, that every particle in the human body possesses a close affinity to particular particles below in the subordinate kingdoms- and that these latter particles, if properly associated and applied would cure any affected portion or organ of the human frame.'[57] It was at this point that Davis was made privy to some sacred revelations. This spiritually evolved being was holding a peculiar looking walking cane. Davis continued to communicate with him telepathically and at his request the spirit-being touched the top of this cane and immediately it broke down into three pieces. Davis described that each of these three pieces was composed of smaller intricate forms that appeared to be shaped like diamonds. On each of these diamond shaped pieces was the name of every disease known to humanity along with its respective cure.[58] This cane provided the inspiration for the title of this biography- *The Magical Staff.* Davis believed that he had spiritually left the world, but remained physically aware of his senses. He mysteriously reappeared in a grave yard where he was visited by both the physician Galen and Emmanuel Swedenborg the philosopher and theologian who would provide the frame work from which Davis would adapt his own ideologies. This revelation of Emmanuel Swedenborg seemed fitting as much of Davis' philosophy seemed derivative of Swedenborgian concepts.

After this mystical experience Davis opened a homeopathic practice through which he clairvoyantly determined people's illnesses and found the corresponding agent necessary to cure it whether it was the magnetic moisture of a rat or the skin of a frog.[59] Davis then embarked on a rigorous lecturing schedule and went on to publish a pamphlet titled 'Lectures on Clairmativeness' in 1845. Despite his success, the memory of the 'sacred staff' from that previous vision consumed Davis. Finally, an important supernatural event occurred involving a floating transparent white sheet that had the following words painted on it:

> Behold! Here is thy Magic Staff: Under all Circumstance keep an even mend. Take it. Try it. Walk With it. Davis seized the mental

cane and began using it to examine the sick. Davis continued a medical clairvoyant passing into trance typically twice daily.[60]

Thus, Davis was given the 'cane of healing' that he had first familiarized himself with in a visionary experience some time earlier. After obtaining this metaphysical staff Davis appointed Samuel S. Lyon a physician from Bridgeport, Connecticut and Rev. William Fishbough as his magnetizer and scribes, and employed them to assist him in lecturing on philosophy while in a trance state. As Frank Podmore noted 'The lectures were actually commenced in November 1845, extended over a period of 1847 in the shape of a large octavo volume of nearly eight hundred closely printed pages, under the title of *The Principles of Nature, Her Divine Revelations, and A Voice to Mankind.*'[61] One of the attendees of this circle was a Princeton scholar and Presbyterian minister named George Bush who also worked as a Professor of Hebrew at the University of New York.[62] Bush suggested that there was a link between Mesmerism and Swedenborgiansm as claimed in his work *Mesmer and Swedenborg* (1847). Bush thought that Davis had begun speaking Hebrew in his trance state which made him intrigued with this controversial character; however, his attitude would inexplicably change for within a few short weeks of the appearance of *Revelations*, Bush published a small 430 paged pamphlet titled 'Davis' Revelations Revealed' which implied that Davis' trances were the result of deceiving spirits.

Revelations was published in December of 1847 by John Chapman who also composed the original preface to this work. *Revelations* focused largely on the advent of a new dispensation 'when the advanced societies of other 'spheres' would effect a transformation of this world' [63] This obsession with the creation of a New World (a utopian society) probably came from Davis through an earlier affiliation with the Millerites who propagated a heavily eschatological view of the world, and believed that Jesus Christ would return in around the year 1843.[64] Davis' abilities became legendary, and some people even believed that on 31 March 1848 he had effectively predicted the future rise of Spiritualism and the phenomena displayed at the Fox house later that year. Though this message was derived from an extremely ambiguous statement, it will be left up to the reader to determine its veracity:

> About daylight this morning, a warm breathing passed over my face, suddenly waking me from a profound slumber; and I heard a

voice, tender and yet peculiarly strong saying: 'Brother! The good work has begun- behold, a living demonstration is born!'...The breathing and the voice ceased immediately, and I was left wondering what could be meant by such a message.[65]

The mystical element of this prophecy rested in its date- it was the same day that the Fox sisters made contact with spirits in Hydesville, New York. In 1847, Davis along with a small group of Universalist ministers gathered together and formed what would become the organ of Davis' philosophy- a journal titled *Univercoelum and Spiritual Philosopher*. As Ann Braude noted in her work *Radical Spirits*, there was a direct connection between this publication, Davis, and the Fox sisters:

> the *Univercoelum*, lasted just long enough to welcome the mysterious noises produced in the presence of the Fox sisters [1848] as evidence truth of Davis's prediction of spirit communication. On hearing of the Rochester rappings, Davis invited the Fox sisters to his home in New York City. Davis investigated the Fox sisters' mediumship himself and explained it to the public in terms of his own philosophy in *Philosophy of Spiritual Intercourse*.[66]

In 1857, Davis had become a leader in the New York Spiritual Association working with the noted spiritualist Emma Hardinge Britten who would become an influential figure in the Theosophical Society during its early days.[67] In 1859, Davis published *The Philosophy of Spiritual Intercourse* which was comprised of his observations and interpretation of events that occurred at the residence of a retired Presbyterian minister Eliakim Phelps in Stratford, Connecticut. He viewed this event as the evidence of the power of spirit and rationalized it as follows:

> That spirit can come into contact with inorganic and material substances, is proved by every man's experience. Railroads and steamboats are made and managed by spirit. Suppose you desire to lift a weight; what is it that performs that labor? I answer, it is your spirit! It is that spirituals principle within you which thinks, feels, loves, and reasons- it is your interior self.[68]

On 25 January 1863, after observing the Christian pedagogical model of Sunday school, Davis created a Spiritualist Sunday school class for children called the Lyceum that met on Sunday mornings.

Olcott employed a similar method when establishing Buddhist Sunday schools on his various tours of Ceylon. Olcott's Buddhist Sunday school could have easily have been influenced by Davis whom Olcott claimed to have met on several occasions.[69] In 1887, Emma Hardinge Britten would devote a weekly article towards discussing the latest developments in various lyceums across the country. This section in *The Two Worlds* was open to 'any lyceum that can send exceptional evidence of progress and activity.'[70]

Davis further concerned himself with social issues which he viewed as an imperative element in the transformation of his utopian society that he envisioned would soon occur. These social issues included abolition, feminism, temperance and peace.[71] In fact, when Spiritualists developed their first national organization, the National Association of Spiritualists in 1864, David used his influence to include not just Spiritualists but also 'progressive reformers' into this organization.

As early as 1867, Davis realized that his Harmonial philosophy was at odds with many modern Spiritualist mediums who profited and preyed upon grief stricken individuals who had had lost a loved one and performed fraudulent communications with spirits in order to cheat people out of their hard earned money. Throughout subsequent years, Davis attempted to reform Spiritualism hoping to focus not on the phenomena but on the philosophy of the movement. In 1870, Davis published *The Fountain With Jets of New Meaning* which 'condemned particular "errors or superstitions" in modern Spiritualism.'[72] This periodical attempted to criticize the modern Spiritualist movement which enticed multiple attacks from various Spiritualists who disagreed with Davis' approach and philosophy. In 1878 Davis sought to separate his philosophical movement from Spiritualism by branching out of mainstream Spiritualism. In this respect, Davis prefigured Blavatsky in that he emerged out of Spiritualism and formed his own society in 1868 called the First Harmonial Association in New York which focused on spreading the idea of 'PERFECT LOVE OF ALL WISDOM.'[73]

In an article written in 1879 for the *Religio-Philosophical Journal* Davis attacked many individual Spiritualists including Henry Kiddle and his latest book which he claimed had originated in the spirit world; Davis argued that it was impossible for any work to originate in the world of the departed spirits. Kiddle is an intriguing character in his own right and he is best known in Theosophical history for a later incident concerning an accusation made against Blavatsky's Koot

Hoomi for plagiarizing from one of his lectures in an event labeled the 'Kiddle incident.'[74] Henry Kiddle (1824 – 1891) developed his fascination for Spiritualism later in his adult life though he soon became influential in various circles of American Spiritualism. Kiddle had received a Master of Arts degree from Union College in 1848 and later become the 'officier d'academie from the University of France in 1878.[75] On 14 May 1879, Kiddle announced his conversion to Spiritualism and noted that this life change could result in a forced retirement from his position which he held as the 'superintendent of public Schools.'[76] Later that same year, Kiddle resigned from this occupation following pressure from the press after releasing his work *Spiritual Communications* in which he claimed to record messages from the spirit land transmitted through the mediums of his son and daughter.[77] Kiddle's claims were incredible and suggested that he had contacted Edgar Allen Poe, Prince Albert, Lord Byron, William Shakespeare and multiple other famous individuals. Also, he held that each of these departed spirits were alive in outer space existing on the various planets of our solar system including Saturn and Jupiter which he attempted to assimilate into his biblical soteriology (view of salvation).[78]

Davis denounced Kiddle's work and spoke openly against it to a reporter declaring that it 'reflected a lower phase of mediumship' and observed that 'the superintendent of schools knew little about what had been done to develop the science and philosophy of Spiritualism and indicated his belief that the communications published in the recent volume by Kiddle and his family had not originated in the world of departed spirits.'[79]

In 1880, Davis became involved with New York Medical College and was later elected as a trustee of this institution impressed by their eclectic view of medicine. After a vicious legal battle which ensued between orthodox medical practitioners and the college, the school's charter was eventually revoked. After this conflict and a bitter divorce which opened Davis to attacks from the media, Davis settled down in Boston, Massachusetts and opened an unorthodox medical practice where he practiced until his death in January 1910. In his later years, Davis withdrew from the Spiritualist media until an editor for the *Banner of Light* wrote favorably about him and connected his influence on what was to became the Spiritualist movement of the nineteenth century noting that 'every idea jostling about among Theosophists, Christian Scientists, and Spiritualists had been foreshadowed by Davis.'[80] Thus, Davis' influence on the early Theosophical

Society was acknowledged even during his lifetime. Ever since his demise in 1910, many have continued to refer to Davis as the 'Father of Modern Spiritualism' for his multiple contributions to the study of American Spiritualism and his fidelity to this cause.

3.7 Davis and the Summer Land

One of Davis' major contributions to the Spiritualist community was the creation of and the idealization of the 'Summer Land' a locality of spheres that existed in the afterlife. Davis believed that this Summer Land consisted of numerous interconnecting spheres that were located in the sky and in the planets. Davis further believed that a portion of this Summer Land was to be found in the Milky Way Galaxy, and that after death the spirit would float up to this location.[81] Davis reconciled his afterlife and its role with the basic tenet of Spiritualism:

> And yet the power of the will of a dweller of the Summer Land to make himself seen and felt at an immense distance, as though he were present in the organs of the medium's person, is almost inconceivable. It is marvelous to the unphilosophical observer. It would seem that the communicating mind was bodily and directly within the circle of your presence. The psychological connection between the medium-brain and the spirit's will is perfect. The characteristics and habits of the spirit may be transmitted to the medium- that is, when the psychological control of the brain organs and though-faculties of the medium is complete. The medium, for the time being, is no self-responsible individual; for the will of the communication spirit gives form, shape, gesture, expression, and speech- all which, to an unprepared observer, looking at the matter sensuously, seems as though the controlling spirit was there embodied, and that the customary proprietor of the 'organism' had departed for a time to some other place.[82]

The composition of the spiritual body in the afterlife was further elucidated by Davis. He asserted that in the Summer Land some of the vital organs and other portions of the body which were no longer needed do not appear within the spiritual body. There are no fluids requiring kidneys, no negative or broken down blood requiring pulmonary air cavities, and people become spiritual hermaphrodites.[83] The Summer Land remained eternal in relation to space and time and in distance and duration. Davis was quick to apologetically explicate that 'inasmuch as you cannot conceive of the origin of something out of nothing, or the existence of effects without preexistent causes, or of physical world of matter which is "no matter," but only a sensation or an illusion of the mind, so you cannot conceive of "another world" without its own appropriate sceneries, continents, climates, societies, brotherhoods, religions, governments, and where the inhabitants can have no other sense of eternity than the flowings of time, and no other sense of infinity than the successions of 'space.'[84] Thus, the Summer Land became the final metaphysical resting place for all eternity and many Spiritualists across the Western world adopted Davis' conceptualization of this heavenly realm.

Blavatsky employed this term in her 'Fragments of Occult Truth' a series of articles published in the *Theosophist* between 1881 and 1882, where she equated the Summer Land with her conceptualization of Devachan though she warned that both of these designations referred to a state and not a locality as Davis had initially claimed.[85] In Mahatma letter No.XXV written by Blavatsky's 'Koot Hoomi' and received on 2 February 1883, the Summer Land was actually equated to Kama-Loka distinct from Devachan:

> Deva Chan is a state, not a locality. Rupa Loka, Arupa-Loka, and Kama-Loka are the three spheres of ascending spirituality in which the several groups of subjective entities find their attractions. In the Kama-Loka (semi-physical sphere) dwell the shells, the victim and suicides; and this sphere is divided into innumerable regions and sub-regions corresponding to the mental states of the comers at their hour of death. This is the glorious 'Summer-land' of the Spiritualists, to whose horizons is (sic) limited the vision of their best seers...[86]

Regardless of this identification of the Summer Land with Kama-Loka in 1883, in her later work *The Key to Theosophy* (1889) Blavatsky became critical of the Spiritualist doctrine of the Summer Land for 'to believe that a pure spirit can feel happy while doomed to witness the sins, mistakes, treachery, and, above all the sufferings of those from whom it is severed by death and whom it loves best, without being able to help them, would be a maddening thought.' Thus, in Blavatsky's conceptualization of paradise or Devachan as she called it, in order for a soul to experience true bliss it had to be separated in a different state far away from the physical plane; however, this belief seemed illogical as even in this later work Blavatsky admitted the possibility for the soul to communicate with the living under two circumstances that will be explained in a later section that will explore Blavatsky's *The Key to Theosophy*.[87]

3.8 Andrew Jackson Davis and His Harmonial Philosophy

It is difficult to make generalizations about Davis' philosophy as his ideas were continuously evolving. Davis was the father of early American Spiritualism and published over thirty works and numerous articles related to American Spiritualism and its ideologies. In these works, Davis boasted a rich and diverse vocabulary though if he could not find a word whose meaning clearly articulated his meaning he was not above making words up on the spot (a trait that was evidenced in the title to one of his first booklets 'Lectures on Clairmativeness'). Another common characteristic of Davis was his tendency to allegorize biblical passages in order to make them relevant to his own philosophy. This allegorical hermeneutic is found continuously throughout the majority of his writings. As alluded to in the biographical section, Davis viewed mainstream theology as being counterproductive to society. Instead he had created a theology that assimilated the tenets of Mesmerism and Swedenborgianism.

Furthermore, there was a direct connection between Spiritualism, the law of progression (which stated that the soul was continually moving towards perfection), social justice and Swedenborg in Davis' conceptualization of soteriology (salvation):

> Andrew Jackson Davis's revelations described a series of six celestial spheres of increasing harmony, beauty, and wisdom through which the soul advances after death. Davis's vision was based on the cosmology of Emanuel Swedenborg, which described six heavens but that the first sphere after earth (the second sphere) was relatively chaotic and so had been misperceived as a hell by Swedenborg....Davis believed the notion of spheres provided a better incentive to lead a moral life on earth than the concept of heaven and hell because the more spiritually advanced one became during life on earth the more advanced would be the sphere one entered death.[88]

Davis found that reincarnation on differing spheres provided humanity with a better reward and punishment for their actions than the 'heaven and hell' of Christian orthodoxy. This soteriological issue would also be discussed in his *Answers to Ever-recurring Questions* published in 1868. Davis noted that:

> Our philosophy is that the deeds of a human being do not die with
> the body, but continue with the undying mind, until the full and
> legitimate effects have spent themselves upon and within the doer.
> The good act and evil thought (not executed) will live, and bear
> fruit away over the grave.[89]

Thus, the 'law of progress' was paramount in Davis' philosophy
which mandated that a human being had to be able to learn from
their wicked deeds. Elsewhere in his *Answers to Ever-Recurring Questions*, Davis told of a spirit he had encountered who explained to him
that 'Memory is eternal...but in the vast future we recall only what
was useful and good in the evil and imperfections of the lower
sphere...It is philosophically impossible for punishment to be inter-
minable. The endless duration of punishment would utterly destroy
the purposes of punishment.'[90]

Davis' refutation of Calvinistic theology with its eternal damnation
seemed paramount in this statement. As noted previously, Davis had
developed his own ideology which he labeled as 'Harmonial Philosophy' which shared affinities with Plato's 'theory of forms' in the belief that the heavenly world (ideal) corresponded to the earthly world
(forms) especially through the characteristics of beauty and goodness:[91]

> Power, goodness, wisdom, mercy. Are various aspects of the
> Truth which is Absolute Being. There are recognized also the law
> of progression; the science of correspondences; the endless chain
> of action, motion, and development throughout Nature; the im-
> mortality of man; a purified and perfect state of existence; the uni-
> ty and harmony of all things....So will the reader comprehend that
> the definition of Harmonial Philosophy is...an unselfish, dispas-
> sionate, divine love of unchangeable principles.'[92]

Thus, Davis' conceptualization of this harmonial philosophy had
to be balanced with his belief in the 'law of progression' which advocated for the eventual establishment of a utopian society on Earth.
This connection was evidenced in his work titled *The Harmonial Philosophy*:

> Under such aegis there will surely come upon our world that New
> Birth which is the passing of an old dispensation into the new,
> bringing a new heaven and a new earth....Meanwhile, man is a
> fixed fact in the universe. When once he is born into being there is
> no way of escape, no door to annihilation...[93] It is to be asked

what is the ulterior object, and what does the Harmonial Philosophy propose to accomplish for man? The answer is, To unfold the Kingdom of Heaven on earth, to apply the laws of planets to individualism a word, to establish in human society the same harmonious relations that are found to obtain in the cosmos...[Thus,] the virtuous and truly great, who as spirits and angels dwell above the earth, are chiefly interested in aiding mankind's growth toward universal peace and harmony."[94]

Davis' fixation on the issues of social justice seemed obvious given his belief that 'the virtuous and truly great, who as spirits and angels dwell above the earth, are chiefly interested in aiding mankind's growth toward universal peace and harmony.'[95] This spiritual goal seemed nearly identical to Blavatsky's explanation for the purpose of her masters who were meant to guide and aid humanity in their evolutionary journey. To Davis, the point of life was to evolve an ideal utopian society full of peace and harmony; therefore, social issues could not afford to be ignored.

3.9 Davis' 'Harmonial Philosophy' and his Conceptualization of Evil

Wouter Hanegraaff noted that 'The underlying belief in spiritual progress based on an individual's own efforts was combined with a marked tendency to dismiss evil as a cosmic category and affirm that 'Whatever is, is right!'"[96] This certainly seemed to be the case with Davis. Davis equated his concept of evil with ignorance and went on to explain in *The Harbinger of Health* (1865) that 'we answer briefly, that the Origin of Evil is Ignorance, and that the Origin of the devil is Evil... Nature is a vast magnetic machine or battery, with a positive and a negative pole, and man is the amature. Man is an intermediate being, and connects the two opposite poles....Our want of development is the only absolute evil.[97] This philosophy was expanded in his work *The History and Philosophy of Evil* (1866) in which Davis clarified his view of evil as a mere predecessor toward progress:

> Sin is the child of Evil; Evil is the child of Error; Error is the child of Ignorance; Ignorance is the first condition of an immortal being, whose whole existence is eternally to be swayed and regulated by the triple Laws, Association, Progression, and Development...But what is this evil? It is the temporal subversion of misdirection of the absolute and omnipresent good. How happened the good to become inverted, diverted, or twisted? First, by man's

ignorance; second, by man's error. Why was man thus ignorant in the beginning? Because man is designed for endless progression. On this principle it will be seen that the inferior must precede the superior; as the alphabet goeth before all scholastic attainment; or as helpless infancy is the basis of manhood's powerful superstructure.[98]

It seemed at this stage in his career Davis was not willing to admit in the existence of evil; instead he made it synonymous with ignorance. This refusal to admit the existence of evil would put him at odds with the zealous African American Spiritualist, Paschal Beverly Randolph.[99] The relationship between Randolph and Davis has been explored by Patrick Deveney in his incredible work *Paschal Bevery Randolph* (1997). Later in his career, Davis eventually accepted the existence of evil, though it became the result of evil trickster spirits that he referred to as *diakkas*. He wrote a work entitled *Andrew Jackson Davis, The Diakka, and their Earthly Victims; being an Explanation of Much that is False and Repulsive in Spiritualism* (1873). These *diakkas* became Davis' way of justifying the widespread practice of fraudulent mediums in an almost identical construction to Blavatsky's elementals. The existence of evil spirits became a popular subject among Spiritualists in the 1880s with the widespread exposure of various mediums.

Blavatsky in her *Theosophical Glossary* noted her own conceptualization of *diakkas* which she later equated with 'phantoms from Kama Loka.'[100] Kama Loka was explained in *Esoteric Buddhism* as an unconscious state of gestation. The term 'loca' was used by Blavatsky to denote a world or sphere. It was connected to the earth in some unspecified way that was never fully expounded. It was here that the fourth principle (the animal soul) was separated from the other parts. The fourth part and some of the fifth part remain in Kama Loca while the rest of the principles continue on in their own spiritual evolution.[101] Kama Loca was also the dwelling place for the astral entities known as elementals. Elementals were the shells of human beings that were capable of being summoned during séances. These elementals are wholly deceptive in nature and aimed to manipulate the medium to do their bidding.[102] Thus, it seemed that Blavatsky had drawn upon Davis' conceptualization of *diakkas* equating them to her belief in elementals.

Davis was also an adamant proponent of 'free love' evidenced in his work *The Genesis and Ethics of Conjugal Love* (1874) in which he defined free love as 'the alleged inalienable right of individual sexual attraction to change its individual sexual conjunctions whenever private conjugal inclinations change, repelling the present one and going out passionately towards another...' One Victorian scholar has noted that the free-love advocated in the Victorian Era simply 'renounced the authority of law over relations between sexes.'[103] This did not necessarily imply that 'free love' sanctioned a promiscuous lifestyle, but instead sought to separate the controls of both the church and the state from issues of sexuality. It seemed that Davis' idea of 'free love' appeared more concerned with the subject of divorce in the Victorian Era than a license for licentious behavior. Davis defined his view of 'free love' as a 'love exercised freely between men and women, unhampered by either statute law or public sentiment' or 'freedom in the gratification of the sexual attraction.'[104]

Curiously, in this work Davis recounted a situation where a *diakka* was working against two lovers that parallels Blavatsky's conceptualization of elementals. An anonymous lady wrote a letter to Davis explaining that her husband went for a psychometrical reading and was told by the medium that he desperately needed to find another wife as his current wife (the writer of this letter) was no longer congenial. The woman explained that up until this point she and her husband had enjoyed a perfectly happy marriage for eighteen years and even produced four beautiful children living in a home on a two acre lot which they owned outright; however, this reading really bothered this anonymous fellow to such a degree that he was having unspecified issues with loving his wife. Davis answered this woman's letter and explained that the *diakka* 'do often times meddle, like the familiar gossips and social ghouls in this world, with the affairs of individuals through mediums correspondingly impressible and inclined...in all cases of spiritual intercourse, a receiver of such information is also unavoidably responsible. He or she is responsible to being weak and credulous enough to be led by meddlesome spirits into false steps and foolish notions.'[105]

There are numerous plausible explanations as to why this man may have told his wife that the psychometrist medium suggested that he leave her to find another mate; however, the point of this story is not to figure out what was happening in this relationship. Rather, what is important for the purpose of this study was that in 1874 Andrew Jackson Davis explained that is was a perfectly normal and common occurrence for a lying and manipulating spirit (*diakka*) to communicate with a medium without the medium being aware of this evil influence. Thus, a strong argument could be made that Blavatsky based the construction of her elementals on Davis' philosophy of *diakka* though it seemed that he believed them to be former human beings as opposed to future beings as Blavatsky's elementals would later become defined in *The Secret Doctrine*. In her 'A Few Questions to HIRAF' published in the 22 July 1875 issue of the *Spiritual Scientist* Blavatsky equated these *diakkas* with her elementals.[106] Thus, if a connection between Davis and Blavatsky could be proven then the theory that Blavatsky borrowed her conceptualization of elementals from Davis could be legitimatized. This conclusion would suggest that Blavatsky's theory of elementals was not her attempt to distance herself from Spiritualism as has often been claimed but instead was derived from her intimate knowledge of Spiritualism. The following section will deal with defining the relationship between Davis and Blavatsky.

3.10 Direct Connections of Davis with Blavatsky

As Olcott's interaction with Andrew Jackson Davis has been mentioned in the first chapter, Davis' relationship with Blavatsky must be realized. Despite the philosophical similarities mentioned above, there seemed to have been a relational connection between Blavatsky and Davis. Davis' opinion of Blavatsky and her connection between evil and elementals was depicted in the following address given to the Spiritualists of New York City on 31 March 1878:

> Of late a rather 'questionable' Magician has appeared in our literature. It is dramatic and slightly farcical. A mysterious magic wand has been waved at Spiritualism…until the great iron doors of perdition seemed about to shut against every chance for immortality. Sinful and brutalized humanity (it is said) become 'Elementary Spirits.' [Isis Unveiled, p. 30]. Which term means the disembodied souls of depraved human beings who have lost their chance of immortality. The Law of Natural Selection gives the world a conspicuous leader of Magical Spiritualism in the person of Mme. Helen P. Blavatsky. She is mentally and metaphysically adapted to present and maintain the startling inaccuracies which constitute the foundations of this fascinating and pretentious movement. She waves her wand (metaphorically, in a large volume) over Earth, Air, Fire, and Water, and lo! forth come gnomes, sylphs, salamanders, undines [See Isis, vol 1, p. 29.]… The Kabbalists call these 'elementals' the forces of nature which may be employed by the disembodied spirits, whether pure or impure, to produce all the

phenomena in dark séances…These elementals creatures were never human; but the 'elementaries' were once human,- but now, having lost their personal immortality, they sustain the position of most abject servants to the intelligent forces (the elements) who come like birds of prey out of Earth, Air, Fire and Water! Co-operating with this magnificently qualified leader, we behold a few persons not unknown to fame; and there are also two or three of great natural powers, and with mediumistic powers combined with accredited inspiration.[107]

This speech was made before the printing of *The Secret Doctrine* in 1888 when Blavatsky claimed that elementals were not depraved former human beings, but future human beings. Despite his sarcasm, Davis recognized Blavatsky as an important reformer of Spiritualism though he seemed to view her attempts at reform as being misguid-ed. In the foot note of this page he admitted that he 'was being criti-cal of them'- Olcott and Blavatsky.[108]

Despite Davis' disregard for the theosophists displayed above, Blavatsky continued to attest that she and Davis had developed a Platonic relationship during her time in New York towards the end of 1874. Marion Meade one of Blavatsky's biographers in the process of taking historical facts and setting them into a narrative seemed to embellish the nature of this particular relationship between Davis and Blavatsky, though it certainly seemed plausible that this could have been the nature of their relationship the evidence does not nec-essarily seem to support the following conclusion:

> Since her friendship with Davis satisfied her craving for intelligent companionship, she fell into the habit of visit him nearly every day. She explained her dilemma of wanting to write but not quite knowing how to go about it, and she must also have been candid about her lack of money and prospects. Eager to be helpful, Davis told her about a Russian friend of his, Aksakov the translator and publisher of his works in German…Alexander Nikolayevich Aksakov was a dedicated Spiritualist who recently had begun a monthly magazine devoted to the serious investigation of psychic phenomena…[109]

Davis had initially inquired to Alexandr Nikolayevich Aksakoff (1832 – 1903) the Russian Spiritualist concerning the integrity and reputa-tion of Blavatsky. Akskakoff replied to him: 'I have heard of Mad-ame Blavatsky from one of her parents, who spoke of her as a rather strong medium. Unfortunately, her communications reflect her morals, which have not been very strict.'

Coincidentally it was Blavatsky who translated this letter from French into English for Davis and took it upon herself to answer Aksakoff. Thus, on 14 November 1874, Blavatsky sent a letter to Aksakoff from her location as 23 Irving place in New York:

> It is barely a week since I wrote to you, and I already bitterly repent it! This morning, as usual, when I was in town, I was sitting with my only friend, Andrew Jackson Davis, who is highly respected by all here; he has received your letter in French, and, as he does not understand the language well, he asked me to read it and to translate it. ...Whoever it was who told you about me, they told you the truth, in essence, if not in details. God only knows how I have suffered for my past. It is clearly my fate to gain no forgiveness upon Earth. This past, like the sea of the curse of Cain has pursued me all my life, and pursues me even here in America, where I came to be far from it and from the people who knew me in my youth.[110]

Blavatsky seemed to believe that Aksakoff knew intimate details about her life in Russia that would discredit her in the eyes of the American Spiritualists. The nature of this issue seemed related to sexuality as hinted at in the following excerpt:

> I have on request to make of you: do not deprive me of the good opinion of Andrew J. Davis. Do not reveal to him that which, if he knew it and were convinced, would force me to escape to the ends of the Earth. I have only one refuge left in the world- it is the respect of the spiritualists of America who despise nothing so much as 'free love.'[111]

Meade further noted the influence that Davis exerted on Blavatsky in her writings though again overstating the nature of this influence in the following quote: 'Doubtless H.P.B. had already read some of his works; there is no question that she read all of them before writing *The Secret Doctrine* because some of her concepts, especially those relating to the origins and evolution of worlds, are reminiscent of his ideas...'[112] Despite the fact that Davis' influence was exerted on *The Secret Doctrine*, it seemed highly unlikely that Blavatsky would have needed to read *all* of Davis' numerous works in order to compose

The Secret Doctrine. Meade continued in her biographical account by focusing on some similarities between these two Spiritualists:

> Davis would influence her in other ways as well, but these would not be apparent for quite some time; she could see that he disdained séance rooms and the more gaudy trappings of Spiritualism, that he was a plain man with high moral objects: the advancement of the race by purification and self-control, a return to simple life, and, the establishment of a brotherhood of mankind.[113]

It remained likely that Blavatsky did not derive all of these ideas mentioned above directly from Davis; however, certainly his influence was apparent in her writings and later philosophical constructions. As already evidenced in this study, during the nineteenth century the subject of social reform and advancement of the race by purification through spirit were common themes found throughout Western esoteric literature especially in the writings of Allan Kardec, Emma Hardinge Britten, and Edward Bulwer-Lytton to name only a few.

Following her move to India and the 'Oriental shift' in her writings that accompanied this excursion, in the first issue of *The Theosophist* published in 1879 Blavatsky asserted the superiority of Eastern texts over Western writings, and diminished the importance of one of the fundamental texts of Spiritualism- Andrew Jackson Davis' *Divine Revelations*:

> To comprehend modern mediumship it is, in short, indispensable to familiarize oneself with the Yoga Philosophy; and the aphorisms of Patanjali are even more essential than the 'Divine Revelations' of Andrew Jackson Davis. We can never know how much of the mediumistic phenomena we *must* attribute to the disembodied, until it is settled how much *can* be done by the embodied, human soul, and the blind but active powers at work within those regions which are yet unexplored by science…[114]

Despite Blavatsky's overall goal to elevate the aphorisms of Patanjali in the esteem of her readers, it remained interesting that she would compare Davis' work to Patanjali claiming that it was 'even more essential than' *Divine Principles* thus evidencing her deep admiration for this work. Thus, Blavatsky held an enormous amount of respect for Davis and his writings and philosophy.

This admiration was confirmed by Michael Gomes who observed that 'following her arrival into America in July 1873, Blavatsky obtained a copy of Andrew Jackson's The Principles of Nature, 'with his inscription "The highest expression of true Religion is Universal Justice" dated July 29, 1874, and H. P. B.'s notation from North Point, Long Island.'[115]

In late January of 1875 after suffering a leg injury that incapacitated her, Blavatsky ordered a complete set of Andrew Jackson's works to pass the time.[116] Around this same time period she read Epes Sargent's *Proof Palpable of Immortality* (which represented materializations as the ultimate proof of Spiritualist communion) whom she fell 'in love with' which she described in a letter to F. J Lippitt on 7 March 1875.[117] Thus, there existed a direct connection between the 'father' of American Spiritualism and the primary founder of Theosophy proving that it was entirely possible that Blavatsky's conceptualization of elementals were in some part derived from Davis' philosophy.

3.11 Allan Kardec (Hippolyte Léon Denizard Rivail- 1804–1869)

In 1848, Spiritualism emerged as a new American religious movement that included the theatrical act of table turning and communicating with spirits though it eventually made its way across the Atlantic to the shores of France. This movement was renamed Spiritism in France as a means of differentiating itself from the term 'spiritualisme' which signified a general philosophical belief system opposite to materialism (though Spiritualism was opposed to materialism this new term distinguished between these two distinct beliefs).[118] The Spiritist belief structure was first systematized in the 1860s by an individual named Hippolyte Léon Denizard Rivail or more commonly known by his pen name- Allan Kardec (1804–1869).[119] Kardec (though retaining some orthodox Christian beliefs) believed in an invisible spirit-world filled with departed spirits that were capable of communicating with the living world with the aid of psychic mediums.[120]

One biography of this renowned figure was composed by Anna Blackwell in 1869 which was taken 'from the lips of his [Kardec's] widow.'[121] Blackwell described Kardec's demeanor and physical appearance as follows:

In person, Allan Kardec was somewhat under middle height. Strongly built, with a large, round, massive head, well-marked features, and clear grey eyes, he looked more like a German than a Frenchman. Energetic and persevering, but of a temperament that was calm, cautious, and unimaginative almost to coldness, incredulous by nature and by education, a close, logical reasoned, and eminently practical in thought and deed, he was equally free from mysticism and from enthusiasm....Grave slow of speech, unassuming manner, yet not without a certain quiet dignity resulting from the earnestness and single-mindedness which were the distinguishing traits of his character...[122]

Kardec was born at Lyons, France on 3 October 1804 to Jean-Baptists Antoine Rivail a magistrate and judge and Jeanne Duhamel.[123] Raised as a devoted Catholic, Kardec attended a school in Switzerland studying under the reformist Jean-Henri Pestalozzi and seemed to have studied medicine to some degree.[124] In 1830, Kardec opened a school where he taught the sciences while his wife Amelie Boudet taught liberal arts in a similar facility. Kardec experimented with various Western Esoteric and scientific organizations including a membership at the Paris Society of Magnetizers and even held office as the secretary of the Phrenological Society.[125]

Kardec attributed some phenomenon to the effects of magnetism a system first systematized by the German physician Franz Anton Mesmer (1734–1815) who employed magnetic powers to cure his patients. Kardec agreed that magnetism revealed the fluidic action and was based primarily on faith; however, Spiritism revealed another power which could be combined with the power of prayer. For Kardec, Spiritism and magnetism remained two distinct belief systems though a person could be healed with the assistance of a magnetizer who was assisted by a spirit.[126] David Hess solidified this connection between Kardec and Mesmerism insisting that 'it is among the shattered fragments of early-nineteenth century Mesmerism that one finds many of the elements of Kardec's Spiritist doctrine. Kardec writes that "magnetism prepared the way for Spiritism," and he adds that he accepted magnetism for decades before becoming a Spiritist...[127] Furthermore, Kardec held similar ideas of spiritual evolution derived from Emmanuel Swedenborg whom he paid tribute to in his selection of a title for his book *Heaven and Hell* (1865) named after Swedenborg's book by the same title.

In January 1858, Kardec founded the Spiritist publication *Revue Spirite* which was a periodical dedicated to communications with the recently deceased. In its first issue, Kardec published a communication given via automatic writing between a bereaved mother and the spirit of her departed daughter Julie. This communication is reprinted below as it provided important information related to the metaphysical gaps that Spiritism was attempting to fill:

> Julie: I no longer have the body that made me suffer so, but I have the same appearance. Aren't you happy that I no longer suffer, since I can speak with you?
> The Mother: If I saw you I'd recognize you, then!
> Julie: Yes, certainly, and you have already seen me often in your dreams.
> The Mother: I have seen you in my dreams, but I thought it was a figment of my imagination, a memory.
> Julie: No, it's me. I am always with you and searching for ways to console you; I even inspired you to summon me here. I have many things to tell you.[128]

One of the main comforts that Spiritism could offer its practitioners were the beliefs that the dead could not only communicate with the living but could even watch over them from the spirit world.

Kardec went on to establish the Society for Spiritist Studies (Societe des etudes spirites) and in 1857 published the *Spirits Book* (*Livre des esprits*). This book was written in a similar style as the Catholic Catechisms that would have been well known to most French citizens; it also classified spirits into three main categories: Imperfect (predominantly matter), Good (more spirit than matter), and Pure (pure spirits).[129] Kardec followed this work with the title *Book of Mediums* (*Livre des mediums*) in 1861. This book provided detailed directions for establishing an autonomous Spiritist group of which the first requirement was to find a small intimate and serious group with a similar belief structure. The content of this work was extremely practical and attempted to answer any questions that the aspiring Spiritist may have wondered about; both of these two works were written as how-to-guides and answered a variety of questions on many diverse topics. Kardec's Spiritism remained accessible and as a result grew to great numbers. In an 1869 edition of the *Revue Spirite* it was estimated that in Europe the Spiritists numbered around one million- six hundred thousand of those residing in France. Few lists of members have survived; however, most groups were quite small, ranging from four to twenty-five members, and as there was no central organization, there was no registry of groups themselves."[130]

In the 1860s Kardec continued to edit the *Revue* while authoring several other writings. He also focused on spreading the doctrines of Spiritism through his missionary-style expeditions across France. Kardec's zeal was exemplified in his recounting of a journey undertaken in 1862 where he traveled cross country visiting various established Spiritist groups along the way. During this excursion he undertook a seven week journey which 'included some twenty stops, including Lyons, Bordeaux, and many of the major towns in between, where Kardec attended over fifty meetings.'[131]

One biographer has noted that though Kardec's presentation of ideas was original, the concepts themselves were not. In fact, many of his doctrines were simply derived from mid-nineteenth century French Romantic Socialist thinkers such as Fourier, Eugene Pelletan and Jean Reynaud who focused on the concepts of charity and the 'law of progress' which both became basic tenets of Kardec's Spiritism. Even his conceptualization of the unusual doctrine of the *perisprit* seemed prefigured in Fourier's idea of the 'aromal body.' Thus, as John Monroe observed, 'to moderately educated readers, therefore, the philosophical system outlined in the *Livre des Esprits* would have seemed familiar.'[132] Kardec also promulgated a unique form of Spiritism which held to a reincarnationist view of the soul as will be observed in the next section. Kardec maintained an assiduous lifestyle propagating the Spiritist movement up until his demise on 31 March 1869 caused by the rupture of an aneurysm; his body was eventually laid to rest in the cemetery of Montmartre.[133]

3.12 Allan Kardec and Madame Blavatsky – The Connection

While residing in Cairo, Egypt in 1871, Blavatsky established a society called the Société Spirite 'for the investigation of mediums and phenomena according to Allan Kardec's theories and philosophy.'[134] This later recollection as recorded by A. P. Sinnett in 1886 noted that Blavatsky had another intention in forming this society:

> She would first give free play to an already established and accepted teaching and then, when the public would see that nothing was coming out of it, she would offer her own explanations. To accomplish this object, she said, she was ready to go to any amount of trouble,—even to allowing herself to be regarded for a time as a helpless medium.[135]

Whether Blavatsky actually believed the above statement in 1871 seemed unlikely; rather, Arthur Lillie commented that despite Blavatsky's later claims that she was only a covert Spiritualist 'fourteen years is rather a long time to keep up the merriest little jest.'[136] Blavatsky's intent eventually became to branch off Spiritualism and form her own 'purer' philosophy which would be labeled as Theosophy though this idea seemed to develop in the 1870s. It will be suggested in the next section that some of Blavatsky's ideologies in constructing her own spiritual evolution especially in her earlier works appear to have been in alignment with Kardec's beliefs (and she would later adapt a form of reincarnation that mirrored Kardec's).

Spiritism provided the background out of which Theosophy would eventually emerge- it should be remembered that it was while investigating Spiritualist 'phenomena' at the Eddy's farmhouse in 1874, that H. P. Blavatsky and Colonel Henry Olcott were introduced to each other. In fact, a strong case could be made that Blavatsky's philosophy was nothing more than a modified view of Spiritualism that employed Eastern terminology. Blavatsky evidenced her awareness of Kardec's Spiritist philosophy in the following letter written on 12 April 1875 to the Spiritualist A. N. Askakoff:

> Since I have been in America I have devoted myself entirely to Spiritualism, not to the phenomenal, material side of it, but to the spiritual Spiritualism, the propaganda of its sacred truths. All my efforts tend to one thing: to purify the new religion from all its weeds…I am only now beginning to collect adepts; I have collected half a dozen and, I say boldly, the best and brightest minds in America…I have decided to devote myself to Spiritualism from the point of view of Andrew Jackson Davis and Allan Kardec (Though I do not believe in reincarnation in the same sense as the French spiritists do)…[137]

Though at this early stage Blavatsky did not agree with Kardec's view of reincarnation, it seemed as though many of her other views stemmed out of his Spiritism. This belief was further illustrated in a different letter written to Hiram Corson on 20 March 1875. Apparently, Corson was intrigued with the French form of Spiritualism and its renowned publication *Revue Spirite* (Spiritism). Blavatsky responded to his inquiries as follows:

> You want to know about the 'Revue Spirite.' I simply with your request the more willingly, for I know well and consider Mr. Ley-

marie the Editor of it- my friend. This journal or periodical is the best in France. It's highly moral and truthful and- interesting. Of course the direction of it is purely Kardec-like, for the book was the creation of the 'Maitre' himself as French Spiritists the Reincarnationsts call Allan Kardec and was left furthermore heirloom by the latter to Leymarie. The widow, madame A. Kardec is one of the noblest and purest women living. The Spiritists have a slight tendency to ritualism and dogmas but this is but a slight shadow of their Catholic education, a habit innate in this people that jumps so quick from Popish slavery whether to Materialism or Spiritualism. Mrs. Corson will not repent if she subscribes for it. I find fault with them but for one thing-not with the 'Revue Spirite' but with the teaching itself; it is, that they are reincarnationists and zealous missionaries for the same. They could never do anything with me in that way, so they gave me up in disgust. But we still are friends with Mr and Madame Leymarie who are both of them highly cultured people and-truthful and sincere as gold.[138]

Thus, Blavatsky articulated that her chief concern with Kardec's Spiritism was his acceptance of reincarnation. This was described in relation to the *perisprit* of Kardec. Kardec believed that each human being was composed of three substances- a physical body, an immaterial soul, and a semi-material link between these two compositions known as a *perisprit* which wrapped around the soul; it was this *perisprit* that allowed the spirit to produce phenomena. In a letter written in February 1876 to C. C. Massey, Blavatsky expounded upon this concept noting that both the spirit and the physical being went through an evolutionary process at the same time with the

> spirit keeping pace with the evolution of matter, and constant tendency of the spirit to an ascendency over, or rather to escape from the bondage of it encompassing matter. When this double evolution has reached a certain point, it is possible for their principle to come into the union with the immortal spirit, which makes of man a Triad. As these emanations were given off, so at the proper time they are drawn back again into the vortex of evolution, and the elementary, dying in the astral light, goes to make the human being-the foetus- the grosser portions furnishing the germ of its body, and its finer ones its astral body, the perisprit of Kardec, or the spirit...while it is true that there is reincarnation in one sense, in the other is untrue.[139]

Thus, Blavatsky admitted that there was some truth to Kardec's theory; however, it appeared to be based on his misunderstanding of the evolution of the spirit. In Blavatsky's conceptualization, the body was reincarnated on a more spiritual world and his astral body took the place of his earthly body in the next sphere. Thus, 'Man's soul...[was] constantly entering into new astral bodies, there is an actual reincarnation; but that when it has once passed through any sphere into a higher one, it should re-enter the lower sphere and pass through other bodies similar to the one it has just quitted.'[140] In other words each reincarnation was in a higher sphere; therefore, it really could not be considered reincarnation but progression. Blavatsky rooted this belief in Western Esotericism noting that this philosophy was ancient being first taught in the eastern Kabbalah, Pythagorean philosophy, and Neo-Platonism. Despite her initial misgivings about the theory of reincarnation Blavatsky would eventually adopt this belief in her 'Fragments of Occult Truth' published in 1882 and in all her publications post-dating these articles.

3.13 Kardec and Blavatsky- Comparing Philosophy
There were two main beliefs that Kardec associated with Spiritism aside from the basic belief that departed spirits could communicate with the living. These included: 1) the belief in the progression of spirits to perfection (divinity) through multiple reincarnations.[141] This belief in progression was also based upon a being's composition and evolution from matter to spirit. The material spirit was equated as being negative and inferior; whereas, the spiritual was viewed as being positive and perfect.[142] 2) The belief that there was an infinite amount of worlds in which the soul could be sent to continue it evolution (including the planets in the solar system).[143] This included the idea that incarnations on the Earth were neither the first nor the last, but that they were of the most material and the 'farthest from perfection.'[144]

Kardec defined his view of time in *Genesis: Miracles and Predictions according to Spiritism* (1868) and its relation to the concept of eternity. In Kardec's view both time and space were eternal in scope and duration.[145] Kardec's systemization of Spiritualism and his infinite view of time and space bore a striking similarity to Blavatsky's views of time in *Isis Unveiled*. Kardec expounded upon his view of eternity:

> Before the creation of humanity there was simply eternity. Beyond earth eternity remains impassive and unmoving although time has

been marching steadily forward on other worlds. On the earth, however, time replaces eternity, and over a given series of generations one will count the years and centuries...Now let us transport ourselves to the final day of that earth, to the hour in which, bowed under the weight of old age, it will be erased from the book of life never to appear again. Here, the chain of events stops, the terrestrial movements that measure time cease and time ends with them...There are as many worlds in the vast expanse as there are different and incongruent times. Outside these worlds, only eternity replaces such ephemeral sequences ... Immensity without boundaries and eternity without bounds: such are the two great properties of the nature of the universe.[146]

This belief appears similar to Blavatsky's view of eternity:

Besides, eternity can have neither past nor future, but only the present as boundless space, in its strictly literal sense, can have neither distant nor proximate places. Our conceptions, limited to the narrow area of our experience, attempt to fit if not an end, at least a beginning of time and space; but neither of these exist in reality; for in such case time would not be eternal, nor space boundless...imagine a point in space as the primordial one; then with compasses draw a circle around this point; where the beginning and the end unite together, emanation and re-absorption meet. The circle itself is composed of innumerable smaller circles.[147]

Beside the infinitude of time and space, Kardec and Blavatsky evidently both viewed the afterlife as consisting of an innumerable number of worlds or spheres. Both believed that the soul (motivated by a desire to become a pure spirit) was reincarnated onto different spheres after death. This reincarnation was intimately connected to the 'law of progression' as Kardec wrote 'that which one can not do in one existence one does in another, it is thus that no one escapes the law of progress, that each is compensated according to his real merit.'[148] Also, both abhorred the idea of eternal punishment and original sin though this was a common tendency among nineteenth century Spiritualists.[149]

In Kardec's philosophy, a great emphasis was placed on the individuality of the soul, a trait that Blavatsky also stressed throughout her works especially in *The Secret Doctrine*. Kardec asserted: 'The fate of each soul must depend on its own personal qualities...Justice demands that each soul should be responsible for its own action; but in order for souls to be thus responsible, they must be free to choose between good and evil.[150] The idea of an 'individual emphasis' is also a common theme found within Theosophical teachings. Blavatsky appeared to have borrowed this theme from Spiritualism and employed it in her own philosophy. Bruce Campbell saw this individuality as one of the main flaws inherent within the teachings of Theosophy:

> Theosophy discusses the destiny of the individual, but teaches little regarding the nature of society. Ironically, its basic teachings do not even include a conception of the role and importance of the Theosophical Society. Absent is any conception analogous to the Christian idea of the Church as the people of God or the Jewish idea of the chosen people.[151]

Another of the main precepts of Spiritism was the evolution of the soul, but it could only progress based upon 'the fruit of their own labor.' In other words, spiritual evolution could only be accomplished after a long series of good actions:

> God has ordained that happiness shall be the result of effort and not of favor, in order that each may obtain it as the result of his own individual merits; each is free to labor diligently, or to do nothing, for his own advancement; he who works hard and quickly gains his wage sooner; he who misemploys his energies, or loses his time, is longer in gaining the promised reward, but has only himself to thank for the delay.[152]

The soul did not automatically ascend to spirituality; rather, progress was always earned.[153] In solidarity, Blavatsky's later view of spiritual evolution was heavily based on her concept of karma which ultimately was exemplified in the karmic law and was based on the golden rule of the Western world- 'do unto others as you would have done unto you.'[154] Thus, these two views on reincarnation appear very similar.

Julie Hall in her article on the inspiration of Blavatsky's septenary doctrine noted that the concepts of the perispirit and of different states were particularly influential on Blavatsky's conceptualization of Kardec's Spiritism. Hall reiterated that in 1871 Blavatsky had set up the Société Spirite in Cairo to teach Kardec's philosophy, but also noted that Blavatsky had mentioned the 'fluidic perisprit' (sic) as the astral soul in *The Secret Doctrine*. Hall concluded this section by noting that 'although early Theosophy is riddled with criticism of Spiritism because it was considered to misunderstand séance phenomena, it is undeniable that Spiritism was an influence on the development of Blavatsky's thought, even though she discusses it relatively little in her works. This silence could be due to her later intention to disavow any connection with Spiritism."[155]

This seemed to be the last identical trait between these two philosophies, though several other elements appear similar. In Kardec's view of the afterlife, following physical death there is a period of confusion that for the moral human is not painful, but 'for those whose conscience is not pure, it is full of anxiety and anguish' that could last hours, days, or years.[156] Blavatsky in her earlier works instituted the 'circle of necessity' which would last longer than Kardec's soteriology ranging anywhere from 1,000–3,000 years—which was a period of purification from matter. It is curious that throughout Blavatsky's later writings and philosophies the 'circle of necessity' seemed to evolve into a non-essential doctrine. In fact, a case could be made that the 'circle of necessity' was replaced by Devachan as Blavatsky's view of reincarnation and karma (after the Oriental shift) started to take center stage. With karma, there would be no need for a place of punishment (avitchi) or a time of limbo (circle of necessity). The next life would provide the 'necessary punishment' for the previous life. No longer did the soul have to wander the earth after death. In Blavatsky's later philosophy the soul was placed directly into an alternative universe of reward (as opposed to wandering in the earthly sphere). This philosophical shift in Blavatsky's philosophy was seen through her later neglect of the term 'circle of necessity.'"[157]

Though Blavatsky's 'circle of necessity' and Kardec's description of a confused state after death are similar concepts, these two views remain distinct especially in Blavatsky's later ideological conceptualizations. In the end both individuals believed that the Spiritist phenomena could be caused by a disembodied spirit wishing to communicate with the living though in Blavatsky's later philosophy this was a rarity (for a full treatment on the basic tenet of Spiritualism in her major writings see the following section). Also of similarity, Kardec divided spirits into three main categories: Imperfect (predominantly matter), Good (more spirit than matter), and Pure (pure spirits).[158] This scale of ascending spirit is also similar to Blavatsky who equated matter as negative and spirit as positive is a central doctrine of Blavatsky.[159] A minor point of difference concerns the place of sun within human evolution. Kardec claimed that the Sun was inhabited by spiritualized beings which Blavatsky contended that only the highest 'Planetary' spirit could access this plane.[160]

Other points where Blavatsky diverged from Spiritism were her beliefs in emanation from the unknown One as opposed to being created by God as explained by Kardec.[161] Also, Blavatsky believed in the possibility of annihilation of the soul in a place called the 'eighth sphere' only if the material constitution outweighed the spiritual constitution—a doctrine which Kardec noted was 'repugnant.'[162] Blavatsky further believed in deceitful spirits called elementals (as opposed to Kardec's imperfect spirits), and in a period of Nirvana which occurred in between the soul's passing from one sphere to another.[163]

In a later article published in *The Theosophist* written in August 1883, Blavatsky described in her own words the distinction between her Theosophy from Kardec's Spiritism:

> The works of Allan Kardec teach a system of ethics which merits the encomiums our correspondent gives it...Since, however, the doctrines of the Spiritist school are not altogether in harmony with those of Occultists, as regards the condition of man after death and the destiny of his monad, we personally have never been enlisted as a follower of the great French philosophy in question. Who inspired Allan Kardec we cannot tell. In some fundamental respects his doctrines are diametrically opposed to ours...With the Spiritists we believe—let us rather say we know—that man is born more than once as a human being; and this not merely upon this earth but upon seven earths in this planetary chain, to say nothing of any other. But as to the rapidity with which and the circumstances under which these reincarnations occur, our Spiritist friends and ourselves are at variance. And yet despite all differences of opinion, including the very great one about the agency of 'departed spirits' in controlling mediums and inspiring books, we have ever been on the friendliest terms with the Kardecists and had hoped always to remain so...[164]

It seemed a curious remark that Blavatsky had claimed that she had never been affiliated or enlisted as a follower of Kardec, yet in Sinnett's biography of her life (and mentioned above) titled *Incidents in the Life of Madame Blavatsky* published in 1886 Blavatsky was said to have started the Société Spirite in Cairo in 1871 which was concerned with ascertaining the teachings of Allan Kardec. Apparently, in 1883 Blavatsky was attempting to distance herself from Spiritism because she had developed her own systematic philosophy in her Theosophy; however, this relationship is continually shifting between conflict and reconciliation (for more information of this shifting for this time period readers should refer to the section 'Fragments of Occult Truth' in the chapter on Blavatsky's Automatic Writings).

One of the main objectives that Blavatsky attempted to achieve through her Theosophical Society was to systematize Spiritualism into an empirically verifiable philosophy in a similar manner as Kardec had achieved for Spiritism in France. Thus, it seemed that her main goal was to carve out her own branch of Spiritualism that contained Western Esoteric elements and was philosophically advanced from the primitive Spiritualism that remained open to blasphemy by fraudulent mediums. As already noted, in order to reconcile the deceptive mediums within her idea of pure Spiritualism, Blavatsky propagated her 'theory of elementals' which stated that that many of the spirits being channeled at séances were not actually the souls of the departed individuals but were instead the lower, animal principles that only acted like the departed spirits in order to manipulate the mediums. The 'theory of elementals' was Blavatsky's attempt at reconceptualizing and intellectualizing Spiritualism, but instead resulted in being ousted by several Spiritualist circles. As a result, the Theosophical Society turned into its own distinct Western Esoteric/Spiritualist organization which after a lack of participation from it important members and its failure to live up to its promises through the lectures of George Felt, soon lost its influence in the world of mainstream Spiritualism. Then Blavatsky decided to move operations to India and the Theosophical Society became intimately intertwined with the history of India through her connection with the Arya Samaj and in her defense of the Eastern religious movements against Christianity. Based upon Blavatsky's involvement with the teachings of Allan Kardec and her familiarity with Spiritism, it seemed that Kardec's influence on Blavatsky could not be overemphasized. Thus, Blavatsky owed much of her philosophical conceptualizations to the Spiritism of Allan Kardec.

One of Blavatsky's later followers Marie Countess of Caithness was an admitted follower of Kardec which paved the way for her Theosophical conversion which in 1884 included the belief in reincarnation and continued the connection between Spiritism and Theosophy. The countess was an avid séance attendee having sat with D. D. Home in the 1860s and continued attending séances up until her death in 1895. She published her *Old Truths in a New Light* which exemplified the influence of Kardec on her philosophy in her distinguishing 'the grosse spiritualism with its "morbid craving for the wonderful", from the purer, more philosophic" "spiritism", or the study of "the soul of things."[165] Thus, the countess provided a direct link between these two organizations and their ideological affinities.

3.14 Connecting Spiritism and the Theosophical Society: Pierre-Gaetan LeyMarie and the French Theosophical Society

Though Blavatsky had studied Kardec and his teachings it seemed that these two public figures had never personally met; however, Blavatsky had been introduced to Pierre-Gaetan Leymarie (1827–1901). Leymarie was interested in the political and social implications of Spiritism and went on to take over as the editor of *Revue Spirite.* Following the death of Kardec, Leymarie attempted to combine Spiritualism and Occultism and through this undertaking came into contact with Blavatsky in 1873 two years before the foundation of the Theosophical Society. This meeting transpired while Blavatsky was visiting her brother Colonel M. Hahan in Rue du Palais and was confirmed by a letter written from L. M. Marquette M.D.[166] In 1879, Leymarie formed the Theosophical Society of French Spiritsts (Societe thosophique des spirites de France) though it seemed that Leymarie remained ignorant of many rudimentary teachings that were taught by the Theosophical Society. Also, apparent was that Leymarie could not memorize the secret signs and passwords necessary to lead a Theosophical 'branch' as Blavatsky explained in a letter written in 4 September 1881 to Adelberth De Bourbon.[167] In 1883, Leymarie aided with translations of Blavatsky's writings came to the realization that Blavatsky denied the reality of the spirits of the dead and reincarnation. Joscelyn Godwin expounded upon this misunderstanding and the incidents that ensued in his wonderful booklet on the establishment of the Theosophical Society in France:

> In 1879 a Branch Society was formed in Paris called the 'Societe Theosophique des Spirites de France.' All the members belonged to the Kardec school. For five years, this society went its way in virtual ignorance of what Mme Blavatsky and others were teaching in The Theosophist and elsewhere. Being quite sufficiently occupied with events in Bombay and Adyar, New York, and London, she thought it best to leave them in peace…At last, in response to the demand by members, some more recent material was translated for them by one of their nummber, (sic) D. A. Courmes. It was an unfortunately chosen 'Fragment', written not by Mme Blavatsky but by A.O. Hume, supposedly expounding the teaching of the Mahatmas. The French group were appalled when they read this,

because they understood from it that the doctrines now coming out of India denied reincarnation, and, worse, asserted that the spiritual ego or Higher self of the human being is annihilated after death—whereas in Theosophical doctrine it is merely the personal ego that is. This led one member, Tremeschini, to write an ill-informed tirade against Mme Blavatsky's teachings, in which he displayed some bizarre misunderstandings (and spellings) of Oriental names and terms.[168]

This sparked a controversy which lasted from March to October of 1883. On 28 June 1883 another branch of the Theosophical Society was established by Marie the Countess of Caithness called the 'Societe Theosophique d'Orient et d'Occident' and Caithness was appointed as the president. Blavatsky and Olcott decided to visit France and arrived in Marseilles on 12 March 1884 eventually traveling to Paris on 28 March. Then on 3 June 1884 it seemed that Blavatsky intended on intentionally infuriating the Spiritist Theosophical societies by canceling the charters of every group except Lady Caithness' 'Societe Theosophique d'Orient et d'Occident' which she adopted as the official branch of the Madras Theosophical Society.[169]

However things may have turned out in France, the involvement of Leymarie with the early Theosophical Society even at a superficial level provided a direct connection between the teachings of Allan Kardec and those of Madame Blavatsky. The belief that a connection existed between the Theosophical Society and French Spiritism was suggested as early as 1885 by W. F. Kirby a contemporaneous reporter for *Time* magazine:

Theosophy does not come before the world as something new. Many of its teachings agree with Platonism, and other philosophies more or less familiar to Western students, and the reported phenomena of Spiritualism (whatever their origin, and Theosophists interpret them differently to Spiritualists) have done much to familiarize the minds of Europeans with the existence of powers in nature which we do not ordinarily perceive, but which are able to manifest their existence to us under favourable conditions. Among the various American and European systems of spiritualist philosophy which there are several, Spiritism, the system taught in France by Allan Kardec and J. B. Roustaing, and which is generally accepted by spiritualists in the Continent (though not in England and America, where its central doctrine, that of successive existences, or reincarnations, in different world, has hitherto met with but little favour), is most closely allied to Theosophy. Indeed, it is admitted in India that Roustaing's 'Gospels explained by their Writers' (apart from its dogmatism, and its specially Christian colouring) actually contains the secret doctrines of the northern Buddhists, although is it stated to have been written through a medium at Bordeaux, who knew nothing of the subject.[170]

A direct connection between Blavatsky and Spiritism existed as observed in the article above. Furthermore, Blavatsky's establishment of her Société Spirite and her utilization of similar ideologies paid homage to the brilliant mind of Allan Kardec and his influence on her philosophy.

3.15 Theosophical Affinities with Spiritualism

Janet Oppenheim discovered some similar ideologies between Spiritualism and Theosophy in her work *The Other World* and noted that 'if spiritualists and Theosophists had only had the veracity of spirit messages to discuss, the chances for cooperation between the two groups would have been slight. On a wide range of other issues, however, Theosophical convictions were scarcely distinguishable from spiritualist arguments.'[171] These issues included a desire to combat materialism which entailed understanding that spirit existed independently of matter, the promotion of a universal brotherhood through shared religious beliefs (see the section on Andrew Jackson Davis), the development of human faculties for their profound capabilities, and an attempt to attach meaning to life and death in a materialist age and culture.[172] Apparently, Theosophists and Spiritualists also shared some specific presuppositions related to the legitimacy of spirit photography which actually provided a point of intersection between these two movements at the close of the nineteenth century.[173]

Another common tenet shared by both Theosophist and Spiritualist alike was the belief that they had discovered (or rediscovered) the base of all other religions. For the 'oriental' Theosophists this wisdom came from a 'pre-Vedic Buddhism,' and to the Spiritualists, Spiritualism was the universal underlying truth or the 'fundamental substratum' of all religions.[174]

As noted in the section comparing Kardec and Blavatsky's philosophy, after the 'Oriental shift' and the establishment of the Oriental Theosophical Society and its relocation to India in 1879, there was an adoption of the doctrine of karma which Blavatsky explained 'creates nothing, nor does it design. It is man who plans and creates causes, and Karmic law adjusts the effects…"[175] This belief would appear to be in partial agreement with the Spiritualist's view of 'eternal progress' in the spirit world which was followed by an unlimited amount of returns. These similar belief structures pushed Oppenheim to note that 'the differences between spiritualists and theosophists in this respect were more apparent than real, for they shared an immensely optimistic view of gradual human progress to spiritual perfection.'[176] Progressive Spiritualists (those who did not adhere to a Christian form of Spiritualism) would have found even more common belief structures with Theosophy including the denial of a personal God, the belief in a corruption of religious priesthoods, and the conviction that each individual created their own future destiny.[177]

Also similar were Blavatsky's conceptualizations of reincarnation which seemed to correspond with some Spiritualist interpretations. Despite the fact that Blavatsky drew more heavily upon the French medium Allan Kardec's view of reincarnationist Spiritism, the idea which was held primarily within American and British Spiritualism was the belief in eternal progress which asserted for countless spiritual reincarnations.[178] Blavatsky's later implementation of physical reincarnations put her at odds with more than a few mediums including Emma Hardinge Britten, though some who were familiar with Kardec's philosophies became apologetic followers of Blavatsky most notably the Marie Countess of Caithness.[179] Oppenheim suggested that:

> Membership in Theosophical associations in Britain from the late 1870s suggests that Theosophy remained doctrinally flexible, or vague, enough to draw spiritualists from both Christian and progressive camps. Whether they were attracted by the Eastern allure of Theosophy, by its emphasis on each person's sole responsibility for his own fate, by the echoes of old occult lore, or by the hope of experiencing reincarnation, numerous British spiritualists moved into Theosophical circles during the 1880s.[180]

Thus, a continuous connection between Spiritualism in Theosophy existed throughout the nineteenth century.

In 1871, Gerald Massey (1828–1907- not to be confused with C. C. Massey) the working-class Spiritualist and mythographer confirmed his agreement with Darwinism and in doing so evidenced an evolutionary expansion which Blavatsky would also incorporate relating to spiritual evolution:

I for one accept the truth of Mr. Darwin's theory of man's origin and believe that we have ascended physically from those lower forms of creation which we find lying around us like chips in the great workshop of Nature...But the theory contains only one-half the explanation of man's origins, and needs Spiritualism to carry it through and complete it. For while this ascent on the physical side has been progressing through myriads of ages, the Divine descent has also been going on- man being spiritually an incarnation from the Divine as well as a human development from the animal creation. The cause of the development is spiritual. Mr. Darwin's theory does not in the least militate against ours- we think it necessitates it; he simply does not deal with our side of the subject.[181]

Blavatsky's view of evolution would seem to align with Massey's view of Darwinian evolution.[182] Blavatsky assimilated Darwin's concept of evolution into her own cosmological construction of the universe, but only up to a certain point as Nicholas Goodrick-Clarke noted:[183]

Contrary to modern evolutionary theory, this doctrine posits the involution of man from 'higher and more spiritual natures.' A 'divine spark' has descended into matter, and once it has reached its densest material level, it begins its ascent back to its source. Blavatsky thus assimilates modern evolutionism into her scheme, but only as the return cycle, and moreover, she rephrases its biological imperative in spiritual terms: 'The human race must be finally physically spiritualized' (I, 296).[184]

Thus, Darwinian evolution was only sufficient to explain life in the material phase of evolution, but not in the larger, grander picture of spiritual evolution that Blavatsky held within her cyclical view of time.[185] This same idea was evidenced in Blavatsky's later work *The Secret Doctrine*: 'As remarked in *Isis Unveiled*, Darwin's evolution began at the middle point, instead of commencing from man, as for everything else, from the universals.'[186] Both Massey and Blavatsky's conceptualization of evolution illustrated what in Theosophy was called the ascent/descent theory. This idea suggested that humanity had descended from spirit into matter and will one day ascend back into spirit.[187]

In the later decades of the nineteenth century the relationship between Spiritualism and Theosophy became a popular subject that held many differing views. None could deny that Theosophy emerged out of Spiritualism and continued to maintain many of their core beliefs. It was not uncommon in the nineteenth century to find individuals who identified themselves as both Theosophists and Spiritualists evidencing that these two belief structures could be harmonized based on the experience of certain individuals. A speech made by Annie Besant in 1898 further evidenced the secondary differences between Theosophical and Spiritualist views on evolution:

> Though they might differ on points of detail they were both aiming at that object by turning the thoughts of men in the direction of spirituality. Theosophists did not care whether they dealt with the souls in or out of the body, and they believed that there were a number of 'evolving souls' in living bodies at the present time. The initial mistake was made when they failed to recognize the fact that the power of 'manifestation' existed in the soul whether of a dead or living body. To the Theosophist there was no such thing as death. *They were all agreed that the soul evolved and that knowledge increased as the soul grew older. What divided them in opinion was not the question of evolution, but only the comparatively subsidiary question- Did that evolution go on by rapid experience on earth alive or did it go on in spheres outside the world?* If they were once united on the fundamental principle of the 'evolution of the soul', they need not take up clubs to each other....In conclusion, she urged that the Spiritualist should treat the Theosophist with less rigour.[188]

Thus, both sides believed in a similar evolutionary model –though the Theosophist claimed that this process occurred in the physical world and other Spiritualists claimed that it occurred in the spiritual world; however, this belief had no bearing on the subject of Spiritualism which was the belief in the ability for the dead to contact the living which both groups continually ascribed.

3.16 Variances with Spiritualism

Perhaps deemed the most incompatible with Spiritualism by most Blavatsky biographers was Blavatsky's belief that most of the spirits being channeled by mediums at séances were lying, deceitful spirits known as elementals; however, it has already been suggested that Blavatsky was not the only Spiritualist to maintain this belief in mischievous and deceitful spirits.[189] In the introduction to *Isis Unveiled*, Blavatsky defined elementals as 'the creatures evolved in four kingdoms earth, air, fire and water and are called by the kabalists gnomes, sylphs, salamanders, and undines...such beings never become men. These elementals are the principal agents of disembodied but never visible spirits at séances, and the producers of all the phenomena except the subjective."[190] As already noted this definition was not original to Blavatsky and it seemed that her understanding of the nature of these 'spirits' was derived from Alphonse Louis Constant's (more commonly known by his pseudonym Eliphas Lévi- 1810-1875) publication of *Dogme et Rituel de la Haute Magie* (1855) to describe 'unemancipated spirits, slaves of the four elements are those which the kabbalists call elementary daimons, and they people the elements which correspond to their state of servitude. Sylphs, undines, gnomes, and salamanders therefore really exist, some wandering and seeking incarnation, others incarnate and living on earth. These are vicious and imperfect men."[191] Lévi was heavily influential on Blavatsky and on her writings, and this influence was further evident in Blavatsky's decision to use this philosophy in order to justify the common occurrences of fraud in the Spiritualist movement.

As one can imagine, Blavatsky's adamant belief that elementals were controlling the majority of mediums made her a target for many contemporary Spiritualists. It was commonly held that it was in *Isis Unveiled* that Blavatsky propagated the idea that mediums were channeling lying deceitful egos of disembodied men called elemental spirits, but in fact this idea was found much earlier in her writings and especially in the lectures of Olcott likely due to the insistence of Blavatsky. Elementals were not actually the deceased people, but instead that were tricking spirits that attempted to allow themselves to be channeled by mediums in order to fulfill their carnal lusts from their dwelling in Kama Loka.[192] Also, apparently at odds with Spiritualism were Blavatsky's continually evolving beliefs in the septenary constitution of the soul, her division of time into root races, rounds and yugas, her evolutionary belief that man had evolved from a mineral into vegetation into an animal and then finally into a man, and her view of the annihilation of the soul under certain circumstances; however, these seemed irrelevant towards the classification of Blavatsky as a Spiritualist as only one belief seems of importance- did she believe that the dead possessed the ability to contact the living? These differences will be expanded in more depth in the next chapter, but at this point a brief examination of Blavatsky and the United States press should be understood.

3.17 Theosophy and Spiritualism in Mainstream United States Newspapers

Newspaper articles remain a relatively untapped resource in understanding the history of this era and also serve to provide an outsider's opinion on the interaction of these two unorthodox movements. Thus, an explanation of the secular press and its connection to this topic must be mentioned. Though these articles are intriguing by their own merit, they do not help in ascertaining the interaction between these two movements as they reflect the same mixed opinions found in the primary sources and writings of the other figures explored throughout this work. What remained curious in these articles was that despite this ambiguity it was not uncommon for writers to define 'Theosophy' as a Spiritualist movement, thus, solidifying the general thesis of this work. Several examples are listed for the reader to understand the differing views concerning the shifting relationship of these two organizations. The first example was written before the Society's 'Oriental shift' and proved that some reporters viewed a very obvious dichotomy between these movements. A 13 November 1875 newspaper article reprinted in the *New York Mercury* described this early dichotomy between Spiritualism and Theosophy:

> The Theosophical Society should not be confounded with spiritualism, say its members. Indeed, it is greatly in conflict with that belief, inasmuch as it offers a different explanation of the cause of the phenomena of mediumistic manifestation and materialization. Already the members have fallen into disfavor with spiritualists, and have been alluded to in public meetings as sorcerers. The Theosophic theory accounts for all the puzzles of spiritualism on the ground that mediums, either knowingly or unconsciously, use their own influence over matter and spirits; in short, that mediums are crude, undeveloped magicians. The lower order of unearthly beings, called 'elementary spirits,' are credited with being most readily summoned, and to them are ascribed most of the phenomena of spiritualism. Materialization, according to the same theory, is simply the calling back from the other worlds of dead persons, through the art of sorcery or magic; and Satan himself may be made to appear in visible form by an elaboration of the same means- a result which the society folk profess to anticipate as an accomplishment at an early day.[193]

Elsewhere around this same time period, Theosophy was (in contrast) equated with Spiritualism and described as 'a bit of medieval Cabbalism ingrafted upon modern Spiritualism, and so awkwardly that the two kinds of bark are not united.'[194] The preceding examples were written before the Oriental shift in 1879; however, it is intriguing that even many years after this shift Theosophy continued to be equated with Spiritualism. This belief was evidenced in the following quotation:

> The New 'Osophy' of Buddhism many intellectual people in this country who have always professed to hold spiritualism in utter indifference are not very much interested in what they call 'psychical research. They are also investigating *a very extraordinary phase of spiritualism called 'theosophy.'* This queer mystery comes to us from oriental lands, and is a mixture of Asiatic gnosticism, medieval magic and modern science.'[195]

Elsewhere it was noted that Theosophy: 'is composed of two Greek words, meaning knowledge of God. *Theosophy is a sort of Spiritualism,* mingled with Buddhism.'[196] Another article described Theosophy as a 'materialistic spiritualism.'[197] An article titled 'Theosophy Reviewed: It is Plainly an Outgrowth of Modern Spiritualism' presented its own obvious opinion:

> 'Theosophy,' as the name is popularly used, is an outgrowth of 'Spiritualism' as that name is popularly used. The older investigators recollect when Blavatsky and Olcott, the reputed parents of 'Theosophy,' were the center of attraction of a knot of credulous Spiritualists who sat on one of the piers of New York harbor beyond the midnight hour, waiting to see a spirit luminously glide over the dark waters in fulfillment of the prediction of one of that class of mediums who, for a fee, will undertake to be channels of communication between the world of matter and the world of spirit- usually out of balance in both worlds. And Olcott's volume with its particularly drawn diagrams of rooms, doors, cabinets, spirit-forms, etc. written in prove the genuineness of 'spirit materializations,' as 'produced' through the Vermont Eddies, is to be found in many public libraries...'Modern Spiritualism' is likewise the source of all the other new theories and faiths, 'Christian Science.' 'Faith Cure,' 'Mind Science,' etc. All have been evolved from and are based upon that consciousness of the continuity of life which could not have been unfolded to the common understanding, so as to grow into popular character, without the phenomenal evidences offered by modern spiritualism; though all the ages of human history have been illuminated by advanced souls who were in this high consciousness in the regular order of the

race's spiritual evolution....Modern theosophy is the natural result and outbirth of the insufficiency of the phenomenal evidences of modern spiritualism, admitting them to be all and even more than the most creduins (?sic) claim for them, to satisfy the cravings of the human mind for knowledge of the immortality of the human soul.[198]

Depending on the individual reporter and the particular source each consulted for their writing, this opinion of the Theosophical Society and its relationship with Spiritualism would differ. While some reporters may have recognized a connection between these two organizations others sought to separate them completely noting that 'theosophy is not spiritualism,'[199] but, nevertheless remained 'often mistaken for spiritualism pure and simple.' A connection was further suggested in that Theosophy:

> ... does not deny the undoubted genuineness of many of the facts of spiritualist, but it refuses to accept the explanation of these given by Spiritualists, who attribute them all to the 'disembodied spirits' of the dead. Theosophy asserts that *most* of the genuine phenomena are to be credited to the activity of the inner or astral body of the medium.[200]

One writer for an unmentioned Boston periodical noted that two currents existed within the Theosophical Society- one that focused upon Spiritualism the other which focused upon Eastern philosophy:

> Theosophy has taken strong root in Boston. There are both its Oriental and Occidental phases,- the Eastern phase of this philosophy being opposed to Spiritualism, and the Western phase admitting the phenomena of Spiritualism as a truth....The difference, or one great difference between the Eastern and the Western schools of theosophy is that the former denies communication between spirits in Devachan and spirits in the flesh (save only under certain conditions and powers), while the latter freely admits all possibilities of it.[201]

Thus, this reporter believed that Theosophy (even after the Oriental shift of 1879) maintained two separate 'schools'- a Western and an Eastern branch.

This section evidenced that the relationship between these two movements remained ambiguous even during this time period and among secular society. There was no agreement on the connection between Theosophy and Spiritualism (though the fact that there was *a* connection was noted by all); however, this section was valuable for the purposes of this study because it proved the ambiguity associated with defining this organization and the fact that many outsiders viewed Theosophy as a Spiritualist movement. Though it seemed evident that the secular press was divided in their opinions of Blavatsky one Spiritualist periodical seemed united on its treatment of Blavatsky as a Spiritualist medium- the *Medium and Daybreak*.

3.18 *Medium and Daybreak* and James Burns

The *Medium and Daybreak* was a weekly Spiritualist newspaper widely circulated in England that enjoyed great success under its founder, editor, and contributor- James Burns. In founding the newspaper, Burns absorbed a provincial paper, *Daybreak* that had appeared a year or two earlier under the editorship of the Reverend John Page Hopps; this paper continued to flourish from 1870 until Burns' death in 1895.[202] Spiritualist historian Frank Podmore recorded that the *Medium* 'had the largest circulation, chiefly in the provinces, of any English Spiritualist paper, and only came to an end a few months after the death of its publisher and founder in 1895.'[203]

James Burns was born into the family of a Scots farmer craftsman and migrated to London as an adolescent seeking employment. Burns soon became devoted to the temperance movement of the nineteenth century which won him a job with a sympathetic publisher at the end of the 1850s- it would was here the he would first encounter books on American Spiritualism.[204] In 1863, Burns founded the influential Progressive Library and Spiritualist Institution which became an important venue for Spiritualists of all sorts. Burns possessed an entrepreneurial mindset and became involved with the area of communications in the Victorian world becoming a leading publisher of books, tracts, booklets, and newspapers. Burns' temperament consisted of a fiery disposition and he went on to become one of the chief proponents of Victorian Spiritualism in the nineteenth century. Through his Spiritualist Institution, Burns helped in launching the careers of many aspiring young mediums including James J. Morse who started his career as a medium by giving weekly séances at the Spiritual Institution in the late 1860s and went on to write a biography titled *Leaves from My Life: A Narrative of Personal Experiences in the Career of a Servant of the Spirits* in 1877 which were based on and inspired by a series of articles which he had published in the *Medium and Daybreak*.[205] Despite Burns' desire to propagate the Spiritualist message he was also known to refuse to publish advertisements issued by the National Association of Spiritualists and in 1870 took steps to prevent a rival publisher E. W. Allen from selling literature at the Cavendish Rooms which made it appear as though he desired to monopolize the Spiritualist press.[206]

Burns became a popular progressive spiritualist and felt no need to reconcile his beliefs with Christianity despite the fact that most other middle-class Spiritualists maintained some diverted form of Christian belief (a wide-held belief called Christian Spiritualism). In fact, his belief structure later known as progressive Spiritualism 'became synonymous with non-Christian spiritualism.'[207] Despite his apparent success, upon his death he had met with difficult financial times as his obituary the *Unknown World* solemnly noted:

> The sudden death of Mr. James Burns, founder and editor of *The Medium and Daybreak*, removes a prominent and peculiar personality from the front rank of Spiritualism, on which, not only by means of his periodical, but also by all forms of public speaking, he exercised a very great and earnest influence for something like thirty years. We understand, with profound regret, that his life closed amidst poverty and almost distress, and that a heavy burden of financial liability devolves upon his son, Mr. James Burns, Jun., who, with all his energy and capacity, is quite unable to deal with it unassisted.[208]

It appeared that following his demise in 1895, Burns' entire communication empire had crumbled leaving his son to deal with the financial implications. Thus, the life of an influential Spiritualist had come to its end and with it a hole was left in the Victorian Spiritualist movement.

3.19 Blavatsky and the *Medium*

Burns described the origination of *Medium and Daybreak* as his first attempt at Spiritual journalism in a lecture given on the *Medium's* anniversary celebration on 31 March 1882:

> The experienced journalist will smile when told that when we set about the first number of the *Medium* we had no contributors, no means, no experience, no ambition, no end to serve. The spirit world required a 'medium' of the press, and we gave it one, by the aid of a kind lady, now in the spirit-world, who came in and laid a £5 note on the counter. Like a little stream at its fountain head,

> our first number was insignificant, and contained no specious
> promises for the future, We felt the shadow of years of suffering
> and toil enveloping us, and moved in our work, as the hands do on
> the face of the clock, with no purpose of their own, but obedient
> to the unseen power within.[209]

In several issues of the *Medium and Daybreak* Blavatsky and her
Theosophical Society were examined; however, these articles described her not as an 'Eastern occultist', but as a 'Western Spiritualist.' To several of the authors in this widely circulated Spiritualist periodical, the phenomena that Blavatsky had produced in Madras, India remained identical to the typical phenomena produced in séance
rooms across the Western world. Thus, Blavatsky was viewed as a
Western medium practicing in an Eastern land.

One particular letter written to the *Medium* and signed by 'Scrutator
Junior' on 1 March 1878 (shortly after Blavatsky had published *Isis
Unveiled*) noted the following critique of Blavatsky's theory of elementals: 'There is not a fact connected with this pretentious theosophy, so far as it has revealed itself, but that may be accounted for by,
and reconciled with, the different phases of Modern Spiritualism...From what we have read, and from what we have heard of
Madame Blavatsky, we conclude that she is just an ordinary physical
medium.'[210] Now, in 1878 Blavatsky would have been viewed this
way by most Spiritualists understanding that her early Society was
comprised of mainly Spiritualist members; however, an article written by the editor James Burns confirmed another point of view
which rooted Blavatsky in Spiritualism even as late as 1889 many
years after her 'Oriental' shift and one year following her publication
of *The Secret Doctrine*. Burns noted the commonality of Blavatsky's
phenomena in Western Spiritualism and that her spirit guides (which
she called masters) also had precedence in Western Spiritualism:

> But that Madame Blavatsky is a powerful medium there can be no
> doubt. Her consciousness of an unseen presence attending her
> from her early years is just what many Spiritualists can testify
> to. Sometimes these guardians become visible to our mediums,
> and perform acts similar to those claimed for the 'Mahatmas" - a
> name without a meaning. That these guides are men living in phys-
> ical bodies in any part of the world Spiritualists know to be false.
> Madame makes an extraordinary claim for a very ordinary circum-
> stance - a claim which is not in accord with the requirements of
> the case...No doubt the will of the medium enters largely into the

means whereby the phenomena are produced. It is not so much that the medium's will *causes* the manifestations, as that it is allowed to become passive, and therefore no longer acting as an obstacle to the operation of the spirits.

Still, her cases of manifestations at will have been eclipsed many times over by the experiences of Spiritualists. In this connection the mediumship of Mrs. Guppy may be adduced. We have been present when everybody in a large circle has had the fruits, flowers, or fish they wished for; and one gentleman asked for a crawfish, which came into the circle, a delicate crustacean, requiring careful handling. It is possible that at one séance we have seen as many manifestations of this sort as Madame has had recorded, due to her power, during the whole course of her experience...much stress is laid on her control of spirits. This is no novelty in Spiritualism. Certain mediumistic people have unlimited power to influence the result of a sitting. This we have observed many times, and even exercised it, not to cause the spirits to perform, but to control their conduct, transforming a boisterous manifestation of terrific power into one of gentleness and condescension. And we have also some experience in asking spirits to produce manifestations [Again Burns proceeded to compare Blavatsky to Mrs. Guppy...]

Now as to the 'philosophy' of this willing or asking the spirits to do certain things as in the case just named and in those peculiar to Madame Blavatsky. It is an error to suppose that the wish or request of the one who speaks is the *cause* of the manifestation. The present writer is certain that he was 'impressed' to make the request: the idea popped into his head, and without thinking of the impropriety of making such a request, the words slipped out of his mouth, and 'no sooner said than done.' The true conclusion of the matter is, that the spirits had previously intended to produce the manifestation of floating Mrs. Guppy, and all the arrangements happened in accordance with that end, and under 'test conditions,' the request of the writer being a part of the pre-arrangement. In like manner Madame Blavatsky's 'spirits' use her to work their wonders, influencing her to act or request in accordance with their pre-arrangements enabling them to comply with the same. Madame Blavatsky in claiming so much in this respect, not only manifests ignorance of the *modus operandi*, but by misrepresenting the true philosophy of mediumship, acts as a barrier to the progress of psychological science. [211]

Burns accomplished three objective in this above article:1) he equated Blavatsky's psychic abilities with a prominent Western medium (who was still alive and could therefore provide verification of her powers), 2) he explained that there was nothing in Blavatsky's philosophy which would have been viewed as contradictory towards Western Spiritualism except her belief that these guides lived in 'physical bodies' which Burns viewed as a misconception, and 3) he concluded that this type of phenomena was 'very ordinary' in Western Spiritualism. Thus, it seemed that James Burns' opinion of Blavatsky was that she was (in agreement with the accusations of the Spiritualist William Emmette Coleman) nothing more than a confused Spiritualist medium obsessed with an unusual theory of elementaries.

William Henry Harrison (editor of the *Spiritualist*) contributed an article in the *Medium* admitting a similar understanding of Blavatsky's phenomena and its relation to Mrs. Guppy- that it was completely in harmony with Western Spiritualism. He further noted that:

> I am willing to admit that she has no superior among strong mediums…The author of *Esoteric Theosophy*, living out in India, seems in the absences of information to think that Madame Blavatsky's phenomena are different to those of all other mediums, and that the latter obtain the same kind of manifestations. It is true that of later years manifestations in London have been inferior in power and interest, and that several professional mediums have been obtaining nearly the same phenomena.

Then Harrison went on to compare Blavatsky and her phenomena to that of Charles Williams, Henry Slade, D. D. Home, and Agnes Guppy-Volckman. Harrison especially noted that Blavatsky's phenomena bore a striking similarity to that produced by Mrs. Guppy (a similar conclusion had been made by James Burns) and claimed that:

> her manifestations were very like those of Madame Blavatsky. Especially in the manner in which solid objects are carried about. The phenomenon of the production of writing on a letter inside a sealed envelope, used to occur in Australia, as reported some time ago in *The Harbinger of Light*. The fluttering down of letters in daylight was once a common occurrence in the house of Mrs. Showers, at Teignamouth, and I have see plenty of such manifestations, but did not see that the facts gave logical proof of the existence of a retired colony of gentlemen in the high Himalayas…Objects said to be permanently duplicated, sometimes in the presence of Madame Blavatsky and not changed by one of the impish pranks common enough, by the powers at the root of some physical man-

ifestations. There are plenty of cases of temporary duplication in the presence of mediums and Mr. Alfred Russel Wallace has recorded one which took place with a wine-glass through the mediumship of Mrs. Guppy-Volckman. Were she in full power, probably the powers about her would take pleasure in repeating all Madame Blavatsky's manifestations, but it is regrettable to state that she has not been in good health for some years.[212]

Harrison also equated Blavatsky's 'knocking' phenomena with a similar feat produced by Kate Fox-Jeneken. Again the idea that Blavatsky was in the same league as these other Spiritualists seemed to be the main argument presented by the author. Furthermore, both of these above contributors noticed a parallel between Blavatsky and the phenomena produced by Agnes Guppy. All of these articles admitted that there was a tremendous depth to Blavatsky's psychical abilities; nonetheless, Blavatsky's phenomena remained consistent with other phenomena produced in the realm of Spiritualism during this time period. Now that the history of Spiritualism has been examined and certain affinities have been noted, a brief interlude must be undertaken to discuss the nature of the Society's teachings and their relationship to Western Esotericism.

Notes

[1] Nicholas Goodrick-Clarke, 'Mystical East', *Theosophical History*, ed. James Santucci, 13:3 (July 2007), 3-28 (p. 4).
[2] The Golden Dawn provided an exception to this statement (though advocating that the preferred religion for all incoming members was Christianity) as Nevill Drury noted that the Golden Dawn was not prepared to admit candidates to the Order who were Mesmerists or Spiritualists or anyone who 'habitually allow[ed] themselves to fall into a completely passive condition of Will.' Nevill Drury, *Stealing Fire From Heaven: The Rise of Modern Western Magic* (Oxford: Oxford University Press, 2011), p. 44.
[3] Nancy Rubin Stuart, *The Reluctant Spiritualist: The Life of Maggie Fox* (Orlando, FL: Harcourt Books, 2005), p. 6.
[4] T. L. Nichols, *A Biography of The Brothers Davenport: With Some Account of the Physical and Psychical Phenomena Which have Occurred in Their Presence, In America And Europe* (London: Saunders, Otley, and Co., 1864), p. 12.
[5] Nichols, *A Biography of The Brothers Davenport*, p. 5.
[6] W. M. Fay, *Davenport Brothers and Professor W. M. Fay: A Pamphlet Containing a Short sketch of the Lives, Travels, & Performances of the Brothers Davenport* (Tamworth, Goslin & Smart, 1877), p. 11.

[7] Nichols, *A Biography of The Brothers Davenport*, p. 83.

[8] Fay, *Davenport Brothers*, p. 11.

[9] [Paschal Beverly Randolph], *The Davenport Brothers: The World Renowned Spiritual Mediums* (Boston, William White and Company, 1869), pp. 269-270.

[10] [Randolph], *The Davenport Brothers*, p. 108.

[11] Simon During, *Modern Enchantments: The Cultural Power of Secular Magic* (Cambridge, MA: Harvard University Press, 2002), p. 114.

[12] Herr Dobler, *Expose of the Davenport Brothers* (Belfast: D & J Allen, 1869), p. 6.

[13] Dobler, *Expose of the Davenport Brothers*, p. 10. A similar critique related to absence of light would be put forth by a captious critic named Thomas Carr who attempted to discredit the Davenport phenomena. Thomas Carr, *Modern Spiritualism Imposture; or, the Davenport Fraternity Unmasked* (London: H. J. Tresidder, 1864), pp. 7-8, 10-11.

[14] Dobler, *Expose of the Davenport Brothers*, p. 11.

[15] Dobler, *Expose of the Davenport Brothers*, p. 14.

[16] Dobler, *Expose of the Davenport Brothers*, pp. 23-25.

[17] Thomas Carr, *Modern Spiritualism Imposture; or, the Davenport Fraternity Unmasked* (London: H. J. Tresidder, 1864), p. 8.

[18] Carr, *Modern Spiritualism Imposture*, p. 9.

[19] Luke Rand, *A Sketch of the History of the Davenport Boys: Their Mediumship, Journeying, and the Manifestations and Tests given in Their Presences By the Spirits* (Oswego: T. P. Ottaway, 1859), p. 30.

[20] Carr, *Modern Spiritualism Imposture*, pp. 9-10.

[21] Carr, *Modern Spiritualism Imposture*, p. 10.

[22] Carr, *Modern Spiritualism Imposture*, p. 21.

[23] Frank Podmore, *Modern Spiritualism: A History and a Criticism*, 2 vols (London: Methuen & Co., 1902), II, p. 60.

[24] See the 'Introduction' in Hiram S. Maxim, *Maxim Versus Maskelyne: A Complete Explanation of the tricks of the Davenport Brothers and their Imitators* (London: Maskelyne & Devant's Entertainment Bureau, 1910).

[25] Emma Hardinge Britten noted that the Davenport Brothers 'endured imprisonment' for being accused as 'jugglers and conjurers' in her work *Modern American Spiritualism: A Twenty Years' Record of the Communion Between Earth and the World of Spirits*, 3rd ed. (New York: Emma Hardinge Britten, 1870), p. 541.

[26] Emma Hardinge Britten, *Nineteenth Century Miracles* (New York: Colby and Rich 1884), p. 461.

[27] Harry Houdini, *A Magician Among the Spirits* (Cambridge: Cambridge University Press, 2011), p. 27.

[28] H. P. Blavatsky, *Isis Unveiled: A Master Key to the Mysteries of Ancient and Modern Science and Theology*, 2 vols (New York: J. W. Bouton, 1877), II, p. 492.

[29] Blavatsky, *Key to Theosophy: Being a Clear Exposition, in the Form of Question and Answer of the Ethics, Science, and Philosophy* (New York: The Theosophical Publishing House, 1889), p. 28.

[30] H. P. Blavatsky, 'Whipped into Admission', *The Theosophist*, 3:6 (March 1882), 163-164 (p. 163).

[31] Patrick Deveney noted that Paschal Beverly Randolph had known the brothers since the mid-1850s and had begun working on this work in July 1864 before he left for New Orleans; however, he was not able to complete this work until 1869 when it was published anonymously. Eventually, the father of the Davenport Brothers (Ira Davenport, Sr.) retained the copyright of this comprehensive book. Deveney noted that 'perhaps by the time it was finished he believed the brothers were 'deliberate impostors'- a position he certainly came to hold.' John Patrick Deveney, *Paschal Beverly Randolph: A Nineteenth-Century Black American Spiritualist*, Rosicrucian and Sex Magician (Albany: State University of New York Press, 1997), p. 354.

[32] [Paschal Beverly Randolph], *The Davenport Brothers: The World Renowned Spiritual Mediums* (Boston, William White and Company, 1869), p. 115.

[33] Robert S. Elwood, 'American Theosophical Synthesis', *Occult in America: New Historical Perspectives*, eds. Howard Kerr and Charles L. Crow (Champaign, IL: University of Illinois Press, 1986), 11-134 (p. 126).

[34] Andrew Jackson Davis, *The Magic Staff: An Autobiography of Andrew Jackson Davis* (New York: J. S. Brown & Co., 1857), p. 32.

[35] Davis, *The Magic Staff*, p. 158.

[36] Charles Partee, *The Theology of John Calvin* (Louisville, KY: Westminister John Knox Press, 2008), p. 128.

[37] Davis, *The Magic Staff*, p. 162.

[38] Wouter Hanegraaff, *New Age Religion and Western Culture: Esotericism in the Mirror of Secular Thought* (Albany: State University of New York Press), p. 438.

[39] Emanuel Swedenborg, *The True Christian Religion Concerning the Universal Theology of The New Church* (Boston: Otis Clapp, 1842), p. 343.

[40] Davis, *The Magic Staff*, p. 134.

[41] Davis, *The Magic Staff*, p. 193.

[42] Davis, *The Magic Staff*, p. 197.

[43] Davis, *The Magic Staff*, p. 198.

[44] Davis, *The Magic Staff*, p. 199.

[45] Davis, *The Magic Staff*, pp. 200-201.

[46] Davis, *The Magic Staff*, p. 202.

[47] Davis, *The Magic Staff*, p. 211.

[48] Davis, *The Magic Staff*, p. 216.

[49] Davis, *The Magic Staff*, pp. 220-221.

[50] Davis, *The Magic Staff*, p. 231.

[51] Davis, *The Magic Staff*, p. 234.

[52] Davis, *The Magic Staff*, p. 235.

[53] Wouter Hanegraaff noted that Davis's cocnetpualziation of this spirit-being was similar to Swedenborg however 'he gave a progressivist and evolutionary twist to it by emphasizing an optimistic prospect of spiritual growth and development, first thourgh six spiritual spheres surrounding earth, and beyond these through higher spiritual realities.' Wouter Hanegraaff, 'Intermediary Beings IV: 18th Century – Present', in *Dictionary of Gnosis and Western Esotericism*, 628-631 (p. 629).

[54] Davis, *The Magic Staff*, p. 235.

[55] Again, one of the five tenets of Calvinism was 'total depravity.' This theological view posited the idea of original sin. It also held the belief that that the entire world was wholly tainted with sin and wickedness. Man was so consumed with original sin that he would never choose God; therefore, God must have chosen those who would be saved.

[56] Davis, *The Magic Staff*, p. 239.

[57] Davis, *The Magic Staff*, p. 239.

[58] Davis, *The Magic Staff*, pp. 240-241.

[59] Davis, *The Magic Staff*, pp. 255-256.

[60] Davis, *The Magic Staff*, p. 263.

[61] Frank Podmore, *Modern Spiritualism: A History and a Criticism*, 2 vols. (London: Methuen & Co., 1902), I, p. 159.

[62] *Appleton's Cyclopedia of American Biography: Volume I*, eds. James grant Wilson and John Fiske (New York: D. Appleton and Company, 1887), p. 474.

[63] Delp, 'Andrew Jackson Davis', p. 45.

[64] *New York Tribune*, (20 August 1847) noted in Delp, 'Andrew Jackson Davis', p. 44. Davis also had a connection to another American religious organization known as the Mormons. Certainly great similarity exists between Davis' *Revelations* and early Mormon philosophy. In fact *The Spirituals Magazine* noted that 'the Spiritualists of America- the disciples of Andrew Jackson Davis giving to them unity in a leading name- have been continuing the spirituals dispensation opened by Joseph Smith fifty years ago.' Thus, there appeared to be a harmony between Davis and these other millenarian movements. Anonymous, *The Spiritualist Magazine: Vol. VI* (London: James Burns, 1871), p. 199.

[65] Andrew Jackson Davis, *Events in the Life of a Seer: Being Memoranda of Authentic Facts in Magnetism, Clairvoyance, Spiritualism* (Boston: Colby & Rich, 1887), p. 100.

[66] Ann Braude, *Radical Spirits: Spiritualism and Women's Rights in Nineteenth Century America* (Indianapolis: Indiana University Press, 2001), pp. 34-35.

[67] Emma Hardinge Britten was an original member of the New York Theosophical Society founded in 1876. Britten apparently joined because 'nearly all the parties connected with the society, including the lady and gentleman (Madame Blavatsky and Colonel Olcott) now universally recognized and named as the founder, were reputed to be Spiritualists, acknowledged as

such, and supposed by their writings and teachings to be such.' 'Jottings', *Light*, 9:465 (30 November 1889), 576 (p. 576).

[68] Robert W. Delp, 'A Spiritualist in Connecticut', *The New England Quarterly*, 53:3 (September 1980), 345-362 (p. 346).

[69] Janet Oppenheim, *The Other World: Spiritualism and Psychical Research in England, 1850-1914* (Cambridge: Cambridge University Press, 1985), p. 101.

[70] Emma Hardinge Britten, 'Chronicle of Societary Work: The Spiritual Lyceum for the Young', *The Two Worlds* 1:1 (18 November 1887), 12.

[71] Delp, 'Andrew Jackson Davis', p. 47.

[72] Delp, 'Andrew Jackson Davis', p. 50.

[73] Andrew Jackson Davis, *The Great Harmonia: Being a Progressive Revelation of The Eternal Principles* (New York: A. J. Davis, 1860), p. 259.

[74] New York *Tribune* (8 May 1879), p. 4.

[75] *Appleton's Cyclopedia of American Biography*, eds. James Grant Wilson and John Fiske, 8 vols. (New York: D. Appleton and Co., 1900), III, p. 532.

[76] 'Converted to Spiritualism', *The Leavenworth Weekly Times* (15 May 1879), p. 6.

[77] Henry Kiddle, *Spiritual Communications: Presenting a Revelation of the Future Life* (New York: The Authors' Publishing Company, 1879), p. 6.

[78] 'Converted to Spiritualism', *The Leavenworth Weekly Times* (15 May 1879), p. 6. Henry Kiddle, *Spiritual Communications: Presenting a Revelation of the Future Life, And Illustrating and Confirming the Fundamental Doctrines of the Christian Faith* (New York: The Authors' Publishing Company, 1879), pp. 121, 233.

[79] Robert W. Delp, 'Andrew Jackson Davis: Prophet of American Spiritualism', *Journal of American History*, 54:1 (June 1967), 43-56 (p. 53).

[80] Delp, 'Andrew Jackson Davis', p. 5.

[81] Andrew Jackson Davis, *A Stellar Key to The Summer Land* (Boston, Colby & Rich, 1867), p. 151.

[82] Davis, *A Stellar Key to The Summer Land*, pp.159-160.

[83] Andrew Jackson Davis, *Views of Our Heavenly Home: A Sequel to a Stellar Key to the Summer-Land* (Boston: Colby & Rich, 1877), p. 182. Blavatsky would also incorporate hermaphrodites into her spiritual evolution as noted in section 2.5.

[84] Davis, *Views of Our Heavenly Home*, p. 150.

[85] A. O. Hume, 'Fragments of Occult Truth III', *The Theosophist*, 3:12 (September 1882), 307-314 (p. 309).

[86] *The Mahatma Letters to A. P Sinnett*, comp. A Trevor Barker (Pasadena, CA: Theosophical University Press, 1992), p. 198.

[87] Blavatsky, *The Key to Theosophy*, pp. 149-151.

[88] Braude, *Radical Spirits*, p. 40.

[89] Andrew Jackson Davis, *Answers to Ever-Recurring Questions From the People* (Boston: William White & Company, 1868), p. 209.

[90] Davis, *Answers to Ever-Recurring Questions*, p. 209.

[91] *Plato's Phaedo*, trans. E.M. Cope (Cambridge: Cambridge University Press, 1875), p. 43. In *Phaedo*, Socrates described these ideas (forms) by looking at the idea of universal beauty: 'there is nothing else that makes (something) beautiful but that ideal beauty, but only to the extent that it is by the absolute beauty that all beautiful things are made beautiful.' See *Plato's Phaedo*, trans. E.M. Cope (Cambridge: Cambridge University Press, 1875), p. 79. In other words, there exists a universal idea (form) of what constitutes beauty by which to say something is beautiful (a general/universal agreement as to what constitutes beauty). Then, in the *Republic*, Socrates attempted to prove his 'theory of forms' to the young Glaucon. Here Socrates used an analogy of God creating the idea of a bed. Though there are many beds, God created the perfect idea (form) of a bed. This is because God 'desired to be the real maker of a real bed, not a particular maker of a particular bed, and therefore He created a bed which by nature is one only.' See *The Republic of Plato: With an Analysis and Introduction*, trans. Benjamin Jowett (Oxford: Carendon Press, 1881), p. 300.

[92] Andrew Jackson Davis, *The Harmonial Philosophy* (Whitefish. MT: Kessinger Publishing, 2003), pp. 419-420.

[93] Davis, *The Harmonial Philosophy*, p. 422.

[94] Davis, *The Harmonial Philosophy*, p. 223.

[95] Davis, *Views of our Heavenly Home*, p. 43.

[96] Hanegraaff, *New Age Religion and Western Culture*, p. 440.

[97] Andrew Jackson Davis, *The Harbinger of Health: Containing Medical Prescription for the Human Body and Mind* (New York: C. M. Plumb & Co., 1865), p. 194.

[98] Andrew Jackson Davis, *The History and Philosophy of Evil* (Boston, Bela Marsh, 1866), pp. 55-56.

[99] Deveney, *Paschal Beverly Randolph*, p. 93.

[100] H. P. Blavatsky, *The Theosophical Glossary* (London: The Theosophical Publishing Society, 1892), p. 101.

[101] A. P. Sinnett, *Esoteric Buddhism*, 3rd ed. (London: Trubner & Co., 1884), pp. 91-92.

[102] The duration of the soul in Kama Loca can last anywhere from minutes to long periods of time. Sinnett, *Esoteric Buddhism*, pp. 88, 102-103.

[103] Norma Basch, *Framing Divorce: From the Revolutionary Generation to the Victorians* (Berkeley: University of California Press, 2001), p. 84. There was a social expectation known as the Victorian code which were cultural norms set by society that maintained particular gender roles. This code maintained that husbands were responsible to take care of their wives, display genteel behavior, and avoid over indulgences, while the wives were charged with taking care of the house and refraining from immodest activities. In some cases a wife may be expected to work, though the Victorian expectations seemed to discourage a woman from pursuing a career. When the gender roles of the Victorian Era are properly understood Helena Blavatsky becomes an intriguing figure- not only the events of her life which are

astounding but also her irascible relationship with Henry Olcott. See Elaine Tyler May, *Great Expectations: Marriage and Divorce in Post-Victorian America* (Chicago: University of Chicago Press, 1983), pp. 26-27, 46.

[104] Andrew Jackson Davis, *The Genesis and Ethics of Conjugal Love* (Boston: Colby & Rich, 1881), p. 51.

[105] Davis, *The Genesis and Ethics of Conjugal Love*, pp. 65-66.

[106] H. P. Blavatsky 'A Few Questions to "HIRAF"', *Spiritual Scientist*, 2:20 (22 July 1875), 236-237 (p. 237).

[107] Davis, *Beyond the Valley*, pp. 129, 131-132.

[108] In his *Collection of Lectures*, Olcott referred to Davis as a 'life-long friend.' Henry Steel Olcott, *A Collection of Lectures on Theosophy and Archaic Religions, Delivered in India and Ceylon* (Madras: A. Theyaga Rajier, 1883), p. 175.

[109] Marion Meade, *Madame Blavatsky: The Woman Behind the Myth* (New York: G. P. Putnam's Sons, 1980), p. 116.

[110] Letter XI in *Letters of H. P. Blavatsky: 1861 – 1879* (Wheaton, IL: The Theosophical Publishing House, 2003), p. 44.

[111] Letter XI in *The Letters of H. P. Blavatsky*, p. 46.

[112] Meade, *Madame Blavatsky*, p. 116.

[113] Meade, *Madame Blavatsky*, p. 116.

[114] H. P. Blavatsky, 'The Drift of Western Spiritualism', *The Theosophist*, 1:1(October 1879), 7-8 (p. 7).

[115] Michael Gomes, *Dawning of the Theosophical Movement* (Wheaton, IL: The Theosophical Publishing House, 1987), p. 36.

[116] Information taken from Andrew Jackson's expense ledger in the Archives of Edgar Cayce Foundation reprinted in Meade, *Madame Blavatsky*, p. 136.

[117] Letter XXV in *The Letters of H.P. Blavatsky*, p. 96.

[118] John Warne Monroe, *Laboratories of Faith: Mesmerism, Spiritism, and Occultism in Modern France* (Ithaca, NY: Cornell University Press, 2008), p. 109.

[119] For a more exhaustive biography of Allan Kardec see Henri Sausse, *Biographie d'Allan Kardec: Discours pronounce a Lyon le 31 mars 1896* (Lyon, 1896) and Andre Moreil, *La Vie et l'oeuvre d'Allan Kardec* (Paris: Sperar, 1961).

[120] For a more in depth connection between Kardec and the Catholic Church see Kardec's Book of Spiritis, pp. 66-69.

[121] Anna Blackwell, 'Madame Anna Blackwell and Mr. Lacroix', *Light*, 9:460 (26 October 1889), 519-520 (p. 519).

[122] Anna Blackwell, 'Preface', *The Spirits Book* (Brasilia, Brazil: International Spiritst Council, 2010), pp. 21-22.

[123] Allan Kardec, *What is Spiritism?* (Brasilia, DF: International Spiritist Council, 2010), p. 8.

[124] Lynn L. Sharp, *Secular Spirituality: Reincarnation and Spiritism in Nineteenth-Century France* (Lanham, MD: Lexington Books, 2006), p. 52.

[125] Sharp, *Secular Spirituality*, p. 52.

[126] Allan Kardec, *The Gospel According to Spiritism* (Brasilia, Brazil: International Spiritist Council, 2008), pp. 389, 552-553. and Allan Kardec, *Experimental Spiritism: Book on Mediums*, pp. 90-91.

[127] Hess, 'Kardec's Book of Spirit', p. 71.

[128] John Warne Monroe, *Laboratories of Faith: Mesmerism, Spiritism, and Occultism in Modern France* (Ithaca, NY: Cornell University Press, 2008), p. 113.

[129] Allen Kardec. *The Spirit's Book* (Brasilia, Brazil: International Spiritist Council, 2010), p. 125.

[130] Lynn L. Sharp, *Secular Spirituality: Reincarnation and Spiritism in Nineteenth-Century France* (Lanham, MD: Lexington Books, 2006), p. 53.

[131] Sharp, *Secular Spirituality*, p. 56.

[132] Monroe, *Laboratories of Faith*, p. 109 and Sharp, *Secular Spirituality*, pp. 60-63.

[133] Blackwell, 'Preface', p. 23.

[134] A. P. Sinnett, *Incidents in the Life of Madame Blavatsky* (New York: J. W. Bouton, 1886), pp. 158, 154-168. For the connection between Blavatsky and Spiritualism see the article by James Burns, 'Madame Blavatsky as a Spiritualist', *The Medium and Daybreak* (London, 15 March 1889), 165 (p. 165). Also see *The Letters of H. P. Blavatsky*, pp. 17-22.

[135] Alfred Percy Sinnett, *Incidents in the Life of Madame Blavatsky* (New York: J. W. Bouton, 1886), p. 158.

[136] Arthur Lillie, *Madame Blavatsky and Her Theosophy: A Study* (London: Swan Sonnenschein & Co., 1895), p. 37.

[137] Letter No. XXXVII in *Letters of H. P. Blavatsky: 1861 – 1879* (Wheaton, IL: The Theosophical Publishing House, 2003), pp. 141-142.

[138] Letter No. XXX in *Letters of H. P. Blavatsky*, p. 113.

[139] Letter CXV in *Letters of H. P. Blavatsky*, p. 247.

[140] Letter CXV in *Letters of H. P. Blavatsky*, p. 248.

[141] Kardec, *The Spirit's Book*, pp.133-137; 164-165, 170; Allan Kardec, *Genesis: Miracles and Predictions According to Spiritism* (Brasilia, Brazil: International Spiritist Council, 2009), p. 44.

[142] Kardec, *The Spirit's Book*, pp. 127, 130, 132.

[143] Kardec, *The Spirit's Book*, pp. 163-164. Both of these tenets were identified in Sharp, *Secular Spirituality*, pp 60-61. Sharp noted that 'Kardec never cited a recent source [for his view of reincarnation] but he had certainly read Fourier, and his ideas seem to follow most closely those of Reynaud, whose *Terre et ciel* had just been published (1854). The similarity between Blavatsky's view in reincarnation on various planets and Kardec's philosophy was also attested to by Wouter Hanegraaff who further noted this same ideology was accepted by none other than the nineteenth century philosopher Immanuel Kant. Hanegraaff, *The Mirror of Secular Thought*, p. 475.

[144] Kardec, *The Spirit's Book*, p. 164.

[145] Kardec, *Genesis*, p. 150.

[146] Kardec, *Genesis*, pp. 140-141.

[147] Blavatsky, *Isis Unveiled*, I, pp. 184, 348.

[148] Quoted in J. Bouvery, *Le Spiritisme et l'anarchie devant la science et la philosophie* (Paris, 1897), p. 158. reprinted in Sharp, *Secular Spirituality* , p. 63.

[149] Kardec, *Heaven and Hell*, pp. 48; 57-58. Blavatsky never supported a view of eternal punishment. In fact, her view of 'hell' is an evolving concept in her writings. In the Mahatma Letters, her concept of 'hell' is expressed as a Buddhist term 'Avitchi' which in the Mahatma Letters is the place of annihilation also called the eighth sphere; however, there is no mention of eternal suffering or punishment. See Mahatma Letter No. LXXIII in Barker, *Mahatma Letters*, p. 396.; In *Isis Unveiled* , the subject of 'hell' is allegorized. See Blavatsky, *Isis Unveiled*, I, pp. 132, 138, 316, 460; II, 13, 89, 506-507. And in her later works 'hell' is transformed into a state and not locality. Blavatsky, *The Voice of Silence*, p. 97. Blavatsky's view of 'original sin' is also allegorized to refer to the act of humanity falling from spirit into matter. See Blavatsky, *The Secret Doctrine*, I, 264; II, 261, 279, 413, 484.

[150] Allan Kardec, *Heaven and Hell: Divine Justice Vindicated in the Plurality of Existences*, trans. Anna Blackwell (New York: The Spiritist Alliance, 2003), p. 18.

[151] Campbell, *Ancient Wisdom*, p. 74.

[152] Kardec, *Heaven and Hell*, p. 67.

[153] Kardec, *Heaven and Hell*, p. 26.

[154] This idea is first hinted at in Blavatsky, *Isis Unveiled*, II, pp. 286-287, 320; Barker, *Mahatma Letters*, pp. 77, 87, 196; Blavatsky, *The Secret Doctrine*, I,171, 188-189, 326, 634,637, 641, II, 248, 249 f.n., 262, 283,302, 411, 621 f.n. In *Isis Unveiled* volume Blavatsky discussed karma on page 346; however, she obviously plagiarized this from R. Spence Hardy, *Eastern Monarchism: An Account of the Origin, Laws, Discipline, Sacred Writings, Mysterious Rites, Religious Ceremonies, and Present Circumstances of the Order of Mendicants Founded by Gotama Buddha* (London: Williams and Norgate, 1860), pp. 5-6. Thus, exemplifying that during *Isis Unveiled* even her Eastern views were taken from Western sources.

[155] Julie Hall, 'The Saptaparna: The Meaning and Origins of the Theosophical Septenary Constitution of Man', *Theosophical History*, 13 (2007), 5-37 (p. 18).

[156] Kardec, *The Spirit's Book*, pp. 158-159.

[157] According to Kardec, after death the soul 'does not become lost in the immensity of the infinite, as is generally believed. It is in the errant state in the spirit world... Since the visible world lives in the midst of the invisible world and is in constant contact with it, it follows that these two react incessantly upon each other.' Allen Kardec, *What is Spiritism?: Introduction to Knowing the Invisible World, that is, The World of Spirits*, trans. Darrel Kimble, Marcia Saiz, and Illy Reis (Brasilia, DF (Brazil): International Spiritist Council, 2010), pp. 160, 212.

[158] Kardec, *The Spirit's Book*, p. 125.

[159] Blavatsky, *Isis Unveiled*, I, pp. 285, 309, 429; II, pp. 112, 275, 320.

[160] Barker, *Mahatma Letters*, pp. 148,176,

[161] Kardec, *The Spirit's Book*, pp. 95-98.

[162] Kardec, *The Spirit's Book*, pp. 521-522. Also see Allan Kardec, *The Gospel According to Spiritism* (Brasilia, Brazil: International Spiritist Council, 2008), pp. 86-88. Allan Kardec, *Heaven and Hell: Divine Justice Vindicate in the Plurality of Existences*, trans. Anna Blackwell (New York: Spiritst Alliance Books, 2003), pp. 15-18.

[163] It has previously been noted that Blavatsky believed that mediums could only conjure up lying and deceitful spirits known as elementals.

[164] H. P. Blavatsky, 'The Teachings of Allan Kardec', *The Theosophist*, 4:11 (47) (August 1883), p. 281. reprinted in *H. P. Blavatsky: Collected Writings: 1883*, ed. by Boris de Zirkoff ,15 vols. (Pasadena: CA: Theosophical Publishing House, 1950-1991), V (1966), pp. 105-106.

[165] Oppenheim, *The Other World*, p. 171.

[166] Olcott, *Old Diary Leaves*, I, pp. 27-28.

[167] H. P. Blavatsky, *HPB Speaks*, 2 vols (Adyar, Madras: The Theosphical Soceity Press, 1951), II, p. 6.

[168] Joscelyn Godwin, *The Beginnings of Theosophy in France* (London: Theosophical History Centre, 1989), p. 7.

[169] Godwin, *The Beginnings of Theosophy in France*, pp. 8-10.

[170] W. F. Kirby, 'The Theosophical Society', *Time*, 12:1 (January 1885), 47-55 (p. 51).

[171] Oppenheim, *The Other World*, p. 166.

[172] Oppenheim, *The Other World*, pp.166-168.

[173] Oppenheim, *The Other World*, p. 174. and Kuhn, *Theosophy*, p. 246.

[174] Oppenheim, *The Other World*, p. 109.

[175] Blavatsky, *The Secret Doctrine*, II, p. 305.

[176] Oppenheim, *The Other World*, p. 170.

[177] Oppenheim, *The Other World*, p. 168.

[178] Oppenheim, *The Other World*, p. 170.

[179] Oppenheim, *The Other World*, p. 171.

[180] Oppenheim, *The Other World*, p. 172.

[181] Gerald Massey, *Concerning Spiritualism* (London: J. Burns, 1872), p. 55.

[182] Nicholas Goodrick-Clarke, *The Western Esoteric Traditions: A Historical Introduction* (New York: Oxford University Press, 2008), p. 216.

[183] Blavatsky clearly favored Alfred Wallace over Darwin in *Isis Unveiled* (having mentioned Darwin 15 times and Wallace 25 times); however, in *The Secret Doctrine*, Darwin (52 times) was mentioned many more times than Wallace (17 times).

[184] Goodrick-Clarke, *The Western Esoteric Traditions*, p. 216.

[185] The connection between Blavatsky and Alfred Wallace will be explained in 'Part VI: Spiritualists Who Critiqued Theosophy.'

[186] Blavatsky, *The Secret Doctrine*, II, p. 153.

[187] Blavatsky believed strongly in an emanationist origin for the world (Blavatsky, *Isis Unveiled*, I, 154, 285, 295.) The word 'emanation' was derived from the Latin term *emanare* which means to flow out, arise, or proceed. Thus, emanation refers to the belief that the creation of the world occurred by a series of creations flowing out from the one supreme God. As this creative flow proceeded onward it gradually descended further away from the divine source; therefore, the early emanations are closer to the divine then the later emanations. This idea had its roots in neo-Platonism specifically in the writings of the third-century philosopher- Plotinus (ca. 205-270 CE): 'matter receives the forms of the elements, later receiving gradual accessions of other forms, so that ultimately matter becomes so buried under forms that it becomes difficult to recognize. It received forms easily because it (already) possesses a form which holds the lowest rank. Likewise, the producing Principle uses a form as a model, and easily produces forms because it consists entirely of 'being' and form; as a result, its work has been easy and universal, because itself was universal. *Complete Works: In Chronological Order Grouped in Four Periods*, trans. Kenneth Sylvan Guthrie, 4 vols. (Alpine, NJ: Platonist Press, 1918), II, pp. 562-563.

[188] 'Theosophy v. Spiritualism', *Daily News* (8 February 1898), n.p.

[189c] ...nevertheless, these figures were *not* the forms of the persons they appeared to be. They were simply their portrait statues, constructed, animated and operated by the elementaries. If we have not previously elucidated this point, it was because the spiritualistic public was not then ready to even listen to the fundamental proposition that there are elemental and elementary spirits. Since that time this subject has been broached and more or less widely discussed. There is less hazard now in attempting to launch upon the restless sea of criticism the hoary philosophy of the ancient sages, for there has been some preparation of the public mind to consider it with impartiality and deliberation. Two years of agitation have effected a marked change for the better.' Blavatsky, *Isis Unveiled*, I, p. 70.

[190] H. P. Blavatsky, *Isis Unveiled: A Master Key to the Mysteries of Ancient and Modern Science and Theology*, 2 vols (New York: J. W. Bouton, 1877), I, p. xxx.

[191] Eliphas Levi, *Transcendental Magic: Its Doctrine and Rituals*, trans. Arthur Edward Waite (London: George Redway, 1896), p. 59.

[192] The destination known as kama loca was a later construct of Blavatsky's philosophy that was attached to her belief in the septenary constitution of the soul and appears to have been created after the Oriental shift of the Society. Kama Loca is an unconscious state of gestation. The term 'loca' was used by Blavatsky to denote a world or sphere. It is connected to the earth in some way though its relation is never fully explained. It is here that the fourth principle (the animal soul) is separated from the others. The fourth part and some of the fifth part remain in Kama Loca while the rest of the principles continue on in their spiritual evolution. Kama Loca is also the home of astral entities known as elementals. Elementals are the shells of

human beings that are capable of being summoned during séances. These elementals are frequently deceptive in nature and try to manipulate the medium to do their bidding. The duration of the soul in Kama Loca can last anywhere from minutes to long periods of time. Astral entities here include humans that have either committed suicide or died premature deaths. Sinnett, *Esoteric Buddhism*, pp. 88, 91-92, 102-103.

[193] Marc Demarest, 'A School for Sorcery: New Light on the first Theosophical Society', *Theosophical History*, 15:1 (January 2011), 15-32 (p. 17).

[194] '"Theosophical" Obsequies', *New York Herald-Tribune* (29 May 1876), p. 4.

[195] 'The New 'Osophy' of Buddhism, *Owyhee Avalanche* (Silver City, Idaho) (19 September 1885), p. 1.

[196] 'Theosophy', *Jackson Citizen Patriot* (25 February 1889), p. 3.

[197] 'Theosophy Unveiled', *Duluth News-Tribune* (Duluth, MN) (3 August 1890), p. 4.

[198] H. N. Maguire, 'Theosophy Reviewed,' *Oregonian* (1 October 1891), p. 6.

[199] 'Omaha Theosophists', *Omaha World Herald* (6 April 1890), p. 7.

[200] 'Disciples of Theosophy', *Macon Telegraph* (16 July 1893), p. 11.

[201] Lilian Whiting, 'Boston Life: A Remarkable Esoteric Wave Sweeping over Every Portion of the Hub', *Cleveland Leader* (reprinted from Boston magazine) (15 May 1887), p. 9.

[202] Oppenheim, *The Other World*, p. 45.

[203] Frank Podmore, *Modern Spiritualism: A History and Criticism*, 2 vols (Methuen & Co., London, 1902), II, p. 165.

[204] Alex Owen, *The Darkened Room: Women, Power and Spiritualism in Late Victorian England* (Philadelphia: University of Pennsylvania Press, 1990), p. 24.

[205] Oppenheim, *The Other World*, pp. 42-43.

[206] Geoffrey K. Neson, *Spiritualism and Society* (London: Routledge & Kegan Paul, 1969), p. 99.; Owen, *The Darkened Room*, p. 24.

[207] Oppenheim, *The Other World*, p. 43.

[208] 'Death of James Burns', *The Unknown World*, 6:1 (15 January 1895), 242.

[209] Emma Hardinge Britten, *Nineteenth Century Miracles, or, Spirits and Their Work in Every Country of the Earth* (London: William Britten, 1883), pp. 209-210.

[210] 'The Conference- Blavatsky-Olcott, Magic', Medium *and the Daybreak: A Weekly Journal Devoted to the History, Phenomena, Philosophy, and Teachings of Spiritualism*, 9: 413 (1 March 1878), 138.

[211] James Burns, 'Madame Blavatsky as a Spiritualist', *The Medium and Daybreak* (15 March 1889), p. 165.

[212] W. H. Harrison, 'Theosophy and Mediumship: The Alleged Himalayan Brothers', *The Medium and Daybreak*, 15:733 (18 April 1884), 246-247, 249-250 (p. 247).

Part IV.
INTERLUDE

4.1 Theosophy, the Occult, and the *Prisca Theologia*

Blavatsky continually defined her teachings as 'occult' or hidden. Although Antoine Faivre's four characteristics of Western Esotericism were explained in the 'Preface' to this work, there is another tendency among occult organizations- a belief in the existence of a pure tradition that God (or the gods) imparted to humanity. This one 'universal philosophy' contained absolute Truth though through the years it has been diluted by priests and rulers who used this tradition to oppress others. The belief in this 'universal tradition' and the idea that it can be recovered by the initiated remained a vital doctrine of the Theosophical Society. This 'tradition' (which Blavatsky eventually defined as a pure form of Spiritualism) was what Blavatsky was hoping to 'unveil' in *Isis Unveiled*, and to teach upon in *The Secret Doctrine*. She believed that her teachings were the reemergence of this 'ancient tradition' that had remained hidden from mainstream humanity from generation to generation. Blavatsky's conceptualization of this 'ancient wisdom tradition' eventually became a fundamental tenet of occultism and resembled an earlier Western Esoteric concept found throughout the ancient philosophy of the Western world (especially during the Renaissance) known as the *prisca theologia* and the *philosophia perennis*. These ideas were rooted in the Hermetic and neo-Platonic writings of Numenius (ca. 140 CE), Plotinus (ca. 205-270 CE), Marsilio Ficino (1433-1499), and George Gemistos Plethon (ca. 1355-1452).[1] Thus, Blavatsky was attempting to root her philosophy into an established historical lineage.

The term *prisca theologia* must be broken down in order to be understood. The term *theologia* is a transliteration and combination of the Greek terms θεός (God) and λόγος (word, discourse, or reasoning). The Latin term *prisca* means ancient. Thus, the term *prisca theologia* refers to an ancient wisdom that contains the idea of a 'continuity' of tradition accessible throughout history, though it also connotes a 'degeneration' of this universal religion that continued to occur as time progresses. The term *philosophia perennis* is a Latin phrase that contains the two words 'philosophy' (*philosophia*) and 'through the ages' (*perennis*). The word *philosophia* is a transliteration of the Greek terms φιλέω (love) and σοφία (wisdom) and means– 'love (of) wisdom.' The term *philosophia perennis* contained the concept that there is in existence an ancient religion or tradition that transcends time and has been available to all initiates throughout world history. The actual use of the term *philosophia perennis* to denote a hidden religion originated in Agostino Steuco's publication of *De perenni Philosophia* (1540).

Though from a comparative view these terms (*prisca theologia* and *philosophia perennis*) might appear similar, there is one major difference between their definitions. The term *prisca theologia* is connected to the idea that only a degenerative form of the universal religion exists; whereas, *philosophia perennis* claims that the one true religion is still accessible in its pristine state. Wouter Hanegraaff observed that the *prisca theologia* was 'reconceptualized in the 16th century as *philosophia perennis*, this theme of an ancient geneaology of divinely inspired philosopher sages became centrally important to the esoteric tradition; reconstructed by nineteenth century occultists under the influence of the "oriental renaissance" and comparative religion, it was finally adopted in the New Age movement.'[2]

Blavatsky's use of the word 'occult' appeared synonymous with the Western Esoteric traditions that included magic, Kabbalah, Rosicrucianism, and Hermeticism. Furthermore, Blavatsky connected her esoteric occult teachings to this ancient wisdom religion (her own conceptualization of the *prisca theologia*) which was obvious in her writings especially in her earlier article in the *Spiritualist Scientist* where she referred to the angels (who were members of 'God's great Theosophic Seminary') who had handed out this 'secret doctrine' (or Oriental Cabala) down to the mortal world. Blavatsky defined this shift from the *philosophia perennis* to the *prisca theologia* and blamed this alteration on Moses who she claimed was the first to corrupt this oral tradition:

> Before that, all the mysterious doctrines had come down in an unbroken line of merely oral traditions as far back as man could trace himself on earth. They were scrupulously and jealously guarded by the Wise Men of Chaldaea, India, Persia and Egypt, and passed from one initiate to another, in the same purity of form as when handed down to the first man by the angels, students of God's great Theosophic Seminary. For the first time since the world's

creation, the secret doctrines, passing through Moses who was initiated in Egypt, underwent some slight alterations.[3]

The belief in an ancient lineage of the wisdom tradition was typically
associated with Hermes Trismegistus who was ordinarily included
into the wisdom lineages. The word 'Hermetic' is derived from the
name 'Hermes' and implied an acceptance and a belief in the teachings of Hermes Trismegistus in the *Hermeticum*. The mythology surrounding Hermes suggested that he was born only a few generations
after the biblical Moses. Renaissance philosopher Marsilio Ficino
considered Hermes to be the fount of the *prisca theologia* and in the
fashion of Augustine he developed a genealogy that traced the *prisca
theologia* from Hermes to Pythagoras to Orpheus to Philolaus and
finally to Plato.[4] Though connecting Hermes Trismegistus and the
prisca theologia was a result of the Renaissance Platonists, legends concerning the Hermes mythology had been formulated much earlier by
the least likely of sources- the ante-Nicene church fathers Clement of
Alexandria (ca. 150-215 CE) and Lactantius (ca. 240-320 CE) and the
later Nicene writer Augustine (354-430 CE).[5] The belief that there
existed a universal wisdom tradition that could be accessed by one
who had been initiated or aware was a central theme in both the
writings of Blavatsky and Renaissance philosophy. Again this belief
was reflected in Blavatsky's two major works- *Isis Unveiled* and *The
Secret Doctrine*.

4.2 Spiritism versus Occultism- A Theosophical View

The Theosophical Society claimed to be an occult organization that
combined a Western Esoteric belief system, Spiritualism, and the
belief in an ancient wisdom tradition as explained above. The main
difference between the Theosophic 'occult' outlook on the nature of
reality and the Spiritist belief seemed to be related to the 'will' of the
practitioner. This distinction between occultism and Spiritism (the
Kardecian version of Spiritualism) was suggested in Lynn Sharp's
study of Spiritism in France during the nineteenth century. Lynn
noted that the main difference between Spiritism and occultism resided in how the world could be changed by the practitioner.[6] In
other words, the Theosophists believed that the world centered
around the concepts of analogies or Plato's theory of forms also
known as correspondences. The human being was the microcosm
and the universe was the macrocosm. The macrocosm could be ma-

nipulated by the occultist through the use of astral fluid on the astral plane. Thus, by merely using ones 'will' reality could be altered.

The Spiritist on the other hand recognized that that the individual worked through a succession of lives to perfect itself and that the environment cooperated with this change. Thus, a minor difference has been noted in these two differing belief structures; however, this point remains curious because Blavatsky appeared to have believed in both of these ideals. In *The Secret Doctrine*, humanity evolved into various root races and rounds until it had reached perfection and at the same time this was only accomplished after a series of incarnations; Blavatsky also held that adepts and initiates possessed the power and ability to manipulate the 'astral light' and communicate with various spirits simply by their individual will. Thus, employing both of these definitions, Blavatsky's Theosophy could be seen as combination of occultism and Spiritism.

Notes

[1] For a general treatment of this subject see Wouter J. Hanegraaff, 'Tradition', in *Dictionary of Western Esotericism and Gnosis*, ed. Wouter J. Hanegraaff (Boston: Brill Academic Publishers, 2005), pp. 1125-1135 (p. 1126). For individual teachings see *Plotinos Complete Works: In Chronological Order Grouped in Four Periods*, trans. Kenneth Sylvan Guthrie, 4 vols (Apline: NJ: Platonist Press, 1918), II, pp. 562-563.; Kenneth Sylvan Guthrie, *Numenius of Apamea: The Father of Neo-Platonism* (London: George Bell and Sons, 1917), pp. 2-3.; Wouter Haanegraaff, 'The Pagan who Came from the East: George Gemistos Plethon and Platonic Orientalism', in *Hermes in the Academy: Ten Years' Study of Western Esotericism at the University of Amsterdam*, eds. Wouter Hanegraaff and Joyce Pijnenburg (Amsterdam, Netherlands: Amsterdam University Press, 2009), pp. 33-49 (p. 40).; and, Michael J. B. Allen 'Introduction', in *Marsilio Ficino: His Theology, his Philosophy, His Legacy*, ed. Michael J. B. Allen and Valery Rees (Boston: Brill, 2002), pp. xiii-xxii (p. xx).
[2] Wouter J. Hanegraaff, *New Age Religion and Western Culture: Esotericism in the Mirror of Secular Thought* (Albany, NY: State University of New York Press), p. 390. This idea is further expounded by Antoine Faivre who notes that *prisca theologia* in the Middle Ages 'was transformed into *philosophia occulta* and *philosophia perennis*, terms that were not interchangeable, but that were applied to a nebula endowed with relative autonomy in the mental universe of the epoch, and detached from theology properly speaking.' Antoine Faivre, *Access to Western Esotericism* (Albany: State University of New York Press, 1994), p. 7.

[3] H. P. Blavatsky 'A Few Questions to "HIRAF"', *Spiritual Scientist*, 2:19 (15 July 1875), 217-218, 224 (p. 224).

[4] Angela Voss, *Marsilio Ficino* (Berkeley, CA: North Atlantic Books, 2006), p. 16.

[5] The astrological books of Hermes are noted in the *Stromata* of Clement of Alexandria (ca.150-ca. 215). Also Lactantius (ca. 240-ca. 320) notes concerning the *philosophia perennis* of Hermes: 'I have no doubt myself that Trismegistus arrived at the truth by some such analysis; he said everything about God the father and much about the son which is contained in the divine secrets.' *Lactantius: Divine Institutes*, trans. Anthony Bowen and Peter Garnsey (Liverpool: Liverpool University Press, 2003), p. 275. Again Hermes is mentioned in relation to his knowledge of philosophy by Augustine. Augustine notes 'as regards philosophy, which professes to teach men something which shall make them happy, studies of that kind flourished in those lands about the times of Mercury, whom they called Trismegistus, long before the sages and philosophers of Greece, but yet after Abraham, Isaac, Jacob, and Joseph, and even after Moses himself.' Philip Schaff, *A Select Library of the Nicene and Post-Nicene Fathers of the Christian Church*, ed. 14 vols., 'Saint Augustin's City of God and Christian Doctrine,' trans. Marcus Dods, (Buffalo, NY: The Christian Literature Company, 1887), V, p. 384.

[6] Sharp, *Secular Spirituality*, p. 187.

Part V.
BLAVATSKY'S 'AUTOMATIC' WRITINGS

5.1 *Isis Unveiled*

Blavatsky's alignment with Spiritualism was further exhibited through her unusual claims of inspiration for her major works which closely resembled the 'automatic writings' associated with Spiritualism. 'Automatic writing' was a practice closely associated with Victorian Spiritualism that eventually found its way into the eleventh edition of the 1910 *Encyclopedia Britannica* and was defined as follows:

> the name given by students of psychical research to writing performed without the volition of the agent. The writings may also take place without any consciousness of the words written; but some automatists are aware of the word which they are actually writing, perhaps of two or three words on either side, though there is rarely any clear perception of the meaning of the whole. Automatic writings may take place when the agent is in a state of trance, spontaneous or induced, in hyster-epilepsy or other morbid states; or in a condition not distinguishable from normal wakefulness.[1]

Automatic writings were commonplace among Victorian mediums across the Western world including the United States, England, and in France. Oppenheim noted that 'Blavatsky openly claimed to receive "precipitated messages" from her masters, not unlike the written exhortation and encouragements mysteriously received by spiritualists from loved ones beyond the veil."[2] In this particular study many of the figures mentioned participated in this unusual practice of 'automatic writing' including the Davenport Brothers (United States), Andrew Jackson Davis (United States), Allan Kardec (France), and William Stainton Moses (England). Allan Kardec explained his own conceptualization of this practice and its rudimentary nature in his work *Books on Mediums* which was used as a text book for aspiring Spiritists (and was translated into English by Emma Wood in 1874):

> Of all the means of communication, writing with the hand- called by some involuntary writing- is, without contradiction, the most

simple, the easiest, and the most convenient, because it requires no preparation, and because, as in ordinary writing, it can be used for the most extended development.[3]

Kardec continued to note that often times the pencil in the medium's hand 'is thrown forcibly to a distance, or the hand, like the basket, is conclusively shaken, and strikes the table with anger even when the medium is perfectly calm, and astonished not to be master of himself.'[4] A similar description of this automatic writing process was exhibited in Blavatsky's writing of *Isis Unveiled* as described by Olcott in his *Old Diary Leaves*: 'Her pen would be flying over the page, when she would suddenly stop, look out into space with the vacant eye of the clairvoyant seer, shorten her vision as though to look at something held invisibly in the air before her, and begin copying on her paper what she saw.'[5] The writing style that Blavatsky employed while writing *Isis Unveiled* appeared to be based on the typical practice of nineteenth-century Spiritism; however, Blavatsky made it a priority to distance her work from Spiritism by claiming the supernatural influence of her masters. This made her style appear to be more of a 'hypnotic trance' than the typical mediumistic trance though the basic premise appears identical- communication with the invisible world through a 'medium's' writing. Again, despite the fact that her method of transmission seemed similar to other automatic writings of her era, Blavatsky believed that her inspiration separated her writings from Spiritualism which seemed legitimized through two circumstances that occurred in her life.

The first circumstance that preceded the publication of *Isis Unveiled* was the formation of a relationship with the noted Spiritualist Emma Hardinge Britten (1823–1899). Though the nature of this relationship will be explored in more depth at a later point in this study, it should be considered that in the fall of 1875 Blavatsky had met up with Britten and her husband William Britten a former Universalist minister. Emma was a strong female personality who adamantly claimed that she was not the author of her soon to be released *Art Magic* but that she was only an editor- Chevalier Louis the learned adept was the real author.[6] This introduction seemed to 'inspire' Blavatsky to create a work similar in nature that had also been given to her from higher being. The result of this inspiration was *Isis Unveiled*.

The second circumstance was seen in Blavatsky's reflection back onto her writing of *Isis Unveiled*, in Sinnett's later publication of the *Incidents in the Life of Madame Blavatsky* in 1886:

> But when I wrote 'Isis,' I wrote it so easily, that it was certainly no labour, but a real pleasure. Why should I be praised for it? Whenever I am told to write, I sit down and obey, and then I can write easily upon almost anything-metaphysics, psychology, philosophy, ancient religions, zoology, natural sciences, or what not. I never put myself the question: 'Can I write on this subject?...' or,' Am I equal to the task?' but I simply sit down and write. Why? Because somebody who knows all dictates to me...My MASTER, and occasionally others whom I know in my travels years ago...Please do not imagine that I have lost my senses. I have hinted to you before now about them...and I tell you candidly, that whenever I write upon a subject I know little or nothing of, I address myself to Them, and one of Them inspires me, i.e., he allows me to simply copy what I write from manuscripts, and even printed matter that pass before my eyes. *In the air, during which process I have never been unconscious one single instant* (emphasis added).

Blavatsky (through her 'conscious' awareness of this hypnotic process) distanced *Isis Unveiled* from any future claims that she had composed this work by utilizing the process of automatic writing; however, one cannot deny a similar element between Blavatsky's writing of *Isis Unveiled* and the widespread practice of automatic writing in Victorian Spiritualism. Brendan French in his doctoral thesis on Blavatsky's conceptualization of the masters noted that 'Blavatsky was careful to assure her readers, particularly those who were members of the nascent Society, that although *Isis Unveiled* was the product of meta-empirical agency, and contained heretofore unpublished revelation, it was not produced by any species of automatic writing.' It seems more plausible that Blavatsky's claim of inspiration by the 'masters' was her attempt to attract Spiritualists to join her philosophically advanced Theosophical Society and further sanctified her writings from the vast amount of automatic writings that were being produced by other mediums in the nineteenth century.

French insisted that 'such demonstrative declarations from Blavatsky are a concerted attempt to contrast the production of her writings from those of Spiritualists such as Moses, and yet at the same time to retain their intrinsic revelatory character as having been generated with supramundane insight.'[7] It seemed that one of the purposes behind Blavatsky's writing of *Isis Unveiled* was to differentiate 'its origins and content from other unorthodox para-psychological and healing movements which she saw as lacking cohesive intellectual defence.[8] Thus, *Isis Unveiled* was Blavatsky's public proclamation to identify her unique branch of Western Esoteric Spiritualism.

5.2 The Writing of *Isis Unveiled*

Blavatsky wrote *Isis Unveiled* primarily while residing at the Lamasery located in downtown New York at 302 West 47th Street between the years 1876-1878.[9] Blavatsky composed this work by using her psychic senses to peer into the astral light guided by her masters. Olcott explained this process in more detail: 'from the Astral Light, and, by her soul-senses, from her Teachers- the Brothers,' 'Adepts,' Sages,' 'Masters,' as they have been variously called. How do I know it? By working two years with her on *Isis*...to watch her work was a rare and never-to-be-forgotten experience.'[10]

Thus, *Isis Unveiled* was claimed to be a supernaturally inspired treatise despite Olcott's insistence that:

> ...nothing could have been more commonplace and unostentatious than the beginning of *Isis*. One day in the Summer of 1875. H.P.B. showed me some sheets of manuscript which she had written, and said: 'I wrote this last night 'by order', but what the deuce it is to be I don't know. Perhaps it is for a newspaper article, perhaps for a book, perhaps for nothing; anyhow, I did as I was ordered. And she put it away in a drawer, and nothing more was said about it for some time. But in the month of September- if my memory serves- she went to Syracuse (N.Y.), on a visit to her new friends Professor and Mrs. Corson of Cornell University, and the work went on...she said she was writing about things she had never studied and making quotations from books she had never read in all her life...[11]

In the early fall of 1875, as noted above, Blavatsky continued to work on *Isis Unveiled* in Ithaca, NY during her three week visit with Hiram Corson, a professor of Rhetoric, Oratory, and English at Cornell University.[12] Blavatsky evidently made quite an impression on Corson and his family during her visit; many years later Corson was able to recollect the events of her visit in an interview with Charles Lazenby:

She wrote a considerable part of *Isis Unveiled* in my house at Ithaca, and living constantly with her for these weeks, she continually filled me with amazement and curiosity as to what was coming next. She had a profound knowledge of everything apparently, and her method of work was most unusual...She would write in bed, from nine o'clock in the morning till two o'clock the following morning, smoking innumerable cigarettes, quoting long verbatim paragraphs from dozens of books of which I am perfectly certain there were no copies at that time in America, translating easily from several languages, and occasionally calling out to me, in my study, to know how to turn some old world idiom into literary English, for at that time she had not attained the fluency of diction which distinguished *The Secret Doctrine*.... The woman was so marvelous and had such mysterious funds of definite knowledge, that I find it much easier to believe her statement than to account for her quotations by any ordinary explanation of memory...The hundreds of books she quoted from were certainly not in my library, many of them not in America, some of them very rare and difficult to get in Europe, and if her quotations were from memory, then it was an even more startling feat than writing them from the ether. The facts are marvelous, and the explanation must necessarily bewilder those whose consciousness is of a more ordinary type.[13]

Corson evidently believed that Blavatsky had utilized sources not to be found in his personal library, though it seemed doubtful that Corson would have been aware of all the footnotes in each of the books at his house. Despite this criticism, Corson held that Blavatsky exhibited some inexplicable 'powers of erudition' that she claimed were derived from her ability to peer into another plane of existence. It appeared that both these mysterious 'powers of erudition' and her ability to cite sources of which Corson remained unaware were explained in a recently discovered letter dated 17 November 1857 allegedly sent to the Spiritualist William Stainton Moses. This letter explained her true activities during her visit with Corson:

I feel guilty indeed towards you. I have received your first letters, on a visit to Professor Corson and wife at Ithaca Cornell University, and was so busy at the time that I had actually no time to acknowledge your favor- I did not wish to make of it merely an interchange of polite ceremonies, for my object in writing you, was to give you all the information that was in my power, and having my book to attend to at the time busy in the university library.[14]

This visit provided Blavatsky with the opportunity to utilize Cornell University's library and information services effectively explaining the two mysteries that Corson had mentioned in his testimony (both the 'powers of erudition' and the books quoted that were not found in his personal library).

Another rumor for the inspiration of *Isis Unveiled* was suggested in an article published in *The Two Worlds* on 12 June 1891:

> One point only is worthy of notice in the early conduct of the society. It had been determined to form an extensive library of rare and classical works. The advertisements of some New York antiquarian book collectors favoured the idea. Hence large collections were made amongst the members with a view of purchasing the literary treasures so eagerly sought for. To the 'corresponding secretary,' who had taken the place of the librarian, the sums collected and the duty of their investment was entrusted, and it is but justice to say that though they said investments were considerable, every member-no less than the world at large-any one, in fact, who is able to pay the price of 'Isis Unveiled,' can have the full benefit of all the literature that was gathered together in the first Theosophical library.[15]

This article suggested that while Blavatsky was writing *Isis Unveiled* that she had access to a large collection of rare and antiquarian sources, and attempted to explain her use of nearly 1,000 books which she referenced in *Isis Unveiled*; however, the veracity of this statement remains speculative. It seems more plausible that this may have been invented by some rival Spiritualists in Emma Hardinge Britten's circle as a propaganda piece created to slander the Theosophists.

It was notable that Blavatsky never claimed that every word in *Isis Unveiled* was channeled by her own abilities, and acknowledged the contributions of Alexander Wilder (1823–1908) the neo-Platonist who edited *Isis Unveiled* and wrote the preface,[16] Charles Sotheran (1847–1902) who suggested the title '*Isis Unveiled*',[17] and Colonel Olcott who contributed by editing, copying, and translating words and phrases into English, and ultimately postulated the idea of dividing the book into two sections: 'Science' and 'Theology.'[18]

Blavatsky's early influences before she reached New York in 1873 remain relatively unknown despite her claims of entering Tibet and learning from the native mystics. Given the difficulty of reaching Tibet during the nineteenth century and the peril that a quest like that would entail for a woman Blavatsky's visit to this foreign land seems fabricated.[19] Though in her earlier years Blavatsky did manage to keep a scrapbook which contained some letters published in her collected writings from before this time period; however, her first major publication was *Isis Unveiled.*

5.3 The Philosophy in *Isis Unveiled*

Isis Unveiled was published in 1877 and totaled 1,300 pages. The subtitle clearly articulated the aim of this work: 'a master-key to the Mysteries of Ancient and modern Science and Theology.' This subtitle communicated Blavatsky's desire to reveal the 'ancient wisdom tradition' which she believed was the underlying current of all world religions (though a more unadulterated form was to be found in the Eastern traditions).[20] *Isis Unveiled* was released as a two-volume set that was a disorganized manual combining Spiritualism, Western Esoteric philosophy, and rudimentary Eastern terminology. The first volume was titled 'Science' and it attempted to validate the numerous accounts of Spiritualist phenomena that were found within the context of nineteenth-century Spiritualism. The second volume was called 'Theology' and it suggested that all the various world religions could be traced back to one universal religious tradition. Numerous subjects were explored throughout this work; some of these subjects included psychometry (which was the process of receiving psychic impressions from holding any object), the existence of a universal wisdom tradition (the belief that all of the world's truth was hidden in the various world religions), an emanationist creation of the world (that the world was created by emerging out of the one god), the existence of a hidden, and highly evolved race of spiritual Masters that possessed supernatural abilities (commonly called mahatmas or adepts), and an allegorical interpretation of Genesis.

Also, in this work Blavatsky attempted to combine scientific evolutionary theories (such as those advocated by Alfred Wallace, Charles Darwin, and Thomas Huxley), prehistory, Eastern religious traditions (through her readings of Louis Jacolliot), and Spiritualism with the philosophy of Eliphas Lévi. Now as all of these diverse subject matters were not compatible with one another, Blavatsky ultimately picked and chose the parts that defended her pre-conceived philosophy which was ultimately 'a rambling tirade' against the materialism of the nineteenth century (the belief that the world can be reduced to natural principles) and Christianity.[21] One biographer sarcastically noted the contributions Blavatsky had given to society in the publishing of *Isis Unveiled*:

> Fundamentally…*[Isis Unveiled]* was the expression of a brilliant and frustrated woman rebelling against the humdrum routine of life, escaping like Alice through a looking-glass into a world where everything was fascinating because it was different, off the normal…she was, in her day, a pioneer in her defense of ancient and especially Oriental civilizations, in promoting recognition of and respect for the achievements of the past…she confidently brought their wisdom and culture to the attention of the rest of the world. She contributed to the leavening influence that is gradually breaking down the old white-man's-burden arrogance in England and the United States and preparing the way for a spirit of internationalism.[22]

Thus, the positive aspects of this work included familiarizing the Western world with Eastern philosophy and pursuing feminist ideals. Even with the imperfections of this work, the first edition of *Isis Unveiled* (which was limited to 1,000 copies) sold out within a ten-day period and within the year two more reprints had managed to completely sell out.

5.4 Reception of *Isis Unveiled*

Blavatsky's writings are heavily plagiarized, and material was continuously taken from a variety of sources without citations. In her final article written shortly before her demise in 1891, Blavatsky admitted to some of the problematic elements in *Isis Unveiled* in an article titled 'My Books' which she sent to *Light* and was published on 15 May 1891 (in direct response to Coleman's allegations of plagiarism printed in the April issue of the San Francisco publication titled the *Golden Way*):[23]

> Of all the books I have put my name to this particular one is, in literary arrangement, the worst and most confused. And I might have added with as much truth that, carefully analysed from a strictly literary and critical standpoint, *Isis* was full of misprints and misquotations; that it contained useless repetitions, most irritating digressions, and to the casual reader unfamiliar with the various aspects of metaphysical ideas and symbols, as many apparent contradictions; that much of the matter in it ought not to be there at all and also that it had some very gross mistakes due to the many alterations in proof-reading in general, and word corrections in

particular. Finally, that the work, for reasons that will be now explained, has no system in it; and that it looks in truth, as remarked
by a friend, as if a mass of independent paragraphs having no connection with each other, had been well shaken up in a waste-
basket, and then taken out at random and--published... For more
than ten years this unfortunate 'master-piece,' this 'monumental
work,' as some reviews have called it, with its hideous metamor-
phoses of one word into another, thereby entirely transforming
the meaning, with its misprints and wrong quotation-marks, has
given me more anxiety and trouble than anything else during a
long life-time which has ever been more full of thorns than of ros-
es.[24]

Blavatsky then continued to give four justifications that were the
cause of these above issues: First, Blavatsky explained, that upon
entering America in 1873 she had not spoken English since she first
learned it as a small child nearly 30 years before. Secondly, she
claimed that she had never received any formal education at a college
or university making her ability to read philosophical and scientific
works in English difficult. Thirdly, she contended that she did not
know any literary rules, stylistic or otherwise. She noted that 'the art
of writing books, or preparing them for print and publication, reading and correcting proofs,' were so many close[d] secrets to me.'[25]
Lastly, Blavatsky explained that when starting to write *Isis Unveiled*
she had no main thesis for this work and was not sure whether she
would publish it either as an essay, pamphlet, book, or an article.
Furthermore, Blavatsky stated:

> But now enemies (referring specifically to the Spiritualist W. E.
> Coleman) have ferreted out unquoted passages and proclaim loud-
> er than ever 'the author of *Isis Unveiled*,' to be a plagiarist and a
> fraud. Very likely more may be found, as that work is an inex-
> haustible mine of misquotations, errors and blunders, to which it is
> impossible for me to plead 'guilty' in the ordinary sense. Let then
> the slanderers go on, only to find in another fifteen years as they
> have found in the preceding period, that whatever they do, they
> cannot ruin Theosophy, nor even hurt me... the language in *Isis
> Unveiled* is not mine, but...may be called only a sort of translation
> of my facts and ideas into English, secondly, it was not written for
> the public.[26]

Based upon these self admissions made by Blavatsky it would seem
futile to embark upon a complete source analysis of *Isis Unveiled*. It

seemed apparent that Blavatsky had borrowed much of her material from other sources as she herself vaguely admitted.

5.5 *Isis Unveiled* and Spiritualism

Aside from the mode of writing employed in *Isis Unveiled* explained above, Blavatsky's connection to Spiritualism (or Spiritism the French version of Spiritualism that held to reincarnation) was further evident in her introduction of a term to the American Spiritualists that she had seemingly derived from Allan Kardec. This term was used to describe a form of 'automatic writing' and appeared to have been translated from Kardec's book *Experimental Spiritism* (1874) - psychography.[27] Psychography was defined by Blavatsky as 'the direct writing of messages by spirits' and appears to have been introduced to American Spiritualists through Blavatsky in this work.[28]

Also, Blavatsky's view of spiritual evolution in *Isis Unveiled* does not appear to diverge from other Spiritualist writings of the nineteenth century. Blavatsky believed that the soul was continually striving towards spiritualization in a theory referred to as the ascent/descent theory of spiritual evolution. Blavatsky believed that the soul (monad) was conceived as a pure spirit though it eventually fell into pure materialism. Now the soul's mission was to continually evolve through a long and arduous journey back into spirit through physical evolution. Thus, Blavatsky's beliefs conformed to Darwin's theory of evolution to a certain degree; however, she explained that:

> according to cyclic law, the living human race must inevitably and collectively return one day to that point of departure, where man was first clothed with 'coats of skin;' or, to express it more clearly, the human race must, in accordance with the law of evolution, be finally *physically* spiritualized. Unless Messrs. Darwin and Huxley are prepared to prove that the man of our century has attained, as a physical and moral animal, the acme of perfection, and evolution, having reached its apex, must stop all further progress with the modern genus.[29]

This descent into matter would be followed by an ascent back to spirit which was based heavily on her conceptions of emanations and Platonic forms.[30] Thus, the idea that the soul was continually moving towards perfection/spirit would be similar to contemporary salvation (soteriological) views of nineteenth century Spiritualism evident in the Spiritualist conceptualization of the law of progression which purported a similar evolutionary scheme. Blavatsky was building on a rudimentary tenet of modern Spiritualism that included the evolution of the human spirit and its ascent from matter as observed by Frank Podmore (in his description of Heinrich Werner- one of the precursors of the Spiritualist movement) in his monumental work- *Modern Spiritualism* (1902):

> There is, he says, but one absolutely immaterial Being- that is God. Below God there is an infinite chain from seraph to grain of sand, form highest self-consciousness to most absolute unconsciousness, each link in the chain having more of earth intermixed with its spiritual nature than that which went before. The soul of man occupies some intermediate position in this universal procession. Would it not, he asks, be a piece of extreme folly and self-conceit to suppose that the spiritual part of man, as soon as it was separated from the body, could be as absolutely immaterial as God Himself?[31]

Andrew Jackson Davis who noted that a very similar spiritual progression occurred in his Summer Land stated that 'pure spirit can never be reached, for it is an infinite distance (in time) removed from the phenomena of mere body. Eternity alone could suffice to complete the empirical process backward and inward to this great center of the Cosmos. But man is pure spirit in his inmost, at once, in consciousness itself.' In this same work Davis' conceptualization of the composition of God was as a divine 'pure spirit.'[32] Thus, Blavatsky's anti-materialist belief of salvation and eternity would have been well received in Victorian Spiritualism. This spiritual evolution represented Blavatsky's particular doctrine of salvation in the absence of a personal God or a Redeemer. Blavatsky's post-mortem spiritual evolution in *Isis Unveiled* was further explicated in her conceptualization of the circle of necessity which would not seem contrary to other contemporary Spiritualist ideologies:

> It is ordained by faith that every soul, whether with or without understanding, when gone out of the body, should wander for a time, though not all for the same, in the region lying between the earth and moon. For those that have been unjust and dissolute suffer there the punishment due to their offences; but the good and virtuous are there detained till they are purified, and have, by expiation, purged out of them all the infections they might have contracted from the contagion of the body...where they must remain for a certain prefixed and appointed time. And then, as if they were returning from a wandering pilgrimage or long exile into their

country, they have a taste of joy, such as they principally receive who are initiated into Sacred Mysteries, mixed with trouble, admiration, and each one's proper peculiar hope.[33]

This belief in the destination of the soul would shift in her later writings (such as *The Key to Theosophy*) when the soul would become immediately placed in Devachan upon its bodily demise except in a couple of unusual circumstances. Blavatsky went on to define the structure of the universe as a 'circle composed of innumerable smaller circles.' The monad's (soul) mission was to traverse these innumerable spheres occasionally stopping for a temporary rest in Nirvana.[34] After death, the monad would wander through the region lying between the earth and moon in order to purify itself to be reborn on another sphere moving towards spirit in the cycle known as the 'circle of necessity'. The overall purpose of this process of spiritual evolution was the progression of the soul/monad and its eventual absorption into Eternal Rest:

> Plato, Anaxagoras, Pythagoras, the Eleatic schools of Greece, as well as the old Chaldean sacerdotal colleges, all taught the doctrine of the dual evolution; the doctrine of transmigration of souls referring only to the progress of man from world to world, after death here. Every philosophy worthy of the name taught that the spirit of man, if not the soul, was preexistent…nothing is eternal and unchangeable, save the Concealed Deity. Nothing that is finite-whether because it had a beginning, or must have an end can remain stationary. It must either progress or recede; and a soul which thirsts after a reunion with its spirit, which alone confers upon it immortality, must purify itself through cyclic transmigrations, onward toward the only Land of Bliss and Eternal Rest, called in the Sohar, 'The Palace of Love,'…in the Hindu religion, 'Moksha'; among the Gnostics, the 'Pleroma of eternal Light.'; and by the Buddhists, Nirvana. The Christian calls it the kingdom of heaven…[35]The soul cannot reach the abode of bliss, unless she has…the re-union of the soul with the substance from which she emanated- spirit.[36]

It appeared that based upon this above quote that it was possible, according to *Isis Unveiled*, for the soul to obtain an eternal rest by being absorbed into the One Being (from which it had emanated) through the reuniting of the soul and the spirit, though this could only occur after multiple cyclical transmigrations. Thus, Blavatsky's philosophy in *Isis Unveiled* appeared to be an assimilation of a West-

ern view of Eastern religions with a hint of medieval Kabalistic beliefs (likely through the teachings of Maimonides). Later on in *The
Secret Doctrine*, Blavatsky would go on promote an eternal evolution
which she seemed to have been developed from H. H. Wilson's
translation of the *Vishnu Purana*. This later view included a complex
idea that included root races, rounds, and reincarnations; thus, the
soul was eternally evolving not just spiritually as other Spiritualists
had suggested but through physical incarnations (materially).

Isis Unveiled appeared to be Blavatsky's most sympathetic work towards mainstream Spiritualism; in it she attempted to prove the legitimacy of Spiritualist phenomena despite her insistence that mediums
were mostly channeling elementals instead of the departed spirits
with whom Spiritualists thought they were communicating. Despite
the obvious implications of this philosophy, Blavatsky's spiritual evolution could have been attested to by both Theosophists and Spiritualists alike though the Spiritualists believed they could communicate
with these souls who went on to the 'temporary nirvana' or what
Andrew Jackson Davis would have referred to as the Summer Land.
One of Blavatsky's early and faithful followers A.P. Sinnett noted in
1885 concerning the relationship between Spiritualism and Theosophy that 'their disagreements are as between themselves, and could
hardly be understood by outsiders quite unconnected with any investigation of truth on the spiritual plane.'[37] Thus, both sides recognized
that the phenomena employed by Spiritualists proved the existence
of a spirit world. If nothing else, *Isis Unveiled* served as proof that
Blavatsky was emerging out of Spiritualism and this publication was
her attempt to define her new movement within this Spiritualist
backdrop.

Blavatsky's semi-Spiritualist view of spiritual evolution in *Isis Unveiled* was confirmed by Colonel Henry Olcott, the co-founder of the
Theosophical Society in his autobiography (despite the belief in annihilation which would have seemed contrary to the law of progression):

> We believed that the man of flesh dies, decays, and goes to the
> crucible of evolution, to be worked over and over again; that the
> astral man... freed from physical imprisonment, is followed by the
> consequences of his earthly deeds, thoughts and desires...He ei-
> ther becomes purged of...earthly grossness, and, finally, after...
> time is joined to his divine spirit and lives forever as an eternity,
> or...he sinks deeper into matter and is annihilated. Man of pure
> life and spirituality...would be drawn towards a more spiritual

realm than this earth…the thoroughly depraved person would have lost his spirit during life, be reduced to a duality instead of a trinity at the hour of death, and become disintegrated; its grosses matter going into the ground and its finer tuning into a…elementary' 'wandering in and about the habitations of men…until its life is burn out…this was the…substance of our teaching at that time about the nature and destiny of man, and shows how infinitely far away from believing in Re-incarnation H.P.B., and I were then.'[38]

Colonel Olcott confirmed Blavatsky's view of spiritual evolution and elementals posited in the quote above, but further explained that when *Isis Unveiled* was written, Blavatsky had not yet adopted the concept of reincarnation which would have placed her in alignment with many of the American Spiritualists especially Emma Hardinge Britten and Andrew Jackson Davis. Blavatsky's philosophy would soon change in regards to reincarnation- this evolution will now be discussed.

5.6 The New Theosophy: A Re-incarnational Evolution

Later critics of Blavatsky would charge that her philosophy in *Isis Unveiled* was inconsistent with her later 'Eastern' belief structure that incorporated both reincarnation on the same sphere and a septenary constitution of the soul. It was true that in *Isis Unveiled*, Blavatsky spoke against the concept of reincarnation on the same sphere (the same world) except for in the most severe cases of idiocy or an early violent death: 'Reincarnation is not a rule in nature; it is an exception…It is preceded by a violation of the laws of harmony of nature, and happens only….in cases of abortion, of infants dying before a certain age, and of congenital and incurable idiocy, natures original design to produce a perfect human being, has been interrupted.'[39]

The theorization that in *Isis Unveiled* Blavatsky seemed opposed to reincarnation on the same sphere was further exemplified in the following quote:

> But this doctrine of permutation, or *revolutio,* must not be understood as a belief in reincarnation. That Moses was considered the transmigration of Abel and Seth, does not imply that the kabbalists—those who were *initiated* at least—believed that the identical spirit of either of Adam's sons reappeared under the corporeal form of Moses. It only shows what was the mode of expression they used when hinting at one of the profoundest mysteries of the

Oriental Gnosis, one of the most majestic articles of faith of the Secret Wisdom.[40]

It became an issue that Blavatsky had not accepted the doctrine of reincarnation during her writing of *Isis Unveiled*, and it seemed that the doctrine of reincarnation only crept into her philosophy after her travels to India. Colonel Olcott wrote to rectify this discrepancy confirming that Blavatsky *had not* been aware of reincarnation before writing of *Isis Unveiled*. Olcott noted:

> there is no Re-incarnation on this Earth, for the three parts of the triune man have been united together, and he is capable of running the race. But when the new being has not passed beyond the condition of monad, or when, as in the idiot, the trinity has not been completed, the immortal spark which illuminates it has to re-enter on the earthly plane, as it was frustrated in its first attempt.[41]

Olcott further wrote concerning Blavatsky's view of reincarnation:

> she told Mr. Walter R. Old- who is my informant- that she was not taught the doctrine of re-incarnation until 1879- when we were in India. I willingly accept that statement, both because it tallies with our beliefs and writings in New York, and, because if she knew it when we were writing Isis, there was no earthly reason why she should have misled me or other, even if she has so desired, which I do not believed.[42]

Blavatsky would have been aware of the Spiritualist reincarnation through the writings of Allan Kardec (evidenced in her 12 April 1875 letter to A. N. Askakoff), so it would be more accurate of Olcott to explain that up to this point Blavatsky remained unaware of the Eastern form of reincarnation until their travels to India in 1879.

Olcott continued to cite specific writings where Blavatsky had definitively taken this stance against reincarnation especially in the 8 February 1878 issue of the *Spiritualist*: 'A dead child is a failure of nature- he must live again; and the same *psuche* re-enters, together with those of congenital idiots are, as stated in "Isis Unveiled," the only instances of human re-incarnation." Can anything be plainer?...the doctrine of Re-incarnation was not publically taught so early as 1879.'[43] Thus, it seemed that reincarnation on the same sphere would become a doctrine that Blavatsky would adopt as her cosmo-logical structure developed and progressed.

5.7 Trichotomy of the Soul

Another philosophical shift in Blavatsky's early philosophical views that would demarcate Theosophy from Spiritualism (and was also connected to the concept of reincarnation) was the septenary consti-tution of the soul. In *Isis Unveiled*, Blavatsky favored a triune division of the soul which was also favored by most Spiritualists (as noted by Blavatsky in her article 'Fragments of Occult Truth);'[44] whereas, in the Mahatma Letters and in *The Secret Doctrine* she accepted a seven-fold division (septenary). Blavatsky defended her beliefs in the septe-nary constitution of the soul in a later article titled 'Fragments of Occult Truth' published in *The Theosophist* in August 1882. Blavatsky was responding to an article written by Charles Massey that had ac-cused her of changing her doctrine on reincarnation. She explained that this apparent discrepancy was related to a simple misunderstand-ing concerning the constitution of the soul.[45] Blavatsky articulated that in *Isis Unveiled* she divided the monad into three parts: body, soul, and spirit, and that these three attributes as a whole could not reincarnate; however, she argued that these three divisions could be divided into even more divisions, thus advocating for the septenary constitution of the monad. This new constitution was divided as fol-lows: the Body was composed or the 1) Sthula-sarira, 2) jiva, and the 3) lina-sarira; The Soul was composed of the 4) kama-rupa and 5) the manas; and the Spirit was composed of the 6) atma and 7) buddhi. Blavatsky then asked the question:

> where is the 'discrepancy' or contradiction? Whether man was good, bad, or indifferent, Group II (the soul consisting of kama-rupa and the manas) has to become either a 'shell,' or be once or several times more reincarnated under 'exceptional circumstances.' There is a mighty difference in our Occult doctrine between an impersonal Individuality, and an individual Personality. C. C. M. will not be reincarnated; nor will he in his next rebirth be C. C. M., but quite a new being, born of the thoughts and deeds of C. C. M.: his own creation, the child and fruit of his present life, the effect of the causes he is now producing. Shall we say then with the Spir-itists that C. C. M., the man we know, will be reborn again? No; but that his divine Monad will be clothed thousands of times yet before the end of the Grand Cycle, in various human forms, every one of them a new personality.[46]

Blavatsky's defense of her inconsistency in relation to reincarnation was explained by her septenary division of the soul. Her argument was that in *Isis Unveiled* she had simply discussed the division of the soul and reincarnation at a higher level. The soul was capable of being divided into even more segments, though it seemed that even Blavatsky herself was unaware of this concept when writing *Isis Unveiled*.[47] Concerning the trichotomy of the soul, Colonel Olcott stated:

> She and I believed, and taught orally as well as wrote that man is a trinity of physical body, astral body (soul- the Greek psuche), and divine spirits. This will be found set forth in the first official communication made by us to the European reading public...our party left for New York for India on Dec. 17, 1878, and a few days previously H.P.B wrote in the *Revue Spirite*, of Paris, an article which appeared in that magazine, Jan. 1, 1879; it was in answer to sundry critics. She now describes man as a four principle...or quaternary...[48]

Olcott continued to translate a portion of this letter: 'Yes, for the Theosophists of New York, man is a trinity, and not a duality. He is however more than that: for, by adding the physical body, man is a tetraktis, or quaternary.'[49] Based on the above information (both in Blavatsky's own words and the testimony of the primary co-founder of the Theosophical Society) it seems fair to conclude that reincarnation and the septenary constitution of the soul were later conceptualizations by Blavatsky in her attempt to harmonize the various world religions.

Haanegraaff, after studying the concept of reincarnation in *Isis Unveiled* concluded that: 'As far as Blavatsky is concerned, it is significant that when reincarnation (or its cognates, transmigration and metempsychosis) is discussed in *Isis Unveiled*, this is done as frequently with reference to occidental as to oriental traditions.'[50] Thus, given the heavy influence of Spiritualism on Blavatsky's view of time as will be noted in the comparative study of her influences and in the following section, in *Isis Unveiled* Blavatsky's chronological structure and chronology appear almost wholly influenced by Western sources and ideologies.

5.8 Blavatsky's Influence: Eastern or Western?

It remains crucial to observe the type of sources that Blavatsky utilized in her writing of *Isis Unveiled* in order to ascertain whether she was influenced primarily by the East as she claimed or by Western sources which seemed more accessible to her during this time period. In the infamous source analysis performed by Blavatsky's greatest critic William Emmette Coleman, it was claimed that Blavatsky wrote *Isis Unveiled* by using only 100 contemporary works that were accessible to Blavatsky.[51] This prompted Nicholas Goodrick-Clarke to observe that the list of a hundred books that Coleman alleged Blavatsky had plagiarized from in her writing of *Isis Unveiled* revealed that Blavatsky's sources were primarily Western.[52] Goodrick-Clarke further noted that Blavatsky's knowledge of Buddhism could easily have been found in the contemporaneous Western publications such as Edward Upham's *The History and Doctrine of Buddhism* (1829), Robert Spence Hardy's *Eastern Monachism* (1850) and *A Manual of Buddhism* (1860), Samuel Beal's *Catena of the Buddhism Scriptures from the Chinese* (1871), and Thomas William Rhys Davids' *Buddhism* (1877).[53] This belief was confirmed by Joscelyn Godwin who noted that 'there is nothing in the many passages on Buddhism in *Isis Unveiled* that could not have been drawn from Western publications, except the skill with which Blavatsky negotiated the pitfalls inherent in the subject.'[54]

Another problematic issue for determining whether Blavatsky's influences were primarily Eastern or Western was her claims to have visited Tibet in her earlier travels. These travels would have enabled her to study Buddhism and Hinduism under the direct guidance of a master or rishi, allowing Theosophy a possible origin in Eastern philosophy. Recently, the factuality of Blavatsky's travels has been disputed. Nicholas Goodrick-Clarke again noted that Blavatsky appeared knowledgeable about the geography and ethnography of Tibet though it is very possible that this knowledge could have been drawn from the following nineteenth-century sources: Abbe Evariste Regis Huc, *Travels in Tartary, Thibet and China during the Year 1844-5-6* (1852), Emil Schlagintweit, *Buddhism in Tibet* (1863), and Clement R. Markham's, *Narratives of the Mission of George Bogle to Tibet and of the Journey of Thomas Manning to Lhasa* (1876).[55]

It seemed that any information Blavatsky may have obtained regarding Eastern lands and practices could have easily been derived from the writings of the Western Orientalists. Based upon the above information it can be reasonably concluded that Blavatsky's sources in *Isis Unveiled* were primarily Western during this early time period. India was clearly already important to Blavatsky in 1877 while writing *Isis Unveiled*; however, it seemed that much of her knowledge of India could have been derived from these above sources along with the twenty-one volume complete works of Louis Jacolliot (1837 – 1890) which had been sent to Blavatsky from John L. O'Sullivan out of Paris, France illustrating that Blavatsky's influences both before and while writing *Isis Unveiled* were consistently Western in origin.[56]

5.9 The Mahatma Letters

The Mahatma letters were physical, written documents that were received by human recipients and were believed to have been 'precipitated' by Blavatsky's supernatural divine 'masters' or 'adepts' (the majority of these letters being written by 'Koot Hoomi' and 'Morya'). These highly evolved 'masters' were described earlier in Blavatsky's work *Isis Unveiled* in 1877. Though the first Mahatma Letter was sent as early as 1870, they appeared more frequently in 1881 and in following years were primarily sent to two individuals- Alfred Percy Sinnett and A. O. Hume. These mysterious letters would come through diverse delivery methods including falling miraculously from the ceiling, being placed inside old books and more mundanely being delivered through the postal system. Obviously these unusual delivery methods provided a sense of mystery to spiritual seekers which produced an obvious appeal.

So, just who was the author of these letters? Were they written by supernaturally evolved 'adepts' or were they simply the work of Blavatsky and her followers (typically referred to as confederates)? This question has stirred much controversy for many years. This present study will continue under the presumption that Blavatsky was instrumental in writing the Mahatma letters though she certainly could not have personally written each individual letter; nonetheless, they reflected her opinions. To be fair, it should be added that the discipline of history does not allow provision for the supernatural or divine. A historian cannot state that a particular book came from a God or the gods, but only that certain people believed that a book was divine. This can be followed with a relating of historical facts; however, the conclusions derived from these facts are simply opinions.[57] The issue with the Mahatma letters was not whether Blavatsky was under divine inspiration or not; rather, it was whether she physically wrote the letters or was involved in the writing of the letters as a historical event. Of course even if the handwriting analysis proved the letters were physically written by Blavatsky, certainly she could have believed the words were being uttered by one of her mahatmas.

It is the opinion of the author that in fact 'KH' and 'M' were indeed 'sub-personalities' of Blavatsky that she had invented as a theatrical tool during her Spiritualist days. Though these 'personalities' had a different name back in the 1860s and 1870s (John King), one should not forget that Blavatsky was a Spiritualist and going into trances and altered states was a common place practice employed in the Victorian era. As Vernon Harrison one of the most recent surveyors of the authorship of these letters has concluded:

> If any of the KH and M scripts came through the hand of Madame Blavatsky while she was in a state of trance, sleep, or other altered states of consciousness known to psychologists and psychiatrists, KH and M might be considered sub-personalities of Helena Blavatsky. To what extent the sub-personalities are independent is a matter for debate; but in no case would conscious fraud or imposture be involved. Nor does this supposition circumvent the difficulty that there are KH letters which even Hodgson had to admit Madame Blavatsky could not possibly have written as she was too far away at the time and communications were bad.[58]

This above conclusion will be adhered to for the purposes of this study, recognizing that the answer to the question of authorship is not as simple or defined as it may initially appear. There exists a whole intricate historical debate about the authorship of these letters and a number of prominent Theosophical historians have written widely on this subject; however, the actual validity of these letters has very little bearing on to Blavatsky's connection with Spiritualism.

Olcott himself (in defending Blavatsky from the 1885 Hodgson report) connected these Mahatma letters to Spiritualist automatic writings in his diary and noted that their resemblance to her hand writings could not disprove their genuineness:

> That even if the resemblances in the handwritings to Madame Blavatsky's had been much more striking than they were, this would have been no proof of her *mala fides*, since every tyro in spiritualistic research known that, whether a psychic message is written on a closed slate, or precipitated on a paper or card laid on the floor, or on the ceiling, or anywhere else at a distance from the medium, the writing will usually resemble that of the medium. The same rule applies to all intermediary agents through whom messages in psychic writings are transmitted.[59]

5.10 Sources of the Mahatma Letters

In the mid 1930s the brothers Harold and William Hare conducted a thorough analysis of the Mahatma letters in *Who Wrote the Mahatma*

Letters (1936) though, as they willingly admit at the beginning of their study, they were not historians of the Theosophical Society.[60] They point out two plagiarisms in these texts. The first discrepancy is found in Mahatma Letter No. X in the translation of the 'first Khandhaka'.[61] This appears to have been crudely copied from a translation made by Rhys Davids.[62] Not only is the wording similar in the Mahatma letter to Davids' translation (aside from some misspellings and a few interpolations), the 'mahatma' also uses the same parenthetical explanations as Davids.[63]

Another translation that appeared to have been used without citation was found in the reference to 'Sukhavati' copied in Mahatma Letter No. XVI.[64] This seemed to have been a deliberately altered version from Beal's *A Catena of Buddhism Scriptures from the Chinese*,[65] as other similarities between these two texts are apparent; however, the 'mahatma's' version interpolates several terms into the text that are not in the original including a list of Arhats, Dhyan Chohans, Bodhisatwas, and the term Devachan.[66] The Hares further mention that a Japanese version of this text was later discovered and translated by Max Mülller. Mülller's translation was very similar to that of Beal and it also did not include the terms that Blavatsky had interpolated.[67] Thus, the Hares had proved Coleman's accusation that Blavatsky had used quotes from these two sources without citing them. What is curious is that Blavatsky inserts her own terms into an ancient text to give them authority and textual precedence.

Beatrice Hastings argued against the Hares that they were not reliable historians and not suitable to give an analysis of the Mahatma Letters: 'The very first "fact" delivered to this public is wrong: The *Letters* were not published "in September, 1923", but in December. But this is an airy trifle compared with the colossal riot of wrong dates ramping through this worthless volume of ignorance and double-dealing.' Hastings closed her critique by publishing a list of misquotations, dating errors, and incorrect conclusions made by the Hares.[68] In reviewing Hastings conclusions, despite the omissions and mistakes that the Hares were accused of by Hastings, in the end their critique of the Mahatma letters still seem legitimate despite these issues of historicity.

5.11 The Philosophy of the Mahatma Letters

It was in these initial Mahatma letters that Blavatsky's conceptualizations begin to associate her Western philosophies with Eastern terminology. This seemed to have been a natural progression given that these letters were being written at the same time the Theosophical Headquarters were established in India. Also, the promulgation of basic ideas that will be expounded in *The Secret Doctrine* first appeared in a rudimentary form within these letters such as rounds, root races, and Devachan. A crucial aspect of these letters was Blavatsky's creation of her cosmology which would be elaborated in *The Secret Doctrine*. Despite claims that these ideas were taken from Eastern religious movements William Hare noted that 'the system of the Letters does not correspond to any doctrine of Indian philosophy known to me. In reading Letters I cannot tell whether the Authors are Vedantists [ ] Sankhyans, Hinayana or Mahayana Buddhists.'[69]

Despite the fact that the Mahatma Letters evidenced an Oriental shift in the Spiritualist views of Blavatsky, they were not published until 1923. In fact, in the nineteenth century and into the first quarter of the twentieth century, theses letters were primarily alluded to only in the writings of Alfred Percy Sinnett specifically in *The Occult World* published in 1881 and in *Esoteric Buddhism* published in 1883. These mysterious letters were eventually compiled and edited by A. T. Barker and published in December of 1923. The reason for their late publication is explicated in Mahatma Letter No. 63 written in the summer of 1884: 'The letters, in short, were not written for publication or public comment upon them, but for private use, and neither M. nor I will ever give our consent to see them thus handled.'[70] Most individuals living in the nineteenth century would have known the contents of the Mahatma Letters solely through their summary and reprinting in *Esoteric Buddhism* which was a compilation of these letters published by Alfred Percy Sinnett in 1883.

5.12 *Esoteric Buddhism*

Esoteric Buddhism (1883) is a fascinating book that addresses reincarnation on different planetary spheres, cosmic cataclysms, and a process of spiritual evolution that spans vast periods of time. This work was A. P. Sinnett's compilation of the Mahatma letters that were covertly written by H. P. Blavatsky as she developed her own cosmological structure of time and spiritual evolution. *Esoteric Buddhism* was based upon the Mahatma letters that he had received between the years 1880 and 1884. Despite the comment made above that Blavatsky's philosophy was found throughout all these letters it should not be presumed that she was responsible for physically writing each individual 'mahatma letter' (though she was behind the composition of the majority of them). Sinnett summarized and organized the Mahatma letters he had received into a methodologically systematic work that would remain accessible to the average reader.

5.13 The Philosophy in *Esoteric Buddhism*

There are two overriding themes in *Esoteric Buddhism* – the nature of the universe and spiritual evolution. This work puts forth a structure of the universe that would be continually expanded upon and modified throughout Blavatsky's subsequent writings. It will be observed that the number seven and its multiples figure prominently in Blavatsky's structure of the universe (root-races, globes, solar manvantaras, etc.) and spiritual evolution (septenary constitution of the monad). Everything in Blavatsky's universe fits into this septenary structure since it is 'the perfect and sacred number of this Maha-Manvantara of ours.'[71] The overall importance of the Mahatma letters (and subsequently *Esoteric Buddhism*) was noted by one scholar who observed that it was in these letters that Blavatsky first introduced her 'system of prehistory' and correlated it with the epochs of paleontology' superseding 'the disjointed information given in *Isis Unveiled*.'[72] In the Mahatma letters and *Esoteric Buddhism* Blavatsky laid out a complicated mythology of origins and prehistory that would be expounded upon later in *The Secret Doctrine*.

In order to understand both the structure of the universe and spiritual evolution (the two basic premises) explained in *Esoteric Buddhism* an explanation of some key terms employed must first be given. They are as follows:

Avitchi- a state of punishment reached only in exceptional cases and by exceptional natures. The commonplace sinner will work his karma out in a rebirth.[73] It is a state of the most ideal spiritual wickedness – there are not many human beings who will ever reach this state.

Devachan- a temporal place of extreme happiness where the levels of intensity and the duration of stay are based on the karma one produces in his/her lifetime.[74]

8th Sphere- is attached to our planetary chain and it is the only globe that is more materialistic than the earth.[75] The Ego in the middle point of the fifth round can be sent to the eighth sphere for annihilation if it has developed a positive attraction to materialism and a repulsion of spirituality.[76] This concept was found in Blavatsky's earlier work of *Isis Unveiled* where the concept is attributed to Plato in his *Phaedrus*.[77]

Kama Loca- is an unconscious state of gestation. As already noted the term 'loca' was used by Blavatsky to denote a world or sphere. It is connected to the earth in some way though its relation is never fully explained. It is here that the fourth principle (the animal soul) is separated from the others. The fourth part and some of the fifth part remain in Kama Loca while the rest of the principles continue on in their spiritual evolution.[78] Kama Loca is also the home of astral entities known as elementals (more fully described in earlier sections). Again, elementals are the shells of human beings that are capable of being summoned during séances. These elementals are frequently deceptive in nature and try to manipulate the medium to do their bidding. [79] The duration of the soul in Kama Loca can last anywhere from minutes to long periods of time.[80] Astral entities here include humans that have either committed suicide or died premature deaths.

Monad- the unified, upper triad Atma-Buddhi-Manas of the seven principles of man.[81] Further, each monad is comprised of seven principles (septenary constitution). These seven parts include three lower principles associated with the body that are destroyed upon a normal death. These are known as the Body, the Physical Vitality, and the Astral Counterpart. The fourth principle is called the *animal soul* the part of the monad that has desire and will. The fifth principle is known as the *human soul* and it is responsible for reason and memory. The sixth principle of a monad is referred to as the spiritual soul. The seventh principle is simply spirit itself.[82] The term monad was probably known to Blavatsky through the writings of Alexander Wilder and the Platonist Thomas Taylor through his work *The Six Books of Proclus, The Platonic Successor, on the Theology of Plato* (1816).

Pralaya- is the period or inactivity that comes after each round. Pralaya is described by Sinnett as a type of sleep, rest, or a time of inactivity.[83] There are three different pralayas mentioned by Blavatsky: 1) The Maha (great) pralaya and manvantara which is followed by a re-evolution of the whole universe, 2) the solar pralaya and manvantara which is equal to seven minor pralayas, and 3) the minor pralaya and manvantara which begins at the end of each round.

Round- consists of a complete rotation around the seven spheres. During each round there is a maximum of 120 incarnations for each monad in each race with the average of 8,000 years between incarnations.[84] Each round is devoted to the perfection of man of the corresponding principle in its numerical order. A round also prepares the monad for assimilation with the next level of spiritual evolution.

These levels will be defined below. Also, each round is known as a minor manvantara in Eastern philosophy.

These are the basic terms used in relation to spiritual evolution in this work. *Esoteric Buddhism* presented a cosmological structure that was a continual spiritual evolution occurring within phenomenal time, even though no definitive numerical figures were given out until Blavatsky published *The Secret Doctrine* (days, months, years, etc.).

One of the first key elements in *Esoteric Buddhism* was that time is eternal- it never ends.[85] Man begins as a monad and continues through seven root races on each of the seven globes. Each race takes roughly one million years.[86] Of those one million years only 12,000 of them will be spent in objective existence i.e. time spent on the globes. The rest of that time will be spent mainly in the subjective sphere of Devachan (though if one was exceptionally bad in one incarnation one might end up in Avitchi for a short period). This meant that out of one million years- 988,000 years are spent reaping the effects of karma.[87] Karma remains the deciding factor in determining where the monad resides upon death, the length of time that it stays in its destination, and the intensity of its afterlife. In *The Secret Doctrine*, karma will become 'center- stage' as the metaphysical solution for reconciling reincarnation and science without depending on the providence of God.

There are three divisions of races on each globe. There are seven root races, but within these seven root races are sub races, and within the seven sub races there are 7 branch races.

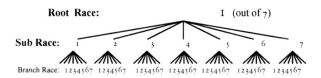

If each monad in each race incarnates once, the total number of incarnations in each globe would be 343 (7 branch races x 7 sub races x 7 root races); however, each monad incarnates typically at a minimum of two times and some even more frequently.[88] In *Esoteric Buddhism* there is no way to ascertain how many incarnations one will have on each globe except that it is more than 343. After death the monad (now stripped down) will enter a period of gestation before reaching Devachan and then the monad is reincarnated.[89] This is the basic structure of spiritual evolution elucidated in *Esoteric Buddhism*.

5.14 *Esoteric Buddhism* and Spiritualism

Sinnett believed that Theosophy and Spiritualism were not diametrically opposed doctrines and believed that they could be reconciled in his 1886 'Introduction to American Edition' of *Esoteric Buddhism*:

> By dwelling on the points of contact between the theosophic teachings and the experience of the higher spiritualism, I think it will be found that the alleged incompatibility of theosophy and spiritualism is much less complete than is supposed.[90]

It seemed that Sinnett when writing in 1886 did not see a contradiction between Spiritualist and Theosophic teachings. In the body of this work Sinnett went on to acknowledge that Theosophy maintained other powers were at work in Spiritualist séances and that the phenomena were not solely a result of elemental spirits:

> But, it may be objected, the 'communicating intelligence' at a spiritual *séance* will constantly perform remarkable feats for no other than their own sake, to exhibit the power over natural forces which it possesses. The reader will please remember, however, that occult science is very far from saying that all the phenomena of spiritualism are traceable to one class of agents. Hitherto in this treatise little has been said of the 'elementals' those semi-intelligent creatures of the astral light, who belong to a wholly different kingdom of Nature from ourselves.[91]

Sinnett expressed his lack of understanding of elementals and their role in this overall cosmological system purported in *Esoteric Buddhism*. The nature of elementals are not explained in this work though Sinnett observed that it would be impossible 'at present to enlarge upon their attributes for the simple and obvious reason, that knowledge concerning elementals, detailed knowledge on that subject, and in regard to the way they work, is scrupulously withheld by the adepts of occultism. To possess such knowledge it to wield power...[92] Despite this ignorance, Sinnett managed to effectively promulgate a unique cosmological structure through his systematic summary of the Mahatma letters.

Arthur Lillie one of Blavatsky's most capable critics noted that the underlying philosophy of this work was remarkably similar to American Spiritualism despite Blavatsky's employment of Buddhist terminology:

> The Buddhist doctrine of karma is pretty well understood. It is held that the causation of good or evil deeds carries a man hereafter to the Domain of Joy or the hell Avitchi, and detains him there until the said Karma is exhausted…But the Buddhism of Koot Hoomi knocks this central support of Buddhism away altogether. He announces that a stay of 'less that fifteen hundred years' in Avichi or the Domain of Joy, is 'quite impossible.' Why is the whole Karma theory thus satisfied? A passage from Mr. Sinnett's book may suggest an answer. 'The person whose happiness of the higher sort on earth has been entirely centred in the exercise of the affections will miss none in Devachan whom he or she loved.'[93] Plainly the very illogical person has given up the main tenets of Buddhism to supply a want felt by the members of the Theosophical Society. By the ordinary rule of karma the mother that the daughter wants to clasp in Heaven might be her little niece, and the elderly departed husband that a fond wife is sighing for might be driving his go-cart in the next square. Buddhism has been transformed into American Spiritualism.[94]

The syncretism of Eastern and Western ideologies was obvious in the writing of *Esoteric Buddhism*. By combining these concepts Blavatsky was creating a new religious movement that sought to pull together the various religions of the world in order to define her 'universal wisdom tradition' and defend the world against materialism. It should be further noted that in *Isis Unveiled* and even into *Esoteric Buddhism* Blavatsky's cosmological structure of the universe shared similar elements with Spiritualism. When Blavatsky had arrived in India in 1879, she was obviously influenced by Eastern philosophies, thus altering Lillie's original observation made in 1884. Instead of saying that 'Buddhism has been transformed into American Spiritualism' the terms should be rearranged and noted that *Esoteric Buddhism* presented a Western Esoteric flavor of Spiritualism that was being explained using Buddhist terminology.

5.15 *Esoteric Buddhism* and *The Secret Doctrine*

The concepts presented in *Esoteric Buddhism* are built upon and expounded in the later publication of *The Secret Doctrine*. There are various philosophical shifts in between these two works that would be expected over the course of a five year period. Primarily these shifts regarded the concept of spiritual evolution. *Esoteric Buddhism* laid down the frame work that *The Secret Doctrine* later filled in. One suggestion that explained the philosophical shifts from *Esoteric Buddhism* to *The Secret Doctrine* was postulated by Arthur Lillie though it resembled a conspiracy theory:

> I have fully noticed other discrepancies, the metempsychosis, the seven and the four principles etc. What was the meaning of this complete change of front? Soon I detected a logic in it. Madame Blavatsky's theosophy had one consistent principle— opportunism. Her 'Esoteric Buddhism' was designed to win over the rich Hindoos, and to do this she was obliged to dethrone Brahma, Vishnu, and Rama, and to put in their places the Mahatmas, the Dhyan Chohans. These Dhyan Chohans made the Kosmos as Mr. Sinnett tells us. But as they are still alive in Tibet they confront us with a difficulty. Without a world there could be no Dhyan Chohans, and without Dhyan Chohans there could be no world. Then Madame Blavatsky had to get rid of the Indian ghost worship. Her mind, as I have often stated, lacks originality. But a book by an eccentric Frenchman gave her a hint. The Abbe Louis Constant, under the pseudonym of Eliphas Lévi, had written several works on magic...Mr. Home came to Paris and quite eclipsed with magician with his marvels. Eliphas Lévi retaliated with a doctrine that he professed to find in the Kabala, the doctrine of shells...[95] Madame Blavatsky seized eagerly on this passage [Lévi's 'Dogme et Rituel de la Haute Magie,' vol. i. p. 262]. At once it played havoc with the visions of her rivals, the Yogis, and swept away the whole army of the Pitris that the Hindoos believed in. Also, it furnished a splendid stick for those wicked spiritualists of America who had snubbed her and accused her of cheating. But Madame Coulomb and Mr. Hodgson broke in upon her Indian day-dreams. Mr. Subba Row, the Sanskrit scholar, who helped her so much, discovered her fraud, and left the society. Mohini and B. J. Padshah "found," says Mr. Coleman, " bundles of blue and red pencils with which the Mahatma letters were written, also packs of Chinese envelopes, and bundles of Tibetan dresses for personating the Mahatmas." Another native, Babajee, made revelations. He confessed that Damodar and Madame Blavatsky exercised so complete an influence over him that he was obliged to attest all they told him. He saw the Russian lady write Mahatma letters, and was told that these great adepts would be very angry if he did not say that he had seen them. Damodar disappeared.[96]

Though Lillie appeared to be overtly critical of Blavatsky's intentions, it remains interesting to note that an intentional shift from *Esoteric Buddhism* to *The Secret Doctrine* was detected by one of Blavatsky's contemporaries. What seems more relevant was that this particular shift had to do with Blavatsky's desire to control her followers and that she managed this through her conceptualization of spiritual evolution. Blavatsky does move away from the concept of annihilation in *The Secret Doctrine*; however, in *Isis Unveiled*, the Mahatma Letters, and *Esoteric Buddhism* the doctrine is clearly presented. This is an interesting evolution because most Spiritualists detested the very concept of the annihilation of the soul favoring an eternal view of progress and spiritual evolution. Blavatsky's evolution away from annihilation after her Oriental shift remains a curious phenomenon. One of the conflicting philosophies between *Isis Unveiled* and *Esoteric Buddhism* concerned the eighth sphere where it is written that if a man is not good enough to live any longer he is sent to the eighth sphere and annihilated.[97]

It is curious to note that in *Isis Unveiled* the eighth sphere was not a permanent place and in some cases the monad (soul) could even leave this sphere after repenting or as Blavatsky noted 'he can, with the help of that glimpse of reason and consciousness left to him, repent...by exercising the remnants of his will-power, strive upward, and...struggle once more to the surface.'[98] However, in *Esoteric Buddhism* the eighth sphere was the end of the line for any monad who was sentenced there as 'this eighth sphere is out of circuit, a *cul de sac*, and the bourne from which it may be truly said no traveler returns.'[99] In *Esoteric Buddhism*, in order for a monad to be sentenced to annihilation the 'Ego must have developed a positive attraction for matter, a positive repulsion for spirituality which is its overwhelming force.'[100] In *The Secret Doctrine*, the entire concept of the eighth sphere would be regarded as a mistake that Sinnett had made in his explanation of the occult doctrine. Regarding annihilation *Esoteric Buddhism* quoted Eliphas Lévi: 'to be immortal in good one must identify oneself with God; to be immortal in evil with Satan...between these two poles vegetate and die without remembrance the useless portion of mankind.'[101] This direct quote illustrated that the soteriology of annihilation was, at the very least, in keeping with the philosophy of Lévi.[102] Blavatsky's use of Lévi's ideas will be explored in a later section.

5.16 *The Theosophist*

When the Theosophical Society relocated to India in 1879, there immediately became an issue with communications both within India and with the Western world. There had to be a method of communicating the Eastern exploits of the Society in a cost-effective manner. It was soon decided that in order to disseminate its teachings and give news updates, the Theosophical Society would create their own publication whose main purpose was to function as the official organ of the Theosophical Society. Thus, they established the *Theosophist* a monthly newspaper which propagated the Society's teachings. Olcott noted in his diary that:

> The *Theosophist* was founded in October 1879 and there appeared its first ten volumes 429 pages (royal 8vo) of translations from the Sanskrit, and 935 pages of original articles on Eastern religious, philosophically, and scientific subjects, mainly by writers of Oriental birth; several hundred lectures were given by myself [Blavatsky]?, besides hundreds more by our colleagues in India, America, and Ceylon.[103]

Blavatsky utilized the literary talents of Sinnett and Olcott to launch her own periodical that would disseminate the teachings of Theosophy. The title of this periodical was *The Theosophist: A Monthly Journal devoted to Oriental Philosophy, Art, Literature and Occultism: Embracing Mesmerism, Spiritualism, and Other Secret Sciences*; thus, solidifying the Oriental shift in Blavatsky's philosophy while still noting an 'embracing' view of Spiritualism. In the first issue, Blavatsky felt a need to distinguish her Western Esoteric Theosophy from Spiritualism and noted some important distinctions:

> The founders of our Society were mainly veteran Spiritualists, who had outgrown their first amazement at the strange phenomena, and felt the necessity to investigate the laws of mediumship to the very bottom. Their reading of medieval and ancient works upon the occult sciences had shown them that our modern phenomena were but repetitions of what had been seen, studied, and comprehended in former epochs...Proceeding in this, the Theosophists though they discovered some reasons to doubt the correctness of the spiritualistic theory that all the phenomena of the circles must of necessity be attributed solely to the action of spirits of our deceased friends...
> The reader will observe that the primary issue between the theosophical and spiritualistic theories of mediumistic phenomena is

that the Theosophists say the phenomena may be produced by more agencies than one, and the latter that but one agency can be conceded namely- the disembodied souls. There are other differences- as, for instance, that there can be such thing as the obliteration of the human individuality as the result of very evil environment; that good spirits seldom, if ever, cause physical manifestations', etc...

Theosophy can be styled the enemy of Spiritualism with no more propriety than of Mesmerism, or any other branch of Psychology...Theosophy with its design to search back into historic records for proof, may be regarded as the natural outcome of phenomenalistic Spiritualism, or as a touchstone to show the value of its pure gold. One must know both to comprehend what is Man.[104]

Thus, Blavatsky viewed Theosophy as the reformation of Spiritualism. A curious correspondence was recorded in the August 1882 edition of the *Theosophist* titled 'Spiritualism and Theosophy' that attempted to explain the differences between these two movements. Through a conversational style format the lines separating Theosophy and Spiritualism were explained through the format of several questions asked from a Calcutta correspondent:

(a) Is Occultism a science akin to Spiritualism? That Theosophy is a very ancient science which Spiritualism is a very modern manifestation of psychical phenomena. It has not yet passed the stage of experimental research

(b) What are the principal points in which the Theosophists and the Spiritualists differ? The difference is in our theories to account for the phenomena. We say they are mainly, though not always, due to the action of other influences than that of the disembodied conscious spirits of the dead. The Spiritualists affirm the contrary.

(c) Can a Spiritualist call himself a Theosophist without altering his faith? and vice versa? Yes; many excellent persons are both, and none need alter his faith.

(d) I understand you do not believe in Spiritualism- then how is it that a Spiritualist has been elected President for the Bengal Branch of the Theosophical Society? We do believe in the phenomena, but not as to their cause – as above remarked. There being no religious or other test- other than that of good moral character and sympathy with the objects of our Society, applied by us to those who seek for admission, the election of the venerable Babu Peary Chund Mittra, as President of our Bengal Branch, was not only most proper, but very desirable. He is certainly the most spiritual Theosophist and most theosophic Spiritualist we have ever met.[105]

It seemed evident that there was no discrepancy in an individual labeling themselves both a Theosophist and a Spiritualist in 1882. In another article published in the supplement to the *Theosophist* (during this same year) written by W. R. Frink , Frink endeavored to answer the claims that the Theosophical Society was established to destroy Spiritualism:

> Now I have carefully read every THEOSOPHIST that has been published since Colonel Olcott and Madame Blavatsky went to India…As to their attempt to supplant Spiritualism, I have seen nothing of the kind in their published speeched or writings. They differ from the Spiritualists in regard to the forces that produce the so-called spiritual phenomena, which they have a perfect right to do until Spiritualism proves itself more infallible than it is at present.[106]

Another example of defining the relationship between Spiritualism and Theosophy was found in an 1882 article written by an unsigned contributor (likely Blavatsky) which further clarified this issue:

> But to conclude for the present, surely there need be no hostility, as some Spiritual writers seem to have imagined between the Spiritualists and ourselves, merely because we bring for the consideration a new stock of ideas,-now, indeed, only as far as their application to modern controversies is concerned, old enough as measured by the ages that have passed over the earth since they were evolved. A gardener is not hostile to roses, because he prunes his bushes and proclaims the impropriety of letting bad shoots spring up from below the graft. With the Spiritualists, students of Occultism must always have bonds of sympathy which are unthought of in the blatant world of earth-bound materialism and superstitious credulity…Let them give us a hearing' let them recognize us as brother-worshippers of Truth, even though found in unexpected places….We bring our friends and brethren in Spiritualism no mere feather-headed fancies, in light-spun speculation, when we offer them some toil-worn fragments of the mighty mountain of Occult knowledge, at the base of whose hardly accessible heights we have learned to estimate their significance and appreciate their worth.[107]

Thus, a distinction between Occultism and Spiritualism was drawn though an acknowledgment that both movements adhered to the same truth as proposed above. In December 1881 an anonymous article was written (here again Blavatsky seemed to have been the likely author) this time evidencing the harmony between Theosophy and Spiritualism. This article described the reception of some of the Spiritualist magazines toward Theosophists and claims that Spiritualism has always been defended and even advocated in the pages of *The Theosophist*:

> From its beginning the THEOSOPHIST, if it has not always advocated, has, at least, warmly defended, Spiritualism, as a careful perusal of its back numbers will show. It has defended it from the attacks of Science, of Journalism, and against the denunciations of private individuals, while the *Spiritualist* has never lost an opportunity of caricaturing us. With Spiritualists as a body, never quarreled, nor do we ever mean to quarrel. Let our esteemed contemporary *Light* give credit for so much as least to those who profess themselves the enemies of Bigots, Hypocrites, and Pharisees.[108]

One of the most influential articles published in the Theosophist was the article 'Fragments of Occult' truth which attempted to distinguish Theosophy from Spiritualism in 1882 and puts forth the septenary constitution of humanity a drastic shift away from the trichotomy explained in *Isis Unveiled* in 1877.

5.17 'Fragments of Occult Truth'

One of Blavatsky's first attempts of dealing with the issues between Spiritualism and her Theosophical Society was found in a series of articles beginning in October 1881 and continuing into 1882 in *The Theosophist* titled 'Fragments of Occult Truth.' These 'Fragments' as they were designated in subsequent issues of *The Theosophist*, were based on the same idea as *Esoteric Buddhism* only summarized by a different recipient- A. O. Hume the noted ornithologist. The 'Fragments of Occult Truth' was a regular column in *The Theosophist* that was based on different mahatma letters received by Hume. These articles remain an integral part of understanding the tenets of the Theosophical Society and its public 'shift' away from American Spiritualism. This series started as a letter from W. Terry and concerned the interaction of Occultism and Spiritualism which was a request for clarification on the role of elementals in séances.

Hume responded to this letter by noting that Theosophists can be categorized into several groups including those who seek to revive their own religious traditions such as Buddhists, Hindus, etc., philosophers, philanthropists, agnostics, atheists, Spiritualists, Spiritists and

Occultists. It was further suggested that the main disagreement between Spiritualists and Theosophists was in their definition of particular terms. In other words, both groups employed the same terms only with differing meanings:

> These latter [the Occultists]are the only' Theosophists' who are really open to out correspondent's accusation and even these, if we look beyond the veil of words which more or less conceals the ideas of both Spiritualists and Occultists, will prove to differ less widely on these points from our correspondent than he seems to suppose. For, in this as in so many other cases, it is in a great measure to the different significations attached to the same terms by the two parties, that their apparent irreconcilable divergence is due. 'Words' as Bacon, we think says, 'mightily perplex the wisdom of the wisest, and like a Tartar's bow, shoot backwards into the minds of those that follow them,' and so here the conflict of opinions between Spiritualists and Occultists is solely due to the fact that the former (who overrate their quality and character) dignify by the name of 'spirits' certain *reliquiae* of deceased human beings, while the Occultists reserve the name of Spirit for the highest principle of human nature and treat those *reliquiae* as mere *eidolons*, or astral *simulacra* of the real spirit.

This argument seemed to be built on definitions; however, whether there was any real disagreement between these two movements remained ambiguous. Next, the harmonization of Theosophy with Spiritualism through a series of semantic arguments was followed by Blavatsky's enigmatic doctrine of the septenary composition of the soul (that was not explained in *Isis Unveiled*) which she claimed was first promulgated in the Chaldean *Book of Numbers*.[109] In the end, these articles were written to illustrate and reconcile the differences between Occultism and Spiritualism though this relationship still remained vague; however, Blavatsky's attitude would soon be revealed in a follow up article.

In an article found in the *Theosophist* in 1882, Blavatsky attempted to reconcile Theosophy with Spiritualism in defending her 'Fragments of Occult Truth' to William Stainton Moses which was in response to the 26 November 1881 issue of *Light* in which Moses noted that:

> The Spiritualist believes that it is possible for spirits of the departed to communicate with this earth. Whatever divergence of opinion there may be among us in respect of other matters, we are

agreed on this, the cardinal article of our faith....The consentient testimony of the most experienced among us agrees that, whether there be, or whether there be not, other agencies at work, the Spirits we know of are human Spirits who have once lived on this earth. To this the *Theosophist* returns the simple answer we are mistaken. No Spirits communicate with earth for the sufficient reason that they cannot. It is idle to argue further.[110]

Now this would appear to be an opportune moment for Blavatsky to clearly affirm this idea and thereby sever and demarcate Theosophy from Spiritualism; however, she replied in the following confusing manner explaining her 'Fragments of Occult Truth:'

> we nevertheless fail to detect in it such passages or ideas as justify M. A. (Oxon) in saying that our doctrine is 'one of complete antagonism with Spiritualism. It is not half so antagonistic as he believes it to be, as we will try to prove. The Spiritualist believes that it is possible for spirits of the departed to communicate with this earth,' says the writer . . . 'and to this the Theosophist returns the simple answer that we are mistaken.' ...Had 'M.A. Oxon.,' slightly modifying the construction of the above-quoted sentence – written instead that 'it is possible for spirits yet embodied on this earth to communicate with the spirits of the departed' – then would there have been hardly any antagonism at all to deplore. What we hold and do maintain is that all of the so-called '*physical* phenomena,' and 'materializations' especially, are produced by something, to which we refuse the name of 'spirit.' In the words of the President of our Berhampore Branch...'We, Hindus- (and along with them the European disciples of Eastern philosophy) are trying to *spiritualize* our grosser material *selves*, while the American and European Spiritualists are endeavouring in their *séance*-rooms to *materialize* spirits.' These words of wisdom well show the opposite tendencies of the Eastern and the Western minds – namely, that while the former are trying to purify *matter*, the latter do their best to degrade *spirit*. Therefore what we say is, that ninety-nine times out of one hundred, 'materializations' so-called, when *genuine*, (and whether they be partial or complete) are produced by what we call 'shells,' and occasionally, perhaps, by the living medium's *astral* body – but certainly *never*, in our humble opinion, by 'disembodied' spirits themselves... As for the rest, we are at one with the Spiritualists with but slight variances, more of form than of substance.[111]

Thus, Blavatsky's main disagreement with Spiritualism (even as late as 1882 well after her 'Oriental' shift) rested on the issue of semantics-Theosophists claimed to spiritualize themselves in order to communicate with spirits where as Spiritualists claimed to materialize the spirits. Either way communication was being achieved with departed spirits fulfilling the basic tenet of Spiritualism. As Blavatsky herself noted 'as for the rest, we are at one with the Spiritualists.' This article again evidenced the shifting attitude that Blavatsky held towards Victorian Spiritualism.

5.18 'Fragments of Occult Truth' Compared to *Isis Unveiled*: Discrepancies or Misunderstandings?

A seeming 'discrepancy' regarding the capability of spirit communications between the teachings presented in *Isis Unveiled* and in this series of articles titled 'Fragments of Occult Truth' was observed by a reader of the *Theosophist* who called themself the 'Caledonian Theosophist.' This reader noted that in 'Fragments' the Ego could not 'span the abyss separating its state from ours, or that it cannot descend into our atmosphere and reach us; that it attracts but cannot be attracted, or, in short, that no departed SPIRIT can visit us.' This reader continued to note that:

> In Vol I., page 67 of 'Isis,' I find it said that many of the spirits, subjectively controlling mediums, are human disembodied spirits, that their being benevolent or wicked in quality largely depends upon the medium's private morality, that 'they cannot materialize, but only project their aetherial reflections on the atmospheric waves.' On page 69: 'Not every one can attract human spirits, who likes. One of the most powerful attractions of our departed ones is their strong affection for those whom they have left on earth It draws them irresistibly, by degrees, into the current of the astral light vibrating between the person sympathetic to them an the universal soul.' On page 325: 'Sometimes, but rarely, the planetary spirits...produce them (subjective manifestations); sometimes the spirits of our translated and beloved friends, &c.'

Blavatsky responded to this allegation by claiming that this reader misunderstood these two ideas because they were 'uniform' as both concepts were derived from the same source 'the ADEPT BROTHERS:'

> Throughout 'Isis'-although an attempt was made in the in the introductory Chapter to show the great difference that exists between the terms 'soul and 'spirit;- one the reliquae of the personal

Ego, the other the pure essence of the spiritual INDIVIDUALI-TY- the term 'spirit; had to be often used in the sense given to it by the Spiritualists, as well as other similar conventional terms, as, otherwise, a still greater confusion would have been caused by our friend, should be thus understood:-On page 67 wherein it is stated that many of the spirits subjectively controlling mediums are human disembodied spirits,' &c. the word 'controlling; must not be understood in the sense of a 'spirit' possessing himself of the organism of a medium; nor that, in each case, it is a 'spirit;' for often it is but a shell in its preliminary stage of dissolution, when most of the physical intelligence and faculties are yet fresh and have not begun to disintegrate, or fade out. A 'spirit;' or, the spiritual Ego, cannot descend to the medium, but it can attract the spirit of the latter to itself, and it can do this only during the two intervals- before and after its 'gestation period'…

Interval the second lasts so long as the merits of the old Ego entitle the being to reap the fruit of its reward in its new regenerated Egoship. It occurs after the gestation period is over, and the new spiritual Ego is reborn- like the fabled Phoenix from its ashesfrom the old one. The locality, which the former inhabits, is called by the northern Buddhist Occultists 'Deva-chan,' the word answering, perhaps, to Paradise or the Kingdom of Heaven of the Christian elect. Having enjoyed a time of bliss, proportionate to his deserts, the new personal Ego gets re-incarnated into a personality when the remembrance of his previous Egoship, of course, fades out, and he can 'communicate' no longer with his fellowmen on the planet he has left forever, as the individual he was there konwn (sic) to be. After numberless re-incarnations, and on numerous planets and in various spheres, a time will come, at the end of the maha-Yug or great cycle, when each individuality will have become so spiritualized that, before its final absorption into the One, its series of past personal existence will marshal themselves before him in a retrospective order like the many days of some one period of man's existence.

… a pure medium's Ego can be drawn to and made, for an instant, to unite in a magnetic (?) relation with a real disembodied spirit, whereas the will of an impure medium can only confabulate with the astral soul, or 'shell,' of the deceased. The former possibility explains those extremely rare cases of direct writing in recognized autographs and of messages from the higher class of disembodied intelligences. We should say then that the personal morality of the medium would be a fair test of the genuineness of the manifestation. As quoted by our friend, 'affection to those whom they have left on earth' is 'one of the most powerful attractions' between two loving spirits- the embodied and the disembodied one.[112]

Thus, the discrepancies between Blavatsky's teachings were again observed by her contemporary readers though the differences between Spiritualism and Theosophy remained an issue of semantics-whether one believed that the 'spirit' came to the medium or the medium went to the spirit communication between the spirit-world and the physical world remained a possibility. Furthermore, Blavatsky's belief that the soul would eventually become absorbed into 'the One' following numberless incarnations illustrated the influence of Hindu and Buddhist traditions which had been combined with her belief in the existence of multiple spheres a popular belief in Swedenborgianism and Spiritualism. This idea of a final absorption would change in *The Secret Doctrine* (1888).

5.19 *The Secret Doctrine*
Advertisements for *The Secret Doctrine* appeared in the *Theosophist* as early as April 1884 claiming that it would be 'a new version of Isis Unveiled' which was supposed to be released 'in monthly parts.'[113] In 1888 Blavatsky compiled these ideas into what became her magnum opus- *The Secret Doctrine*. This two-volume set was a monumental work that consisted of roughly 1,500 pages and 'contained an explanation of four ideals: evolution; man's septenary constitution; karma and reincarnation; and after death states.'[114] This work exemplified Blavatsky's apparent shift away from Spiritualism towards occultism and Orientalism. Blavatsky wrote *The Secret Doctrine* as her vindication from the various attacks being waged on her from all sides including the Kiddle plagiarism of 1883, the testimony of Emma and Alexis Coulomb who went public in 1884 accusing Blavatsky of manipulating her followers through the fabrication of phenomena, and Richard Hodgson and his highly degrading investigative report written for the Society of Psychical Research published in 1885 (which also claimed that Blavatsky was a Russian spy).[115] This book provided Blavatsky an opportunity to prove that the Theosophical Society was not built merely on acts of phenomena (whether legitimate or otherwise); rather, it was the custodian of an ancient wisdom tradition derived from a global network of hidden adept 'masters' that had authorized Blavatsky for the first time in the history of humanity to reveal *The Secret Doctrine*. Despite this extraordinary claim, the method that Bla-

vatsky employed in writing *The Secret Doctrine* would have precedence in Spiritualism as noted below.

5.20 The Language of *The Secret Doctrine*

Blavatsky employed a similar method in composing *The Secret Doctrine* as she did with her *Isis Unveiled*; however, no longer did Blavatsky receive messages through the receipt of mysterious letters precipitating out of thin air, she now peered directly into the astral light and was able to transcribe an ancient metaphysical manuscript that contained the abstruse stanzas of Dzyan:

> *The Secret Doctrine* was copied from a mysterious book that is described in its opening chapter: An Archaic Manuscript- a collection of palm leaves made impermeable to water, fire, and air, by some specific unknown process- is before the writer's eye...The Stanzas which form the thesis of every section are given throughout in their modern translated version, as it would be worse than useless to make the subject still more difficult by introducing archaic phraseology of the original, with its puzzling style and words. Extracts are given from the Chinese Thibetan and Sansrkit translations of the original Senzar Commentaries and Glosses on the Book of Dzyan- these being now rendered for the first time into a European language.[116]

The Secret Doctrine was largely a commentary on stanzas found in the Book of Dzyan which were originally written in an unknown language that Blavatsky identified as Senzar. This strange language appeared to have been a fictitious Eastern-style of alphabet.

The discovery of mystical objects with strange writing was a common element in the development of nineteenth-century Western religious movements. A similar experience was described in the story of Joseph Smith and the origination of the book of Mormon. It was claimed that on 22 September 1827 Joseph Smith was directed to a series of golden plates buried in the mountains of western NY. Upon examining these mysterious plates, Smith realized that he was unable to understand the strange language referred to only as 'Reformed Egyptian.' It was only with the aid of a pair of glasses made from stone that Smith was able to translate this strange language and went on to publish the contents of these plates in 1830 under the title the Book of Mormon. Thus, the discovery of an unknown language had precedence in the religious climate of this time period.

Senzar was not exclusively found in the astral light. It has been recorded in her letters to Sinnett, that Blavatsky actually used this language to write hidden messages that at one time confounded Mrs. Coulomb who mistook Senzar for a Russian code which she believed Blavatsky (working as a spy) was using to communicate with her Russian commanding officers:

> Coulomb stole a 'queer looking paper' and gave it to the missionaries with the assurance this was a cipher used by the Russian spies (!)…."It is one of my Senzar MSS,' I answer. I am perfectly confident of it for one of the sheets of my book with numbered pages is missing I defy anyone but a Tibetan occultist to make it out, if it is this.[117]

Blavatsky's employment of an unknown language that only she could decipher appeared to be a common element in pre-Spiritualist philosophies as prefigured by Frederica Hauffe the Seeress of Prevorst (1801-1832). Hauffe referred to an 'inner voice' indecipherable by most. She best explained the type of language as 'bear[ing] close resemblance to the Eastern tongue.'[118] It is curious to note that this was not the only connection between the Theosophical Society and the Seeress of Prevorst as Frank Podmore noted in his *Modern Spiritualism*.

Podmore noted three characteristics of Hauffe's psychic abilities: 1) the proofs of her clairvoyant abilities in fortune telling and communicating with ghosts, 2) 'the physical disturbances which were observed in her presence', 3) and her extraordinary revelations on things spiritual.'[119] Thus, Blavatsky's translation of an unknown 'Eastern tongue,' her ability to cause phenomena or 'physical disturbances', and her psychic 'revelations' which she could see through the 'astral light' were all prefigured in the career of Frederica Hauffe the Seeress of Prevorst back in 1832. Also, worth observing was Hauffe's belief in historical cycles 'which had relation apparently to spiritual conditions and the passage of time.'[120] Hauffe suggested a cyclical view of time which Blavatsky first promulgated in *Isis Unveiled* and developed more fully in *The Secret Doctrine*.[121] Though it seemed that Blavatsky may have derived her view of cyclical time from Hauffe, Blavatsky never attributed her cyclical cosmology to this seeress. Instead, Blavatsky chose to connect her view of cyclical time with the Western Orientalists such as Charles Coleman and his *The Mythology of the Hindus With Notices of Various Mountain and Island Tribes* (1832) in

Isis Unveiled and in *The Secret Doctrine* she associated her cyclical cosmology with H. H. Wilson's translation of the *Vishnu Purana: A System or Hindu Mythology and Tradition* (1864). Despite this 'Orientalist' connection, Blavatsky seemed familiar with Hauffee as mentioned in page xxiv in the introduction to *Isis Unveiled* and through Olcott's articles printed in the 1886 volume of the *Theosophist*.

5.21 The Writing of *The Secret Doctrine*

The method of writing *The Secret Doctrine* was described by the Countess of Wachtmeister- Blavatsky's housemate during her residency in Wurzburg from 1885 until her departure on 8 May 1886:

> when I walked into HPB's writing room, I found the floor strewn with sheets of discarded manuscript. I asked the meaning of this scene of confusion, and she replied: 'Yes, I have tried twelve times to write this one page correctly, and each time Master says it is wrong. I think I shall go mad, writing it so often; but leave me alone; I will not pause until I have conquered it, even if I have to go on all night.[122]

Blavatsky's 'masters' took an active role in the compilation of *The Secret Doctrine*. Blavatsky explained that her part in this writing process of this enigmatic work:

> I make what I can only describe as a sort of vacuum in the air before me, and fix my sight and will upon it, and soon scene after scene passes before me like the successive pictures of a diorama, or, if I need a reference or information from some book, I fix my mind intently, and the astral counterpart of the book appear and from it I take what I need. ... Master says it is right now, so let us go in and have some tea.[123]

As for the historical events surrounding the actual publication of *The Secret Doctrine*, Kirby Van Mater articulately summarized these details in his article 'The Writing of The Secret Doctrine':

> HPB had long been disappointed with her financial arrangements with J. W. Bouton of New York for the publication of *Isis Unveiled* and, in consequence, she was determined to have financial control of *The Secret Doctrine* in both the United States and England. In May 1888 she asked W. Q. Judge to secure copyright in her name in the United States for her book, and to publish it in the U.S. either from 'stereo plates, or only the moulds' sent from England.

Judge, after consultation with J. W. Lovell, wrote Bert Keightley that the best method to follow for 1,000 sheets or more was for London to ship printed sheets, to be folded, collated, and bound in the U.S. Copyright could be obtained in HPB's name as she was an American citizen, if all particulars about the book were furnished as requested. However, HPB was to understand 'that the emission of the American and English editions should be simultaneous'. After delays in England the sheets, folded and collated, for 1,000 copies of the first volume of the SD arrived in New York City on the steamer *Britannia*, Friday, October 19th. Judge wrote that the deadline of October 27th for 'publishing' probably could not be met by him. Finally, on October 31st H. P. Blavatsky cabled Judge asking 'Have you published?' Judge cabled back 'Yes, Book Out Nov 1'. Volume II was published December 28th.[124]

The Countess Wachtmeister recorded a detailed account of the events surrounding the writing of *The Secret Doctrine* in her work *Reminiscences of H. P. Blavatsky and The Secret Doctrine* published in 1893. One of most memorable characteristics that impressed the countess about Blavatsky was her perseverance. The countess vividly recounted the words of Blavatsky after reading the *Report of the Society for Psychical Research*. Blavatsky cried, 'I am the scapegoat. I am made to bear all the sins of the Society, and now that I am dubbed the greatest impostor of the age, and a Russian spy into the bargain, who will listen to me or read *The Secret Doctrine?*'[125] Blavatsky's concern for her integrity seemed like a legitimate response to this investigation which went so far as to accuse her of being a spy for the Russian government. In February of 1886 similar emotions emerged with the printing of Blavatsky's handwritten 'confession' to Solovyoff. These were difficult years for the Theosophical Society, but as Blavatsky eventually came to realize her opportunity for vindication would be through the publication of her magnum opus- *The Secret Doctrine*. In a letter written to Sinnett in October 1885, Blavatsky expressed her feelings that this book would be her redemption:

> I am very busy on Secret D. The thing at New York is repeated-only far clearer and better. *I begin to think it shall vindicate us.* Such pictures, panoramas, scenes, antediluvian dramas, with all that! Never saw or heard better. Your calculations, 'the best and truest that can be given at this end of the 5000 y. of Kaliyug.' Watch your impressions and turn your back on the S.P.R. and its rabid idiots (emphasis added).[126]

There were two individuals who were particularly instrumental in preparing and organizing *The Secret Doctrine*- the Cambridge educated physician Archibald Keightley (1859-1930) and his cousin (who was also studied law at Cambridge) - Bertram Keightley (1860–1944). Bertram, in recollecting his initial view on *The Secret Doctrine*, stated that '*The Secret Doctrine* was destined to be by far the most important contribution of this century to the literature of Occultism; though even then the in choate and fragmentary character of much of the work led me to think that careful revision and much re-arrangement would be needed before the manuscript would be fit for publication.'[127] This appeared to have been an understatement since, as Bertram pointed out there was a supreme lack of a central thesis and consecutiveness. Archibald concurred with Betram's sentiments 'What I saw was a mass of MSS with no definite arrangement, much of which had been patiently and industriously copied by the Countess Wachtmeister.'[128] Archibald went on to conclude that 'all through the summer Bertram Keightley and I were engaged in reading, re-reading, copying and correcting.'[129] After dealing with this work for nearly eight years, Blavatsky eventually arrived at the point where she 'washed her hands' entirely of the manuscript placing the difficult task of editing this grandiose manuscript into the hands of the Keightley cousins. The Keightleys developed a plan for organizing this unorganized work, dividing it into three parts: 1) the Stanzas and Commentaries, 2) Symbolism, and, 3) Science.[130]

5.22 Contents of *The Secret Doctrine*

The Secret Doctrine was written to establish three fundamental positions: 1) That an omnipresent, eternal, boundless, and immutable supreme being existed that is the infinite and eternal cause- the root of all that was, is, or ever shall be, 2) the eternity of the universe is a boundless plane that is periodically the playground of numberless universes that are cyclically appearing and disappearing; and, 3) the identity of all souls with the universal soul, and the spiritual evolution through the cycle of incarnation in accordance with the cyclic and karmic law through the whole term.[131] Carl Jackson noted this book's relation to *Isis Unveiled*: '*Isis* had outlined Theosophy's major teachings; *Secret Doctrine* attempted to provide a systematic explanation.'[132] This work was divided into two volumes 1) Cosmogenesis which dealt with the origin of the universe and 2) Anthropogenesis which explained the evolution of humanity.

The first volume 'Cosmogenesis' was concerned with disseminating Blavatsky's elaborate cosmology. The entire universe was said to follow a cyclical time pattern of millions of years divided into 'yugas' and 'kalpas' based on the cosmology exhibited in H.H. Wilson's *Vishnu Purana*. The entire cyclical universe revolved around two main periods of existence- activity which Blavatsky labeled using the Eastern terms 'days and nights of Brahma' and the intermittent 'rests' were called Pralayas (this same terminology was earlier employed in *Isis Unveiled* and *Esoteric Buddhism*). The concept of rounds, root races, and the astral light were further explicated from their initial appearance in *Esoteric Buddhism* in connection with the seven spheres and planets. The sevenfold (septenary) constitution of the soul was also expanded to apply to the entire universe except the One Supreme Being who remained outside of human comprehension. Blavatsky in a very circular manner explained the process of emanation from the divine which included her ascent/descent theory and the creation of a celestial hierarchy of various mediations and a varying level of planetary spirits. Included in this cosmology was Blavatsky's Eastern idea of *fohat* which provided the link between matter and spirit and was the electric ever-propelling life force of the universe. Blavatsky continued expanding many of the basic ideas put forth in *Esoteric Buddhism* in this first volume including the evolution of the soul beginning as an elemental and then incarnating through the various 'kingdoms' of life from mineral to vegetable to animal to man and then eventually into a god-like being.

Another main theme found in this first volume was the concept of 'maya' an Eastern term denoting an illusion which 'is an element which enters into all finite things, for everything that exists has only a relative, not an absolute, reality, since that appearance which the hidden noumenon assumes for any observer depends upon his power of cognition.'[133] Despite Blavatsky's use of the Eastern term 'maya' a similar theory was purported by her contemporary- Mary Baker Eddy in her *Science and Health*. In fact, in her work Eddy used the word 'illusion' over seventy times indicating the importance of this theory in her nineteenth-century religious movement known as Christian Science. Eddy in solidarity with Blavatsky noted that 'Illusion says, 'I am man;' but this belief is far from actuality. From beginning to end mortals are composed of human beliefs.'[134] An article in the *Woman's Herald* revealed that it was not unheard of in the nineteenth century for people to confuse Christian Science as a branch of Theosophy likely because of their similar ideas of reality.[135]

The second volume 'Anthropogenesis' set forth the subject of personal evolution and the history of each individual root race. The classification of root races was similar to the basic structure explained in *Esoteric Buddhism*. This volume also dissected the chronology of the universe focusing on prehistoric ages and continually challenged the Darwinian theory of evolution throughout its pages. Furthermore, this work expounded upon Blavatsky's complicated racial anthropology and attempted to pinpoint the true origin of humanity. Also, Blavatsky developed and validated the ascent/descent theory mentioned in *Isis Unveiled* concerning the soul's descent into matter and its subsequent ascension back into a spirit composition. Blavatsky further attempted to assimilate the various world religions and chronologies into her own universal tradition; therefore, Jesus, Osiris, and Hermes were all the same soul reincarnated at different stages in the history of the world based on the all pervading septenary law.[136] Thus, this belief evidenced that Blavatsky viewed *The Secret Doctrine* as comprising the one universal tradition which served as the perfect form from which all the world religions had been derived.

Underlying both of these volumes was the philosophical framework of Eliphas Lévi (1810–1875), the influence of Alexander Winchell's *World-Life* (1883), and H. H. Wilson's *Vishnu Purana*. Drawing on an allegorical biblical hermeneutic, Blavatsky created her own complex narrative of world history and prehistory by combining ancient philosophy and world mythologies into one super religion-Theosophy. Karma appeared as the guiding principle through this eternal cosmological structure of life and death, reward and punishment. Wouter Hanegraaff the respected Western esoteric scholar came to the following realization relating to Blavatsky's conceptualization of karma in this work:

> If souls progressed through many lives (whether on earth or not), could that process be explained in 'scientific' terms acceptable to a modern science? I suggest that Blavatsky had not yet solved this problem when she wrote *Isis Unveiled*, but subsequently realized that karma provided the long sought-for answer. The index to *Isis Unveiled* lists a considerable number of references to metempsychosis, reincarnation and transmigration, but only three to karma (plus a fourth to the appendix added in 1886...) In *The Secret Doctrine*, on the others hand, karma had definitely moved to center stage, while reincarnation and its cognates are mentioned far less often.[137]

Bruce Campbell attempted to summarize the overall theme of this influential work:

> *The Secret Doctrine* is a treatise on individual human destiny, one that places moral problems on individual development against the backdrop of cosmic evolution and, in fact, makes the development of inner man the heart and reason of evolution…*The Secret Doctrine* combined ideas from Asian religions with a cosmological framework that gave meaning to individual destiny within an involuntary and evolutionary framework. [138]

5.23 *The Secret Doctrine* and Spiritualism

While *Isis Unveiled* devoted an entire section towards validating Spiritualist phenomena, *The Secret Doctrine* focused on the deeper metaphysical questions such as the origin of the universe, the cosmological cycles, and the nature of the One unknowable being.

Another purpose for writing *Isis Unveiled* appeared to have been Blavatsky's opportunity to define the 'unique' belief structures of the Theosophical Society and set it further apart from other Spiritualist mainstream groups.[139] In *The Secret Doctrine*, Blavatsky was less concerned with differentiating between her group and other organizations and instead created an extensive philosophy based upon contemporaneous scientific theories, her interpretation of ancient texts, Eastern belief structures, allegorizing biblical passage, and reinterpreting her earlier work. Blavatsky assimilated the writings of the most notable scientists of her day including Huxley, Darwin, and Lyell. Blavatsky's *The Secret Doctrine* fully represented the 'Oriental shift' in Blavatsky's Theosophical Society and rarely referenced the subject of Spiritualism within its pages; however, there are some instances where allusions are made.

One reference to Spiritualism in particular, proved that for a short while Blavatsky disconnected with the main tenet of Spiritualism- the belief that the living could contact the dead through her belief that mediums could only channel Nirmanakayas [an Eastern term for a guardian angel]:[140]

> Many are those among the Spiritual Entities, who have incarnated bodily in man, since the beginning of his appearance, and how, for all that, still exist as independently as they did before, in the infinitudes of Space…To put it more clearly: the invisible Entity may be bodily present on earth without abandoning, however, its status and functions in the supersensuous regions. If this needs explana-

tion, we can do no better than remind the reader of like cases in Spiritualism, though such cases are very rare, at least as regards the nature of the Entities incarnating, or taking possession of a medium."[141]

Blavatsky noted that it was possible for a Nirmanakaya to possess a medium though only in rare cases. There was a foot note in the above section clarifying this idea: 'The so-called 'Spirits' that may occasionally possess themselves of the bodies of mediums are not the Monads or Higher Principles of disembodied personalities. Such a Spirit can *only* be either an Elementary, or – a Nirmanakaya (emphasis added)."[142] A Nirmanakaya was a soul that had been given the choice between entering a state of bliss or reincarnating on the earth 'for the sake of doing good to the world."[143]

Blavatsky's dogmatic assertion that a departed 'ego' was not able to contact the living was slightly amended in her 1889 *The Key to Theosophy* where this possibility became possible though again under rare circumstances:

> during the few days that follow immediately the death of a person and before the Ego passes into the Devachanic state. Whether any living mortal, save a few exceptional cases—(when the intensity of the desire in the dying person to return for some purpose forced the higher consciousness *to remain awake,* and therefore it was really the *individuality,* the "Spirit" that communicated)—has derived much benefit from the return of the spirit into the *objective* plane is another question. The spirit is dazed after death and falls very soon into what we call '*pre-devachanic* unconsciousness.'

This silence concerning Spiritualism seemed related to the soul's post-mortem evolution. In *Isis Unveiled* and *Esoteric Buddhism* there was a circle of necessity following physical death followed by an entrance into either Avitchi, Devachan, or the eighth sphere; in *The Secret Doctrine* the soul was immediately placed in the region of Devachan where it could not return under any circumstances.

Blavatsky's main goal in *The Secret Doctrine* appeared to be the setting forth of her own philosophical ideas which she defended by proving that they were not original to her and had historical precedence in ancient and modern sources. In propagating her ideas Blavatsky drew upon multiple conflicting ideologies and harmonized them to fit into her own world view. To Blavatsky, Theosophy was empirically verifiable (through science, psychic powers, and history).

Theosophy was not simply a religion, but a scientifically provable theory. Brendan French made the following summarization:

> [Theosophy was] announced as scientifically-generated, historically verifiable, and empirically-testable: in short, *as fact*. Recognising that hers was an age characterised by concerns over facticity, Blavatsky asserted that teachings had been mediated to her by document so remarkable...antiquity, and –crucially- by a Brotherhood of Masters whose perennial task it was to oversee human development. Theosophy, thus was presented as nothing less than an empirically-verifiable revelation.[144]

Thus, *The Secret Doctrine* was really not a secret at all; it had existed across the world both in the scriptures of its major movements and in the new discipline of physical science and evolutionary theory- the real secret was how to harmonize these conflicting world views into one unified philosophy.

5.24 *The Key to Theosophy*

In 1889, while engaged in writing a third volume to *The Secret Doctrine* and editing the French Theosophical periodical *La Revue Theosophique*, Blavatsky wrote a conversational, question-and-answer style, 310-page work called *The Key to Theosophy* that explained the basic tenets of the Theosophical Society. This work employed a similar literary style to Colonel Olcott's 1881 book *A Buddhist Catechism* which disseminated Buddhist philosophy to the Western world. *The Key to Theosophy* was not intended to be an all inclusive treatise of the Theosophical Society; rather, it was only a simple explanation of some of the basic tenets of the Society. The subject of this work included the septenary constitution of man, reincarnation, karma, the afterlife state of the soul, and an explanation on the unity of all things.

Blavatsky mentioned the 'apologetic' nature of this work in a letter written to Jirah D. Buck during her stay in Fontainebleau, France in 1889: 'Unfortunately, my *Key to Theosophy* is not yet ready, since I received the last proofs; but there seems to be some hitch with Judge. Whether he has secured the copyright in America or not, I do not know...This 'Key' will answer many an objection; there are some 250 pages of it of an 8vo volume.[145]

5.25 Spiritualism and the *Key to Theosophy*

In this work 'some care had been taken in distinguishing some part of what is true from what is false in Spiritualistic teachings as to the post-mortem life, and to showing the true nature of Spiritualistic phenomena."[146] Again the relationship between Theosophy and Spiritualism remained undefined even in 1889 fourteen years after the establishment of the Theosophical Society which illustrated the long standing ambiguity associated with these two movements. It seemed that multiple people could not understand their distinctions including their own leaders. Also, adding to this confusion was that Blavatsky herself shifted between harmonizing Spiritualism and Theosophy while at other times attempting to separate them distinctly. There are several sections in this work that attempt a bold resolution concerning the relationship between Theosophy and Spiritualism. The question was direct posited: Do you believe in Spiritualism? -to which Blavatsky replied:

> If by 'Spiritualism' you mean the explanation which Spiritualists give of some abnormal phenomena, then decidedly *we do not*. They maintain that these manifestations are all produced by the 'spirits' of departed mortals, generally their relatives, who return to earth, they say, to communicate with those they have loved or to whom they are attached. We deny this point blank. We assert that the spirits of the dead cannot return to earth—save in rare and exceptional cases, of which I may speak later; nor do they communicate with men except by *entirely subjective means*. That which does appear objectively, is only the phantom of the ex-physical man. But in *psychic*, and so to say, 'Spiritual' Spiritualism, we do believe, most decidedly.[147]

> Do you reject the phenomena also? 'Assuredly not—save cases of conscious fraud.' How do you account for them, then?
> In many ways. The causes of such manifestations are by no means so simple as the Spiritualists would like to believe. Foremost of all, the *deus ex machina* of the so-called 'materializations' is usually the astral body or 'double' of the medium or of some one present. This *astral* body is also the producer or operating force in the manifestations of slatewriting, 'Davenport'-like manifestations, and so on.[148]

> This means that you reject the philosophy of Spiritualism *in toto*?
> If by 'philosophy' you mean their crude theories, we do. But they have no philosophy, in truth. Their best, their most intellectual and earnest defenders say so. Their fundamental and only unimpeachable truth, namely, that phenomena occur through mediums controlled by invisible forces and intelligences—no one, except a blind materialist of the 'Huxley big toe' school, will or *can* deny.[149]

Thus, in this excerpt Blavatsky revealed that the one undisputed truth of Spiritualism was that phenomena occurred through mediums by the workings of invisible forces, to which she expressed her solidarity. Blavatsky then continued on to define the establishment of the Theosophical Society in relation to Spiritualism:

> I was told that the Theosophical Society was originally founded to crush Spiritualism and belief in the survival of the individuality in man?

> You are misinformed. Our beliefs are all founded on that immortal individuality. But then, like so many others, you confuse *personality* with individuality. Your Western psychologists do not seem to have established any clear distinction between the two. Yet it is precisely that difference which gives the key-note to the understanding of Eastern philosophy, and which lies at the root of the divergence between the Theosophical and Spiritualistic teachings. And though it may draw upon us still more the hostility of some Spiritualists, yet I must state here that it is Theosophy which is the *true* and unalloyed Spiritualism, while the modern scheme of that name is, as now practised by the masses, simply transcendental materialism.[150]

> I understand to a certain extent; out I see that your teachings are far more complicated and metaphysical than either Spiritualism or current religious thought. Can you tell me, then, what has caused this system of Theosophy which you support to arouse so much interest and so much animosity at the same time?[151]

> Pray understand me. I do not speak against real Spiritualism, but against the modern movement which goes under that name, and the so-called philosophy invented to explain its phenomena.[152]

It seems here (again) that Blavatsky was recanting her earlier alignment with Spiritualism. The following section illustrates why Blavatsky disagreed with the process of channeling spirits through materializations:

> Finally, I say, what I have never ceased repeating orally and in print for fifteen years: While some of the so-called 'spirits' do not know what they are talking about, repeating merely—like poll-parrots—what they find in the mediums' and other people's brains, others are most dangerous, and can only lead one to evil. These are two self evident facts. Go into spiritualistic circles of the

Allan Kardec school, and you find 'spirits' asserting re-incarnation and speaking like Roman Catholics born. Turn to the 'dear departed ones' in England and America, and you will hear them denying re-incarnation through thick and thin, denouncing those who teach it, and holding to Protestant views. Your best, your most powerful mediums, have all suffered in health of body and mind. Think of the sad end of Charles Foster, who died in an asylum, a raving lunatic; of Slade, an epileptic; of Eglinton—the best medium now in England—subject to the same. Look back over the life of D. D. Home, a man whose mind was steeped in gall and bitterness, who never had a good word to say of anyone whom he suspected of possessing psychic powers, and who slandered every other medium to the bitter end. This Calvin of Spiritualism suffered for years from a terrible spinal disease, brought on by his intercourse with the 'spirits,' and died a perfect wreck. Think again of the sad fate of poor Washington Irving Bishop. I knew him in New York, when he was fourteen, and he was undeniably a medium. It is true that the poor man stole a march on his 'spirits,' and baptised them 'unconscious muscular action,' to the great *gaudium* of all the corporations of highly learned and scientific fools, and to the replenishment of his own pocket. But *de mortuis nil nisi bonum;* his end was a sad one. He had strenuously concealed his epileptic fits—the first and strongest symptom of genuine mediumship— and who knows whether he was dead or in a trance when the *postmortem* examination was performed? His relatives insist that he was alive, if we are to believe Pveuter's telegrams. Finally, behold the veteran mediums, the founders and prime movers of modern spiritualism—the Fox sisters. After more than forty years of intercourse with the 'Angels,' the latter have led them to become incurable sots, who are now denouncing, in public lectures, their own life-long work and philosophy as a fraud.[133]

Thus, Blavatsky believed that channeling elementals would eventually lead to physical ailments. Despite this attempt to distance herself from Spiritism (and Spiritualism), in *The Key to Theosophy* Blavatsky still admitted that it was possible for 'the communication of the living with the disembodied spirit?'

> Yes, there is a case, and even two exceptions to the rule. The first exception is during the few days that follow immediately the death of a person and before the Ego passes into the Devachanic state. Whether any living mortal, save a few exceptional cases—(when the intensity of the desire in the dying person to return for some purpose forced the higher consciousness *to remain awake,* and

THE THEOSOPHICAL SOCIETY

therefore it was really the *individuality*, the 'Spirit' that communicated)—has derived much benefit from the return of the spirit into the *objective* plane is another question. The spirit is dazed after death and falls very soon into what we call '*pre-devachanic* unconsciousness.' The second exception is found in the *Nirmanakayas*... It is the name given to those who, though they have won the right to Nirvana and cyclic rest—*(not* 'Devachan,' as the latter is an illusion of our consciousness, a happy dream, and as those who are fit for Nirvana must have lost entirely every desire or possibility of the world's illusions)—have out of pity for mankind and those they left on earth renounced the Nirvanic state. Such an adept, or Saint, or whatever you may call him, believing it a selfish act to rest in bliss while mankind groans under the burden of misery produced by ignorance, renounces Nirvana, and determines to remain invisible *in spirit* on this earth. They have no material body, as they have left it behind; but otherwise they remain with all their principles even *in astral life* in our sphere. And such can and do communicate with a few elect ones, only surely not with *ordinary* mediums.

Thus, despite any other philosophical debates or disagreements about reincarnation or the septenary division of the soul it seemed that Theosophy still made provision for the basic tenet of Spiritualism; therefore, no matter how articulately Blavatsky attempted to demarcate between Theosophy and Spiritualism, her written philosophy still remained aligned with the basic requirement of Spiritualism as late as 1889. Blavatsky seemed to admit to this fact later in the *Key to Theosophy*:

> Is M.A. Oxon a Spiritualist? Quite so, and the only *true* Spiritualist I know of, though we may still disagree with him on many a minor question. Apart from this, no Spiritualist comes nearer to the occult truths than he does. Like any one of us he speaks incessantly 'of the surface dangers that beset the ill-equipped, featherheaded muddler with the occult, who crosses the threshold without counting the cost.' Our only disagreement rests in the question of 'Spirit Identity.' Otherwise, I, for one, coincide almost entirely with him, and accept the three propositions he embodied in his address of July, 1884. It is this eminent Spiritualist, rather, who disagrees with us, not we with him.[154]

Blavatsky believed her Theosophy was a purer form of Spiritualism. She further claimed that the Theosophical Society had no qualms with Spiritualists; rather, it seemed that the animosity came primarily

BLAVATSKY'S 'AUTOMATIC' WRITINGS

from the Spiritualists towards the Theosophists. Though Blavatsky accepted the Spiritualist phenomena as the work of supernatural agents; nonetheless, she maintained that these spirits were not the same beings that the mediums were seeking to communicate with and continued to hold that Theosophy was superior to Spiritualism throughout her writings. The point of this work is to determine whether Theosophy remained in alignment with Spiritualism.

5.26 One Spiritualist's Review of *The Key to Theosophy*

One reviewer (referred to only as an 'authority') noted the 'Key to Theosophy' and its importance to the ongoing debate between Theosophists and Spiritualists in *Light* published 23 November 1889:

> It might have been called a Catechism of Theosophy, and in that aspect is far ahead of most handbooks. Its fourteen sections discuss, in the form of question and answer, various points on which we crave enlightenment, and (of course) omit several which seem to us important....And though we may recur to some of them hereafter and discuss them in more detail, our impression is that a careful analysis would show that the crucial points in the divergence between Spiritualists and Theosophists still need light.[155]

Again the ambiguity between these two movements was revealed in this above review as no consensus on the role of Theosophy within the Spiritualist movement had been derived even as late as November 1889. One public (secular) reporter was not as kind in their review of this work though they still noted a relationship between Theosophy and Spiritualism:

> It is impossible to make very clear and simple that which is so strange to the average modern reader that it requires in part for its expression a new vocabulary. Briefly and in modern terms this philosophy is a spiritualized Pantheism. It makes the universe the emanation or reflection of the Divine, Universal Spirit, and man, as a spark of the Divine fire, capable in his higher development of becoming one with it. As to universal processes it accepts the modern theory of physical evolution, and extends it to a spiritual evolution. Theosophy combats modern Spiritualism as commonly held and explained by it votaries, while admitting certain elements of genuineness in some of its phenomena but referring them to different causes. ...Anyone who wishes to become familiar with the leading features of Theosophical doctrine will find them set

forth in this book about as clearly as the nature of the subject permits.[156]

5.27 *The Voice of Silence*

The Voice of Silence was published in 1889 just a few months apart from *The Key To Theosophy*. *The Voice of Silence* was based upon 'The Books of the Golden Precepts' the same source that the Book of Dzyan was allegedly derived from and by which Blavatsky supposedly based her *Secret Doctrine* upon; however, this particular metaphysical manuscript was engraved on thin oblong squares that appeared within the astral light. Boris de Zirkoff wrote an article on the writing of *The Voice of Silence* noting key events that occurred during this time period in the life of Blavatsky. Through this investigation, Zirkoff observed a two-fold reason that necessitated the publication of this work: 1) a more accessible version of the Theosophical philosophy and tenets of faith was necessary for any who did not have the time, disposition, or patience to wade through the denser *Isis Unveiled* or *The Secret Doctrine* and 2) this work was pragmatic in nature and attempted to illustrate the practicality of the Theosophical teachings. Though Blavatsky's health began to deteriorate while writing this work from London, she decided to travel to Fontainebleau a commune (village) just outside of Paris where the majority of *The Voice of Silence* was actually composed though it has been suggested that she had started this work before leaving London.[157]

In an undated letter sent to G.R.S. Mead, Blavatsky noted a possible format for this publication: 'I have finished my Key to Theosophy & my 1st Series of Fragments from the 'Book of the Golden Precepts,' 'The Voice of the Silence.' Annie Besant says it ought to be published in letters of gold & even Sinnett's eyes sparkled when he read it; he said it was very beautiful. It will be ready for sale in about a month.'[158] An excerpt taken from the Theosophical periodical *Lucifer* described the process by which this work was written in the midst of a counter attack against William Coleman: 'I can testify that she used none of the books named [by Coleman], nor any others, but wrote straight on, rapidly, page after page, now and then pausing and looking up, as though to recall something to memory. The notes were later done with the help of books.'[159] It is interesting that no mention of Senzar squares was alluded to in this description.

Nearing the end of her life, Blavatsky wrote a letter to her sister Vera pleading for her to translate these practical works into Russian:

My *Key to Theosophy* will bring many new proselytes, and the *Voice of Silence*, tiny book though it is, is simply becoming the Theosophists' bible. They are grand aphorisms, indeed, I may say so, because you know I did not invent them I only translated them from Telugu, the oldest South-Indian dialect. There are three treatises, about morals, and the moral principles of the Mongolian and Dravidian mystics. Some of the aphorisms are wonderful deep and beautiful. Here they have created a perfect *furore*, and I think they would attract attention in Russia, too. Won't you translate them? It will be a fine thing to do.[160]

5.28 The Philosophy of *The Voice of Silence*

Philosophically, *The Voice of Silence* presented a practical approach to the great inaccessible books previously written by Blavatsky- it only consisted of 100 pages. This work was further divided into three sections: 'The Voice of Silence', 'The Two Paths, and 'The Seven Portals.'

This work represented a culmination of all of Blavatsky's experiences which at this later stage appeared far removed from Spiritualism and attested to her Eastern views of contemplative meditation. This book evidenced more clearly than any previous work the affinities between Blavatsky's Theosophy and Eastern religious beliefs. A connection between this book and what was called the 'Heart Doctrine' of the Mahayana was first noticed by Alice Cleather and Basil Crump in their editorial foreward to a 1927 reprint of this famous work. This same doctrine was observed by Nancy Reigle who went on to expound this idea in more depth:

> What is the Heart Doctrine spoken of by the Panchen Lama? In the *Voice of Silence* H.P. B. distinguishes between the Head Doctrine and the Heart Doctrine in Fragment Two title 'The Two Paths' where she says: Learn above all to separate Head-learning from Soul-Sidom, the 'Eye' from the 'Heart' doctrine...even ignorance is better than Head-learning with no Soul-wisdom to illuminate and guide it...'Great Sifter' is the name of the 'Heart Doctrine,' O disciple....True knowledge is the flour, false learning is the husk...[161]

Reigle then continued to note the important characteristics of this in the Mahayana tradition concluding that '...in Mahayana Buddhism we find works that serve as guides for our own training in the same noble ethics and compassion that H. P. B. urged us to practice in

The *Voice of Silence*.[162] Here the Oriental shift in Blavatsky's writings seemed obvious.

5.29 The Basic Tenet of Spiritualism in the Writings of Blavatsky

The basic tenet of Spiritualism held that a departed soul could maintain communications with the world of the living. At this juncture, an examination of Blavatsky's major writings and their treatment of this one basic Spiritualist belief will be explored (*The Voice of Silence* has been omitted because it does not directly deal with this question).

-Isis Unveiled

In *Isis Unveiled* Blavatsky attributed phenomena to the 'will' of the practicing medium:

> We will now only again assert that no spirit claimed by the spiritualists to be human was ever produced to be such on sufficient testimony. …Thus every so-called 'materialization'- when genuine- is either produced (*perhaps*) by the will of that spirit whom the 'appearance' is claimed to be but can only personate at best, or by the elementary goblins themselves, which are generally too stupid to deserve the honor of being called devils.[163]

Now if this were all that was written *Isis Unveiled* would remain incompatible with Spiritualism; however, Blavatsky continued to expound:

> Upon rare occasions the spirits are able to subdue and control these soulless beings, which are ever ready to assume pompous names if left to themselves, in such a way that the mischievous spirit 'of the air', shaped in the real image of the human spirit, will be moved by the latter like a marionette, and unable to either act or utter other words than those imposed on him by the 'immortal soul,' But this requires many conditions generally unknown to the circles of even spiritualists most in the habit of regularly attending séances. Not everyone can attract human spirits who likes. One of the most powerful attractions of our departed ones is their strong affection for those whom they have left on earth. It draws them irresistibly, by degrees, into the current of the Astral Light vibrating between the person sympathetic to them and the Universal Soul.[164]

Blavatsky made provision for Spiritualism in *Isis Unveiled* implementing two laws: 1) that departed souls are attracted to their loved ones even after death and 2) that some human souls can use 'mischievous spirits' to convey their message for them. Either way communication with the spirit world could be achieved.

A letter appeared in *Light* on 20 September 1884 titled 'Theosophy and Spiritualism.' In this letter it was explained that the Oriental Theosophy was at odds with the earlier form of Theosophy explained in *Isis Unveiled*. This belief evidenced that *Isis Unveiled* was viewed by Blavatsky's contemporaries as being more favorable to Spiritualists than her later teachings were. The writer quoted from both Arthur Lillie and *Isis Unveiled*:

> I feel anxious that all readers of 'LIGHT' should know that the Theosophy taught in the pages of the Theosophist is quite at variance with the Theosophy taught in 'Isis Unveiled'; and consequently cannot be inspired by the same school of thought, unless Mr. Arthur Lillie is correct in saying that their (the Mahatmas') opinions change with the times. Speaking of objective phenomena on p. 596, Vol. II., 'Isis Unveiled,' we are told the phenomena are generally,' and without discrimination, attributed to disembodied spirits, where- as bid one-third of them may be produced by the latter, another third by elementals, and the rest by the astral double of the medium....' It is scarcely necessary for me to say that these words express the exact opinion of most, if not all the advanced Spiritualists of to-day; and that the particular brother, Mahatma, or Adept, who either inspired or precipitated those words, should come forward and save his reputation from his Theosophical friends. Again, on p. 597 of the same volume, we read as follows respecting subjective phenomena: 'They are mostly, and, according to the moral, intellectual, and physical purity of the medium, the work of the elementary, or, sometimes, VERY PURE HUMAN SPIRITS; elementals have nought to do with subject manifestations.' Let these words be printed in large type, sir, because there is but one interpretation that will apply to them, viz., that 'very pure human spirits' can and do 'sometimes' communicate to mortal man. I ask Mr. Sinnett, who is at present in London, to answer this question: 'Why have the Theosophists ignored the inspired teachings of "Isis Unveiled"?' Because, at p. 172 of 'The Occult World,' 1st Ed., he says: 'But once realise the real position of the authors or inspirers of 'Isis,' and the value of any argument on which you find them, launched, is enhanced enormously.... This fact alone will be of enormous significance for any reader who, in indirect ways, has reached a comprehension of the authority with which they are entitled to speak." This, sir, in my humble opinion, is only a fair question in the face of this assertion.—Yours, &c.,[165]

Thus, it seemed that the teachings put forth in *Isis Unveiled* were not at odds with contemporary Spiritualism on the Victorian Era at least according to this reader. A similar conclusion was admitted by Alvin Boyd Kuhn in his work *Theosophy* (1930) based on his PhD dissertation presented at Columbia University:

> In 1876, the writing of *Isis* was committing her [Blavatsky] to a stand which made further compromise with Spiritualism impossible. Her statements reveal what she would ostensibly have labored to do for that movement had it shown itself more plastic in her hands. She would have striven to buttress the phenomena with a more historical interpretation and a more respectable rationale. In this context, however, the following passage is a bit difficult to understand. It seems to make a gesture of conciliation toward the Spiritualistic hypothesis after all. She says 'We are far from believing that all the spirits that communicate at circles are of the classes called "Elemental," and "Elementary." Many —especially among those who control the medium subjectively to speak, write, and otherwise act in various ways—are human, disembodied spirits. Whether the majority of such spirits are good or *bad*, largely depends on the private morality of the medium, much on the circle present, and a great deal on the intensity and object of their purpose. But, in any case, human spirits can *never* materialize themselves in *propria persona.*'
>
> If this seems a recession from her consistent position elsewhere assumed, it must be remembered that she never, before or after, denied the possibility of the occasional descent of genuinely human spirits "in rare and exceptional cases."[166]

Thus, Kuhn admitted that Blavatsky continually shifted in her opinion of Spiritualism; however, he also observed that the Theosophical Society consistently remained inclusive of Spiritualists throughout its various stages through its acceptance of its basic tenet. Though Kuhn suggested that the 'writing of *Isis* was committing her to a stand which made further compromise with Spiritualism impossible' it should be understood that Blavatsky attempted to merely reform Spiritualism through re-conceptualizing terms and re-institutionalizing its order to provide safeguards against fraudulent practices. This reformation was evident in *Isis Unveiled* where communication of departed spirits with the living was included in Blavatsky's philosophy.

-The Mahatma Letters

In the correspondence between Hume, Sinnett, Morya, and Koot Hoomi now infamously known as the 'Mahatma letters' the subject of spirit communications were brought up on several occasions. The first occasion was found in the undated Letter XVI probably received around July of 1882 written by Koot Hoomi:

> Many of the subjective spiritual communications- most of them when the sensitives are pure minded- are real; but it is most difficult for the uninitiated medium to fix in his mind the true and correct pictures of what he sees and hears. Some of the phenomena called psychography though more rarely are also real). The spirit of the sensitive getting odylised, so to say, by the aura of the Spirit in the Devachan, become for a few minutes that departed personality, and write in the hand writing of the latter, in his language and in his thoughts, as they were during his life time. The two spirits become blended in one; and, the preponderance of one over the other during such phenomena, determines the preponderance of personality in the characteristics exhibited in such writings, and 'trance-speaking.' What you call rapport, is in plain fact an identity of molecular vibration between the astral part of the incarnate medium and the astral part of the disincarnate personality...[167]

In this same letter Koot Hoomi was attempting to explain that mediums could actually hurt the spirits that they were channeling:

> The rule is, that a person who dies a natural death, will remain from 'a few hours to several short years,' within the earth's attraction., i.e. in Kama-Loka....For in grasping them, and satisfying their thirst for life, the medium helps to develop in them- is in fact the cause of- a new set of Skandhas, a new body, with far worse tendencies and passions than was the one they lost...were the mediums and Spiritualists but to know, as I said, that with every new 'angel guide' they welcome with rapture, then entice the latter into an Upadana which will be productive of a series of untold evils for the new Ego that will be born under its nefarious shadow, and that with very séance- especially for materialization- they multiply the causes for misery, birth, or be reborn into a worse existence than ever- they would perhaps, be less lavishing their hospitality.[168]

The belief that departed souls could communicate with the living seemed obvious in this above quote (and in *Isis Unveiled*) though the qualifications are slightly altered. In these letters, it is only those who died premature deaths i.e. suicides and violent or accidental deaths that are able to make their way through to the mediums:

> Our first doctrine is that the majority of objective phenomena were due to shells, 1 ½ and 2 ½ principled shells, i. e. principles entirely separated from their sixth and seventh principles. But as further (1) development we admit that there are some spirits, which also may be potent in the séance room. These are spirits of suicides and the victims of accident or violence. Here the doctrine is that...all spirits prematurely divorced from the lower principles, must remain on earth, until the foredestined hours of what would have been the natural death strikes. Now this is all very well but this being so, it is clear that in *opposition to our former doctrine, shells will be few and spirits many* (2).[169]

Here the italics refer to particular passages that Koot Hoomi had underlined in blue colored pencil. In a return letter from Koot Hoomi, referred to as letter No. XXc sent sometime in August 1882, K.H. elaborated upon this idea:

> In no case then,- with the exception of suicides and shells, is there any possibility for any other to be attracted to a séance room. And it is clear that 'this teachings is not in position to our former doctrine' and that while 'shells' will be many,- Spirits very few."[170]

This letter (now labeled Letter No. XXI) was received back on 22 August 1882 with Koot Hoomi's marking on it in italics:

> But there is another kind of spirit we have lost sign of,- the suicides and those killed by accidents. Both kinds can communicate and both have to pay dearly for such visits...'
> *Correct.*

> As to the victims of accident these far still worse...unhappy shades...cut off in the full flush of earthly passions...they are the *pisachas* etc...They not only ruin their victims etc...
> *Again correct. Bear in mind that the exceptions enforce the rule*

> And if they are neither very good nor very bad the 'victims of accident or violence,' derive a new set of skandhas from the medium who attracts them.

> *I have explained the situation on the margin of the proofs. See note....*

On margin I said 'rarely' but I have not pronounced the word 'never'. Accidents occur under the most various circumstances; and men are not only killed accidentally, or die as suicides but are also murdered- something we have not even touched upon. ...Bear always in mind that there are exceptions to every rule, and to these again and other side exceptions, and be always prepared to learn something new...The majority- nether very good nor very bad, the victims of accident or violence (including murder)- some sleep, others become Nature pisachas, and while a small minority may fall victims to mediums and derive a new set of skandhas from the medium who attracts them. Small as their number may be, their fate is to be the most deplored...Remember still even in the case of suicide there are many who will never allow themselves to be drawn into the vortex of mediumship, and pray do not accuse me of 'inconsistency' or contradiction when we come to that point.[171]

So it seemed that the possibility of spirit communications were an acceptable doctrine in these early writings from the Indian Mahatmas.

-*Esoteric Buddhism*

Esoteric Buddhism and its relationship with the basic tenet of Spiritualism was derived solely from the Mahatma Letters already treated above. It is important to again note that access to the Mahatma Letters was not widespread until the early 20th century, so most individuals would have only known about the contents of these letters through Sinnett's *Esoteric Buddhism* and through the occasional letter that was reprinted in the *Theosophist*. The following passages are reprinted so that the reader can begin to ascertain how Sinnett used them in his writing. The words in italics align with the mahatma letter from which they were derived:

For once in Devachan there is very little opportunity for communication between a spirit, then wholly absorbed in its own sensations and practically oblivious of the earth left behind, and its former friends still living. 'Whether gone before or yet remaining on earth, those friends, if the bond of affection has been sufficiently strong, will be with the happy spirit still, to all intents and purposes for him, and as happy blissful, innocent, as the disembodied dreamer himself. It is *possible*, however, for yet living persons to have visions of Devachan, though such visions are rare, and only one-sided, the entities in Devachan, sighted by the earthly clairvoyant, being quite unconscious themselves of undergoing such observation. The spirit of the clairvoyant ascends into the condition of Devachan in such rare visions, and thus becomes subject to the vivid delusions of that existence. It is under the impression that the spirits, with which it is in Devachanic bonds of sympathy, have come down to visit earth and itself, while the converse operation has really taken place. The clairvoyant's spirit has been raised towards those in Devachan. Thus *many of the subjective spiritual communications—most of them -when the sensitives are pure-minded—are real, though it is most difficult for the uninitiated medium to fix in his mind the true and correct pictures of what he sees and hears. In the same way some of the phenomena called psychography (though more rarely) are also real. The spirit of the sensitive getting odylized, so to say, by the aura of the spirit in the Devachan becomes for a few minutes that departed personality, and writes in the handwriting of the latter, in his language and in his thoughts as they were during his lifetime. The two spirits become blended in one,*[172] and the *preponderance of one over the other during such phenomena, determines the preponderance of personality in the characteristics exhibited [...].* Thus, it may incidentally be observed, what is called *rapport, is, in plain fact, an identity of molecular vibration between the astral part of the incarnate medium and the astral part of the disincarnate personality.*[173]

Elsewhere, the belief that souls which have suffered violent deaths could be contacted was also purported in Sinnett's writing:

The elementary…which finds itself in Kama loca, on its violent expulsion from the body is not a mere shell- it is the person himself who was lately alive, minus nothing but the body… Certainly elementaries of this kind may communicate very effectually at spiritual séances at their own heavy cost; for they are unfortunately able, by reason of the completeness of their astral constitution, to go on generating Karma, to assuage their thirst for life at the unwholesome spring of mediumship. Cut off in the full flush of earthly passions which bind them to familiar scene, they are enticed by the opportunity which mediums afford for the gratification of these vicariously.[174]

Curiously in an appendix added to *Esoteric Buddhism* in the sixth edition published in 1887 the ideology that the loved ones can pull the ego back to the earth seemed to be the prominent idea (not the Mahatma letters of violent deaths):

The more frequently it is appealed to by the affection of friends still in the body to avail itself of the opportunities furnished by the mediumship for manifesting its existence on the physical plane, the more vehement will be the impulses which draw it back to physical life, and the more serious the retardation of its spirituals progress. This consideration appears to involve the most influential motive which leads the representative of Theosophical teaching to discountenance and disapprove of all attempts to hold communication with departed souls by means of the spiritual séance. The more such communications are genuine the more detrimental there are to the inhabitants of Kama loca concerned with them.[175]

The idea of shells was further expanded:

> The shell which the real Ego has altogether abandoned may even in that state be mistaken sometimes at spiritual séances for a living entity. It remains for a time an astral looking-glass, in which mediums may see their own thoughts reflected, and take these back, fully believing them to come from an external source. These phenomena in the truest sense of the term are galvanized astral corpses; none the less so, because until they are actually disintegrated a certain subtle connection will subsist between them and the true Devachanic spirit; just as such a subtle communication subsists in the first instance between the Kama loca entity and the dead body left on earth. That last-mentioned communication is kept up by the finally-diffused material of the original third principle, or linga sharira, and a study of this branch of the subject will, I believe, lead us up to a better comprehension than we possess at present of the circumstances under which materializations are sometimes accomplished at spiritual séances. ..it is enough to recognize that the analogy may help to show ho, between the Devachanic entity and the discarded shell in Kama loca a similar connection may continue for a while, acting, while it lasts, as a drag on the higher spirit, but perhaps as an after-glow of sunset on the shell.[176]

-The Secret Doctrine

In 1888, Blavatsky produced her major work *The Secret Doctrine* which was her explanation for her ideologies that she associated with the ancient wisdom tradition (her reconceptualized *prisca theologia*). As noted above, *The Secret Doctrine* did not seem to make any provision for communication with the deceased; however, an agreement made with William Stainton Moses in 1888 illustrated that during the same year that this work was published Blavatsky became more open towards re-associating with other Spiritualists.

-Key to Theosophy

Blavatsky's dogmatic assertion that a departed 'ego' was not able to contact the living was slightly amended in her 1889 *The Key to Theoso-*

phy where this communication becomes possible though only under rare circumstances:

> during the few days that follow immediately the death of a person and before the Ego passes into the Devachanic state. Whether any living mortal, save a few exceptional cases—(when the intensity of the desire in the dying person to return for some purpose forced the higher consciousness *to remain awake,* and therefore it was really the *individuality,* the 'Spirit' that communicated)—has derived much benefit from the return of the spirit into the *objective* plane is another question. The spirit is dazed after death and falls very soon into what we call *'pre-devachanic* unconsciousness.' The second exception is found in the *Nirmanakayas...*

Blavatsky's major works spanned from 1877–1891. Looking at the evolution of some of her ideologies and the subsequent omissions of some of these doctrines in her later writings, it seemed that the reason for these changes could have been as Lillie suggested- the agenda of an 'opportunist', or they could have been Blavatsky's attempt to build an eclectic Society that incorporated all religious movements in an attempt to make good on her later goal of the Society- to build a universal brotherhood. Despite this questionable motivation, it deserves to be noted that it was only in *The Secret Doctrine* that the basic tenet to Spiritualism was denied; however, this idea (perhaps based on the alliance made with William Stainton Moses) was soon corrected in *The Key to Theosophy.* Throughout these years provision had been made for this basic Spiritualist doctrine which did not seem to be coincidental by any means. There remains a continual connection between Blavatsky's theories and Spiritualism, not only in their methods of transmission which appear similar to the process known as automatic writing , but also through their belief structures. Now that many of these similarities have been addressed attention will be paid to the early critics of the Theosophical Society. These following individuals have been chosen for their arguments related to the Theosophical Society and Spiritualism.

Notes

[1] *The Encyclopedia Britannica: A Dictionary of Arts, Science, Literature and General Information,* 11th edition, 29 vols (Cambridge: Cambridge University Press, 1910), III, p. 47.

[2] Janet Oppenheim, *The Other World: Spiritualism and Psychical Research in England, 1850-1914* (Cambridge: Cambridge University Press, 1985), p. 173. It appeared that Oppenheim was referencing Constance Wachtmeister's claims in *Reminiscences of HP Blavatsky and The Secret Doctrine*, p. 38.

[3] Kardec, *Experimental Spiritism: Book on Mediums, or, Guide for Mediums and Invocators*, trans. Emma A. Wood (Boston: Colby and Rich, 1874), p. 199.

[4] Kardec, *Experimental Spiritism*, p. 220.

[5] Henry Steel Olcott, *Old Diary Leaves: The true Story of The Theosophical Society* (New York: G. P. Putnams Sons, 1895), I, pp. 208-209.

[6] Marion Meade, *Madame Blavatsky: The Woman Behind the Myth* (New York: G. P. Putnam's Sons, 1980), p. 149.; Gertrude Marvin Williams, *Madame Blavatsky Priestess of the Occult* (New York: Lancer Books, Inc., 1946), p. 117.

[7] Brendan James French, *The Theosophical Masters: An Investigation into the Conceptual Domains of H. P. Blavatsky and C. W. Leadbeater*, 2 vols (unpublished doctoral thesis, University of Sydney, August 2000), I, pp. 113-114.

[8] Gary W. Trompf, 'Macrohistory in Blavatsky, Steiner, and Guenon', in *Western Esotericism and the Science of Religion*, ed. By Antoine Faivre and Wouter J. Hanegraaff (Leuven, Belgium: Peeters, 1998), pp. 269-296 (p. 279).

[9] For more information concerning the Lamasery see Anonymous, 'The Theosophical Society: The Lamasery at New York. Interviews with Madame Blavatsky the Wonderful Author of the Book of Wonders, "Isis Unveiled" etc.', *Hartford Daily Times*, 2 December 1878, p. 1. and Michael Gomes, *The Dawning of the Theosophical Movement* (Wheaton, IL: The Theosophical Publishing House, 1987), p. 199.

[10] Olcott, *Old Diary Leaves*, I, p. 208.

[11] Olcott, *Old Diary Leaves*, I, pp. 202-203.

[12] Boris de Zirkoff noted that Blavatsky 'seems to have left New York, September 15, 1875, going by the evening boat to Albany, N. Y. Either the next day or the 17th, she arrived at Ithaca. By the second week in October, she was back in New York.' Boris de Zirkoff, 'Introductory: How Isis Unveiled Was Written', in *Isis Unveiled: Collected Writings 1877*, 1st Quest Edition, 2 vols. (The Theosophical Publishing House, 1972), I, pp. 1-61 (p. 5).

[13] Charles Lazenby, 'Isis Unveiled: Anecdotes about HP Blavatsky', *The Path*, 1:1 (July 1910), 9.

[14] Joscelyn Godwin, 'From the Archives: H.P.B. to M.A., Oxon', *Theosophical History*, 4:6-7 (April – July 1993), 172-177 (p. 173).

[15] E. H. Britten, 'Theosophy: its Origin and Founders', *The Two Worlds*, 187:4 (12 June 1891) 359-360 (p. 359).

[16] Blavatsky claimed that: 'it is Professor Wilder who did the most for me. It is he who made the excellent Index, who corrected the Greek, Latin and Hebrew words, suggested quotations and wrote the greater part of the Introduction "Before the Veil"…it was Dr. Wilder's express wish that his name should not appear except in footnotes.' Helena Blavatsky, 'My Books,'

in H. P. Blavatsky, *Collected Writings: 1890-1891*, comp. Boris De Zirkoff, 15 vols (Pasadena: CA: Theosophical Publishing House, 1966), XIII, 191-193 (p. 198). Though Alexander Wilder noted a different opinion: 'I would hesitate, likewise, to be considered in any noteworthy sense as an editor of the work. It is true that ...I was asked to read the proof sheets and make sure that the Hebrew words and terms belonging to other languages were correctly given by the printer, but I added nothing, and do not remember that I ventured to control anything that was contributed to the work. Without her knowledge and approval, such action would have been reprehensible.' Alexander Wilder, 'How "Isis Unveiled" Was Written', *The Word*, 7:2 (New York: Theosophical Publishing Co., 1908), 77–87 (p. 83).

[17] J. W. Bouton, 'Cuttings and Comments', *The Theosophist*, 22:5 (February 1901), 314-320 (p. 318).

[18] Blavatsky, 'My Books', p. 198.

[19] Blavatsky's claim to have visited Tibet in her earlier travels seems unlikely thought these travels would have enabled her to study Buddhism and Hinduism under the direct guidance of a 'master' or 'rishi', allowing Theosophy a possible origin in Eastern philosophy. Nicholas Goodrick-Clarke noted that Blavatsky appeared knowledgeable about the geography and ethnography of Tibet though it is very possible that this knowledge could have been drawn from the following nineteenth-century sources: Abbe Evariste Regis Huc, *Travels in Tartary, Thibet and China during the Year 1844-5-6* (1852), Emil Schlagintweit, *Buddhism in Tibet* (1863), and Clements R. Markham's, *Narratives of the Mission of George Bogle to Tibet and of the Journey of Thomas Manning to Lhasa* (1876). Nicholas Goodrick-Clarke, 'Mystical East', *Theosophical History*, 13:3 (July 2007), 3-28 (p. 21).

[20] Blavatsky's term 'wisdom tradition' was her reconceptualization of the prisca theologia. The term prisca theologia is a Latin term that means literally ancient theology/tradition. This term is used by the Greek historian Lucius Mestrius Plutarchus (ca. 45-120 CE) in his De Animae Procreation in Timaeo in reference to pre-Platonic philosophers as teachers of religious wisdom. The Latin term theologia is a transliteration and combination of the Greek terms θεός (God) and λόγος (word, discourse, or reasoning). The Latin word prisca means ancient. Thus, the term prisca theologia refers to an ancient wisdom that contains the idea of a 'continuity' of tradition accessible throughout history, though it also connotes a 'degeneration' of this universal religion that continues to occur as time progresses. See Wouter J. Hanegraaff, 'Tradition', in *Dictionary of Western Esotericism and Gnosis*, ed. Wouter J. Hanegraaff (Boston: Brill Academic Publishers, 2005), 1125-1135 (p. 1126). Blavatsky claimed an eastern origin for her reconceptualization of the ancient wisdom tradition as opposed to the Renaissance Platonists who maintained an occidental origin. See Blavatsky, *Isis Unveiled*, I, pp. 33-34, II, p. 123. Blavatsky viewed the ancient wisdom as providing the hermeneutical key to interpret scientific data: 'our work, then, is a plea for the recognition

of the Hermetic philosophy, that anciently universal Wisdom Religion, as the only possible key to the Absolute in science and theology.' Blavatsky, *Isis Unveiled,*, I, pp. vii, xi, 131, 162, 436; II, pp. 99, 142.

[21] Nicholas Goodrick-Clarke, *The Occult Roots of Nazism: Secret Aryan Cults and Their Influence on Nazi Ideology* (New York: New York University Press, 1992), p. 18.

[22] Gertrude Marvin Williams, *Priestess of the Occult, Madame Blavatsky* (New York: A. A. Knopf, 1946), p. 114.

[23] Marion Meade questioned the dating of this letter in her work and noted 'In my opinion, the date of this article, 27 April 1891, is erroneous because on that date H. P. B. was mortally ill. Presumably it was written sometime before the twenty-sixth.' Meade, *Madame Blavatsky*, p. 498.

[24] Helena Blavatsky, 'My Books', in H. P. Blavatsky, *Collected Writings: 1890-1891*, comp. Boris De Zirkoff, 15 vols (Pasadena: CA: Theosophical Publishing House, 1966), XIII, 191-193.

[25] Blavatsky, 'My Books', p. 197.

[26] Blavatsky, 'My Books', p. 201.

[27] The Spiritualist, William Stainton Moses, in *Light Magazine* believed that Blavatsky had 'introduced this word to the movement'; however, it appeared in Kardec's 1884 work Experimental Spiritism. Given Blavatsky's familiarity with Kardec, it seems logical to deduce that Blavatsky had borrowed it from Kardec. See William Stainton Moses, 'Our Contemporaries', *Light*, 40:1 (8 October 1881), 323 (p. 323).

[28] Blavatsky, *Isis Unveiled*, I, p. 367.

[29] Blavatsky, *Isis Unveiled*, I, p. 296.

[30] Blavatsky, *Isis Unveiled*, I, pp. 51, 294-296.

[31] Frank Podmore, *Modern Spiritualism: A History and a Criticism*, 2 vols (London: Methuen & Co., 1902), I, p. 107.

[32] Andrew Jackson Davis, *A Stellar Key to The Summer Land* (Boston, Colby & Rich, 1867), pp. 55-56, 89; 140, 181.

[33] Blavatsky, *Isis Unveiled*, II, p. 284.

[34] Nirvana means and absorption into God's own essence and being. See Blavatsky, *Isis Unveiled*, II, p. 310. The word monad is derived from the Greek word μονάς meaning one. It is defined as 'the immortal part of man which reincarnates in the lower kingdoms, and gradually progresses through them to Man and then to the final goal Nirvana.' H. P. Blavatsky, The Theosophical Glossary (London: The Theosophical Publishing Society, 1892), p. 216.

[35] Blavatsky, *Isis Unveiled*, II, pp. 279-280.

[36] Blavatsky, *Isis Unveiled*, II, p. 281.

[37] A.P. Sinnett, 'Kama Loca and the Bearings of The Esoteric Doctrine on Spiritualism', *The Theosophist*, 6:5 (February 1885), 106-110 (p. 108).

[38] Olcott, *Old Diary Leaves*, I, p. 281.

[39] Blavatsky, *Isis Unveiled*, I, p. 351.

[40] Blavatsky, *Isis Unveiled*, II, pp. 152-153, 280.

[41] Henry Steel Olcott, *Old Diary Leaves: The True Story of The Theosophical Society* (New York: G. P. Putnams Sons, 1895), I, p. 280.

[42] Olcott, *Old Diary Leaves*, I, p. 280.

[43] Olcott, *Old Diary Leaves*, I, p. 284.

[44] Emma Hardinge Britten, *Nineteenth Century Miracles: or, Spirits and Their Work in Every Country of the Earth* (New York: William Britten, 1883/4), p. 18.

[45] 'Koot Hoomi' explained this discrepancy in Mahatma Letter No. LII received in Simla in Autumn of 1882: 'we thought it was premature to give the public more than they could possibly assimilate, and before they had digested the "two souls";- and thus the further subdivision of the trinity into 7 principles was left unmentioned in Isis.' *The Mahatma Letters: to A. P. Sinnett*, comp. A. Trevor Barker, (Theosophical University Press, 1975), p. 290.

[46] Helena Blavatsky, '*Isis Unveiled* and *The Theosophist* on Reincarnation,' *Collected Writings: 1882-1883*, comp. Boris De Zirkoff, 15 vols. (Pasadena: CA: Theosophical Publishing House, 1966), IV, pp. 183-186.

[47] See Mahatma Letter Nos. XXIVb and LII in Barker, *The Mahatma Letters*, pp. 182-183, 290.

[48] Olcott, *Old Diary Leaves*, I, p. 283.

[49] Olcott, *Old Diary Leaves*, I, p. 283.

[50] Wouter J. Hanegraaff, *New Age Religions and Western Culture* (Albany, NY: State University of New York, 1998), p. 471.

[51] William Emmette Coleman, 'The Sources of Madame Blavatsky's Writings', in *Modern Priestess of Isis* by Vsevolod Solovyoff (London: Longmans, Green, and Company, 1895), 353-366 (p. 358).

[52] Nicholas Goodrick-Clarke, *Helena Blavatsky* (Berkeley, CA: North Atlantic Books, 2004), p. 52.

[53] Nicholas Goodrick-Clarke, 'The Theosophical Society, Orientalism, and the "Mystic East": Western Esotericism and Eastern Religion in Theosophy', *Theosophical History*, 13: 3 (July 2007), 3-28 (p. 21).

[54] Godwin, *Theosophical Enlightenment*, p. 326. Also, Wouter Hanegraaff noted that 'up to the publication of her first major work, Isis Unveiled (1877), it was not an Indian but an "Egyptian" atmosphere which prevailed in the Theosophical Society.' Hanegraaff went on to quote Carl T. Jackson as evidence for this supposition. See Hanegraff, *New Age Religion and Western Culture*, pp. 452-453.

[55] Nicholas Goodrick-Clarke, 'Mystical East', p. 21.

[56] Blavatsky, *Isis Unveiled*, I, p. 594. For a detailed biographical account of Jacolliot see Daniel Caracostea, 'Louis-François Jacolliot (1837-1890)', *Theosophical History*, 9:1 (January 2003), 12-39.

[57] Dipesh Chakrabarty, a Marxist historian, notes that 'history's own time is godless, continuous, and...empty and homogeneous. By this I mean that in employing modern historical consciousness (whether in academic writing or

outside of it), we think of a world that…is already disenchanted. God's, spirits, and other 'supernatural' forces can claim no agency in our (the historian's) narratives.' See Dipesh Chakrabarty, *Provincializing Europe: Post Colonial Thought and Historical Difference* (Princeton: Princeton University Press, 2000), p. 76.

[58] Vernon Harrison, *HP Blavatsky and the SPR*, Theosophical University Press, 1997 <http://www.theosociety.org/pasadena/hpb-spr/hpbspr-o.htm> (accessed on 25 August 2011) [para. 9 of 12]

[59] Olcott, Old Diary Leaves, III, p. 106.

[60] Harold Edward Hare and William Loftus Hare, *Who Wrote the Mahatma Letters?* (London: Williams and Norgate, 1936), p. 16. Beatrice Hastings argues that the Hares were not reliable historians and not suitable to give an analysis of the Mahatma Letters: 'The very first "fact" delivered to this public is wrong: The Letters were not published "in September,1923", but in December. But this is an airy trifle compared with the colossal riot of wrong dates ramping through this worthless volume of ignorance and double-dealing.' Hastings ends her critique by publishing a list of misquotations, dating errors, and incorrect conclusions. Beatrice Hastings, *Defence of Madame Blavatsky* (Worthing, Sussex: The Hastings Press, 1937), pp. 22; 23-26.

[61] Barker, *The Mahatma Letters*, pp. 58-59.

[62] "The Mahavagga" trans. T. W. Rhys Davids in *Sacred Books of the East*, ed. Max Muller, 50 vols (Oxford: Clarendon Press, 1881), XIII, pp. 73-78.

[63] Hare, *Who Wrote the Mahatma Letters*, pp. 105-108. This Letter No XVI is also referred to as 'The Devachan Letter.'

[64] Barker, *The Mahatma Letters*, pp. 99-100.

[65] Samuel Beal, *A Catena of Buddhist Scriptures from the Chinese* (London: Trubner & Co., 1872), pp. 379-381.

[66] Hare, *Who Wrote the Mahatma Letters*, pp. 108-111.

[67] Hare, *Who Wrote the Mahatma Letters*, p. 110.

[68] Beatrice Hastings, *Defence of Madame Blavatsky: Volume 1* (Worthing,Sussex: The Hastings Press, 1937), pp. 22; 23-26.

[69] William Loftus Hare, 'The Mahatma Letters to A. P. Sinnett: A Note,' *The Occult Review*, 39 (April 1924), p. 218.

[70] Barker, *The Mahatma Letters*, p. 357.

[71] H. P. Blavatsky, *The Secret Doctrine: The Synthesis of Science, Religion and Philosophy*, 2 vols, (Adyar: The Theosophical Publishing Company, 1888), II, p. 602. 'This septenary doctrine had not yet been divulged to the world at the time when Isis was written.' Barker, *The Mahatma Letters*, p. 183.

[72] Joscelyn Godwin, *Atlantis and the Cycles of Time: Prophecies, Traditions, and Occult Revelations* (Rochester, NY: Inner Traditions, 2011), p. 70.

[73] A. P. Sinnett, *Esoteric Buddhism*, (3rd ed. (London: Trubner & Co., 1884), p. 83. The 1884 third edition has been cited for all quotations as it contains the same pagination and text as the original 1883 first edition.

[74] Sinnett, *Esoteric Buddhism*, p. 82.

[75] Sinnett, *Esoteric Buddhism*, p. 32.

[76] Sinnett, *Esoteric Buddhism*, pp. 137, 128.

[77] H. P. Blavatsky, *Isis Unveiled: A Master Key to the Mysteries of Ancient and Modern Science and Theology*, 2 vols (New York: J. W. Bouton , 1877), I, pp. 328; 219 f.n., 493.

[78] Sinnett, *Esoteric Buddhism*, pp. 91-92.

[79] Sinnett, *Esoteric Buddhism*, pp. 102-103.

[80] Sinnett, *Esoteric Buddhism*, p. 88.

[81] *Theosophical Glossary*, p. 216.

[82] The septenary (seven) constitution of man was first explained to the world by the publication of another recipient of the Mahatma letters- Allan Octavian Hume, a retired civil servant and former secretary to the Government of India residing in Simla. Hume explains that each monad is comprised of seven separate principles: 1) the physical body, 2) the vital principle, 3) the astral body, 4) the astral shape, 5) the animal consciousness (ego), 6) the spiritual intelligence, and 7) the spirit. A. O. Hume, 'Fragments of Occult Truth: Number One', *The Theosophist* (1881) pp. 17-22. Sinnett changes these slightly in *Esoteric Buddhism*: 1) body, 2) physical vitality, 3) astral counterpart, 4) animal soul, 5) human soul, 6) spiritual soul and 7) spirit. Sinnett, *Esoteric Buddhism*, p. 21.

[83] Sinnett, *Esoteric Buddhism*, pp. 171-172; 248-253; Barker, *The Mahatma Letters*, p. 93.

[84] Sinnett, *Esoteric Buddhism*, p. 120.

[85] Sinnett, *Esoteric Buddhism*, p. 181.

[86] Sinnett, *Esoteric Buddhism*, pp. 119-120. Sinnett is quick to remind the reader that this is a rough number and serves more as an illustration that as an exact figure.

[87] In Mahatma Letter No. XIV (9 July 1882) written to A. O. Hume, this number appears to be slightly different. It is said that 'each man will live in all his lives upon our planet (in this Round) but 77,700 years he has been in the subjective spheres 922,300 years,' Barker, *The Mahatma Letters*, p. 83. It appeared that Sinnett had altered this number, switching the term 'race' with a 'round.'

[88] Sinnett, *Esoteric Buddhism*, pp. 50-51, 117. In the Mahatma letters it is also said that 'one life is lived in each of the seven root-races; seven lives in each of the 49 sub-races- or 7 x 7 x 7 = 343 and add 7 more. And then a series of lives in offshoot and branchlet races; making the total incarnations of man in each station or planet 777,' Barker, *The Mahatma Letters*, pp. 83, 119. The reason behind the change here is unknown.

[89] Sinnett, *Esoteric Buddhism*, pp. 88-89.

[90] A. P. Sinnett, *Esoteric Buddhism*, 5th ed. (Boston: Houghton, Mifflin, and Company, 1886), p. 23.

[91] Sinnett, *Esoteric Buddhism*, p. 97.

[92] Sinnett, *Esoteric Buddhism*, p. 96.

[93] Sinnett, *Esoteric Buddhism*, p. 71.
[94] Arthur Lillie, *Koot Hoomi Unveiled; or, Tibetan "Buddhists" versus the Buddhists of Tibet* (London: The Psychological Press Association, 1884), p. 5.
[95] Arthur Lillie, *Madame Blavatsky and Her Theosophy* (London: Swan Sonnenschein & Co., 1895), p. 182.
[96] Lillie, *Madame Blavatsky and Her Theosophy*, p. 183.
[97] Sinnett, *Esoteric Buddhism*, pp. 32; 104-105; 127.
[98] Blavatsky, *Isis Unveiled*, I, pp. 352-353. The rule that monads could escape the eighth sphere would change in *Esoteric Buddhism*.
[99] Sinnett, *Esoteric Buddhism*, p. 104.
[100] Sinnett, *Esoteric Buddhism*, p. 137.
[101] Sinnett, *Esoteric Buddhism*, p. 129. The source from which this quote is taken is not cited in *Esoteric Buddhism*. In every other 'acknowledged' source cited in *Esoteric Buddhism* the author and the book is given. It is interesting that this one is not. This quote was taken from Eliphas Levi's, 'Death' in *The Theosophist: A Monthly Journal Devoted To Oriental Philosophy, Art, Literature and Occultism*, 3, (1881), 13-14 (p. 14).
[102] The concept of reconciling Levi's views of annihilation with Blavatsky's philosophy was a subject of much discussion in the Mahatma letters. Blavatsky maintained that her philosophy was in line with Levi's. Possible 'disagreements' between these two philosophies were expelled with the writing of Mahatma Letter's 20b and 20c. Lillie does not accept this defense and notes that a "not very logical person has again tried to reconcile Southern Buddhism, which teaches that annihilation is the reward of the just, and Eliphas Levi, who this time in the teeth of the Kabbalah, asserts that annihilation if the punishment of the wicked." Lillie, *Unveiling Koot Hoomi*, p. 4.
[103] Olcott, *Old Diary Leaves*, III, p. 335.
[104] H. P. Blavatsky, 'The Drift of Western Spiritualism', *The Theosophist*, 1:1 (October 1879), 7-8 (pp. 7-8).
[105] 'Correspondence', *The Theosophist*, 3:11 (August 1882), 272.
[106] W. R. Frink, 'Kind Words From Stranger Friends', Supplement to *The Theosophist*, 4:2 (November 1882), 3.
[107] Unknown, 'Spiritualism and Occult Truth', *The Theosophist*, 3:5 (February 1882), 113-115 (p. 115).
[108] Unknown, 'What is a Fact?', *The Theosophist*, 3:3 (December 1881), 70-71 (p. 71).
[109] Goodrick-Clarke, *Helena Blavatsky*, p. 17.
[110] M.A. Oxon [William Stainton Moses], 'Notes By The Way', *Light*, 1:47 (26 November 1881), 376.
[111] 'It is Idle to Argue Further', *The Theosophist*, 3:4 (January 1882), 90-92 (p. 91).
[112] 'Seeming "Discrepancies:" To the Editor of the Theosophist', *The Theosophist*, 3:9 (June 1882), 225-226 (p. 226).
[113] 'Advertisements', Supplement to *The Theosophist*, 5:7 (April 1884), 68.

[114] Goodrick-Clarke, The Western Esoteric Traditions, p. 224.

[115] Emma Coulomb, *Some Account of My Intercourse With Madame Blavatsky From 1872 to 1884: With A Number of Additional Letters and a Full Explanation of the Most Marvellous Theosophical Phenomena* (London: Elliot Stock, 1885). and Richard Hodgson, 'Account of Personal Investigations in India and Discussion of the Authorship of the "Koot Hoomi" Letters,' *Proceedings of the Society for Psychical Research*, 3 (1885), 209-317.

[116] Blavatsky, The Secret Doctrine, I, p. 23.

[117] *Letters of H. P. Blavatsky to A. P. Sinnett*, p. 76.

[118] Justinus Kerner, *The Seeress of Prevorst: Being Revelations Concerning the Inner Life of Man* (London: J. C. Moore, 1845), p. 22. The idea of interpreting an unknown language or angelic tongue was a common element in mainstream Spiritualism having already been prefigured in Andrew Jackson Davis' magic staff which 'contained writing in characters which he had never before seen and yet he was able to translate them without hesitation.' Davis, *The Magic Staff*, p. 235.

[119] Podmore, *Modern Spiritualism*, p. 100.

[120] Podmore, *Modern Spiritualism*, p. 107.

[121] In 1886 Olcott attempted to compare the spheres of Theosophical literature with the spheres put forth by the Seeress of Prevorst. See H. S. Olcott, 'The Seeress or Prevorst', *Theosophist*, 8:86 (November 1886), 104-111.

[122] Constance Wachtmeister, Reminiscences of H. P. Blavatsky and The Secret Doctrine (London: Theosophical Publishing Society, 1893), p. 32.

[123] Wachtmeister, *Reminiscences of H. P. Blavatsky*, p. 33.

[124] Kirby van Mater, 'The Writing of The Secret Doctrine', An Invitation to the Secret Doctrine (Theosophical University Press, 1988) < http://www.theosociety.org/pasadena/invit-sd/invsd-4.htm > [accessed on 13 September 2011]

[125] Wachtmeister, *Reminiscences of H. P. Blavatsky*, p. 26.

[126] Alfred Percy Sinnett, *Incidents in the Life of Madame Blavatsky* (London: The Theosophical Publishing Society, 1913), pp. 236-237.

[127] Bertram Keightley, 'Mr. Bertram Keightley's Account of the Writing of The Secret Doctrine', *Reminiscences of H.P. Blavatsky and The Secret Doctrine*, comp. Constance Wachtmeister (London: Theosophical Publishing Society, 1893), 89-95 (pp. 89-90).

[128] Archibald Keightley, 'Dr. Archibald Keightley's Account of the Writing of The Secret Doctrine,' *Reminiscences of H.P. Blavatsky and The Secret Doctrine*, comp. Constance Wachtmeister (London: Theosophical Publishing Society, 1893), 96- 100 (p. 97).

[129] Archibald, Keightley, 'Dr. Archibald Keightley's Account of the Writing of The Secret Doctrine,' p. 98.

[130] Bertram Keightley, 'The Writing of The Secret Doctrine', p. 91.

[131] Blavatsky, *The Secret Doctrine*, I, pp. 14-17.

[132] Carl T. Jackson, 'Theosophy', in *Oriental Religions and American Thought: Nineteenth-Century Explorations* (Westport, CT: Greenwood Press, 1981), 157-177 (p. 166).

[133] Blavatsky, *The Secret Doctrine*, I, p. 39.

[134] Mary Baker G. Eddy, *Science and Health with Key to the Scriptures*, 14th ed. (Boston: Mary Baker Eddy, 1889), p. 412.

[135] Miss Dodge, 'A Short Sketch of What Christian Science is and is Not', *Woman's Herald* (18 April 1891), p. 402.

[136] Blavatsky, *The Secret Doctrine*, II, pp. 358-359.

[137] Hanegraaff, *New Age Religion*, p. 482.

[138] Campbell, *Ancient Wisdom Revived*, p. 45, 48.

[139] Brendan French confirmed this belief: 'Blavatsky turned her attention to the writing of The Secret Doctrine. In fact, the project to produce a compendium of Theosophical doctrine, incorporating an anthropology and a cosmology, had been in Blavatsky's mind for some years. French, *The Theosophical Masters*, I, p. 144.

[140] H. P. Blavatsky, *The Theosophical Glossary* (London: The Theosophical Publishing Society, 1892), p. 231.

[141] Blavatsky, *The Secret Doctrine*, I, pp. 233-234.

[142] Blavatsky, *The Secret Doctrine*, I, p. 233.f.n.

[143] Blavatsky, *The Secret Doctrine*, I, p. 132.

[144] Brendan French, 'The Mercurian Master', *Aries*, 1 (2001), 168-205 (p. 169).

[145] De Zirkoff, 'Introductory: How The Voice of Silence Was Written', *Voice of Silence: Being Extracts from the Book of the Golden Precepts* (Wheaton, IL: Theosophical Publishing House, 1992), 11a-39a (p. 19a).

[146] H. P. Blavatsky, *The Key to Theosophy: Being a Clear Exposition, in the Form of Question And Answer of the Ethics, Science, and Philosophy* (London: The Theosophical Publishing Company, 1889), p. xii.

[147] Blavatsky, *The Key to Theosophy*, p. 27.

[148] Blavatsky, *The Key to Theosophy*, p. 28.

[149] Blavatsky, *The Key to Theosophy*, p. 31.

[150] Blavatsky, *The Key to Theosophy*, pp. 32-33.

[151] Blavatsky, *The Key to Theosophy*, p. 35.

[152] Blavatsky, *The Key to Theosophy*, p. 193.

[153] Blavatsky, *The Key to Theosophy*, pp. 194-195.

[154] Blavatsky, *The Key to Theosophy*, p. 152.

[155] 'An Exposition of Theosophy: By an Authority', *Light*, 464: 9(23 November 1889), 558-559 (p. 559).

[156] 'Current Literature: The Key to Theosophy, *San Francisco Bulletin* (5 October 1889), p. 1.

[157] Boris de Zirkoff, 'Introductory', *The Voice of Silence: Being Extracts from the Book of the Golden Precepts* (Wheaton, IL: The Theosophical Publishing House, 1992), 11a-39a (p. 17a).

[158] Zirkoff, 'Introductory', pp. 19a-20a.

[159] 'On the Watch Tower', *Lucifer*, 16:93 (15 May 1895), 177-184 (p. 180).

[160] HP Blavatsky, 'Letters of H. P. Blavatsky XIII', *The Path*, 10:9 (December 1895), 267-270 (p. 268).

[161] Nancy Reigle, *The Works and Influence of H.P. Blavatsky: Conference Papers* (Edmonton: Edmonton Theosophical Society, 1999), pp. 107-108.

[162] Reigle, *The Works and Influence of H.P. Blavatsky*, pp. 107-108.

[163] Blavatsky, *Isis Unveiled*, I, p. 68.

[164] Blavatsky, *Isis Unveiled*, I, pp. 68-69.

[165] John Ridley, 'Theosophy and Spiritualism', *Light*, 194:4 (20 September 1884), 386.

[166] Alvin Boyd Kuhn, *Theosophy: A Modern Revival of Ancient Wisdom* (New York: Henry Holt and Company, 1930), p. 99.; Blavatsky, Isis Unveiled, I, p. 67.

[167] Barker, *The Mahatma Letters*, p. 101.

[168] Barker, *The Mahatma Letters*, p. 113.

[169] Barker, *The Mahatma Letters*, p. 123.

[170] Barker, *The Mahatma Letters*, p. 132.

[171] Barker, *The Mahatma Letters*, p. 136.

[172] This excerpt is nearly identical to Mahatma Letter No. XVI in Barker, *The Mahatma Letters*, p. 101. except for a few altered words and phrases.

[173] Sinnett, *Esoteric Buddhism*, pp. 85-86.

[174] Sinnett, *Esoteric Buddhism*, pp. 101-102.

[175] Sinnett, 'Appendix', *Esoteric Buddhism*, 5th ed. (Boston: Houghton, Mifflin, and Company, 1892), pp. 316-317.

[176] Sinnett, Appendix', *Esoteric Buddhism*, 1892, pp. 320-321.

Part VI.

SPIRITUALISTS WHO CRITIQUED THEOSOPHY

6.1 Arthur Lillie (1831-1912?)

Arthur Lillie (1831-1912?) is an elusive figure that history has nearly forgotten. Despite publishing over twenty-five books on a wide range of diverse topics, little has been published on this intriguing figure's background and life. A small glimpse into this underappreciated Victorian author will now be undertaken.

6.2 Military Career

Lillie was the son of Major-General Sir John Scott Lillie a Peninsular veteran,[1] and entered the literary world as an author of mediocre romance novels.[2] Lillie appeared to have been a talented croquet player having become the honorary Secretary for Croquet, All England Lawn-tennis and Croquet Club in 1897,[3] and also served as an officer in the English army serving in the British colony of India. Lillie described one of his Indian adventures that occurred while enlisted in the British forces during the autumn of 1854. Lillie had embarked on his first detachment duty under the leadership of Lieutenant Turnbull, and both he and Turnbull were the only two English officers the rest of the army was composed of Sepoys (native Indian soldiers who worked for England). Lillie elucidated that:

> We reviled our sad fates, I recollect, at having to serve in India when the epoch of romance and adventure had closed. In three years, poor Lieut. Turnbull was lying in the terrible well that served as a cemetery to the ill-fated garrison of Cawnpore. And the thicket of tress where our camp-kettles simmered was fated at the same moment to be red with the blood of gallant British force, which had attempted to relieve my friend Mr. Wake at Arrah. Vincent Eyre was then to reach the same thickets and fight his gallant fight with Koer Singh and the sepoys. And, eventually I myself, whilst serving with the little column of Lord Mark Kerr, had the honour of taking part in another severe action against these my old Dinapore comrades, when Lord Mark Kerr defeated Koer Singh at Azimgurh. The poor torn colours of the 13th Light Infantry were exposed to a fire on that

day, according to the Duke of Endinburgh, such as a few other English regiments have ever witnessed.[4]

The above story illustrated the traumatic events that transpired during Lillie's involvement in the British military, and the type of combat that he endured during his deployment in India. Surely these events heavily influenced Lillie's conceptualization of Eastern culture.

One source noted that during Lillie's enlistment in 1847 he served in the Bengal Infantry, and served through the Santal and Mutiny Campaigns until he was removed because of an injury in 1863.[5] The Santal rebellion was a low casualty conflict for the British forces that was the result of insurgence caused by the high caste Santal people. The Santals were a tribal group in Bengal and Bihar who rebelled against both the British and nonlocal Indians in 1855.[6] According to the tribal leaders, this insurrection was instigated as the result of a supernatural revelation. Legend stated that both Sido and Kanhu the two leaders of the indigenous tribe that organized this revolt received a divine vision in which their god appeared to them in the form of a white man dressed in native style; on each hand he had ten fingers and held a white book with 20 pieces of paper.[7] This vision persisted each day until the meaning eventually became clear to these two tribal leaders- Thakoor their deity would favor their rebellion.[8] This insurgence lasted only 6 months commencing on July 1855 and ending in January of 1856. In his work *The Influence of Buddhism on Primitive Christianity*, Lillie described the religious practices of the Santals during his role in squelching their rebellion:

> In India before the Mutiny I was employed with a force sent to put down the rebellion of the Santals. These, a branch of the Kolarias, represent the early races that the Arya displaced. And their institutions were singularly like those of the Jews. They worshipped in 'high places' rude circles of upright monoliths. They worshipped in 'groves;' and on one occasion we came across a slaughtered kid still warm, that under the holy Sal tree had been sacrificed to obtain the help of Singh Bonga against us. They had, like the Jews, twelve tribes… When we met them in action a chief came forward like Goliath with gestures and shouts of defiance. Like the Jews they were stiff-necked in their conservatism.[9]

This smaller Santal rebellion was overshadowed by the Great Indian Rebellion of 1857 in which Lillie apparently participated.[10] The

Indian Rebellion (or India's First War of Independence as it was more commonly known) started early in the year 1857. In tracing the causes for this high casualty war, it is important to note that there was no one cause for such a violent conflict but rather an accumulation of multiple factors. This bloody insurrection was primarily due to the expansion of and the control that the East India Trading Company exerted on India and the economic policies that it endorsed. This was a devastating war for both sides that lasted from 10 May 1857 to 20 June 1858 though it was especially tragic for the native Indians which suffered from an extremely high casualty count of anywhere from several hundreds of thousands to the latest theorized figure of ten million Indian casualties (though this high number seems exaggerated).[11] Despite this inflated number, it remained obvious that the Great Indian Rebellion was an especially brutal rebellion that resulted in the genocide of many indigenous Indian tribes of which Lillie participated. The actual extent and position that Lillie served in this battle remains unknown; however, this conflict must have also impacted Lillie's opinion of the Indian civilization and religion.

It was curious that in an interview for the *English Morning News* of Paris Blavatsky suggested her own supernatural explanation for the end of this war and the British victory which coincidentally negated the military action of Britain and of course the service and sacrifice of Arthur Lillie:

> The English owe more than they know to the religious bodies in India - to the old faiths. A few men in spiritual authority stopped the Mutiny: it was not stopped by the British army - how could England have held all these millions in check? But wise men saw that the time had not yet come for the English to go, and their expulsion would bring back the old anarchy and the old despotism; so the word was passed round, and the Mutiny stopped. And you have no idea how quickly such an order travels in India. It is what you would call miraculous. Officers have often told me that news of any event reached the common people, from the Himalayas to the sea, long before it reached the Government. There were occult arts before the telegraph, you may be sure of that. The English ought to take warning by what happened in the Mutiny and lower their tone of patronage to men immeasurably their superiors in every kind of knowledge.[12]

6.3 The Diversified Writer

Arthur Lillie drew upon his military experiences in India and went on to write a number of books related to Eastern religious practices that included: *Buddha and Early Buddhism* (1881), *The Popular Life of Buddha: Containing an Answer to the Hibbert Lectures* (1883), *Buddhism in Christendom: or, Jesus the Essene* (1887), *Buddha and his Parables* (1890), *The Influence of Buddhism on Primitive Christianity* (1893), *Buddha and Buddhism* (in the series Epoch-Makers of the World, 1900), *India in Primitive Christianity* (1909), and *Rama and Homer: An Argument That In the Indian Epics Homer Found the Theme of His Two Great Poems*, ed. G. Keith Murray (1912).

In addition to his publications in which Lillie theorized on comparative religion and Eastern religious traditions, he also published a couple of fictional stories set in India. These included *Out of the Meshes: An Indian Novel* (1869) and *An Indian Wizard* (1887) which was apparently a fictional account based on his service in the British Army during the Santal rebellion. Lillie did not allow himself to become limited to only Eastern settings and wrote numerous other fictional romance novels throughout his lifetime including *The Enchanted Toasting-Fork: A Fairy Tale* (1869), *The King of Topsy Turvy* (1870), *Puppets Dallying: A Novel* (1872), *The Railway Fortress* (1875), and *The Cobra Diamond* (1890). Lillie even incorporated Blavatsky into this final work *The Cobra Diamond* which contained a character that was an obvious representation of Blavatsky. The woman's name in the novel is Lady Puffendorff. In this book, Puffendorff communicates with secret adepts, has traveled to Tibet, and is continuously being chased by elementary spirits. And if any doubt that Puffendorff represented Blavatsky still lingered in the mind of the reader, Lillie included a description: 'short lady, very stout, very lethargic, very swaddly in her walk. Her eyes were very small and usually half closed. Perhaps it was the contrast between her fat, sleepy manner and the unexpected and astounding remarks that she was in the habit of giving vent to that struck a stranger most.'[13]

As evidenced in his criticism of Blavatsky, Lillie was concerned with exposing modern fraudulent religious movements and published several works revealing his opinion on modern movements including: *Modern Mystics and Modern Magic* (1894), *Madame Blavatsky and her 'Theosophy': A Study* (1895), *The Worship of Satan in Modern France* (1896) (the sequel to *Modern Mystics*), *The Worship of Religions* (1906), *Spiritualism Vs. Psychical Research* (1910), and the pamphlet written against *Esoteric Buddhism* titled- 'Koot Hoomi Unveiled' (1883).

Not only was Lillie a published fictional writer and a philosopher of religion as mentioned above he was also a talented croquet player publishing several works on this challenging sport: *The Book of Croquet: It's Tactics. Laws and Mode of Play* (1872), *The Laws of Croquet* (1875), *Croquet: Its History, Rules, and Secret* (1897), *Kingball: A Game For Garden Parties* (1897), and *Croquet Up to Date: Containing the Idea and Teachings of the Leading Players* (1900).

Lillie's religious publications on Buddhism and Christianity appeared to have been successfully received leading him to become accepted into the Royal Asiatic Society and provided him with the opportunity to lecture on his writings along with such noted nineteenth century scholars as George Rawlings, James Legge, Frederic Balfour, and Samuel Beal.[14] It should seem obvious that Lille possessed many talents physical, literary, and philosophical that would make him a lethal opponent against Blavatsky.

6.4 Lillie's Writings against Theosophy
In 1884, prompted it seemed by Blavatsky's misunderstanding of Eastern religions, Lillie published a booklet called *Koot Hoomi Unveiled* (1884) that questioned the mahatmas along with their writings. Through this publication Lillie opened himself up as a target for the irascible Madame Blavatsky. His works against Blavatsky will be discussed in the paragraphs below.[15]

6.5 Henry Kiddle (1824-1891)
Arthur Lille in his work *Madame Blavatsky and Her 'Theosophy': A Study* (1895) (and earlier in his 1883 booklet 'Koot Hoomi Unveiled') expounded upon the infamous issue of 'Koot Hoomi's' plagiarism from a discourse given by Henry Kiddle on 'The Present Outlook of Spiritualism' delivered at Lake Pleasant Camp Meeting on Sunday, 15 August 1880.[16] Even the most apologetic follower of Blavatsky upon reading a side by side comparison of these two works cannot disagree that one of these sources copied from the other. Since the Mahatma letter in question was written in June 1881 (nearly one year after the lecture was given by Mr. Kiddle), the suspicion falls on the mahatmas. A response came directly from Koot Hoomi, the author of the Mahatma letter in question that was rather amusing:

The letter in question…was framed by me while on a journey and on horseback. It was dictated mentally in the direction of and precipitated by a young *chela* not yet expert at this branch of psychic chemistry, and who had to transcribe it from the hardly visible imprint. Half of it, therefore, was omitted, and the other half more or less distorted by the 'artist.' When asked by him at the time whether I would look over and correct it, I answered -imprudently I confess – 'Anyhow will do, my boy; it is of no great importance if you skip a few words.' I was physically very tired by a ride of forty-eight hours consecutively, and (physically again) half asleep. Besides this, I had very important business to attend to psychically, and therefore little remained of me to devote to that letter. When I awoke I found it had already been sent on, and as I was not then anticipating its publication, I never gave it from that time a thought… Yet had I dictated my letter in the form it now appears in print, it would certainly look suspicious, and however far from what is generally called plagiarism, yet in the absence of any inverted commas it would lay a foundation for censure. But I did nothing of the kind, as the original impression now before me clearly shows.[17]

This quote proved that the concept of plagiarism was known even to the mahatmas though their understanding of what plagiarism entailed seemed to be rather vague. Darrell Erixson has written an article absolving Blavatsky from any claims of plagiarism noting that there was 'no legal precedent for the era' and that 'one must excuse Blavatsky's borrowing' since 'many people can have the same idea.'[18] Furthermore, he argued, the term *'plagiaries'* in the Latin refers to 'kidnapper' and since Blavatsky admitted that she was simply trying to reveal the *prisca theologia* that was created in the 'immemorial past…one cannot classify Blavatsky's borrowing as definitive plagiarism.'[19] Despite Erixson's best attempt, it cannot be denied that there was a sense of plagiarism in this 'era' which is illustrated by both the mahatmas vague understanding of it, but, more importantly, by the very fact that the Kiddle Incident had enough legitimacy to have been taken seriously.[20] If there was no conceptualization of plagiarism in the Victorian Era then both the Kiddle incident mentioned here and William Coleman's later accusations of plagiarism would have produced little negative impact on the Theosophical Society and would have instantly been categorized as illegitimate critiques-such was not the case.

One of Blavatsky's followers, Alfred Percy Sinnett offered an explanation to this incident claiming that both individuals might have consulted the same original source; this defense would seem plausible only if this original source could be produced antedating Kiddle's speech.[21] Blavatsky's own defense of the 'Kiddle incident' appeared in a letter to Sinnett sent on 27 September 1883:

> See the grin and fiendish sneer of M.A. Oxon [i.e. Stainton Moses] in *Light* of Sept. 8, against the Kiddle accusation. Olcott has answered it before his departure and he gave it nice to the great medium of 'Imperator' K. H. plagiarizing from Kiddle!! Then I have a letter from him, written a year before I knew you and in Professors A. Wilder's (*Phrenological Journal*) article written *seven or eight months later* I found about 20 lines verbatim from K. H.'s letter; and now Olcott found in the last *Nineteenth Century* (July I think, or August) an article 'After Death' by Norman Pearson (or something like that) a passage about God something like 18 lines taken *verbatim* to every comma, from a letter of K. H. written three years ago.[22] Has Norman Somebody plagiarised it from a letter he has never seen?...And fancy, of what a philosophical importance these Kiddle lines, to be worthy of plagiarism! Next to 'John, bring me my dinner,' '*ideas that travel or rule the world,*'-have been mentioned since the days of Plato thousands of time. The 'Eternal Now' is a sentence I can show to you in Mrs. Harding Britten's lectures and in an article of mine in the *Spiritual Scientist* nine years ago, from which she took or perhaps and most probably *did not* take it, but simply got it from astral impressions. It makes me sick all your Western wickedness and malice.[23]

Blavatsky was clearly stating that the terms she employed in Mahatma Letter No. VI were commonly used elsewhere and that this situation does not warrant plagiarism.[24] This was the same excuse Erixson had insisted upon- that many people could have the same idea. From the above quote it was apparent that Blavatsky did not concede that using a source without citing it constituted plagiarism when this occurred within an astral vision. The very idea was 'Western wickedness and malice.' In attempting to prove that copying ideas was a common occurrence, she cites an article by Norman Pearson and described how he borrowed eighteen lines (even the commas) from a Mahatma letter written three years earlier; however, to verify which Mahatma letter this statement is referring to would be extremely difficult since no specific date is given, no addressee is assigned, and the only description of its contents was that it concerned 'God'. [25]

There remains one more issue of a quote that may have been derived from Henry Kiddle's *Spirit Communications* (1879) found in Mahatma Letter No. XIX (12 August 1882). Here Blavatsky quoted an excerpt from the poem *A Hymn from the Inner Life* (1848) written by the Spiritualist prophet Thomas Lake Harris (1823 – 1906): 'No curtain hides the spheres Elysian, Nor these poor shells of half transparent dust; For all that blinds the spirit's vision, Is pride and hate and lust. *(Not for publication).*'[26] Though the poem was not reprinted word for word, there is little room for disagreement that it was derived from Harris. Now it can only be suggested that Blavatsky had taken this poem from Kiddle's work, but given the fact that Blavatsky had quoted Kiddle before without citing him, it seemed very likely that this could have occurred again.[27]

6.6 Eliphas Lévi (1810-1875)

In 'Koot Hoomi Unveiled,' Lillie accused Blavatsky of deriving most of her philosophy from a known French occultist who called himself Eliphas Lévi (1810-1875).[28] Lillie explained that the Buddhism of Theosophy is not the 'Buddhism of Tibet at all. It is the Buddhism of the South altered, and indeed, stultified to fit in with the teaching of a French book of magic written by a gentleman under the pseudonym of Eliphas Lévi.'[29]

Lévi's real name was Alphonse-Louis Constant and though he considered himself a magician, his philosophy was rooted in Catholicism. Lévi's obedience to the Catholic Church was explained in his work titled *The Key to the Great Mysteries*: 'there will always be a gap between the known and the unknown which science cannot bridge. Mankind needs an act of faith to bridge the gap in a meaningful way. But faith must be directed so as to give human life a moral meaning and purpose, and for this it is a necessary to have the absolute and invariable affirmation of a dogma preserved by an authorised hierarchy. It is necessary to have an efficacious cult, giving, with an absolute faith, a substantial realization to the symbols of belief. The priesthood, Lévi says, who are the guardians of this dogma, must be respected.[30] Thus, Lévi legitimized the Catholic Church and their dogma. This will differ from Blavatsky who seemed to disagree primarily with the institution of the church and not its philosophy:

> I have no animus. On the contrary, I have the greatest admiration
> for the Christianity of Christ, identified with Jesus of Nazareth and

embodied in the Sermon on the Mount. On the other hand, in perfect agreement with 'Leo,' I have the greatest contempt for 'Church' Christianity, or 'Churchianity,' so-called by Mr. Laurence Oliphant—that which 'Leo' so aptly describes in his criticism as a 'combination of feeble ignorance and bigotry.'[31]

Thus, it appeared that Blavatsky was provoked more by the organization of religion (such as the Catholic Church) than with the message of Jesus promulgated in Protestant Christianity.

Even with this blatant theological difference; nevertheless, the claim that Blavatsky had taken most of her concepts from Eliphas Lévi was a common theme among the early opponents of Theosophy. This idea was promulgated by Vsevolod Sergyeevich Solovyoff in his book *Modern Priestess of Isis* (1895). Solovyoff noted that Blavatsky was known to take direct quotations from Lévi's books without giving any citations or indication that these were from Lévi.[32] Though this allegation was suggested by Solovyoff, no specific examples were cited for the reader to verify the validity of this statement. William Coleman also accused Blavatsky of relying heavily upon Eliphas Lévi when writing *Isis Unveiled* (1877) having taken many of her ideas directly from *Dogme et Rituel de la Haute Magie* (1855), *La Science des Esprits* (1865), *La Clef des Grands Mysteres* (1861), and *Histoire de la Magie* (1860).[33] This accusation by Coleman showed that by the time the Mahatma letters were being written Blavatsky was already aware of Lévi's philosophy having adopted much of it in her previous work.[34] Here, again, no mentioning of specific examples of plagiarism was listed for verification.

Arthur Lillie in *Madame Blavatsky and Her 'Theosophy'* went on to claim that Blavatsky had stolen her doctrine of shells or elementals from Eliphas Lévi's *Dogme et Rituel de la Haute Magie*.[35] Lillie viewed the adaptation of 'shells' as proof that Blavatsky stole many of her concepts from this French mage:

> Her mind, as I have often stated, lacks originality. But a book by an eccentric Frenchman gave her a hint. The Abbe Louis Constant, under the pseudonym of Eliphas Lévi, had written several works on magic...Mr. Home came to Paris and quite eclipsed with magician with his marvels. Eliphas Lévi retaliated with a doctrine that he professed to find in the Kabala, the doctrine of shells...[36]Madame Blavatsky seized eagerly on this passage [Lévi's 'Dogme et Rituel de la Haute Magie,' vol. i. p. 262].

6.7 Arthur Lillie and Madame Blavatsky

In his article titled 'Madame Blavatsky and Her Theosophy,' Lillie noted the continual contradictions presented by Blavatsky over the course of her writings:

> Theosophy, through Madame Blavatsky, has announced that there is a God, that there is no God; that Nirvana is annihilation, that Nirvana is not annihilation; that the metempsychosis is a fact, that the metempsychosis is a fiction; that vegetarianism is necessary for psychic development, that vegetarianism is not necessary; that the dead are split in half and that the better halves 'can never again span the abyss that separates their state from ours'; that the better halves can span the abyss; and so on through a hundred contradictions, to be seen in my little work.[37]

Lillie went on to label Blavatsky as a common Spiritualist medium even after the apparent Oriental shift in the Theosophical Society:

> In the year 1872, Madame Blavatsky earned her bread as a professional 'medium.' From a box, called a 'cabinet,' she could cause to issue a form with a beard and turban, the spirit, she affirmed, of a pirate who died more than two hundred years ago. In the year 1883, we find her at Adyar, in Madras. Again she has a box, which she calls this time a 'shrine.' Again a figure emerges with beard and turban. This time is it announced to be a 'Buddhist' from Tibet, who some years back instructed Madame Blavatsky in the secrets of Esoteric Buddhism.[38]

Lillie identified a direct link between Blavatsky's earlier Western Spiritualism and her later Eastern occultism. Furthermore, he seemed especially interested in exposing Blavatsky's Spiritualist background to the world despite her later insistence that she had never been associated with this movement. Lillie dedicated his writing career towards exposing Blavatsky as both an opportunist and a fraud focusing upon the inconsistencies in her teachings and in her biographical accounts. He went on to demystify her own personal history noting that Blavatsky was simply an elevated Spiritualist: 'In the month of September, 1856, it is alleged that she went to Tibet, and remained there about six months. There she learned the secrets of Eastern occultism from one Koot Hoomi Lal Singh, the overstating of Spiritualism being, as I have said, one of his objects in teaching her.'[39] Lillie criticized that the early Theosophical Society was originally 'announced to be a spiritualistic Society' and noted the inconsistency of her later teachings observing that in her early career Blavatsky was an ardent Spiritualist and 'at this time the dangers that result to Spiritualists from 'Shells' and Elementaries' did not seem to disturb her much.'⁴⁰ In her earlier career, there seemed to be no mention of any harm associated with the mediumistic act of channeling departed spirits as Blavatsky would later claim in her *Key to Theosophy* published in 1889.

In his 'Koot Hoomi Unveiled,' Lillie professed three objectives which he believed Koot Hoomi was attempting to achieve; how he arrived at these conclusions remains unknown. Only the first of these objectives appears relevant to this particular study- (1) To convert Spiritualists by proving to them that none but the most degraded spirits can communicate with them, the mere smoke and smell of the blown-out candle.'⁴¹ Lillie went on to connect Koot Hoomi to the common materializations being produced in Spiritualist circles around the Western world:

> Let us see how he [Koot Hoomi] sets to work to compass object No. 1. He selects a lady who is a medium, and believes that her dead father can come back to her. Is not this arming the Spiritualists with a dilemma that has two cruel prongs? They may ask: Were the miracles of Madame Blavatsky, when she was a medium, real miracles, or only cheats? If they were genuine, and the buccaneer John King, two hundred years after death could really bring medals of honour from her father's tomb to her, it is plain that she has proved instead of disproving Spiritualism. If they were frauds and due to sham beards and sleight of hand, why may not the appearances of Koot Hoomi and his brooches and breakfast cups be due to similar imposture?⁴²

Thus, Lillie accused Koot Hoomi of being nothing more than an impostor created using the same methods that certain fraudulent Spiritualists employed in producing human materializations. Though Lillie never blatantly accused Theosophy of becoming a modified form of Spiritualism based on the above insinuations this critique seemed to be the basic premise of his argument and was continuously implied throughout his writings.⁴³ Despite Lillie's borderline 'conspiracy theory' view of Blavatsky his critiques legitimate the central thesis of this work –that in the nineteenth century Blavatsky was viewed as a Spiritualist medium especially by her contemporaneous critics.

6.8 Lillie's Gnostic 'Buddh-ianity'

Arthur Lillie's personal belief structure could be categorized as a combination of Gnosticism and theosophy; however, Lillie's view of theosophy differed from the 'Theosophy' proposed by Blavatsky. His own personal convictions were elucidated in *Modern Mystics* that:

> for years I have been a patient student of the real Indian Theosophy, and I think that the old Indian books are destined, at no distant date, to breathe life once more into the dead theologies of Europe. But before we attempt building it is necessary to get the ground firm under foot. Buddhism, or, Buddhism Gnosticism, whether by Ananda, St. Paul. Or Mirza the Sufi, is the most purely spiritual religion yet given to man. The word simply means knowledge of spirit.[44]

Thus, 'knowledge of spirit' was a key component of Lillie's belief structure. In short, Lillie believed in a *prisca theologia* the belief that there was an original religion which had become corrupted through time. This original religion Lillie called higher Buddhism (and Higher Christianity) was eventually corrupted into its lower form of Buddhism which was the form that was practiced by the majority of Buddhists during this time period.

Lillie went on to expand upon this idea noting its Gnostic roots. He told the story of a friend of his who had visited Nepal, and while there he had met a:

> learned old Buddist, Amirta Nanda Bandhya. This individual, reticent at first, was at last persuaded to disclose … the inner teaching of his religion. He revealed a creed to like the lofty Gnosticism of Philo and Clemens Alexandrius, that writers like Mr. Rhys Davis contend that Nepaulese Buddhism is Christianity imported from the West. [This] gnostic school is called, on the other hand, the Buddhism of the North… I may mention that I entered upon the study without bias, and that my conclusions have been gradual…There was a higher Christianity and a higher Judaism both very like Buddhism, for transcendental wisdom must always be one the old Buddhists believed the higher Buddhism and the higher Christianity to be the same religion, an idea which seems also to have been held by St. Paul, for he talks of a gospel as having already been 'preached to every creature under heaven' at a time when outside Jerusalem, a small Romish congregation comprise almost all the Gentile converts of the historical apostles.[45]

Thus, Lillie maintained that there was one true philosophy underlying both Christianity and Buddhism and that this was the higher form mentioned above. Most of Lillie's works on Buddhism were comparative in nature and attempted to reconcile his Western views of Buddhism with Judaism and Christianity. In combining these differing theologies, Lillie focused upon the affinities of these belief systems including the worship of a triune God, the birth narratives, the teachings of Buddha and the Sermon on the Mount. The concept of comparing Eastern and Western religious elements was not a novel concept in the nineteenth century, nor was combining this idea with a belief in an ancient wisdom tradition having already been attempted in the unreliable histories of both Kersey Graves' *The World's Sixteen Crucified Saviors* (1875) and Godfrey Higgin's *Anacalypsis* (1833).[46]

Lillie demarcated between the higher forms of religion which were associated with the original form of the *prisca theologia* and their subsequent lower corrupted form.[47] Lillie had been raised as a Christian though he maintained a Gnostic belief system which assimilated Christianity and Buddhism.[48] He held that Buddha and Christ 'taught much the same doctrine… that religion was the religion of the individual, as discriminated from religion by body corporate.'[49] One of Lillie's core disagreements with Theosophy was their belief of transmigration:

> But in point of fact, whether we adopt the metempsychosis in its full Indian absurdity, or whether we improve upon it, as most Theosophists do, according to their fancy, that scheme, instead of promoting spiritual perfection, would make the spiritual growth almost impossible.[50]

Lillie believed in spiritual progression which would also put him at odds with Blavatsky's view of annihilation. Lillie held that after death the soul could not be either annihilated or reincarnated but instead went directly into a heavenly realm:

> It is to be confessed that many graver teachers in India and the West have held some of these views; but the original Mahabharata knew nothing of the modern misty doctrines of Moksha and Nirvana. The hero goes to the eternal heaven of God, a heaven tenanted by the seven great legions of dead men made wise (vidyadharas).[51]

Furthermore, Lillie believed in the existence of this 'higher' universal tradition and the fact that Christianity, Judaism, and Buddhism all held the key to this truth. It seemed curious that Lillie would have so voraciously attacked Blavatsky given their similar belief structures based on the existence on the *prisca theologia* and their appreciation for Eastern religions; however, Lillie's main disagreements apparently stemmed from the fact that Blavatsky claimed to teach Eastern philosophy while her teachings seemed to be merely a perversion of Western Spiritualism. Though this same Western persuasion could be alleged about Lillie, nonetheless, he spent much of his time and energy attempting to expose Blavatsky to the world and remained an exceptionally vicious opponent to the early Theosophical Society.

6.9 William Emmette Coleman: A Disgruntled Spiritualist

William Emmette Coleman was one of the most vocal adversaries of Blavatsky in the nineteenth century and he also claimed to be a loyal Spiritualist. Coleman had devoted three years of his life towards analyzing Blavatsky's major works and writings and published his critiques in such noted Spiritualist publications as *The Golden Way* , *The Carrier Dove*, and the *Religio-Philosophical Journal*. One of Coleman's articles was also published as an appendix to Vsevolod Solovyoff's book *A Modern Priestess of Isis* (1895) entitled 'The Sources of Madame Blavatsky's Writings.' In his writings, Coleman argued that Blavatsky had plagiarized most of her information from Western sources. Coleman mentioned his intention to publish a book that would fully 'expose of theosophy as a whole' by expounding upon his ideas set forth in this article.[52] Despite his eagerness to expose Blavatsky, this book never saw publication. In his article 'The Sources of Madame Blavatsky's Writings' Coleman noted a long list of sources that Blavatsky had plagiarized from along with the number of quotations that Blavatsky had stolen; however, he rarely cited specific examples of this plagiarism which makes many of his assertions too vague to verify. This is not to conclude that Coleman was incorrect in his assumptions only that many of his accusations were never specified. Coleman's claims, though extensive, are vital for ascertaining the writings of Blavatsky and her sources.[53]

6.10 Coleman's Critique of *Isis Unveiled*

Coleman demonstrated that Blavatsky had plagiarized from a number of sources in her writing of *Isis Unveiled*. Blavatsky would later admit to this fact in her last article 'My Books,' written before her demise in 1891. Nonetheless, Coleman had started the process of analyzing Blavatsky's sources. He noted the following works were continuously used by Blavatsky:

> Mackenzie's *Masonic Cyclopaedia*, King's *Gnostics*, and the works of S. F. Dunlap, L. Jacolliot, and Eliphas Levi. Not a line of the quotations in *Isis*, from the old-time mystics, Paracelsus, Van Helmont, Cardan, Robert Fludd, Philalethes, Gaffarel, and others, was taken from the original works; the whole of them were copied from other books containing scattered quotations from those writers. The same thing obtains with her quotations from Josephus, Philo, and the Church Fathers, as Justin Martyr, Origen, Clement, Irenaeus, Tertullian, Eusebius, and all the rest. The same holds good with the classical authors, - Homer, Ovid, Horace, Virgil, Plato, Pliny, and many others. The quotations from all these were copied at second-hand from some of the 100 books which were used by the compiler of *Isis*.
>
> In a number of instances Madame Blavatsky, in *Isis* claimed to possess or to have read certain books quoted from, which it is evident she neither possessed nor had read... Here follows a list of some other of the more extensive plagiarisms in *Isis*. It includes the names of the books plagiarised from, and the number of passages in them that were plagiarized.[54]

Coleman went on to identify some of the key works that Blavatsky consulted in her work both cited and uncited. These works included: Eliphas Levi's *Dogme et Rituel de la Haute Magie, La Science des Esprits, La Clef des Grands Mysteres,* and *Histoire de la Magie;* Max Muller's *Chips,* vols. I and II, Taylor's *Eleusinian and Bacchic Mysteries* (1875 ed.), Mackenzie's *Masonic Cyclopedia.* Jacolliot's *Christna et le Christ, Bible in India* (English translation), *Le Spiritisme dans le Monde,* Ennemoser's *History of Magic* (English translation), Emma Hardinge's *Modern American Spiritualism,* Gasparin's *Science and Spiritualism, Report on Spiritualism of the London Dialectical Society* (1873), Randolph's *Pre-Adamite Man,*[55] Peebles's *Jesus: Myth, Man, or God, Around the World, Principles of the Jesuits* (1893), *Septenary Institutions* (1850), Higgins's *Anacalypsis,* Bunsen's *Egypt,* and Wallace's *Miracles and Modern Spiritualism.*[56]

Coleman's inclusion of such noted Spiritualists as Emma Hardinge Britten, James Peebles, and Alfred Wallace evidenced the strong influence that Spiritualism exerted on Blavatsky's *Isis Unveiled.* Nicholas Goodrick-Clarke has made a stunning realization concerning Coleman's accusations towards understanding Blavatsky's sources:

'What is important in Coleman's analysis is not his charge of unat-tributed quotations and plagiarism, but the identity of her nine-teenth-century sources. Coleman's list of sources from which she took most passages in the compilation of *Isis Unveiled* indicates her chief inspiration in histories of ancient religion, magic, Gnosticism, Hermeticism, Neo-Platonism, Kabbalah, Freemasonry, and modern spiritualism.'[57]

6.11 Coleman's Critique of *Esoteric Buddhism* and the Mahatma Letters

William Coleman went on to analyze both *Esoteric Buddhism* and the Mahatma letters noting some of the primary sources consulted by Blavatsky:

> *Esoteric Buddhism*, by A. P. Sinnett, was based upon statements in letters received by Mr. Sinnett and Mr. A. O. Hume, through Madame Blavatsky, purporting to be written by the Mahatmas Koot Hoomi and Morya, - principally the former.... I find in them overwhelming evidence that all of them were written by Madame Blavatsky, which evidence will be presented in full in my book. In these letters are a number of extracts from Buddhist books, alleged to be translations from the originals by the Mahatmic writers themselves. These letters claim for the adepts a knowledge of Sanskrit, Thibetan, Pali and Chinese. I have traced to its source each quotation from the Buddhist scriptures in the letters, and they were all copied from current English translations, including even the notes and explanations of the English translators. They were principally copied from Beal's *Catena of Buddhist Scriptures from the Chinese*. In other places where the adept (?) is using his own language in explanation of Buddhistic terms and ideas, I find that his presumed original language was copied nearly word for word from Rhys Davids's *Buddhism*, and other books. I have traced every Buddhistic idea in these letters and in *Esoteric Buddhism*, and every Buddhistic term, such as Devachan, Avitchi, etc., to the books whence Helena Petrovna Blavatsky derived them. Although said to be proficient in the knowledge of Thibetan and Sanskrit, the words and terms in these languages in the letters of the adepts were nearly all used in a ludicrously erroneous and absurd manner. The writer of those letters was an ignoramus in Sanskrit and Thibetan; and the mistakes and blunders in them, in these languages, are in exact accordance with the known ignorance of Madame Blavatsky thereanent. *Esoteric Buddhism*, like all of Madame Blavatsky's works, was based upon wholesale plagiarism and ignorance.[58]

Though Coleman's conclusion seems harsh, he brought to light several key sources used in writing these Mahatma letters- Rhys Davids' *Buddhism* (1877) and Samuel Beal's *Catena of Buddhist Scriptures from the Chinese* (1871). These authors were both mentioned in Mahatma Letter No. XVI along with Émile-Louis Burnouf a professor at the French School in Athens and a noted Orientalist and anti-Semite.[19] Many of the Eastern terms used in *Esoteric Buddhism* can be found in either Beal or Rhys David's works. These include Avitchi, Devachan, Kama Loka, Rupa Loka, and Arupa Loka; however, the Western terms such as kingdoms, monads, and the eighth sphere are noticeably absent in these 'Orientalist' writings.

In an article published in the Chicago based *Religio-Philosophical Journal,* William Emmette Coleman declared that *Esoteric Buddhism* had nothing to do with Buddhism at all, but was rather simply a concoction of Western ideas mixed together by Blavatsky:

> The name 'Esoteric Buddhism' applied to the system of thought known as theosophy is a misnomer. It is not Buddhism. Nearly the whole of it is borrowed from sources alien to Buddhism. A portion is Brahmanism, and the remainder is taken from Paracelsus, Eliphas Levi, the Kabbala, Spiritualism and Christianity. It is doubtful if there is anything distinctively Buddhistic in it, save the use of a few Sanskrit terms. Its doctrine of Karma approximates the Brahmanic idea more than it does the Buddhistic, and its reincarnation is more Brahmanic than Buddhistic. In fact, theosophy has no title whatever to the name of Buddhism, exoteric or esoteric, and its appropriation of the name is in keeping with all the rest of its false pretensions, perversions and distortions. From top to bottom, from stem to stern, theosophy is one mass of falsehood, tergiversation, pretense, imposture, fraud. As a humbug it has perhaps never been excelled.[60]

6.12 Coleman's Critique of *The Secret Doctrine*

The Secret Doctrine was written while Blavatsky resided in India and it had the appearance of being heavily influenced by Eastern philosophy; however, many Western Esoteric scholars now believe that this Eastern influence was more apparent than actual.[61] When examining her sources that Coleman analyzed in relation to *The Secret Doctrine* it seemed as though she was largely influenced more by Western philosophy and Western views of Eastern ideas. Coleman noted that *The Secret Doctrine* 'permeated with plagiarisms, and is in all its parts a rehash of other books.'⁶² He went on to note the major victims of Blavatsky's plagiarism:

> A specimen of the wholesale plagiarisms in this book appears in vol. ii., pp. 599-603. Nearly the whole of four pages was copied from Oliver's *Pythagorean Triangle*, while only a few lines were credited to that work. Considerable other matter in *Secret Doctrine* was copied, uncredited, from Oliver's work. Donnelly's *Atlantis* was largely plagiarised from. Madame Blavatsky not only borrowed from this writer the general idea of the derivation of Eastern civilisation, mythology, etc., from *Atlantis*; but she coolly appropriated from him a number of the alleged detailed evidences of this derivation, without crediting him therewith. Vol. ii., pp. 790-793, contains a number of facts, numbered *seriatim*, said to prove this Atlantean derivation. These facts were almost wholly copied from Donnelly's book, ch. iv., where they are also numbered *seriatim*; but there is no intimation in The *Secret Doctrine* that its author was indebted to Donnelly's book for this mass of matter.
>
> In addition to those credited, there are 130 passages from Wilson's *Vishnu Purana* copied uncredited; and there are some 70 passages from Winchell's *World Life* not credited. From Dowson's *Hindu Classical Dictionary*, 123 passages were plagiarised. From Decharme's *Mythologie de la Grece Antique*, about 60 passages were plagiarised; and from Myer's *Qabbala*, 34. These are some of the other books plagiarised from: Kenealy's *Book of God*, Faber's *Cabiri*, Wake's *Great Pyramid*, Gould's *Mythical Monsters*, Joly's *Man before Metals*, Stallo's, *Modern Physics*, Massey's *Natural Genesis*, Mackey's *Mythological Astronomy*, Schmidt's *Descent and Darwinism*, Quatrefages's *Human Species*, Laing's *Modern Science and Modern Thought*, Mather's *Cabbala Unveiled*, Maspero's *Musee de Boulaq*, Ragon's *Maconnerie Occulte*, Lefevre's *Philosophy*, and Buchner's *Force and Matter*.

Despite this list of plagiarisms which remain accessible and in print for any interested individual to confirm, many of her followers still attempt to circumvent these allegations by attacking Coleman and his critiques.⁶³

Aside from the charge of plagiarism, Coleman noted some philosophical issues with *The Secret Doctrine* and its claims to have compiled the religious traditions of the world into one system was nonsense and was really more 'Blavatskyism' than any established religious belief:

> They write sweetly about universal truth, the good in all religions, the divine wisdom; but when you make them plainly and squarely

confess what they really believe in, you find that the divine wisdom, the universal truth, consists of reincarnation, karma, the teachings of the mahatmas, and all the other rubbish of Madame Blavatsky. They prate about Jesus and the other reformers being theosophists; did Jesus, Paul, Zoroaster, Confucius, teaching reincarnation, karma, the doctrines of 'shells,' elemental and elementary spirits, devachan, or any other part of the 'Secret Doctrine' of Madame Blavatsky? Did Buddha teach any of this except reincarnation and karma? The conclusion of the whole matter is, try to disguise it as some theosophists may, present-day theosophy is Blavatskyism all through. Its teachings are primarily derived from her; her labors and her writings are the main-spring and fountainhead of the whole movement. She bestowed the name of theosophy upon the movement started by her, and all other theosophists adopted the name from her. From her every theosophist has his being, and from her nearly all other forms of present day occultism and mysticism, not calling themselves theosophic, have been derived. All phases of the occultism and the mysticism of the present day can be summed up in one word - Blavatskyism; and that is virtually a synonym of imposture as well as of mystical rubbish; and I repeat, the sooner the whole of this fanfaronade of nonsense and corruption is buried in oblivion the better for humanity.[64]

6.13 Coleman's Critiques of *The Key To Theosophy*

Coleman does not have all that much to say about Blavatsky's *Key to Theosophy*, though he does briefly note the following vague report: 'The *Key to Theosophy*, by Helena Petrovna Blavatsky, being a compendium of doctrines. Its plagiarisms consists in the ideas and teachings which it contains rather than in plagiarized passages from other books.'[65] Given Coleman's lack of analysis connected with this work, it seemed that this work was the most original of Blavatsky's and her best cited work. *The Key to Theosophy* was a summary of Blavatsky's basic belief systems and though she had borrowed ideas from other sources it remained distinctively 'Blavatskian.'

6.14 Coleman's Critiques of *The Voice of Silence*

Coleman's critiques of the *Voice of Silence* were equally vague as his analysis of the *Key to Theosophy*:

> The *Voice of the Silence*, published in 1889, purports to be a translation by Helena Petrovna Blavatsky from a Thibetan work. It is said to belong to the same series as the *Book of Dzyan*, which is true; as, like that work, it is a compilation of ideas and terminology from

various nineteenth-century books, the diction and phraseology being those of Madame Blavatsky. I have traced the sources whence it was taken, and it is a hotch-potch from Brahmanical books on Yoga and other Hindu writings; Southern Buddhistic books, from the Pali and Sinhalese; and Northern Buddhistic writings, from the Chinese and Thibetan,- the whole having been taken by Helena Petrovna Blavatsky from translations by, and the writings of, European and other Orientalists of to-day. In this work are intermingled Sanskrit, Pali, Thibetan, Chinese, and Sinhalese terms, - a manifest absurdity in a Thibetan work. I have traced the books from which each of these terms was taken. I find embedded in the text of this alleged ancient Thibetan work quotations, phrases, and terms copied from current Oriental literature. The books most utilised in its compilation are these: Schlagintweit's *Buddhism in Thibet*, Edkins's's *Chinese Buddhism*, Hardy's *Eastern Monachism*, Rhys Davids's *Buddhism*, Dvivedi's *Raja Yoga*, and *Raja Yoga Philosophy* (1888); also an article, 'The Dream of Ravan,' published in the *Dublin University Magazine*, January, 1854, extracts from which appeared in the *Theosophist* of January, 1880. Passages from this article, and from the books named above, are scattered about in the text of the *Voice of the Silence*, as well as in the annotations thereon, which latter are admitted to be the work of Blavatsky. Full proofs of this, including the parallel passages, will be given in my work on theosophy; including evidence that this old Thibetan book contains not only passages from the Hindu books quoted in the article in the *Dublin Magazine*, but also ideas and phrases stolen from the nineteenth-century writer of said article. One example of the incongruity of the elements composing the conglomerate admixture of terms and ideas in the *Voice of the Silence* will be given. On p. 87, it is said that the Narjols of the Northern Buddhists are 'learned in Gotrabhu-gnyana and gnyana-dassana-suddhi.' Helena Petrovna Blavatsky copied these two terms from Hardy's *Eastern Monachism*, p. 281. The terms used in Northern Buddhism are usually Sanskrit, or from the Sanskrit; those in Southern Buddhism, Pali, or from the Pali. Hardy's work, devoted to Sinhalese Buddhism, is composed of translations from Sinhalese books, and its terms and phrases are largely Sinhalese corruptions of the Pali terms are unknown in Northern Buddhism. The two terms in the *Voice of the Silence*, descriptive of the wisdom of the Narjols, are Sinhalese-Pali corruptions, and therefore unknown in Thibet. Narjol is a word manufactured by Helena Petrovna Blavatsky, from the Thibetan Nal-jor, which she found in Schlagintweit's work, p. 138, - the *r* and *l* being transposed by her. [66]

Coleman suggested that underlying this Eastern philosophical book were the multiple writings of the Western 'Orientalists' though he again failed to provide instances where these plagiarisms had occurred. Coleman further believed that Blavatsky had created her own term 'Narjol' which he claimed had been derived from the Tibetan word 'Nal-jor.' An article printed in an 1895 issue of *Lucifer* disputed this idea and noted that 'in the Sacred Texts Series of Prof. Max Muller you will observe a curious mode of transcription is used. There *g* is used in the place of *j*. Hence it is likely to write Naljor as Nalgor, and then change *r* for *l* to get Nargol.' Despite this apologetic article written against Coleman's critique, the very fact that Blavatsky had utilized Muller's work again illustrated that Blavatsky was largely influenced by Western sources in 1889.[67] Coleman further believed that Blavatsky had derived her concept of 'Gotrabhu-gnyana and gnyana-dassana-suddhi' from Robert Spence Hardy's *Eastern Monachism* which seemed legitimate given the fact that Blavatsky had relied heavily on this source in her earlier writing of *Isis Unveiled*. In *Isis Unveiled* Blavatsky mentioned karma in volume one on page 346; however, she plagiarized this from *Eastern Monarchism* (p. 6) nearly word for word without giving any credit to Hardy.[68] Though the majority of Coleman's accusations remain too vague to verify this should not illegitimate his accusations that Blavatsky had committed plagiarism. Furthermore, Coleman's analysis of Blavatsky's sources illustrated her Western influence during the composition of this work.

6.15 Analyzing Coleman

William Coleman's analyses have stirred much controversy since their initial publication. Many who remain sympathetic to Theosophy have attempted to disprove Coleman's above analysis by attacking his personal character. It has been noted that Coleman held a humble position as a clerk in the Quartermaster Department of the U.S. Army.[69] Michael Gomes noted that out of the long list of credentials that Coleman boasted in his article 'The Sources of Madame Blavatsky's Writings' (the American Oriental Society, the Royal Asiatic Society of Great Britain and Ireland, and the Pali Text Society) none of his contributions in these fields are known.[70] Gomes also recorded a thorough analysis of Coleman's charges leveled against Blavatsky (including his rare articles in *The Golden Way* and *Light*) and further noted that in 1890 Coleman was pursuing a theory that the scholarly part of *Isis Unveiled* was taken from a manuscript which he believed might have been left de Baron De Palm—an early member of the Theosophical Society.[71] Sylvia Cranston rightfully scrutinized Coleman's own literary reputation noting that he himself had been accused of plagiarism by William Burr:

> Coleman himself did not always practice what he had preached concerning giving credit to secondary sources. In his essay 'Sunday Not Being the Real Sabbath', he borrowed without credit numerous quotations from a paper on the subject by William Henry Burr…(Cranston goes on to quote an article written by Burr)…W.E.C has borrowed from my little work all that he has quoted or summarized from Irenaeus, Clement, Tertullian, Victorinus, Origen, Eusebius, Jerome, Luther, Melanchthon, Baxter, Ileyin, Milton, Paley,and Neander. Every reference given by him to the aforesaid authorities is borrowed from me, and has added nothing from their works which he did not find in my work.' Nor did Coleman acknowledge that Burr's booklet existed. Burr also cites which parts Coleman had plagiarized.[72]

Cranston roundly concluded that 'Coleman overreaches himself and loses all rights to credibility as an honest researcher.'[73] Despite personal opinions about Coleman's ability to perform this analysis, it should be noted whether he was correct in his claims or not. Bruce Campbell confirmed Coleman's analysis and the detrimental implications of this charge on Blavatsky's philosophy:

> [after quoting Coleman's article 'The Sources of Madame Blavatsky's Writings'] a sample of several dozen of the alleged plagiarisms were checked in the research for this book (*Ancient Wisdom Revived*, 1980). In every case, I found the passage from *Isis* verbatim in the source given by Coleman. Many of these quotations were of a single sentence, though sometimes there were two or more plagiarized sentences in one paragraph from the same paragraph of a single source. One might argue that the total is a small amount of a two-volume work that runs to many hundred pages, or that her unattributed borrowing was consistent with some nineteenth-century standard of attribution. Still, the number two thousand suggests plagiarism on a large scale and, more to the point, challenges the Theosophical interpretation of the source of Madame Blavatsky's writings. Coleman's evidence suggests neither inspiration by Masters nor familiarity with the vast range of literature cited in *Isis*.[74]

Gomes performed his own source analysis of Blavatsky with the following result:

> In verifying Coleman's charges of plagiarism given in their most detailed form in the 1891 Golden Way articles, I found the quotes in question were often only a few words or a sentence, almost always referring to some obscure text of the medieval or classical period. When used in Isis, they are far from being lifted word for word as he suggests. There is a similarity to an original source and that is all.[75]

Though Gomes continued to provide one instance where Coleman's allegations were mistaken, Gomes also failed to acknowledge the instances where Coleman was correct. Thus, giving the impression that Coleman was wrong in all of his claims which seems unfair.[76]

These two points of view reflect the divided opinions in Theosophical studies on Blavatsky's sources; however, the truth likely rests somewhere between these differing views. Blavatsky would have been viewed as a plagiarizer (as she herself admitted in her final article 'My Books') due to her tendency for taking material from secondary sources and citing it as primary, her neglect to use quotation marks when using direct quotes (many instances of this are proved throughout this study), and her inability to cite many of her direct quotes. However, in some of Coleman's allegations, Blavatsky does use her sources correctly, and does not appear to plagiarize them.[77] Thus, the answer is that Blavatsky did plagiarize often, though not in every case that Coleman has suggested.

6.16 Coleman and Spiritualism

Coleman began his investigation of Theosophy seemingly open-minded as evidenced in an article written in 1881 for the *Religio-Philosophical Journal* in which he noted the potential benefits of Theosophy in promoting the Spiritualist cause:

> There is a foundation of truth in the vagaries of Theosophy. Spirits in the body do perform some of the phenomena attributed to the spirits disembodied. If the Theosophists would drop their absurdities about elementaries and elementals and go to work to demonstrate the action of the occult forces of the human spirit on earth, they would be doing valuable work --- work much needed. But as it is the little truth they have is so encumbered with nonsense and charlatanry that their influence upon the world is more

injurious than beneficial. Occultism and Theosophy rightly directed would be eminently serviceable to Spiritualism and the
world. Let us hope that in time its services may be thus utilized.[78]

Coleman in suggesting the heavy influence that Spiritualism exerted on Blavatsky observed that she was originally a Spiritualist medium before creating her Theosophical Society which was at its inception 'an offshoot from Spiritualism; and from this source was a large
part of her theosophy taken. I find that its teachings upon some 267
points were copied from those of spiritualism.'[79] Michael Gomes
noted that 'Coleman in a series on the early history of the T.S., 'Spiritualism and the Wisdom Religion' (*The Carrier Dove*, San Francisco,
Nov. 1891, p. 298)... sought to prove that the Founders were really
renegade spiritualists.'[80]

These articles which Gomes alluded to above were compiled and
printed in a rare pamphlet published in Bombay, India in 1892 as
Blavatsky Unveiled. This series of articles were derived from a *New
York Sun* column allegedly written by Elliott Coues and published on
20 July 1890. Coleman took large pieces of this article and mixed it
with his own commentary. In this article Blavatsky was charged with
exploiting Spiritualism though it was not copied in Coleman's article
derived from a sub-title in this column:

> Whatever the nature of the instructions from Russia under which
> she was ostensibly exploited in spiritualism then, as before and
> since. But we first hear of anything to your present purpose after
> she had met Olcott in Vermont in the fall of 1874. And been
> written up by him. ...At this time, as we have seen, Mrs.
> Blavatsky-Metrovich-Bettanely had not been metempsychosed
> into a theosophist. She was simply exploiting as a spiritualist
> medium, setting a style and fashion later developed into a fine art
> by New York by Delia Ann O'Sullivan, better known as the Dis-
> Debar woman.[81]

Furthermore, Coleman noted a duality in Blavatsky's beliefs related
to Spiritualism as exemplified in the Kiddle incident of 1883-84.

> A person who, while pretending to despise Spiritualism, and while
> belittling and ridiculing its lecturers, would steal from a Spiritualist
> lecturer's printed address some sixty lines of said lecturer's
> language, and by slight manipulation, adapt it to another subject,
> and then palm it off as an original production; who, when
> discovered in this literary theft, would manufacture or cause to be

made a forged document to sustain a totally false defense of said theft; and who would deliberately invent a tissue of falsehoods like that composing the so-called explanation of Koot Hoomi, - a person who could be guilty of all this is morally despicable, and worthy only of the scorn and contempt of every lover of truth, honor, and honesty. One who could falsify in this wholesale manner is unworthy of credit on any subject; his or her assertions or teachings are, in themselves, absolutely worthless in all matters. No reliance can be placed in a single word emanating from such a corrupt and constitutionally untruthful source. The mind that produced the Koot Hoomi writings in this matter has falsehood, deception, craft, and low, cunning trickery ingrained in its innate constitution; it is saturated with steeped in, mendacity, forgery, and fraud.

Despite the personal attacks implied in this above article, Coleman was correct in noting the irony in the accusations that the 'master' had plagiarized his letters from a Spiritualist despite Blavatsky's shifting opinion in the danger of this movement. Coleman went on to publish an article in the *Two Worlds* which attempted to paint the Society from a Spiritualist point of view though he viewed it as being harmful to the cause:

In 1875 an organized movement, called Theosophy, was instituted in New York City, by Madame H. P. Blavatsky and Col. H. S. Olcott; and from the inception of this movement to the present time it has been brought into connection, more or less, with modern spiritualism....At no time during these fifteen years has the attitude of the founders of theosophy, and its leading workers, as well as the fundamental bases of its philosophy, been otherwise than inimical to the central principles of spiritualism... During these earlier years it was not denied by the founders of theosophy that a small part of the spiritual phenomena was caused by the direct personal action of good and pure disembodied human spirits. But shortly after the transfer of the theosophical headquarters to India in 1879, a new theory of the constitution of man, and to some extent of the sources of the spiritual manifestations was broached by the theosophic leaders... According to these theories, no genuine human spirit call communicate with earth, and the whole of the manifestations so far as they are produced by spirits, are due to the influence of low, degraded, vicious, demoralizing intelligences, or semi-intelligences. In consonance with this, mediumship has been persistently denounced and discouraged by the theosophists as demoniacal and degrading, a species of black magic...[82]

Coleman continued to conclude that Spiritualism answered the same questions that Theosophy attempted:

> There is nothing of value to be gained from theosophy that cannot be found in spiritualism. Every truth that is in theosophy is also in spiritualism. The former prates largely of soul culture, of development of man's higher nature, and of culture of the latent psychic powers in man. All this has formed a component of the spiritual philosophy from its beginning, with this distinction: The soul culture of spiritualism is rational, healthful, scientific, and adapted to man's highest uses; while that of theosophy is largely impracticable, fanatical, and leading the mind into extravagances calculated to injure rather than benefit those indulging in this fantastic kind of culture. I regard theosophy as the greatest enemy of modern spiritualists. Spiritualists should consider well the many startling contrasts between the doctrines of theosophy and Spiritualism, a few of which have been enumerated above…Theosophy says this world is the realm of causes, the spirit world that of effects; that there is no progress in the spirit world there being, for the most part, nothing but a period of protracted dreaming, of thousands of years duration, between nearly 6,000 different incarnations; that progress pertains to the successive earth lives, in each of which we develop a new *karma*, with which we start again at our next re-birth in a physical body.[83]

Thus, Coleman's eventual conclusion was that Theosophy was a perversion of Spiritualism and became based upon the eclectic and continuously shifting opinions of its foremost leader Madame Blavatsky and should more appropriately be titled 'Blavatskyism.' This Blavatskyism was a philosophically eclectic belief that remained connected to Spiritualism in some of its ideologies and its phenomena.

6.17 Richard Hodgson (1855–1905):
Theosophy from the Other Side

The decline of Spiritualism in the 1870-1880s was not the result of mere coincidence; rather, it was during this time period that scientific research groups were established to investigate the claims of Spiritualism. These groups applied the scientific method towards psychic investigations and attempted to empirically verify the claims of mediums and their phenomena. The development of these scientific organizations resulted in the exposure of countless mediums. One of the more well known of these organizations was the Society for Psychical Research (S.P.R.) established in 1882 by Henry Sidgwick a professor at Cambridge University. The S.P.R. would be the same organization that in 1884 would commission Richard Hodgson to travel to India to investigate the Theosophical phenomena occurring at their headquarters in Madras, India. Hodgson's report was officially published in 1885 and caused irreparable damage to the reputation and integrity of both Blavatsky and her Theosophical Society. In order to fully understand Hodgson's conclusions some biographical details should first be considered.

Richard Hodgson was born on 24 September 1855 in Melbourne, Australia. He grew up as a Nonconformist and as a young man he was known to give his testimony at Methodist meetings.[84] He attended the University of Melbourne where he received a Bachelor of Arts (1874), Bachelor of Law (1885), Master of Arts (1876), and a Doctorate of Law (1878). Hodgson maintained an intimate love interest with his cousin Jessie Turner Dunn causing his parents to directly interfere with his personal life which led to a harsh break up.[85] In 1879, just four years after this dissolution, Jessie died and Hodgson remained unmarried for the rest of his life. It seemed curious that it was during the same year of his lover's death that Hodgson attended his first séance.

Meanwhile, Hodgson continued to further his education enrolling at St. John's College at Cambridge University where he received a Bachelor of Arts degree in 1882 and a Master of Arts degree in 1893. Hodgson had specifically chose St. John's for one of its most famous alumni- William Wordsworth the Lake Poet whom Hodgson greatly admired.[86] In 1881, Hodgson became a professor of poetry and philosophy at Cambridge University Extension and in 1884 accepted a fulltime position as a professor of philosophy at Cambridge University. Hodgson became obsessed with the paranormal and its phenomena. F. B. Smith noted the influence of the supernatural upon Hodgson:

> Since 1879 he had participated in the séances arranged by the Sidgwicks, F. W. H. Myers and other Cambridge investigators and in 1882 he had become an early member of the Society for Psychical Research. His supernatural experiences began in September 1884 with the touch of disembodied hands in the dark in his room at St John's. About this time too he was experimenting with hallucinatory drugs. He afterwards became convinced that he

had received premonitions of the deaths of three friends and of his mother.[87]

The use of mind altering drugs and narcotics to produce phenomena was a common occurrence in the nineteenth century as noted throughout the 1881 volume of *Light* and in the pages of *Two Worlds*.[88] Opium provided a legal alternative to somnambulistic faculties and could be purchased in large quantities as late as 1897 through mail order from the Sears Roebuck catalog.[89]

Despite this avowed interest in phenomena; nonetheless, Hodgson in 1887 noted that many Spiritualists were indeed 'fraudulent' and 'inconclusive' and many used 'trickery' to perform their phenomena. It was during this same time period that he moved in to his headquarters at 5 Boylston Place in downtown Boston, MA in order to fill the position of executive secretary in the American branch of the Society of Psychic Research. This same year (1887) Hodgson made the following observation concerning mediums:

> It has been considered by perhaps the majority of Spiritualists, not only that the recorded testimony to these physical phenomena is enough to establish their genuineness, but that any honest investigator might establish their genuineness to his own satisfaction by personal experience. I agreed in a great measure with this opinion when, some ten years ago, I attended my first séance; but hitherto my personal experiences, though not by any means extensive, have been almost precisely of the same nature as Mr. Sidgwick's...the physical phenomena which I have witnessed were either clearly ascertained by my friends and myself to be fraudulent, or they were inconclusive and accompanied by circumstances which strongly suggested trickery.[90]

As for his own domicile, Hodgson moved in to some inexpensive rooms on Charles Street which contained only a bedroom and a sitting room full of books, papers, pipes, tobacco cans, and cheap cigars- though greatly respected by his peers Hodgson rarely ever entertained visitors in his house.[91] In May 1887, Hodgson had been requested by R. Pearsall Smith to investigate the workings of one Leonora Piper (1857 – 1950), a Spiritualist medium. It seemed that Smith's motivation for this request stemmed from his desire to see Hodgson expose Piper as a fraud.[92] Hodgson was intrigued and William James immediately scheduled an 'anonymous' appointment with Mrs. Piper; however, when Hodgson arrived for his sitting he was told that Mrs. Piper was not available at the moment but instead went on to reschedule for a sitting two days later. At this point Hodgson remained unaware, but his negative attitude towards Spiritualism expressed above was about to become dramatically changed.

6.18 Richard Hodgson and the Strange Case of Mrs. Piper

Hodgson found what he had been looking for through his membership in the S.P.R.- genuine proof of the afterlife through the examination of the trance medium- Mrs. Leonora Piper. Piper was said to have gone into trances described as follows:

> She is obliged to hold someone's hand in order to go into a trance. She holds the hand several minutes, silently, in half-darkness. After some time- from five to fifteen minutes- she is seized with a light spasmodic convulsion, which increase, and terminate in a very slight epileptiform attack. Passing out of this, she falls into a state of stupor, with somewhat stertorous breathing; this lasts about a minute or two; then, all at once, she comes out of the stupor with a burst of words. Her voice is changed; she is no longer Mrs. Piper, but another personage.[93]

Leonora Piper grew up in Nashua, NH and moved to the Beacon Hill area of Boston after marrying her husband William Piper at the age of twenty, and three years later gave birth to her first daughter Alta Piper.[94] Piper had been raised within the Congregational church even though her impressive psychical abilities manifested themselves during childhood. Piper managed to suppress her psychic talents throughout her formative years and into adulthood. It wasn't until her husband William started having inexplicable attacks of pain from an earlier injury that these dormant powers were finally reactivated. After her husband had been cured, Mrs. Piper became an active Spiritualist medium being especially adept in producing automatic drawings and channeling various spirit personalities which she called 'controls.' These 'controls' were spirit personalities who would indwell (control) her body; these included a number of allegedly 'historical' personalities such as G. P. and Phinuit, as well as some more famous spirits including Martin Luther and Abraham Lincoln.

Upon being introduced to the Society of Psychical Research through William James, Mrs. Piper went to some extreme measures in order to allow her sittings to be analyzed including performing in controlled environments all in the interest of science. Piper was eventually hired by the S.P.R. at a sum of 200 pounds a year and was placed under the direct supervision of Richard Hodgson.[95] Hodgson's periodical reports on Mrs. Piper and her phenomena evidenced a progression in his confidence relating to this medium. In 1891, Hodgson denied that Mrs. Piper had the ability to communicate directly with the deceased but that 'the evidence here presented, together with that previously published, is very far from sufficient to establish any such conclusion' though he did note that it may have been possible for Piper to receive some indirect communications.[96] In an addendum published on May 1892 Hodgson concluded that 'Mrs. Piper has given some sittings very recently which ...render some form of the 'spiritistic' hypothesis more plausible.'[97] What he meant by this statement was not expounded upon until a later publication in 1898 which further illustrated this evolution in his belief system:

> At the present time I cannot profess to have any doubt but that the chief 'communicators' to whom I have referred in the forgoing pages, are veritably the personalities that the claims to be, that they have survived the change we call death, and that they have directly communicated with us whom we call living, through Mrs. Piper's entranced organism.[98]

This change of belief marked Hodgson's conversion to Spiritualism which was celebrated by Spiritualists far and wide as a milestone in the science; Piper continued to give Hodgson readings that comforted him including news of his mother and dearly beloved Jessie D. and most importantly confirmation that Blavatsky's 'spirit was in the deepest part of Hell.'[99] In 1895 Mrs. Piper channeled another control that claimed to be the roaming spirit of William Stainton Moses the noted and recently deceased Spiritualist. This spirit-control helped confirm Hodgson of the legitimacy of Spiritualism. Mark Antony De Wolfe in his very personal account of Richard Hodgson referred to Richard by his nickname 'Dick' and noted a letter that had been sent to him in 1901 concerning his level of metaphysical faith in Spiritualism and Piper's control of Imperator [Moses]:

> I seem to understand clearly the reasons for incoherence and obscurity, etc. and I think that if for the rest of my life from now I should never see another trance or have another word from Imperator or his group, it would make no difference to my

knowledge that all is well, that Imperator, etc., are all they claim to
be and are indeed messengers that we may call divine.[100]

Hodgson's conversion to Spiritualism seemed legitimate, and, in the
end Hodgson implicitly believed in the Imperator controls basing his
entire life on the teachings of this spirit-guide which was channeled
by Mrs. Piper.[101] Hodgson's belief system has often been classified as
a non- religionist view of Spiritualism. He held to the belief of a
'dualist hypothesis' which advocated the survival after death of the
non-physical component of the human mind, and that this discarnate
mind could at times communicate through a medium.[102] The
important aspect of this conversion was that Hodgson had come to
accept the existence of a supernatural spirit world and came to
believe that Spiritualism was the key towards understanding the
afterlife; however, this realization did not occur until 1892.

6.19 Hodgson's Influence
On 20 December 1905 Richard Hodgson suffered a heart attack
while playing a game of handball. He died immediately, and this (as
Baird noted in his hagiography) appeared to be a 'fitting end for a
muscular Christian manqué.'[103] Hodgson was decidedly influential in
the Spiritualist world of the late nineteenth century, especially on the
noted historian of Spiritualism Frank Podmore and his foremost
Modern Spiritualism: a History and a Criticism published in 1902. By
Podmore's own admission this entire work was 'based, as the reader
will see, almost exclusively on Dr. Hodgson's writings, supplemented
by his criticisms and suggestions on the completed chapters.'[104] The
influence of Podmore's history on the study of Spiritualism even in
modern academia cannot be underestimated, yet it was all based on
the writings and reports of Richard Hodgson.[105]

Podmore began his study on such prominent figures as John Dee
and followed the history of witchcraft into the Salem witch trials.
Then he noted the prevalence of poltergeists and their influence on
Mary Jobson, the Wesley household and Angelique Cottin. Next,
Podmore tackled the great Western Esoteric thinkers Paracelsus
(Philippus Aureolus Theophrastus Bombastus von Hohenheim),
William Maxwelll and Robert Fludd (Robertus de Fluctibus) and ob-
served some common characteristics that they each employed which
included Platonic correspondences, magnetism, and spiritual belief.
This was followed by an examination of Antoine Mesmer and a brief
history of his philosophy and writings. Podmore then attempted to

survey the roots of modern Spiritualism in France before 1848 noting some key cases of phenomena attached to the concept of telepathy (thought transference). Podmore connected these early cases to the Modern Spiritualist movement as holding the basic belief that would eventually become the foundation of nineteenth century Spiritualism- communications with the dead.

Even after his demise in 1905, Hodgson's spirit played an intricate role in Spiritualism becoming a frequent guest at séances across the Western world. Hodgson made post-mortem appearances to the Professor James Hyslop (1854–1920) of Columbia University and, as early as one week after his death, to his own beloved Mrs. Piper.[106] Mrs. Piper claimed to be able to communicate with Hodgson and continued to contact his spirit for 60 sittings until 1 January 1908; she maintained this relationship with Hodgson through her spirit guide 'Rector'.[107] Thus, after a life full of skepticism dealing with dishonest mediums Hodgson found what he was looking for in the personage of Mrs. Piper. Perhaps, he was tired of searching, or maybe he found something truly supernatural in the readings of Mrs. Piper whatever it was it seemed that after becoming acquainted with the teachings of Mrs. Piper, Hodgson's soul had finally found peace.

6.20 The Society of Psychical Research and the Hodgson Report 1885

While Hodgson attended St. John's of Cambridge in 1882 he joined the undergraduate Society for Psychical Research, and when the Society of Psychical Research was founded that same year Hodgson immediately joined. As noted at the beginning of this section, the late 1870s and early 1880s were a time when Spiritualist mediums were being continuously exposed as frauds. For this reason this scientific society was assembled in order to investigate the claims of all psychic phenomena. It was founded by Henry Sidgwick (1838–1900) who explained its goals and purposes in his first presidential address:

> My interest in this subject dates back to nearly twenty years, and I quite remember that when I began to look into the matter, nearly every educated Spiritualist that I came across, however firmly, convinced, warned me against fraud, and emphasised his warning by impressive anecdotes. It is merely a question of degree, and I think it would be generally admitted that recent experiences have changed the view of many Spiritualist with regard to the degree...I think that even educated and scientific Spiritualists were not quite prepared for the amount of fraud which has recently come to light,

nor for the obstinacy with which the mediums against whom fraud had been proved have been afterwards defended, and have in fact been able to go on with what I may, without offence, call their trade, after exposure no less than before. And this leads me to the point which is chiefly characteristic of the method of investigation which our Society will, I hope, in the main use. Though it would be a mistake to lay down a hard and fast rule that we may not avail ourselves of the services of paid performers for paid mediums, still we shall, as much as possible, direct our investigation to phenomena where no ordinary motive to fraud,- at any rate I may no pecuniary motives- can come in.[108]

Shortly after its establishment in 1882, the S.P.R became intrigued with tales coming in from the East regarding Blavatsky, the Theosophical Society, and its phenomena. Blavatsky's Eastern phenomena and the phenomena of Western Spiritualism appeared similar in the mind of Henry Sidgwick who observed the following connection in his 'Foreward':

But we cannot separate the evidence offered by the Theosophists for projection of the 'astral form', from the evidence which they also offer for a different class of phenomena, similar to some which are said by Spiritualists to occur through the agency of mediums, and which involve the action of 'psychical' energies on ponderable matter; since such phenomena are usually described either as 1) accompanying apparitions of the Mahatmas or their disciples, or 2) at any rate as carrying with the manifest reference of their agency.[109]

From this above quote it seemed that the S.P.R. initially focused on the Theosophist claims of phenomena because of their similarity to the phenomena being produced in the West by Spiritualist mediums. Given this statement and the belief that genuine phenomena were being produced by the Theosophists in India, in December of 1884 the S.P.R. drew up an initial report and decided that these reports could no longer afford to 'be ignored.'[110] An occasional meeting was held on 30 April at Queen Anne's Mansion attended by both Henry Olcott and Mohini Chatterji –the subject concerned Damodar's astral travels. This same year Hodgson had procured a position at the University Extension however it was during this time that he was called by the S. P. R. to travel to Madras, India to investigate Blavatsky and the Theosophical Society's claim of phenomena.[111] Hodgson was picked as a neutral investigator and 'had been very justly accepted by both parties as an impartial inquirer, had had opportunities which no one else had enjoyed of learning the facts from every quarter.[112] Hodgson arrived in India on November 1884 and carried on an intensive investigation returning in April of 1885. There are many differing ideas as to Hodgson's primary goals in commencing his investigation; however, it seemed that many scholars would agree that he began as an impartial observer. Hodgson's intent in traveling to India was clarified by Sidgwick who noted that:

> with instructions to examine, and have examined by experts, the Blavatsky-Coulomb letters to ascertain, so far as possible, the degree of value that was to be attached to the statements of certain important native witnesses; and to examine localities and witnesses with a view to ascertaining whether various phenomena, such as the falling of letters from the ceiling, and appearances of Mahatmas, could be accounted for by fraud in the ways that had suggested themselves to the members of the Committee, or in other ways. This, Mr. Hodgson has done.[113]

Hodgson's conclusions are noted below though it should be observed that Hodgson's appointment to Madras was due to a fascination with one peculiar phenomenon that was housed in the Theosophical House- the shrine. In a cupboard, Blavatsky had placed a shrine which was a statue of a 'master'. Sinnett described the functioning of this supernatural cupboard as follows:

> Here she had established some simple occult treasures- relics of her stay in Tibet- two small portraits she possessed of the Mahatmas and some other trifles associated with them in her imagination...'the shrine' was used a dozen times for the transaction of business between the Masters and the chelas connected with the Society for every once it was made to subserve the purpose of any show phenomenon.[114]

The shrine served as a connection between the masters and the Theosophists. Sinnett further noted in his autobiography that this shrine had actually provided inspiration to him during his writing of *Esoteric Buddhism* published in 1883:

> I had been writing at *Esoteric Buddhism* in a lower room and as the work advanced I set down various questions to submit to the Masters when opportunity served. My wife one morning came in to speak to me and I gave her some such questions, asking her to

give them to Madame Blavatsky for transmission at convenience. She, it appears, took them upstairs at the opposite side of the room from 'The Shrine'. Madame Blavatsky told my wife to put my questions in the shrine which she did, remaining in the room talking to 'the old lady' as we always called her. In about 10 minutes Madame Blavatsky told my wife that the Master had already sent some answer. My wife went to the shrine and there found a reply to my questions from the Master, or rather a few lines in his writing promising an answer the next day. The incident was very simple but very complete in its phenomenal character. Madame Blavatsky had not moved from her seat at the writing table during the ten minutes referred to.[115]

Again it seemed evident that this shrine and cupboard were used by the masters to deliver their messages to the world, or at least this was what Blavatsky had claimed- Hodgson believed this to be otherwise. He noted 'that, in particular, the Shrine at Adyar, through which letters purporting to come from Mahatmas were received, was elaborately arranged with a view to the secret insertion of letters and other objects through a sliding panel at the back, and regularly used for this purpose by Madame Blavatsky or her agents.'[116] Despite Hodgson's opinions regarding the function of the shrine at the Theosophical Headquarters, when he arrived at the compound the original shrine had been destroyed. Hodgson believed that 'Babula had concealed or destroyed it in compliance with instructions from Madame Blavatsky, as it was on the night of September 20th that the removal of the Shrine had been effected.'[117] Thus, any opinions Hodgson may have derived regarding the function of this device were based on the testimonies of the Theosophists and the Coulombs.

Another reason specified by Sidgwick behind Hodgson's deployment to India concerned the Mahatma letters and certain allegations made by the Coulombs- Alexis and Emma Coulomb. Emma Coulomb (then Emma Cutting) had originally met Blavatsky in Cairo, Egypt in 1872, and had at that time loaned some money to Blavatsky. Then when Blavatsky left for Odessa, Cutting married one Alexis Coulomb, a Frenchman whose family ran a local hotel. The couple fled the country after an attempt at fraudulent bankruptcy, turning up in Calcutta in 1874 and moving on to Ceylon. The Coulombs joined the Society on April 3 on the eve of the Founders' first tour of Ceylon and Col. Olcott asked Mme. Coulomb to take over the household duties.[118]

Coulomb had managed to work her way back into Blavatsky's inner circle of confederates, though she would eventually detract and go on to publish some letters and accusations that were absolutely devastating to Blavatsky and her Theosophical Society in 1884.

This brief pamphlet was entitled *Some Account of My Intercourse With Madame Blavatsky From 1872 to 1884: With A Number of Additional Letters and a Full Explanation of the Most Marvellous Theosophical Phenomena* and was published in 1885 in which Coulomb admitted her role in the duping of certain Theosophical Society members. Coulomb explained some of the desperate measures that Blavatsky employed in order to cloak these Mahatma letters with a sense of mystery. The first involved a mango tree and a letter which observers claimed fell 'perpendicularly through the air:'

> The letter did not fall, as it is here stated, from the open air, but from a branch of a mango-tree which, though growing in the garden of the terrace below, was not only reaching the high terrace, but also dominating a part of it, and some of the branches overhung where the letter fell; and anyone in Bombay can ascertain for himself the truth of this by going to the Crow's Nest bungalow, where he will also find a wooden staircase close by this tree, which was on this occasion the hiding place for the servant who, by pulling the string, which had previously been prepared on one of the branches, caused the letter to fall.[119]

Coulomb also reprinted a series of letters that Blavatsky had sent to her that related to trickery and the sending of certain 'Mahatma letters':

> *Letter II*: I cannot and dare not write anything to you. But you must understand that it is absolutely necessary that something should happen in Bombay while I am here. The King and Dam. must see one of the Brothers, and receive a visit from him; and, if possible, the first must receive a letter which I shall send. But to see them [the Brothers] is still more necessary. The letter must fall on his head like the first, and I am begging Koothoomi to send it to him. We must strike while the iron is hot.[120]

> *Letter III*: My Dear Friend, I have not a minute to reply. I beg you to send this letter (here enclosed) to Damodar in a miraculous way. It is very important. Oh. My dear, how unhappy I am! On every side unpleasantness and horror. Yours entirely, H.P.B.[121]

Letter IV: Be good enough, O sorceress of a thousand resources, to ask Christofolo [the life sized doll used to trick people into thinking they saw a master from a distance] when you see him, to transmit the letter herewith enclosed, by an aerial or astral way, or it makes no matter how. It is very important. (My Love) to you, my dear; I embrace you. Yours faithfully, Luna Melanconica [a pseudonym used by Blavatsky in her correspondence with Coulomb]. I beg you DO IT WELL.[122]

Letter V: For the love of St. Joseph do the thing well. There are two letters and a parcel, the two must be delivered to their address. If it were possible that the letter and the parcel should fall at the same moment on the nose of the King, it would be magnificent. As to the other- I do not care! I leave it to your discretion...I have bought a box for _____' how are they? I shall send him one of these days box and letter by astral letter. But how to make the box reach you? Do not speak of it to him yet. All yours, H.P.B.[123]

Hodgson considered these allegations and the testimony made by Coulomb in his report. Despite the negative tone apparent in the above excerpts, it seemed that Hodgson began this investigation believing that the Mahatma Letters were indeed the product of genuine psychic phenomena. Hodgson did acknowledge the warmth and kindness that the Theosophical Society exhibited to him in their hospitality and in their allowance of him to interrogate their members. Through a series of investigations and interviews with several prominent Theosophists including Damodar, Mohini, and Olcott, Hodgson eventually concluded that:

> From these Blavatsky-Coulomb documents it appears that the Mahatma Letters were prepared and sent by Madame Blavatsky, that Koot Hoomi is a fictitious personage, that supposed 'astral forms' of the Mahatmas were confederated of Madame Blavatsky in disguise- generally the Coulombs; that alleged transportation of cigarettes and other objects, 'integration' of letters, and allied phenomena...were ingenious trickeries, carried out by Madame Blavatsky, with the assistance chiefly of the Coulombs... I finally had no doubt whatever that the phenomena connected with the Theosophical Society were part of a huge fraudulent system worked by Madame Blavatsky with the assistance of the Coulombs and several other confederates, and that not a single genuine phenomenon could be found among them all.[124]

Hodgson left India disappointed by the results of his investigations and may have even harbored feelings of bitterness towards Blavatsky and her confederates for violating the trust of the other Theosophists.[125] Hodgson wrote his report publishing an initial private conclusion in the Society's *Journal* in December of 1884 and then his official report was published in the *Proceedings of the Society for Psychical Research* in 1885. This report was devastating to the Theosophical Society and destroyed Blavatsky's reputation even to this day. As the devoted Theosophist Alfred Percy Sinnett recorded in his *Autobiography*, the Hodgson report 'had the effect of completely shattering the Society, which melted away until it was only represented by a few faithful adherents- the Arundales, Varleys, Keightleys and some others.'[126]

6.21 A Western Investigation of Eastern Phenomena

What remained absent in the Hodgson report was any revelation of inclination that Blavatsky may have had for allowing the S.P.R to visit her Society headquarters. After all, it seemed that Blavatsky maintained credibility in the East, so why would she risk exposure from the West? Though it can only be conjectured at this late stage it seemed plausible that there were some unsettled feelings that Blavatsky held towards contemporary Spiritualism following the Kiddle plagiarism incident in 1883-84 that transpired several years before Hodgson's visit to the Theosophical commune. Blavatsky's feelings likely stemmed from the inexorable treatment which she endured from the opinions of the Western Spiritualist Press during that incident. Janet Oppenheim astutely commented upon Blavatsky's relationship to Spiritualism in her monumental work *The Other World* noting that 'uncharitable critics might well assume that, having failed to establish herself in the first rank of mediums, she decided to adopt even bolder means to achieve world fame.'[127] This would suggest a motive for allowing the S.P.R. to investigate her Society which had nearly fallen off the radar of Western Spiritualism until this report (and is indicative of Lillie's 'opportunist' view of Blavatsky). Thus, it seemed that Blavatsky was seeking recognition of her psychic powers from the Western world. This theory notwithstanding, the decision to submit to this investigation was influenced largely by Henry Olcott. Olcott recorded how the Theosophical Society became known to the S.P.R. in a diary entry:

There had been the making of acquaintances between us and the S.P.R; entire cordiality and unsuspicious friendliness on our part; an equally apparent sympathy on theirs; agreeable social meetings at the houses of their leaders, and, finally a consent on my part to be examined by a Committee of the S.P.R. The sky was purely blue, without the tiniest cloud to indicate the hurricane in preparation for us. So those were joyous days in London and Paris, and H.P.B. and I were in exuberant spirits. On the 11th May (1884) I had my first sitting and examination with Messrs. F. W. H. Myers and J. Herbert Stack.[128]

It is important to note that Olcott remarked that 'H.P.B. and I were exuberant'- their time for vindication from the Kiddle incident had arrived. Olcott went on to record the nature of this initial conversation mentioned above which included a conversation on such topics as the appearance of phantasms, astral projection of the double, communications with adepts, and other paranormal activities. Olcott had initially persuaded Blavatsky to allow the Theosophical Society to become investigated as noted in the following dramatic letter sent to Olcott from Blavatsky explaining that she would never forgive him for 'thrusting out phenomena upon the attention of the gentlemen scientists of the P.R.S [S.P.R.].' Olcott took this letter as a personal attack; his motivation in inviting the S.P.R. to India appeared to be his sincere desire to share Theosophy and its phenomenon with the Western world evidencing that he remained credulous to a fault.[129]

An informal meeting was held on 2 May 1884 at the house of F. W. H. Myers at Cambridge 'for the purpose of taking such evidence as to the alleged phenomena connected with the Theosophical Society as might be offered by members of that body at the time in England or as could be collected elsewhere.'[130] This led to an official meeting on the 11th of May that was described by Olcott above to which he noted that both he and Blavatsky were exuberant. This was in turn followed by a regular stream of correspondence throughout the months of May and June. During this time Olcott, Mohini and Sinnett were interviewed by such noted members of the S.P.R as Frank Podmore the Spiritualist historian and Herbert Stack. The S. P. R. asked of these members a series of impromptu questions gathering enough testimony to justify the June 30 general meeting of the S. P. R during which time Herbert Stack read a "Further Report on phenomena attested by members of the Theosophical Society." A large group of interested Theosophists attended, including the Sinnetts, Miss Arundale, Col. Olcott and Mme. Blavatsky.'[131]

Alfred Percy Sinnett in his autobiography recorded this last event relying upon his wife's diaries meticulously kept during these early days. Sinnett noted that on 30 June 1884 he, Olcott, and Blavatsky attended a meeting of the Psychical Research Society. Then in the middle of this meeting Olcott did something unprecedented- he began addressing the board in what Sinnett explained as 'an extraordinary tactless character' explaining that he could prove that astral projection was possible and as proof he started waving a cream colored scarf which he claimed had materialized before his very eyes by his Indian guru. Sinnett elucidated that the leaders of the Psychic Research Society were intensely careful to keep all its proceedings on the level of the upper class culture. Now Colonel Olcott with all the goodness and devotion to the cause was not in tune with the taste of cultivated Europeans. Sinnett's wife Patty made the following notes in her diary: 'Colonel Ol. Made a dreadful goose of himself and made O.L. furious and ashamed [O.L. stood for 'Old Lady' referring to Blavatsky].[132]

The Theosophists decided to retire to the Sinnett's home during which time Blavatsky publically and acrimoniously chastised Olcott prompting Sinnett to record in his autobiography that 'her face was white from the intensity of her emotion; she spoke so loudly that I was afraid she would disturb the neighbours and she reviled the unfortunate Colonel until he was driven to ask her if she wanted him to commit suicide.'[133] Sinnett insisted that all of the Society's later troubles could be traced back to this one event that occurred on this one fateful evening when Olcott spoke out of turn. Sinnett further articulated that 'The Psychic leaders had all their teeth set on edge by the Colonel's unhappy outbreak. All of this were the 'fruits of that miserable evening, the 30th June 1884.'[134]

So it was through Olcott's disagreeable interactions with this organization that led the S.P.R. to investigate the T.S. headquarters at the request of the president Henry Sidgwick. The very fact that Blavatsky subjected herself to the investigations of this Western pseudo-scientific research organization which had been established at a university that was (and remains) the very pinnacle of Western intelligence (Cambridge University) evidenced her desire for acceptance back into the embraces of Western Spiritualism.

In the history of the S.P.R. leading up to its investigation of the Theosophical Society in India it should be noted that all of its previous test cases had been performed on Western Spiritualist mediums and haunted houses. It remains intriguing that following Hodgson's report Blavatsky had been molded into what she so vehemently despised – an exposed 'fraudulent' medium who denigrated the name of her movement. The limits of the S.P.R's investigations into India were recognized in the first volume of the *Journal* which was written on 28 May 1884 noting that certain issues would limit their ability to reproduce these Eastern phenomena especially their distance which affected their ability to follow up on certain claims, and the timing and test conditions of such phenomena. Despite these issues it was observed that

> ...with reference to the incidents of modern Spiritualism and of Indian Theosophy, the policy of the Society is in the main distinct. The Spiritualists not only record an immense mass of abnormal facts as having occurred under certain conditions in the presence of certain sensitives or mediums, but they assert that these phenomena will probably recur should the same conditions be observed, and in presence of the same mediums. Instead, therefore, of collecting and collating the immense mass of marvels recorded as having occurred in the presence of mediums, and attested by many respectable writers, including living witnesses, the better course seems to be to institute practical investigations, with a hope of their recurrence under our own eyes and with strict securities against collusion or fraud. Our attitude towards the Theosophists must be, to a great extent, the same. Their marvels do not belong only to the past; they recur, as they assert, daily, and at the will of those who direct and guide the Theosophical Society. We are, therefore, not obliged to exhaustively examine their records, if we can, through their courtesy, secure the repetition in England or India, under satisfactory tests, of the abnormal incidents they report as being within their power.[135]

It was summarized elsewhere that 'these narratives though of a different order from those which the Society has so far collected, possess sufficient points of analogy to suggest many interesting questions.'[136] Thus, the above quotes noted that the Society was interested in these events for their similarity of occurrence in Western Spiritualism though they could not thoroughly investigate these reports because of the distance factor; however, it was eventually decided that a trip to India had to be made to witness these extraordinary acts of phenomena.

Some Theosophists have claimed that one of their own members, George Lane-Fox (who arrived at the Society headquarter in February 1884) was in fact a spy for the S.P.R. The evidence that is cited for this belief suggested that Lane-Fox became a member of S.P.R. in 1882 which meant that he may have attended a meeting and possibly have paid some dues though this could not imply that he was a saboteur or retained any direct affiliation with this organization during his time in India. In fact, 'membership' in any Spiritualist organization at this time was loose at best. Despite this fact, it was admitted that:

> the S.P.R. was founded in February 1882, and Mr. Lane-Fox's name appears on the second published list of S.P.R. members in December 1883, and also as a Council member, presumably coopted by the Council. (S.P.R. Proceedings 1 322, 320.) In 1884-5, he was a member, but not on the Council. (Proc. 2 319, 331.) In 1887 he had dropped out of the S.P.R., but returned in 1889 as an Associate. (Proc. 5 600). He continued thus until becoming a full member in 1897, and so could become a member of the Council, as he did. (Proc. 12 358, 366). It was in the late 1890s that he adopted the surname of Pitt. Until his resignation from the Council in 1920, Lane-Fox-Pitt attended 68 out of about 250 meetings. 'Not really a bad record' comments Mr. Nicol, 'for most meetings were poorly attended.'[37]

Lane-Fox was not present at the meeting when Olcott presented Damodar's phenomena nor are there any records of his collusion with Hodgson. There was another member of the S.P.R who did exert a certain level of influence on Hodgson's final report- John Herbert Stack.

Herbert Stack was a 'great friend' of Alfred Percy Sinnett as both he and his brother Henry Stack had introduced Sinnett to the two loves of his life: The first was his future wife the young Patty Endensor, and the second, through the recommendation of Herbert Stack, Sinnett had read Blavatsky's *Isis Unveiled*.[138] Stack had been previously employed as Sinnett's editor-in-chief at the *Globe* and they continued to share a close friendship spending Sundays on the river at Kensington.[139] Together they joined the South Middlesex Corps commanded by Lord Ranelagh and would often times dine at Hooper's in Bedford Gardens in Kensington. Due to his participation in carrying on a love affair with a married woman, Stack was fired from his post as editor at the *Globe* though he managed to take an editorship at the *Birmingham Daily Gazette*.[140] The *Globe* was soon discontinued after which time Sinnett followed Herbert Stack to the *Gazette*. Despite this previous relationship it seemed that after the publication of the Hodgson report neither Stack nor Sinnett wished to identify this friendship openly.

In Stack's obituary printed in the May 1892 issue of the *Journal of the Society of Psychical Research* it was noted that 'Mr. Stack gave cordial co-operation to the Society's work from the time of its foundation. His strong sense and marked fairness of mind were or especial value to the "Committee on Alleged Marvels Connected with Theosophy" on which he served in 1885. He will be much regretted by many friends.'[141] This seemed to be a very peculiar obituary and the very suggestion that Stack possessed a 'fairness of mind' especially in relation to the Theosophical investigations evidenced a deeper story underlying this obituary. One possible reason is explored in the following paragraph below.

Herbert Stack had the unique opportunity of editing the draft of the preliminary report of the Committee before it was circulated (this was circulated privately to SPR members only and should not be confused with the final report). Thus, Stack wrote some of his own comments and suggestions next to each point. Stack made multiple suggestions though two are especially relevant for understanding the uniqueness of these Eastern phenomena over the typical phenomena being produced by Western mediums- these have been reprinted in capital letters below:

> (10) It is curious as regards the dropping of letters that the instances are all, or nearly all, confined to India or in Europe to railway carriages. Indian ceilings are not generally plastered—they are often even in first-class houses made of rough boards with chinks. A railway carriage is a very easy place for the 'chucking up' of a letter so as to make it fall from the ceiling. Nobody sees a letter fall from an '*English* ceiling while he is quite alone.' IRRELEVANT POINT IS THAT OLCOTT IS INVOLVED.[142]

> 13) We must bear in mind that Theosophy has made very few converts amongst Englishmen in India—notwithstanding the conversion of Mr Hume, Mr Sinnett General Morgan, Colonel Gordon and perhaps one or two more. English people in India have ample opportunities of judging the leaders and the phenomena. The slow progress of the cause amongst Anglo-Indians many of whom are highly educated and its rapid progress

amongst uneducated, superstitious and credulous natives is *prima facie* against it. UNIMPORTANT.[143]

It seemed that both of these facts were pertinent to this case; however, Stack felt as though they should be left out of the report. These particular facts mentioned above have tremendous bearing on understanding the 'unique' place of Blavatsky's phenomena in the eyes of the Western world. The falling of letters did not occur in the West because the West had plastered ceilings rendering this phenomenon near impossible. Secondly, the fact that the Theosophical Society had few converts outside of India revealed 1) that Theosophy flourished among the uneducated (an idea that will be repeated by Emma Hardinge Britten in the next section) and 2) a confirmation of Blavatsky's desire for acceptance in the Western world. It seems possible that if the membership rolls of the Theosophical Society contained more Western members Blavatsky would have been less likely to allow the S.P.R. to investigate her society. Despite the importance of these two facts, Stack attempted to stifle them from public view. This could have been due to his 'fairness of mind' mentioned in the strange fashion in his obituary or this could have been merely in the interest of being concise.

6.22 The Results of Hodgson's Report
It remains imperative for the reader to understand that Hodgson was incorrect in many of his assumptions which have been recently examined in publications by the handwriting expert Vernon Harrison and the Theosophical historian Michael Gomes (especially in his claim that the Theosophical Society was really a covert operation to hide the fact that Blavatsky was a Russian spy); however, these false conclusions should not distract the reader from his analysis of her phenomena. Hodgson's report was an attempt to expose the Theosophical phenomena and present the public with a report of its operations; however, it seemed that his report managed to induce an opposite effect. This report provided Blavatsky with two things: 1) this publicity heightened people's awareness of Blavatsky leading many people to become interested in her teachings and 2) this news made her an infamously intriguing character in the Victorian media.

This report paved the way for her comeback in the West following the publication of *The Secret Doctrine* in 1888. A November 1889 issue of the *Theosophist* noted that it was 'really surprising to see how vivid an interest there is in Theosophy throughout the United Kingdom.

The Hodgson Report, so far from crushing the movement seems to have only stimulated public curiosity."[144] Theosophy began to flourish in the West despite Hodgson's best attempts to extinguish it. Also, adding to the rise in popularity was the conversion of Annie Besant in 1889 at the height of her public popularity. Besant was a well known social reformer and atheist who had become interested in Theosophy following a close reading of *The Secret Doctrine*. In her autobiography Besant explained that she went to the headquarters on Landsdowne Road to inquire of Blavatsky about membership. Blavatsky responded that she would not allow Besant to join until she had thoroughly read the Society for Psychical Research report issued by Richard Hodgson. So Besant quickly:

> borrowed a copy of the report, read and re-read it. Quickly I saw how slender was the foundation on which the imposing structure was built. The continual assumptions on which conclusions were based; the incredible character of the allegations; and-most damning fact of all- the foul source from which the evidence was derived. Everything turned on the veracity of the Coulombs, and they were self-stamped as partners in the alleged frauds.[145]

The next day after reading this report 'not hesitating even as long as she had done before yielding to previous and less extreme conversion' Besant joined the Theosophical Society and received her diploma of membership on 21 May 1889.[146]

6.23 A Letter of Response

Following this investigation Blavatsky sent a letter to Hodgson pleading with him to remember the English presumption of innocence which maintained a person was 'innocent until proven guilty.' Her main source of frustration seemed related to Hodgson's accusation that she was working as a Russian spy. In an undated letter likely sent immediately following Hodgson's report, Blavatsky requested:

> Only a fortnight ago I had an affectionate regard for yourself whom I believed impartial and just...I thank you also for your additional fling at an innocent and absent woman who has never done you any harm, in saying that you believed her a woman capable of every and any crime...I defy any mortal man to bring valid proof that I have ever written one line or received one from the Russian Govt. for the last 15 years...I expect from you a

> written statement over your signature of all you heard from the Coulombs about my being a spy that led you to form such a conclusion.[147]

Despite Blavatsky's open hostility towards Hodgson and his report to the S.P.R. it does seem that she raised a valid dispute in claiming that they had overstepped their bounds of judgment which she explained in a later letter to Sinnett sent on 19 August 1885:

> The only right that the S.P.R has- is to proclaim that all their investigations notwithstanding, they got no evidence to show that the phenomena were all genuine; that there is a strong presumption from the scientific and logical, if not legal stand-point, to suspect that there many have been exaggerations in the reports, suspicious circumstance attached to their production, etc.- never deliberate fraud, deception and so on.[148]

Despite the feeling Blavatsky may have felt towards Hodgson it seemed that she would bounce back stronger than ever several years later following the printing of her *Secret Doctrine* in 1888 and her move back to England after which she seemed to cease performing all phenomena.

6.24 Emma Hardinge Britten (1823–1899)

Emma Hardinge Britten (1823–1899) was an influential Spiritualist and occultist in the Victorian Era though her life remains a much neglected topic in the history of Western Esotericism despite her own autobiography published in 1899. Some brief works have been written on the life of this fascinating medium including the reports of such noted academics as Patrick Deveney, Marc Demarest, Robert Mathiesen, and Joscelyn Godwin; however, as of yet, no exhaustive work has been written. Emma was born as Emma Floyd in Bethnal Green London in 1823. At age eleven her father died leaving a financial burden for Emma and her family to carry.

The lot fell to Ann Sophia, Emma's mother to provide for the family which provided Emma with adequate time to practice and prepare for her musical career which occurred in 1838 four years after her father Ebenezer's demise. It is believed that Emma even published music under the name 'Ernest Rienohld' during this time in Bristol England.

Eventually she was discovered by a mystical circle in the 1840s called the 'Orphic Society' which was joined by prominent figures in the history of Western Esotericism including Edward Bulwer-Lytton (1805–1873) the well known occult author, Richard James Morrison (1795–1874) the astrologer who went by pseudonym Zadkiel, and the British diplomat Sir Charles Wyke to name a few.[149] Britten wrote about her involvement with this society in her 'Occultism Defined' in the 18 November 1887 issue of *Two Worlds*:

> When quite young, in fact, before I had attained my thirteenth year, I became acquainted with certain parties who sought me out and professed a desire to observe the somnambulic faculties for which I was then remarkable. I found my new associates to be ladies and gentlemen, mostly persons of noble rank, and during a period of several years, I, and many other young persons, assisted at their sessions in the quality of somnambulists, or mesmeric subjects... I should have known but little of its principles and practices, as I was simply what I should now call a clairvoyant, sought out by the society for my gifts in this direction, had I not, in later years, been instructed in the fundamentals of the society by the author of 'Art Magic.' When modern spiritualism dawned upon the world, for special reasons of my own, the fellows of my society gave me an honorary release from every obligation I had entered into with them except in the matter of secrecy. On that point I can never be released and never seek to be; but in respect to the statements I am about to make, my former associates . . . not only sanction, but command me to present to the candid enquirer...[150]

This 'matter of secrecy' may have referred to the sexual abuse she endured by some of the Society's members. Rape was not uncommon in the Victorian era especially for younger women as no laws protecting women against their employers were established during this time period.[151] The historian, Joscelyn Godwin learned of this sexual assault in 1989 through a conversation with the late Mr. Mostyn Gilbert, Dr. E.J. Dingwall's fellow psychical researcher in London; however, even with this insight the exact nature of this 'matter of secrecy' must remain speculative though this would explain her resignation from the Theosophical Society which she inferred was due to the implementation of a secrecy oath.[152]

Britten began her career as a child actress in Bristol until 1840 and then moved to London and became involved with the Covenant garden company, Princess' Theatre, Sadler's Wells, Adelphi, Royal Surrey, and then in 1854 went on a tour of France as a member of the company of J. W. Wallack who had rented the Imperial Theater in Paris for several weeks. When this arrangement had expired she signed up to become a Broadway actress in New York from September 1855 through May 1856.[153] After this time Britten retired from acting to focus upon her career as a Spiritualist medium. In 1855 she arrived in the States with her mother, and went on to revive her own somnambulistic abilities after being introduced to American Spiritualism by a fellow occupant of a theatrical rooming house.[154]

Around this time from June 1856 – May 1857 Britten connected with the Society for the Diffusion of Spiritual Knowledge holding séances as a medium. This society was chartered on 10 June 1854 and appeared to have been the first legally organized Spiritualist society in the United States of which any record has survived.[155] Britten eventually took over the editorship of *The Christian Spiritualist* which circulated up until May 1857 leaving her without an income and forcing her to rely upon her musical abilities putting out advertisement as a 'musical governess... accomplished in every branch of Polite Literature.'[156]

Before and during the United States' Civil War (also known as the War between the States) which waged from 1861–1865 Britten became a social reformer, concerned with the treatment of *magdalens* (prostitutes and other 'fallen' women looking to reform their lives) and the abolition of slavery evidenced in the publication of her work *The Great Funeral Oration on Abraham Lincoln* in 1865.[157] Shortly following her involvement with the war, from 1865 – 1868 Britten began writing *Modern American Spiritualism* and on 11 October 1870 she married the gentleman William Britten and moved to Boston.[158] It was during this same year that she would self-publish her influential and well received work *Modern American Spiritualism: A Twenty Years' Record of the Communion Between Earth and The World of Spirits* (1870).

In 1872 Britten released her own periodical the *Western Star* a Spiritualist magazine which was well received; however, this success was short lived as many of her financial backers' suffered tremendous losses from the Boston fires of 9-11 November 1872.[159] Left with little financial resources, the Brittens moved back to New York.

In 1875, Britten and her husband William established their own galvanic medicine practice using electricity to cure patients. During this time she published a manual *The Electric Physician; or, Self-Cure Though Electricity* in which the cure for dysentery was to 'wrap a tin electrode wound with this piece of sponge; tie this and use it, P. placing it against the entrance to the rectum. Sit on this, and lay a large, very hot plate, N. over the bowels ten minutes. Then keep the plate over the bowels, P, and place another opposite to it across the lower part of the back, N, for ten minutes.'[160] Given these unusual methods of healing it seemed little wonder that this galvanic practice could not sustain itself. Mathiesen in his study of Britten noted that: 'The Britten's medical practice must have been something of a side-line, or perhaps it never became very profitable, because 1875 and 1876 were also the years of Emma's greatest public involvements with occultism in the United States.'[161] The failed practice will become important when understanding Britten's relationship with Blavatsky and her connection to the early Theosophical Society.

Britten and her husband Dr. William Britten were an integral part of the early Theosophical Society allowing the Society to meet in their reception rooms on 16 and 30 October 1875 at their house on 38th Street, New York before it had rented rooms in Mott Memorial hall on 17 November. It was while meeting at the Britten's home that the Theosophical Society's Preamble and Bylaws were drawn up and passed and the major leaders were voted into office.[162]

In 1879 Britten published one of her most popular and republished works (during her lifetime) *The Faiths, Facts and Frauds of Religious History* (1879) which dealt with 'the primal source from whence have been derived the various systems of theology' and attempted to reduced the various world religions into its core archetypes.[163] In 1883 Britten went on to publish her history of Spiritualism titled *Nineteenth Century Miracles* which by its own admission was 'a concise historical summary of the spiritual movement as it has transpired in various countries on the earth, from the commencement of the nineteenth century.'[164] From 1887-1892 Britten founded and edited her own weekly periodical *The Two Worlds* which published articles that related generally to the Spiritualist movement though it was also unique for its attempt to demarcate Spiritualism from Theosophy. Then in 1892 she commenced a new monthly magazine similar to *The Two Worlds* called *The Unseen Universe* though this periodical only enjoyed a short run lasting only for a year. On 24 November 1894 her husband William died at the age of 73 from heart disease greatly aggravated by lung and liver difficulties.[165] Five years later on 2 October 1899 at 76 years of age Emma Hardinge Britten would join her husband in the afterlife meeting her own demise after a year of poor health and drained energy.[166]

6.25 *Art Magic* (1876)

Emma Hardinge Britten was a founding member of the first Theosophical Society and went on to publish a work titled *Art Magic* which was announced for subscription during the same time period as the inauguration of the original Theosophical Society in 1875. Olcott discussed the coincidental nature of these two events in his diary:

> The coincidence consisted in the fact that the book and our Society simultaneously affirmed the dignity of ancient Occult Science, the existence of Adepts, the reality of and contrast between White and Black Magic, the existence of the Astral Light, the swarming of Elemental races in the regions of air, earth, etc. the existence of relations between them and ourselves, and the practicability of bringing them under subjection by certain methods long known and tested.[167]

It could even be argued that given Britten's relationship with the Theosophical Society that her work *Art Magic* was originally created as a textbook to promote the early agenda of the Theosophical Society. There were claims to this effect made by various journals and newspapers of the time; however, the question remains 'Were those claims accurate?' Marc Demarest noted that 'there was no reason for anyone to suppose that *Art Magic* was not, in some way or other, in service of a Theosophical agenda that undermined that spirit' though whether this was the initial purpose of *Art Magic* remains unknown.[168] Britten did not claim authorship of this work; rather, she explained that this was an editorial for Louis de B____ who Britten identified as an adept whom she had become acquainted with in Europe.[169] This 'style' of authorship would go on to heavily influence Blavatsky who made a similar claim regarding her later publication of *Isis Unveiled* (1877).

Art Magic attempted to educate the reader on how to manipulate the three orders of spirits that existed: submundane, mundane, and supermundane.[170] This work dealt with some of the basic metaphysical questions of life including the origin of humanity and the universe and the nature of God. In answering these questions Britten combined Western Esoteric elements and Spiritualism promulgating a belief in a grand hierarchy of mediations complete with angels and spirits of varying degree, the emanation of the human soul from Deity, and a belief that the ancient Eastern writings antedated the biblical accounts, and of course the existence of a *prisca theologia* which could be read through a study of nature and astrology.[171] Many of the elements found in *Art Magic* would become rudimentary doctrines in the later works of Blavatsky. Demarest had noted the following summary which identified the fundamental purpose behind writing *Art Magic*:

> At the most fundamental level then, *Art Magic* works with a body of knowledge — a peculiar cosmology, Mesmerism and Freemasonry — that is neither occult, in the traditional sense of that term, nor Spiritualistic per se. Magnetism, psychology and ancient Freemasonry are the science and history on which the epistemic claims of *Art Magic* are based. And the epistemic claims of the text are, largely, in the service of its political objective, which is masked, but present and, to my way of thinking, ambitious. *Art Magic* seeks to dismantle Christianity's claim to privilege or uniqueness.[172]

Despite Britten's claim that *Art Magic* would only have a limited run of 500 original printings, it seemed that this was an exaggeration as Olcott noted and claimed that indeed 1,500 copies were actually printed for circulation.[173] Charles Sotheran in the journal *Woodhull and Claflin's Weekly* managed to get a copy and reviewed it as 'simply a rehash of books accessible to any student of even limited means, and (which) can be readily found in almost any book-store, or on the shelves of any public library, Ennemoser's *History of Magic*, Howitt's *Supernatural*, Salverte's *Philosophy of Magic*, Hargrave Jenning's *Rosicrucian*, Barrett's *Magus*, Agrippa's *Occult Philosophy*, and a few others are the real sources of this wretched compilation, which is full of bad grammar and worse assumptions. We unhesitatingly assert that there is not a single important statement in the book which cannot be discovered in already-printed books.'[174] Marc Demarest expanded upon this basic premise and identified several other sources which heavily influenced *Art Magic* including Kersey Graves' *The World's Sixteen Crucified Saviors, or Christianity Before Christ* (1875), Abisha S. Hudson's *The Masculine Cross and Ancient Sex Worship* (1874), and G.C. Stewart's *The Hierophant, or Gleanings from the Past* (1859) though these ideas were rooted in the methodologies first applied by Godfrey Higgins in his two volume work *Anacalypsis: An Attempt to Draw Aside the Veil of Saitic Isis* (1833, 1836).[175] Despite the plagiarism obvious in this particular publication, *Art Magic* exemplified the ideas that Blavatsky was engaging and would build upon with her *Isis Unveiled* in 1877 and went on to become a defining work in the history of Western Esotericism.

6.26 Excerpts from *The Two Worlds* –
Britten's Afterthoughts on the Theosophical Society

Beginning in 1887, Britten published her own weekly paper titled *The Two Worlds: A Journal Devoted To Spiritualist, Occult Science, Ethics, Religion and Reform*. Following the demise of Helena Blavatsky in 1891, Britten thought it appropriate to reprint the early history of this Society in the pages of her periodical. It had been sixteen years since they had all first met in Britten's home in New York in 1875 and her history described the Society and the events that led to the 'Oriental shift' with some bitterness:

> Soon after the society removed from Dr. Britten's reception-rooms in Thirty-eighth Street, New York, to the Mott Memorial Hall, the allegations of one of the original members of the society against the character and aims of the corresponding secretary, Madame Blavatsky, as before stated, caused the remaining members to expel the party in question, pledge themselves to repel the charges alleged, and form themselves into a secret society. As time passed on and dull, fruitless meetings succeeded, varied only by the introduction of new members and the payment of entrance fees and subscriptions, it was evident that the claims of its founders were baseless…As to the founders (or 'conspirators' as some scrupled not to call them), they had nothing to add to the revelations of 'Art Magic,' then just published…The said founders realizing that some 'new departure' was necessary, the original Theosophical members having set them an unmistakable example in that respect, proceeded in the same marked duality in which they had hitherto sustained each other, to exchange the poor New York upper flat lodging for the splendours of a Hindoo bungalow, and a docile following of Hindostanee curiosity hunters. After this change of base having brought into existence a full *corps* of 'Mahatmas', at too great a distance from their own scene of action to be accessible to any prying eyes except in *their astral bodies*, they carried on a prosperous trade in unpronounceable names- 'astral bodies, astral letters, astral shrines, and astral crockery,' &c. &c.,. until in the plenitude of old Hindoo traditions and scraps of antediluvian philosophy they found it expedient to share their wealth of Oriental lore with those European branches whom Carlyle has described in language more plain than recondite, but whom we prefer to call *persons somewhat easy of belief*.[176]

Thus, Britten claimed that Blavatsky had moved her Society to India in order to trick people who were of 'easy belief' or in other words-naïve. She continued expounding her skeptical view of the Society's early history:

> Whilst we may, and do admire the talent of the few, we have but small sympathy with the masses they control; but that for which the present writer has given this analysis is to show that when the founders of Theosophy entered upon their wide-spread but perfectly human task of hypnotization they could not be contented to leave their former associates, the Spiritualists, alone; but in order to rear up what they claims to be a superstructure on the well-attested and proven FACTS of Spiritualism, they must needs strive to demolish those facts altogether, even though, Samson like, they might pull the entire fabric over their own heads by attempting to shake its foundations. They seemed possessed in fact with the idea that Theosophy could not live in the presence of the stern practical demonstrations of Spiritualism...

So it seemed that Britten claimed Blavatsky had made the conscious decision to separate her Theosophical Society from Spiritualism. She continued by further examining the nature of this relationship:

> 'Spiritualist of many years standing' as she had once professed to be- she was so no longer when she became a Theosophist, and openly taught by pen and voice, that no spirit ever had, or could come to earth, and that all the millions of her quondam associates in Spiritualism were only being gulled, ruined, and degraded by ghouls, corpse lights, and emanation from dead bodies.[177]

Britten accused Blavatsky of inventing her theory of elementals for the sole intention of causing chaos in the ranks of Spiritualism which seemed ironic given that Britten herself adhered to a similar doctrine as noted in her view of elementary spirits exhibited in section XVII of her *Art Magic*. Britten's dramatic claim that Blavatsky did not believe in the possibility that deceased spirits could contact their loved ones was contrary to most Theosophical teachings and could have stemmed from two ideas: 1) a deliberate misrepresentation of Theosophical doctrine which Britten seemed to be using to instigate other Spiritualists to shun the Theosophical Society or 2) a focus on Blavatsky's teachings as recorded in *The Secret Doctrine* which was seemingly counteracted by a deal made with William Stainton Moses in 1888. This deal consisted of an intentional truce between Spiritualism and Theosophy and as a result, Blavatsky was to make the Theosophical Society more accepting of Spiritualism. It seemed that Britten's intention for these anti-Theosophical articles was to employ them as Spiritualist propaganda advocating against uniting with the Theosophical Society in any form. This motive seemed exhibited in the following paragraph:

> We know that on more occasion than on efforts have been made to show that Theosophy and Spiritualism were one and the same belief, and although we have written again and yet again in denial of this monstrous and IMPOSSIBLE alliance, that common rumour (which Dr. Johnson so well and aptly defined as 'a common liar') has reiterated the statement as nauseam. It is in the true interests of Spiritualism, therefore, and no doubt in what Theosophists will acknowledge to be the same for their cult, that we shall once more show in our next and concluding article (and that without the lease reference to personality of the founders of Theosophy) that its doctrines and teachings are as widely opposed to Spiritualism as is the now risen spirit from the burnt-out ashes of the form that once constituted the personality of Madame H. P. Blavatsky.[178]

In the third and final installment of this series another attempt was launched to demarcate between Spiritualism and Theosophy. The writer started by noting: 'The only connection that ever existed between these two cults, the Editor has plainly detailed in the early history of the latter movement.' And then she went on to define Spiritualism which was derived from previous published leaflets put out by *The Two Worlds* and taken from 'countless millions of well-attested facts' as the ability of mortals to communicate with spirits using a variety of means including but not limited to signals, psychological influence, etc. This was an accurate definition of the main tenet of Spiritualism though its philosophy was expanded to include the following:

> Whilst it is admitted that bad or undeveloped spirits can communicate as readily as the good and true, it is taught by spirits, as well as reason, that no bad spirit can compel a mortal to of wrong any more than a bad human companion can do so....Spiritualism is a ceaseless incentive to practice good, it re-unites the friends separated by death, strengthens the easy and desolate by the presence of angel guidance and protection, cheers the afflicted with the certainty of another and better world, where justice will be done and every wrong will be righted...[179]

In another article titled 'The Impassable Lines of Demarcation Between Spiritualism and Theosophy,' Britten attempted to differentiate between Spiritualism and Theosophy by focusing upon their unverifiable claims. This was initially suppose to be a lecture given through a panel discussion with both Olcott and Britten speaking in turn; however, Olcott declined her invitation leaving Britten to rant unchallenged:

> At that time, the lecturer alleged, nearly all the parties connected with the society, including the lady and gentleman now universally recognized and named as the founders and chiefs of the Theosophical Society, were reputed to be spiritualists; acknowledged as such, and supposed by their writings and teachings to *be* such. For the several months, during which the first members of the society came together, there was not a single idea promulgated of the doctrines now alleged to be the basis of the Theosophists' belief. At the various meetings which after the first few inaugural gatherings, took place in a hired hall and for reasons slightly touched upon, had been resolved into 'a secret society,' the teachings of the lecturers were all spiritualistic, and the doctrines discussed were the same. Some hired mediums exhibited the phenomena usual amongst spiritualists, and no hint was breathed by any parties connected with the society of any other source for those phenomena, than such as is now accepted by spiritualists. For reasons of a purely personal nature, however, the society, as founded and conducted in New York, was distasteful to the generality of its members, and after duly paying their fees, finding nothing of interest to reward them and no information to be derived from their continued association, they one after another quietly withdrew.

> ...the society- as originally constituted amongst *shrewd-thinking Americans*- virtually died out, and was deemed by the majority at least, of its original members as defunct. To some of these members, however, including the present speaker, it was hardly a matter of surprise to find the founders of the society, after the New York adventure, enlisting the sympathies of a very different class of disciples, namely, the *native* population of India... They [The Theosophists] either give their own *opinions*, the beliefs of antiquity (totally regardless of proofs concerning their value), or the opinions of unknown, invisible, and all too doubtful brotherhoods, the only evidence of whose existence is boldly alleged by a published and uncontradicted mass of testimony, to have been the result of vile trick and deception.[180]

Again the argument was made that the Theosophical Society was not able to withstand the critical nature of its original, sophisticated American audience and therefore had to relocate to India to entertain a simpler and naïve audience. There is a clear biased evident in Britten's writings; however, two points are worthwhile to note: 1) it was asserted that no tangible evidence for the existence of the masters was made available; and, 2) that Blavatsky had 'failed' as a Spiritualist and therefore retreated to India. Britten's feelings towards teaming up with Theosophical Society and Spiritualism on the basis of common goals were explored in another article. A letter was received in the *Two Worlds* written by R.M. noting that 'Both spiritualist and theosophist agree as far as can be gathered from their published writings, that given a medium, physical phenomena are produced by the operation of psychic and spiritual manifestations of disembodied personalities.'[181] This was responded to by the writer (possibly Britten):

> As we have shown again and again in this journal, and that from the literature of both parties, spiritualism and theosophy are as wide apart, and as likely to remain so, at the poles of the earth. Spiritualism claims as its revelator unnumbered hosts of spirits who prove their identity with human beings who once lived in earth by tests, such as ages, names, dates, expressions, and revelations known only to those the world calls dead- in fact, by a vast range of varied phenomena, the great bulk of which could not be imitated by any human beings under similar conditions. These spirits, moreover, prove the truth and human origin by repeating their tests all over the world, trough countless mediums, strangers to each other, under totally unprepared conditions, and in great varieties of languages.[182]

> Now theosophists, although they put forth very fine philosophic talk about universal brotherhood, good, truth, science, &c., &c., &c., and every good thing that every other sect in the world has taught before them, when they come to speak or write of spiritual things and existence, deny every item named above, as taught by spirits. They cut up the one man into seven parts; bury some, drift off others to states where they are to lose all consciousness of their past lives, quench their identity, and become utterly unable 'ever to return to earth again,' except to the very highest adepts-favoured beings of whose existence no proof has ever yet been rendered. Out of the seven cut-up items of the one soul they only allow one to return to earth, and these are only corpse lights, grave

emanations, horrible loathsome 'reliquae of the dead,' and in returning or attending the séance rooms, they are only there to do
mischief, teach every conceivable vice, and lower the mediums
through whom they come, so as 'to ruin them body and soul.'
And these are the horrible spooks that the make of our beloved
spirit friends, and these are the shameful slanders that they launch
against the many good, pure living, and spiritualized persons who
are to be found in the ranks of the spiritual mediums.[183]

The writer failed to reply directly to the comment explained in the
above letter: If both sides agreed on the basic tenet of Spiritualism
then weren't both organization on the same side philosophically?
Based on this article, Britten seemed to be mostly intolerant for the
philosophy that Blavatsky attached to her eclectic form of Spiritualism especially in her septenary division of the soul. Furthermore, a
misunderstanding of Blavatsky's doctrines seemed obvious in the
above article- Blavatsky believed that it was possible for the soul of
the departed to contact the living. Though this was an evolving concept that started as a common occurrence in Blavatsky's earlier writings (especially related to loved ones and suicides) and became less
frequent in her later works nonetheless it still remained possible in
rare cases. Britten's failure to recognize this belief showed that she
was either attempting to cast Theosophy in an inferior light or she
remained ignorant to this doctrine. Given the fact that Britten was
continuously denigrating the Theosophical Society and Blavatsky, the
former statement seems closer to the truth.

The writer continued to record a statement which was powerful
for its implication- the general belief in the relationship between
Spiritualism and Theosophy: 'We receive constant assurances that
theosophy and spiritualism are one, and the interest of believes in
both ranks ought to be fraternally shared and united. To this we reply everlastingly, No.'[184] Despite the biased against Theosophy explicated above, the very fact that the writer observed that the *Two
Worlds* received 'constant assurances' that these two organizations
were compatible implied that they received steady correspondences
wishing for Britten to ease up on her attacks of the Society. The
writer of this article continued his defamation of the Society by focusing upon the philosophical differences between Theosophy instead of the similarities:

Our souls are not cut up into seven bits at death, and no part of us
loses consciousness, identity, love of kindred, or memory of earth-

life. No part of us *does* remain on earth hovering about séance rooms only to do mischief, ruin the mediums body and soul, and incite those that listen to them to every evil. Few, if any spirits, really proved to be such, ever taught the doctrine of re-incarnation; and, all alike in every country and through all sources return to do good, incite humanity to progress, and help to open up endless vistas of knowledge of spiritual things and spiritual science. Now in fine, when our theosophist friends can give one ,well-proven fact as susceptible of demonstration as those which have convinced, say, one such mind as that of Judge Edmonds, or William Howitt, we will say here may be some common ground of belief between the two parties; until then. Theosophical theories and spiritual facts are- once again- as widely sundered as the poles; although as friends and students in the newly discovered realms of the spiritual universe, they may walk and-in-hand and personally be friends as loving as the Hebrew Jonathan and David…[185]

Despite Britten's reluctance to acknowledge the affinities, it seemed that the common ground which she shared with the Theosophical Society was their belief in the basic tenet of Spiritualism- the possibility for the deceased to communicate with the living. The main value in examining the articles in *Two Worlds* is not found in what is written but in what is implied- If Spiritualism and Theosophy were really very distinct from one another there would be no reason to publish articles like the ones cited above. Everyone would know their differences and articles clarifying their relationship would garner very little interest; however, it seemed that this connection was a continual point of controversy throughout the publishing of *Two Worlds*. It seems plausible that these two movements shared an intimate connection that Britten hoped to sever due to a personal conflict that occurred between herself and the co-founder of this movement Madame Blavatsky. In order to prove this theory, an understanding of this relationship must be explored.

6.27 Blavatsky and Britten: A Confused Connection

Before Blavatsky landed in the United States, she had previous experience in Spiritualism evidenced in her alleged conversion by D. D. Home in 1858 and through her understanding of French Spiritism and the teachings of Allen Kardec which she admitted to in *Incidents of Madame Blavatsky* and revealed in her subsequent formation of the *Société Spirite* in Cairo, Egypt in 1871. Her advanced understanding of Spiritualism seemed evident in her articles published in the *Spiritual*

Scientist which appeared theoretically advanced to the writings of many contemporary American Spiritualists most notably in her assimilation of Western Esotericism.

Many of the events in Blavatsky's early personal life have already been explored in the biographical section at the opening of this study; however, during Blavatsky's initial entrance into the States in 1873 she had very limited resources and lived at a women's tenement located in 222 Madison Street, New York. Also, her impulsive marriage to Michael Bettanelly in 1875 and their eventual divorce in 25 May 1878 along with the events of the Philadelphia fiasco set the background for her introduction to Emma Hardinge Britten.

Britten was first connected to Blavatsky through their mutual acquaintance- Henry Olcott. Emma Britten maintained an ambiguous relationship with Olcott for some years prior to 1875 though the nature of this relationship remains unknown it seemed that they had been introduced through a mutual acquaintance- J. J. Mapes. Mapes had been Britten's housemate and Olcott's teacher in the 1850s and provides a link between these two personalities. Olcott eventually reached out to Britten in an unpublished letter dated 4 October 1875 in order to locate an apartment for Blavatsky somewhere in New York City following her stay with Hiram Corson (though this seemed to be unsuccessful as she ended up moving in with Olcott at 433 West Thirty Fourth Street in New York City).[186] In his biography, Olcott expressed an admiration for the teachings of Britten noting that 'there are fine, even brilliant passages in it' and that he was 'deeply impressed' with Britten's knowledge exemplified in this work *Art Magic.* Indeed, he even appeared to pay double the price to receive one of the original limited printings of 500 copies self published by Britten using the printers Messrs. Wheat and Cornett in New York.'[187] As suggested in the previous section *Art Magic* could have been intended as the first publication of the Theosophical Society which evidenced the intimacy of Britten's relationship with the early Theosophical Society.

This seemed possible as during the fall of 1875 Britten had attempted to re-enter the mainstream Spiritual movement after her farewell speech to the Boston Spiritualist Association in 1873 where she noted her divergence with American Spiritualism over the issues of free love and reincarnation.[188] For 'she denounced with especial earnestness the doctrine of free love as repulsive to every instinct of humanity....One of the worst features with which Spiritualism is charged is the dark, the baleful doctrine of re-incarnation as taught by Allen (sic) Kardec of France… In closing, Mrs. Britten bid her friends farewell, perhaps for but a season, perhaps forever."[189] Britten had temporarily set aside her career as a Spiritualist in favor of starting an unsuccessful galvanic medicine practice. This practice was a futile enterprise and in the fall of 1875 Britten returned to Spiritualism as a means of providing her with an income. Britten's early connection with the Theosophical Society was recognized by Marc Demarest in his introduction to *Art Magic*: 'So it comes as no surprise that she [Britten] was welcomed into the unruly fraternity that progressed, in the latter half of 1875, from a "Miracle Club" to the Theosophical Society, or that she was treated by that group as a knowledgeable occultist, and a senior partner in the enterprise."[190] Britten had teamed up with Blavatsky and these two outspoken women had to share the spotlight as the only two female members of the original Theosophical Society.

In the 1870s there was talk of a decline (whether actual or imagined) in the Spiritualist movement across the Western world due primarily to the rise of countless exposures of 'reputable' mediums.[191] Evidence of this decline was suggested by Frank Podmore the historian of Spiritualism and in the public's general attitude as summarized in the following New York Times article titled 'A Decline in Spiritualism' published on 23 February 1875:[192]

> … From the 'eight to eleven millions' of men and women in the country, who, according to the assertion of Mr. Alfred Wallace, a noted English writer, may be classed as believers in Spiritualism there has come up no great declaration of belief…The decline, once fairly begun, will be rapid. Of course there were never as many as eleven, or even eight millions of American men and women, who became firmly and fairly convinced, after due exercise of reason, that the phenomena in which modern mediums delight to deal are produced by supernatural influences. It is fair to doubt whether there were ever as many American interested in Spiritualism at all…When the indifferent masses are quite certain that all the later 'manifestations' have been swindles, and when they see that even ardent defenders of Spiritualism as a science cannot help laughing at the ridiculous and vulgar tricks of the 'materializers,' the indifference will become scorn. There will be mourning in the house of the Eddy's, and these rustic brethren will there after gain their bread by exclusive attention to following the plow.[193]

This 'decline' would impact both Britten and Blavatsky who were attempting to establish themselves as reformers of this fading movement and to institutionalize this religious tradition both philosophically and methodologically. In essence, they were attempting to instigate a revival of Spiritualism. In order to accomplish this goal, these two women needed to procure impressionable and dedicated converts who would take a philosophical interest in the ideals of Spiritualism not just by attending the occasional séance, but by ordering books, attending lectures, and paying dues. Thus, the Theosophical Society was formed out of this desire to revitalize Spiritualism and to organize it philosophically. Their personal justifications for attempting this bold reformation seemed to have been overstated by Arthur Lillie in a previous section though his observations remain seemingly accurate- these women were attempting to fund their individual propagandist campaigns associated with this religious movement.

Blavatsky was extremely intelligent though not in any academic sense having never attended college or university; however, she did maintain a charismatic personality which coupled with her extensive experience in world travel and in mystical religious practices made her an ideal leader of this eclectic movement.[194] Britten, on the other hand, had an equal claim towards the leadership of this organization having been well diversified and knowledgeable in the various aspects of Spiritualism and through her networking organized an impressive list of influential Spiritualist connections through her peripatetic tour of the United States from 1857-1875. Also, her 1870 work *Modern American Spiritualism* provided Britten with recognition as an early historian of this movement. Despite the individual strengths that each of these two women brought to the Society it seemed that Britten appeared to possess some occult knowledge that had intrigued Blavatsky evidently making Britten a valuable asset to the early Theosophical Society.

At this stage in their early relationship, Blavatsky appeared to submit to the younger vivacious Britten as implied in the following undated letter sent to Britten written shortly after the establishment of the Theosophical Society:

> To E. Hardinge Britten
> To Mrs. H. B.---, with the kindest regards and sincere friendly love of a poor Buddhist pilgrim, daily stoned in the Free State of New York. M. [sic] P. Blavatsky

'Neither naked nor clothed, barefoot nor shod,' I knock thrice for admission at the 'inner door' of the temple. Let your heart be Jachin and Boaz, the main pillars of Solomon's Temple, and allow a poor candidate with the left breast, knee and foot naked pass through, that the unity added to the Binary might produce the sacred Friend or Trinity but shut tight your heart against the rest of the cunning craft. Amen.

Remember, O, my sister fellow of the Theosophical Society, that the cable toe [tow] encircling the Mason's waist is twin brother of the sacred Brahminic cord. And to the modern Mason who may doubt, chant the following Hindoo hymn and ask him what it means: Thou, O wise god Varuna, Lord of all, of heaven and earth, listen on thy way: That I may live, take from me the upper rope, close the middle rope and remove the lower rope.
---Hymn to Varuna, R.V. 1:25

Apparently, Britten possessed some superior occult understanding which Blavatsky desired to extract from her; one such possibility was suggested by Patrick Deveney -the doctrine of an astral double discussed more fully below. It seemed Britten appreciated this temporal submission especially by such a strong and formidable personality as Blavatsky. Given the complexities of this relationship, there must have been issues concerning leadership in the early Theosophical Society prompting Britten to reluctantly join the Theosophical Society.

Around this same time, came Blavatsky's acceptance of the 'theory of elementals' to explain fraudulent phenomena. It seemed that both women had agreed to accept this explanation as the logical justification for the wide spread practice of fraudulency among some Spiritualist mediums. After all the decline of the Spiritualist movement was largely due to the deceitful practices of unsavory and dishonest mediums in the press; thus, in order to revive the Spiritualist movement its basic tenets and the nature of spirits had to be reconceptualized. This included an expansion of basic doctrines including the survival of the soul after death, its ability to communicate with the dead, the need for an Order and institution, and the ability to hold practitioners to a regulated standard. Thus, the Theosophical Society modified Spiritualism into a slightly different philosophical framework which included elements of Western Esotericism and Orientalism which would provide safeguards against the fraudulent behavior that was rampant in the Spiritualist movement of the 1870s.

Despite this objective, Blavatsky soon became sidetracked with *Isis Unveiled* which resulted in the shirking of her responsibilities in the

Society and as a result many of the Spiritualists resigned as noted by Olcott:

> H. P. B. then working night and day upon her first book, 'Isis Unveiled,' soon refused to even attend our meetings, let alone do so much at them as make the smallest phenomenon- though she was continually astounding her visitors with them at her own house- and so, naturally enough, the leading Spiritualists in the Society became dissatisfied and dropped out. Forced, contrary to all my expectations to keep up the interest at the meetings and carry the whole load myself, while at the same time attending to my professional business and helping H. P. B. on 'Isis,' I did what I could in the way of getting psychometers, clairvoyants, mesmerisers, and spiritual mediums to show us sundry phases of psychical science.[195]

All of these events along with a lack of strongly defined leadership pushed many of the Spiritualists to resign from the Society and forced the Theosophists to seek recognition in the East.

As alluded earlier, John Patrick Deveney suggested another reconceptualized Spiritualist philosophy created by both Britten and Blavatsky in his *Astral Projection or Liberation of the Double and the Work of the Early Theosophical Society*. In this article, Deveney made a compelling argument that the early Theosophical Society was interested in the occult principle of astral projection and the ability to project the conscious or the astral body into another person's body. He further connected this idea to Britten:

> It is well known that one of the changes wrought in spiritualism by the 'occultism' introduced by Colonel Olcott, H.P.B. and Emma Hardinge Britten in the mid-1870s was the notion of 'elementals' and 'elementaries' as responsible, at least partially, for the phenomena of the séance room, but *beyond this was the notion of the role of the double of the living 'adept' as controller or instigator of the phenomena and the related notion that spiritualism itself as a movement was the creation of such living adepts...*[196]

> The fundamental key to this 'occultism' that transformed spiritualism in the mid-1870s was the conclusion that man even now while living is as much a spirit as he will ever be after death and can accordingly, in proper circumstances and with proper training, do now as an embodied human everything that he will be able later to do when he has dropped his body in death, including consciously projecting his double. In the words of Emma Hardinge Britten,

'There are no phenomena produced by disembodied spirits, which may not be effected by the still embodied human spirit, provided a correct knowledge of these powers is directed by a strong and powerful will.' Britten, one of the original formers of the Theosophical Society, was the proximate introducer of this idea into spiritualism.[197]

Deveney went on to trace the origination of this idea back to Britten who was one of the first people credited with the founding concept of the astral double in Spiritualism (and therefore seemingly introduced this idea into the Theosophical Society as well) during this time period. Deveney further claimed that the Lamasery was a training school for astral projection which seemed plausible. A belief in the astral double would not contradict the basic tenet of Spiritualism but could rather confirm the idea that if the soul could be separated and communicate with other beings in life it could certainly maintain this ability post-mortem.[198] This idea may have been the reason why Blavatsky treated Britten as a superior in some of her earlier communications.

In November of 1875 Britten became a resolute member of the Theosophical Society, yet in December she was attempting to distance herself and her *Art Magic* from the Society.[199] She wrote an article noting that 'little pugs' had tried to connect her with Olcott, Blavatsky, and the Theosophical Society which she called a 'rank falsehood.'

I have no desire to injure them by allowing my work to be fastened upon theirs, nor do I wish to be injured in return by suffering their views, names or proceedings, to be mixed up with my undertaking…I am now compelled to say I WILL NOT ALLOW IT TO BE SO, and, furthermore, I must add that my husband and myself find the reiteration of this petty and mischievous slander persisted in by whisperers who dare not openly confront us; finding, moreover, that those who communicate it are [Banner of Light] subscribers, and claim their authority from your correspondents, Mr. Editor, we have felt it our duty to lay the case before an eminent New York legal gentleman, who has instructed us to say publicly that free as this country may be to do what each one pleases [sic], it is not free enough to allow the circulation of injurious libels, and whilst this same legal functionary has instructed us on the award which the law of this free but JUST country renders to the libeller [sic], we have instructed him to proceed immediately against anyone who hereafter shall assert, publicly or privately, that the work I have undertaken — namely, to become Secretary to the publication of Art Magic, or Mundane, Sub-Mundane, and Super-Mundane Spiritualism [sic] — has anything to do with Col. Olcott, Madame Blavatsky, the New York Theosophical Society, or any thing or person belonging to either those persons or that Society. Further, I insist that the work was prepared in Europe by a gentleman who is wholly unknown to the persons and Society named above, and that, though two or three of the Society, as individuals, have sent in their names as subscribers, they, too, are entirely ignorant of the author, his name, standing or the character of his work.[200]

After the dissolution of this professional relationship between Britten and Blavatsky it seemed that neither side had any desire to reconcile this friendship. In a letter written on July 1876 and published in the *Spiritualist Scientist*, Britten alluded to the 'secret order' of the Theosophical Society and seemingly suggested that this new secret organization of the Society had become her public reason for resigning even though this seemed to be a rather insignificant issue (this seemed an ironic reason for leaving as C. C. Massey wanted the Society to remain secretive).[201] Though her actual reasons for resignation remain unclear one thing was certain- Britten left the Theosophical Society.

In Robert Mathiesen's brief biography of Emma Hardinge Britten, he observed an element of the Blavatsky-Britten connection that seemed strangely coincidental which he believed may have an unknown explanation. There seemed to be more behind the dissolution of this relationship than either party had suggested. Mathiesen's coincidence involved the fact that upon disagreeing with the future of the Theosophical Society these two outspoken figures went in complete opposite directions abandoning the United States:

> After the Earlier Theosophical Society ceased to meet in November, 1876, H. P. Blavatsky and H. S. Olcott decided to leave the United States and start over again. They left New York harbor on December 17-19, 1877, and traveled eastward across the Atlantic, first to England, but then to India. It is a striking fact that Emma Hardinge Britten and her husband, William Britten, left New York, and then the United States, at about the same time, although they traveled in the opposite direction. Sometime in 1877, only a few months after the Earlier Theosophical Society ceased to meet, the Brittens began their most extensive lecture tour ever, first going overland to California, where they remained for several months.

On January 21, 1878, the Brittens left San Francisco harbor and sailed westward across the Pacific, stopping at Hawaii, Australia and New Zealand. Neither the Brittens nor Blavatsky and Olcott ever spent much time in the United States again. Blavatsky remained in India until 1885; in that year she moved to Europe and then to England, where she died in 1891. The Brittens returned to San Francisco on December 31, 1879; having spent several months on the west coast, they slowly traveled overland to New York. Early in 1881 they left the United States for England, where they remained until his death in 1894 and hers in 1899.

Such a symmetry suggests that we may not yet have fully understood the motives for each departure, which may be more complex than either woman ever admitted in print. It may, of course, simply come down to this: in their conflict the two strong-willed, visionary occultists mutually shattered one another's hopes for the Earlier Theosophical Society at the same time, and hastily abandoned the scene of their mutual defeat. Or there may be other reasons, as yet wholly unsuspected, why all parties left New York, and the United States, so rapidly.[202]

It seemed that an unspecified event may have occurred which caused these women to get as far away from each other as possible though nothing is specifically mentioned.

Marc Demarest in his unpublished *Revising Mathiesen* noted that Britten left the States 'in 1881 under a cloud (after being contradicted, during a trance lecture, by one of the subjects of her lecture, who happens to be in her audience) and she does return to the US, in 1884, for the camp meeting season, remaining some six months in the US. This final 'transition' in 1884 is significant, as her reception in the US in 1884 did much to convince EHB, I believe, that her future lay in England, or in quiet seclusion.'[203] Britten had left the States only to return again for a brief period and immediately departing once again. There appears to be grounds for this blow out between these two women with strong personalities which seemed suggested by Mathiesen. Returning to the earlier premise posited in the last section that 'It seemed plausible that these two movements shared an intimate connection that Britten hoped to sever due to a personal conflict that occurred between herself and the co-founder of this movement Madame Blavatsky.' This conflict suggested by Mathiesen seemed to justify Britten's later goal of completely separating from the Theosophical Society in her *Two Worlds* periodical and the animosity that Britten exhibited towards Blavatsky even after her demise in 1891.

Though this may seem to be a stretch of the evidence who could deny that the possibility exists? No matter what occurred both women were destined for great things in the advent of Spiritualism. Madame Blavatsky went on to reinstitutionalize the Theosophical Society with an Oriental shift and Emma Hardinge Britten became the founder of the Spiritualist National Federation in 1891.

6.28 Alfred Wallace, the Victorian Scientist, Spiritualist ... Theosophist? (1823–1913)

In concluding this examination on the relationship between Theosophy and Spiritualism it should be ascertained that some prominent Victorians found their names associated with certain Spiritualist groups in order to lend validity and prestige to these individual organizations even if the individual had never joined. This was certainly the case with the respected scientist Alfred Russel Wallace whose name became associated with the Theosophical Society. Wallace found himself used as a pawn by Blavatsky in order to lend credibility to both her own organization and ideas, but, the question remains, what was the actual nature of their relationship? This section will give some biographical details in the life of one of the world's most prominent scientists and his connection to Theosophy.

6.29 The Scientist

Alfred R. Wallace (1823–1913) is best remembered for his role as the independent co-founder for the theory of natural selection alongside Charles Darwin, the father of evolutionary theory. Although Darwin and Wallace had never contacted each other before 1858, both men had independently worked out similar theories related to natural selection and evolution. Darwin explained how he had discovered Wallace's theory in the following letter written to the noted geologist Charles Lyell (1797-1875) written on 18 June 1858:

> My dear Lyell,-Some year or so ago you recommended me to read a paper by Wallace in the 'Annals', which had interested you, and, as I was writing to him, I knew this would please him much, so I told him. He has today sent me the enclosed, and asked me to forward it to you. .. You said this, when I explained to you here very briefly my views of 'Natural Selection' depending on the struggle for existence. I never saw a more striking coincidence; if Wallace had my MS. sketch written out in 1842, he could not have

made a better short abstract! Even his terms now stand as heads of my chapters. Please return me the MS., which he does not say he wishes me to publish but I shall, of course, at once write and offer to send to any journal. So all my originality, whatever it may amount to, will be smashed.[204]

Thus, it appears that one of the greatest scientific discoveries of the nineteenth century was in fact first published by Alfred Wallace. This discovery placed Wallace in a prestigious position among his peers and the scientific community of this day. This status would enable Wallace to promote his scientific theories and religious ideas, no matter how unusual or unorthodox they may have appeared.

In May 1864 Wallace published an article in the *Anthropological Review* entitled 'The Origin of Human Races and the Antiquity of Man Deduced from the Theory of Natural Selection.' He observed that on ancient Egyptian sculptures and paintings (dating at least 5,000 years ago) there were depictions of humanity that displayed nearly identical features to modern man. Their depiction of racial traits seemed to have remained unchanged over this long period.[205] Commenting on Darwin's own concept of natural selection, Wallace here proposed a new theory based on the differences between humanity and the animal kingdom: Man was subject to natural selection until the point that he evolved into a conscious being.[206] Thenceforth man was emancipated from the process of natural selection by using his mind to invent various items (i.e. the discovery of weapons, clothes, houses, etc.). First published in 1864 this essay was reprinted in 1870 in the work entitled *Contributions to the Theory of Natural Selection* and published in anticipation of Darwin's publication of *Descent of Man* in 1871. *Contributions to the Theory of Natural Selection* reflected Wallace's belief in a higher intelligence and contained a revised version of 'The Origin of Human Races and the Antiquity of Man Deduced from the Theory of Natural Selection' which appeared under the title 'The Development of Human Races under the Law of Natural Selection.' There was one major change italicized below:

But while these changes had been going on, his mental development had, from *some unknown cause*, greatly advanced, and had now reached that condition in which it began powerfully to influence his whole existence, and would therefore become subject to the irresistible action of 'natural selection.' At length, however, there came into existence a being in whom that subtle force we term *mind*, became of greater importance than his mere bodily structure. Though with a naked and unprotected body, *this* gave him clothing against the vary-ing inclemencies of the seasons…a grand revolution was effected in nature, a revolution which in all the previous ages of the earth's his-tory had had no parallel, for a being had arisen who was no longer necessarily subject to change with the changing universe—a being who was in some degree superior to nature, inasmuch as he knew how to control and regulate her action, and could keep himself in harmony with her, not by a change in body, but by an advance of mind… Man has not only escaped 'natural selection' himself, but he is actually able to take away some of that power from nature which before his appearance she universally exercised. We can anticipate the time when the earth will produce only cultivated plants and do-mestic animals; when man's selection shall have supplanted 'natural selection;' and when the ocean will be the only domain in which that power can be exerted, which for countless cycles of ages ruled su-preme over all the earth (emphasis added).[207]

The principal revision was the addition of the phrase 'some un-known cause' highlighted above with the implication that something supernatural was responsible for the origin of humanity. Wallace believed that the evolution of the 'mind' in human beings absolved them from the process of natural selection: 'Though with a naked and unprotected body, *this* (mind) gave him clothing against the vary-ing inclemencies of the seasons.'[208]

Wallace (in contrast to Blavatsky's views) further theorized that there would be little need for any future physical evolutionary chang-es in humanity except for the features of the head and face. This mental evolution in humanity's development effectively answered the question 'Why did man's body, with the exception of his skull, so closely resemble the bodies of extant apes, while his skull and mental capacities (were) so widely diverged from those of the same apes?'[209] Wallace's thesis that the mental evolution of humanity was caused by unknown supernatural agents placed him at odds with Darwin. [210] In 1871, Darwin in *The Descent of Man*, explained that sexual selection was the superior replacement for natural selection (though this was hinted in *Origin of Species*).[211] Although Darwin had inferred (as had Wallace earlier) that selection was based upon efficiency Wallace later believed humanity had evolved under the controlling action of such higher intelligences. It should be noted that Wallace's idea of natural selection was continuously changing throughout his writings. One scholar has noted that 'it is sometimes hard to follow Wallace's be-liefs concerning the impact of natural selection on human development because, several times, they changed dramatically during the second half of the nineteenth century."[212]

Wallace further theorized that humanity had evolved over long intervals of time, but that its physical evolution was minimal compared to mental evolution. Once the mind had evolved, humanity stopped physically evolving. Also, Wallace was a monogenist and believed that races of humanity were varieties of a single species. This fitted Wallace's unique view of natural selection:

> Here, then, we see the true grandeur and dignity of man. On this view of his special attributes, we may admit that even those who claim for him a position as an order, a class, or a sub-kingdom by himself, have some reason on their side. He is, indeed, a being apart, since he is not influenced by the great laws which irresistibly modify all other organic beings. Nay more; this victory which he has gained for himself gives him a directing influence over other existences.[213]

Wallace viewed the earth and humanity as unique occurrences within the universe. This was contrary to the contemporaneous theories of Percival Lowell (1855-1916), who theorized that intelligent life existed elsewhere in this universe and inhabited the planet of Mars.[214] Wallace specifically disputed Lowell's theory in his book entitled *Is Mars Habitable?* (1907). Wallace maintained that the earth was the center of the universe along with our unique, life-producing sun.[215] Earlier in *Man's Place in the Universe* (1904), Wallace laid down the earliest foundation for the theory that would later be labeled the anthropic principle. This principle was based upon the unique characteristics of the earth and argued that it appeared to be the ideal place for the emergence of intelligent life. Wallace also noted the possible existence of other universes, though he maintained that man was the apex of intelligent creation and appeared to be against the belief that any other intelligent beings existed in the universe.[216]

To summarize Wallace's scientific views at this point: He believed that the evolution of humanity was unique for the reason that man had evolved a mind which protected him from the laws of natural selection. This unique evolution was the result of unknown forces working within the universe. Also, Wallace was a monogenist – he believed that humanity evolved from a single species. Furthermore he viewed humanity and the earth as unique occurrences within a cyclical universe. Now that Wallace's scientific views have been explored, focus will now be placed upon his religious beliefs as a Spiritualist.

6.30 The Spiritualist
In a letter to his brother-in-law Thomas Sims written on 15 March 1861 Wallace wrote the following noting his agnostic belief system:

> I am thankful I can see much to admire in all religions. To the mass of mankind religion of some kind is a necessity. But whether there be a God and whatever be His nature; whether we have an immortal soul or not, or whatever may be our state after death, I can have no fear of having to suffer for the study of nature and the search for truth, or believe that those will be better off in a future state who have lived in the belief of doctrines inculcated from childhood, and which are to them rather a matter of blind faith than intelligent conviction.[217]

However, this agnostic, materialist belief would soon be challenged in the summer of 1865 when Wallace first encountered Spiritualism. This experience is recorded in his own words:

> July 22nd, 1865- Sat with my friend, his wife, and two daughters, at a large loo table,[218] by daylight. In about half-an-hour some faint motions were perceived, and some faint taps heard. They gradually increased; the taps became very distinct and the table moved considerably, obliging us all to shift our chairs. Then a curious vibratory motion of the table commenced, almost like the shivering of a living animal. I could feel it up to my elbows. These phenomena were variously repeated for two hours. On trying afterwards, we found the table could not be voluntarily moved in the same manner without a great exertion of force, and we could discover no possible way of producing the taps when our hands were upon the table.[219]

Thus, did Wallace begin his journey into Spiritualism. He would not be the only scientist to join the ranks of Spiritualism. There were several other well known scientists who believed in the basic tenets of Spiritualism during this time period as well. These included: Sir William Crookes (1832-1919), chemist, Sir Oliver Lodge (1851-1940), physicist, Richard Norris Wolfenden (1854-1926), physiologist and oceanographer, and Cromwell Fleetwood (C. F.) *Varley* (1828-1883), engineer, to name but a few.

Malcolm Kottler notes a drastic change in Wallace's writing during this time period which he attributed to his new-found belief in Spiritualism:

> In 1864 Wallace was firmly committed to the action of natural selection alone in the development of man. In 1869 he first expressed publicly his new point of view that natural selection was unable to explain the origin of man and that higher intelligences guiding man's development were required. Something happened between 1864 and 1869 to change his mind: the crucial event was Wallace's conversion to spiritualism.[220]

Wallace would go on to attend séances as noted in his book *Miracles and Modern Spiritualism*. In September 1865, he began a series of visits to Mrs. Marshall, the noted British medium.[221] The phenomena that he witnessed there consisted of mostly levitation and inexplicably moving objects. Wallace assured his readers that in these events 'there was no room for any possible trick or deception.'[222] Wallace also received communications from the other side via a ouija board style of divination. In November 1866, Wallace's sister discovered that she had been living with a woman who possessed 'the power of inducing loud and distinct taps and other curious phenomena.'[223] Thus, Wallace began to set up his own group for performing séances in 1866 with the aid of his sister and her housemate.

Aside from the notoriety that Wallace had achieved in the scientific world he was soon reputed as a prominent Spiritualist. Wallace was especially intrigued with the subject of mesmerism and phrenology. Mesmerism was a systematic belief system based upon the findings of Franz Anton Mesmer (1734 – 1815), the noted healer who used magnetic powers to cure his patients. Mesmer had founded what he defined as 'animal magnetism' which explained that a physical force was directly connected to physical ailments. Mesmer studied medicine at the University of Vienna and published a dissertation in 1776 which attempted to explore the subject of the microcosm and macrocosm- the idea that events in the solar system could correspond with the physical ailments of individuals. This work was titled *De influx planetarum in corpus humanum* (The influence of the planets in the human body) and argued for the existence of an 'invisible, universally distributed fluid that flowed continuously everywhere and served as a vehicle for the mutual influence among heavenly bodies, the earth, and living things.'[224] Mesmer was a legitimate medical doctor who used unorthodox treatments to cure his patients including his patented 'baquet'- a wooden tub that was filled with iron filings and bottles holding magnetized water.[225]

In the nineteenth century, mesmerism started to become associated with the new theory of phrenology. Phrenology is a pseudo-scientific belief that the measurements of a person's cranium can reveal insights to their character. Alan Gauld noted that:

> Both mesmerism and phrenology gained greatly from the union...Phrenology began to gain momentum in Britain in the early 1820s and a national Phrenological association was started in 1838...throughout the 1830s and with increasing rapidity after 1840, phrenology...became a movement whose greatest strength was among the artisans and radical working class. It soon came to permeate many of the progressive social movements.[226]

Thus, the appeal for Wallace appears to have been that both mesmerism and phrenology attempted to label themselves as scientific. Both of these 'sciences' depended upon the 'microcosm and macrocosm' which implied that a supernatural being had created humanity and the universe to correspond with each other; this belief in a supernatural creator would boast an obvious appeal for Wallace. Wallace's affinity with phrenology was noted by Joel Schwartz in the following observation:

> Wallace's belief in phrenology allowed him to discard natural selection as an influence on the human body when he wrote his paper on man in 1864. In it such expressions as faculties, propensities and feelings were employed in a phrenological style. For example, Wallace's use of the term 'faculties' (which developed, according to him, when man's brain had become fairly complex and his physical form and structure ceased to be influenced by natural selection) was the same as that of the phrenologists, who assigned such 'faculties' to man but not to animals.[227]

Wallace was one of the earliest members of the Society for Psychical Research (SPR) in 1882, though his opinion of this Society would later change. In a letter written to Mrs. Fisher on 14 September 1896 Wallace made a comment that the majority of the active members within the Psychical Research Society were 'absurdly and illogically skeptical.'[228]

The SPR were examined more thoroughly in the earlier section on Richard Hodgson for their role in the publication of a report in 1884 which was heavily detrimental to the Theosophical Society.[229] The 'Hodgson Report' (as it was known) suggested that Blavatsky had forged the Mahatma letters and would accuse her of fraud among many other dishonorable offenses. Having briefly exhibited Wallace's background in Spiritualism and established his membership in the Psychical Research Society, attention will now be focused upon his philosophical views.

6.31 His Philosophy

Wallace stated his views of soteriology in his writing *The Scientific Aspect of the Supernatural*:

> At death it (the spirit) quits the body for ever. The spirit like the body has its laws, definition limited to its powers. The spirit which has lived and developed its powers clothed with a human body, will, when it leaves that body, still retain its former modes of thought, its former tastes, feelings, and affections. The new state of existence is a natural continuation of the old one…it is the same in character as before, but it has acquired new physical and mental powers, new modes of manifesting the moral sentiments, wider capacity for acquiring physical and spiritual knowledge…[230]

Accordingly, after death the human spirit does not change drastically but remains in a state very similar to that before death, although it now has use of new 'physical and mental powers.' In Wallace's view, death was not very different from life. The purpose of earthly life was further clarified by Wallace in his final publication *The World of Life* in 1910:

> Man was here for the very purpose of developing diversity and individuality, to be further advanced in a future life. That we see more clearly the whole object of our earth-life as a preparation for it. In this world we have the maximum of diversity produced, with a potential capacity for individual educability, and inasmuch as every spirit has been derived from the Deity, only limited by the time at the disposal of each of us. In the spirit-world death will not cut short the period of educational advancement. The best conditions and opportunities will be afforded for the conscious progress to a higher status, which all the diversities produced here will lead to an infinite variety, charm, and use, that could probably have been brought about in no other way.[231]

Wallace believed that the human spirit would continue to evolve even after death.[232] His view of the afterlife appeared very different than the prevalent orthodox Christian view. This is evidenced in the following excerpt:

> Equally at variance with each other are the popular and the spiritu-
> alistic doctrines as regards the Deity. …in the teaching of the 'spir-
> its' there is not a word of all this; They tell us they commune with
> higher intelligences than themselves, but of God they really know
> no more than we do. They say that above these higher intelligenc-
> es are others higher and higher in apparently endless gradation, but
> as far as they know, no absolute knowledge of the Deity himself is
> claimed by any of them.[233]

Wallace believed in higher spirits though his belief in orthodox Christianity remains unclear. In a letter written to Rev. J. B. Hender-son on 10 August 1893 Wallace noted that: 'although I look upon Christianity as originating in an unusual influx, I am not disposed to consider [it] as essentially different from those which originated oth-er great religious and philanthropic movements. It is probable that in your sense of the word I am not a Christian- Believe me…'[234] Though clearly distancing himself from Henderson it seemed that Wallace did possess a continuous belief in God that prompted one of his biographers Martin Fichman to note that 'Wallace believed in God but avoided allegiance to any traditional, doctrinal, or institu-tional position. Moreover, Wallace never asserted that God's exist-ence is provable.'[235] By his own admission Wallace believed in an 'Unknown Reality' which was infinite, and eternal as well as all-knowing, but not necessarily omnipotent.'[236]

Wallace held to the moral teachings of Spiritualism which he ex-plained in his work entitled *On Miracles and Modern Spiritualism*:

> 1) Man is a duality, consisting…of a spiritual form, evolved coin-
> cidentally with and permeating the physical body. 2) Death is the
> separation of this duality, and effects no change in the spirit, mor-
> ally or intellectually. 3) Progressive evolution of the intellectual and
> moral nature is the destiny of individuals; the knowledge, attain-
> ments and experience of earth-life forming the basis of spirit life.
> 4) Spirits can communicate through mediums though their com-
> munications are fallible.[237]

It is curious to note that, Wallace believed the constitution of humanity was dichotomous- spirit and body. Also, Wallace believed that mediums were fallible in their teachings; he eventually condensed Spiritualism into one essential teaching:

> that all of humanity was in every act and thought, helping to build up a mental fabric which will be and constitutes ourselves, more completely after the death of the body than it does now. Just as this fabric is well or ill built, so will our progress and happiness be aided or retarded….in proportion as we have developed our higher intellectual and moral nature, or starved it by disuse and by giving undue prominence to those faculties which secure us mere physical or selfish enjoyment, shall we be well or ill fitted for the new life we enter on.[238]

It is evident that Wallace's philosophy focused largely on the future life of the human spirit. Each life provided an opportunity for the spirit to advance. Thus, Wallace believed that happiness and progression were based upon works and actions (cause and effect).

In Wallace's final work, he embraced a spiritualistic form of evolution in *The World of Life* (1910) that occurred within an infinite number of worlds:

> If, as I here suggest, the whole purport of the material universe (our universe) is the development of spiritual beings who, in the infinite variety of their natures- what we term their characters,- shall to some extent reflect that infinite variety of the whole inorganic and organic worlds through which they have been developed; and if we further suppose…that such a variety of character could have been produced in no other way, then we may reasonably suppose that there may have been a vast system of cooperation of such grades of being, from a very high grade of power and intelligence down to those unconscious of almost unconscious 'cell-souls' posited by Haeckel, and which, I quite admit, seem to be essential coadjutors in the process of life-development.[239]

Thus, Wallace viewed the material world as a prepatory world for the spirit that was guided by a higher being. Now that Wallace's philosophy has been explained the question that next arises is why was Wallace attracted to Spiritualism?

6.32 Why Spiritualism?

James Marchant in his compilation of Wallace's letters made a profound analysis of Wallace's attraction to Spiritualism:

> It was, in short, his peculiar task to reveal something of the Why as well as the How of the evolutionary process, and in doing so verily to bring immortality to light. The immediate exciting cause of this discovery of the inadequacy of evolution from the material side alone to account for the world of life may seem to many to have been trivial and unworthy of the serious attention of a great scientist.[240] How, it might be asked, could the crude and doubtful phenomena of Spiritualism afford reasonably adequate grounds for challenging its supremacy and for setting a limit to its range? But spiritualistic phenomena were only the accidental modes in which the other side of evolution struck in upon his vision. They set him upon the other track and opened up to him the vaster kingdom of life which is without beginning, limit or end; in which perchance the sequence of life from the simple to the complex, from living germ to living God, may also be the law of growth. It is in the light of this ultimate end that we must judge the stumbling steps guided by raps and visons (sic) which led him to the ladder set up to the stars by which connection was established with the inner reality of being. That was the distinctive contribution which he made to human beliefs over and above his advocacy of Darwinianism.[241]

This commentary identifies Wallace's inquisitive nature as the stimulus leading him to investigate Spiritualism. In Spiritualism, Wallace would find the answers that would fill in the metaphysical gaps that his scientific theories had left unfilled. Spiritualism appeared to be an obvious religion for any scientist based upon Wallace's view that 'Spiritualism is an experimental science and affords the only sure foundation for a true philosophy and a pure religion...it, and it alone, is able to harmonize conflicting creeds...it appeals to evidence instead of faith, and substitutes facts for opinions.'[242]

6.33 Helena Blavatsky and Alfred Wallace: The Connection

In *Isis Unveiled* (1877), Blavatsky was greatly concerned with ascertaining the correct process of evolution. In the first volume of this work titled 'Science', Blavatsky continually attempted to refute Darwin's materialistic, evolutionary theories purported in his *On The Origin of Species*.[243] It becomes obvious that while refuting the materialist conclusions that could be derived from Darwin's work, Blavatsky also attempted to assimilate Darwin's concept of evolution into her cosmological construction of the universe. This was where Blavatsky's appreciation for Wallace becomes apparent. Wallace was a respected scientist and a co-founder (along with Darwin) of the 'modern' evolutionary theory of natural selection, but he was also a Spiritualist. In Blavatsky's opinion it seemed that Wallace's conversion to Spiritualism legitimized this belief structure and her own Theosophy which (in 1877) appeared to be simply a modified form of Spiritualism.

6.34 Blavatsky's Misquotations of Wallace

Blavatsky's treatment of Wallace's works allows the reader to understand the way in which Blavatsky used her sources. Blavatsky did not read a work and then contrive an idea based upon her reading; rather, it seemed that Blavatsky began with a presupposed idea and used a source to defend her preconceived belief even if it did not fit.

Blavatsky continuously referred to Wallace throughout *Isis Unveiled*, typically in relation to her idea of the spiritual evolution of the soul. The main problem arose when she took Wallace's theories and applied them to different contexts, allowing herself to speculate and derive incorrect assumptions. One such example of these assumptions is found in the following misquotation of Wallace's belief in a 'slow development over long evolutionary cycles':

> In the recent work of Mr. Alfred R. Wallace, *The Geographical Distribution of Animals*, we find the author seriously favoring the idea of 'some slow process of development' of the present species from others which have preceded them, his idea extending back over an innumerable series of cycles. And if animal why not animal man, preceded back by a thoroughly 'spiritual' one- a 'son of God'.[244]

Blavatsky took Wallace's theory that all animal species could be traced back to original 'parent forms' and applied this concept to humanity. She speculated that humanity could trace its lineage back to an original spiritual parent, form, or emanation. Thus, Blavatsky took Wallace's theory of an original parent species and applied it to humanity and her view of emanations and evolution from a spirit-like race. This statement appears to have been derived from a misunderstanding of Wallace's work. The above quotation corresponded to Wallace's statement that 'naturalists have now arrived at the conclusion, that by some slow process of development or transmutation, all animals have been produced from those which preceded them."[245] Though Wallace did concur that the development and distribution of animals was a lengthy process (he stated well before 50,000 to 100,000 years ago), he never used either the term 'innumerable' or 'cycle(s)' anywhere in *The Geographical Distribution of Animals* (1876). Based upon his later works, Wallace did believe in the concept of innumerable worlds where spiritual evolution could occur, but it was not related to physical evolution in a material world which was clearly referenced in the above quote.[246] Thus, it appeared that either Blavatsky mistakenly read something into Wallace's work that never existed or she simply fabricated this belief and attached Wallace's name to her own theory to give it some validity. Not only did she misunderstand Wallace, but she also took his quote that applied to the animal kingdom and speculated that this theory could also apply to humanity.

Another instance of Blavatsky applying Wallace's theories to a different context is exhibited in the next quote also taken from *Isis Unveiled*. Previous to this quote, Blavatsky had printed a large excerpt from Wallace pertaining to his belief in the future mental progression of humanity. Blavatsky clarified that:

> Still, what he [Wallace] says above clashes in no way with our kabbalistic assertions. Allow to ever-progressing nature, to the great law of the 'survival of the fittest', one step beyond Mr. Wallace's deductions, and we have in the future a possibility- nay, the assurance of a race, which, like the Vril-ya of Bulwer-Lytton's Coming Race, will be but one remove from the primitive 'Sons of God.'[247]

Again, Blavatsky takes one of Wallace's theories (in this case the mental development of the human race) and expounds upon it to defend her own belief that humanity is evolving into a supernatural race. The reference to Bulwer Lytton's Vril-ya is important to understanding Blavatsky's soteriology. In his science fiction novel *The Coming Race* (1871), Bulwer-Lytton noted an advanced race called the Vril-ya that lived in the earth and was an advanced form of beings indwelled with supernatural powers of healing and telekinesis.[248] They are described as having faces similar to men, but distinct from any known extant race. This being had a face similar to 'the sculptured sphinx—so regular in its calm, intellectual, mysterious beauty, its colour was peculiar. More like that of the red man than any other variety of our species' it had 'black eyes, deep and brilliant, and brows arched as a semi circle. The face...[contained] a nameless something in the aspect, tranquil...'[249] Thus, Blavatsky attempted to connect the scientific theories of Wallace with her own concept of an ancient Golden Age race of supernatural beings. Throughout the pages of *Isis Unveiled* (as previously noted), Blavatsky expressed her determination to reconnect Science and Theology, by interpreting Wallace's evolutionary ideas in a manner consistent with esoteric speculations of spiritual advance; however, what she achieved by combining these two elements was the development of her own unique tradition known as Theosophy. Thus, Blavatsky attempted to connect Wallace to her own Western Esoteric ideology.

In *Isis Unveiled* Blavatsky relied primarily upon Wallace as her champion against Darwinism, and remarkably never spoke negatively of him or his theories:[250] 'Mr. Alfred R. Wallace argues with sound logic, that the development of man has been more marked in his mental organization than in his external form. Man, he conceives to differ from the animal, by being able to undergo great changes of conditions and of his entire environment, without very many alterations in bodily form and structure.'[251]

There is a definitive similarity between Wallace's soteriology and Blavatsky's in *Isis Unveiled* as acknowledged in the following quote by Janet Oppenheim: 'Wallace's views on progress after death were very close to Blavatsky's;' however, despite this similarity regarding spiritual evolution, Blavatsky's later conceptualization of reincarnation would put her at odds with Wallace.'[252] Wallace openly spoke against the Theosophical concept of reincarnation put forth in Blavatsky's later writings in his article entitled 'Have We Lived on Earth Before? Shall We Live on Earth Again?' printed in *The London* in November 1904. Wallace noted that:

> the theosophical doctrine of the re-incarnation—the only thoroughly worked-out system answering our questions in the affirmative—asserts that this process of re-embodiment only began after the human form was perfected, and the human soul, or 'manas,' became incarnated in it, and that it was really essential for soul-development. The difficulty as to the early generations of men finding bodies in which to live a second time is overcome by the theory of devachan, an intermediate state of existence in which the lessons of earth-life fructify through contemplation and communion with other souls in the same condition; and as this state may continue for very long periods the actual commencement of re-

incarnation was at a later period when there was considerable population with a large and continuous supply of births. Thenceforward it is supposed that all, or almost all, souls in due course became re-incarnated for purposes of development in the grades of spirit existence. If this theory be true, it undoubtedly follows that, speaking broadly, we have all lived on earth before, and shall live on earth again, at all events till man is far more advanced morally and intellectually than he is now. But is it true? So far as I can learn, it is a pure speculation, and can appeal to no direct evidence in its support. But there is, on the other hand, a considerable body of evidence which renders it in the highest degree improbable, if it does not absolutely demonstrate its fallacy, as I shall now endeavour to show.[253]

Though Wallace had dealt with Blavatsky's final conceptualization of reincarnation in her later work *The Secret Doctrine* (1888) and her subsequent writings it is important to consider that Wallace's opinion of Theosophy's concept of reincarnation appeared to echo his conclusion on Theosophy as a whole: 'it is a pure speculation, and can appeal to no direct evidence in its support.'

6.35 Blavatsky's Connection to Wallace: Friendly or Fake?

The relationship between Alfred Wallace and Blavatsky remains ambiguous though there has been a trend in Theosophical studies to claim that Wallace was a member of the Theosophical Society.[254] This connection was also attested by Colonel Olcott in a lecture given at the United Service Institution of Indian at Simla on 7 October 1880: 'Edison is our member, and Wallace, and Camille Flammarion, and Lord Lindsay, and Baron du Potet and octogenarian Cahagnet, and scores of men of' that intellectual quality.'[255] In her study of Occultism and Spiritualism in the nineteenth century, Oppenheim questioned Wallace's membership in the Theosophical Society noting the fact that Theosophy could not have held Wallace's interest for very long.[256] The legitimacy of Wallace's membership as a member of the Theosophical Society will be commented upon below, but it is important to define the relationship between Wallace and Blavatsky. Several letters attempt to shed some light onto this vague connection. According to an apologetic letter written by Blavatsky on 7 November 1877, Wallace was presented with a complimentary copy of *Isis Unveiled*. This letter contained Blavatsky's justification for choosing the title *Isis Unveiled* and demonstrated its universal importance for both 'those who advocate and those who oppose the study of spiritualism.'[257]

Wallace responded in the following letter written to Blavatsky from Rosehill, Dorking, Surrey, on 1 January 1878:[258]

> Dear Madam,
> I return you many thanks for the handsome present of your two very handsome volumes. I have as yet only had time to read a chapter here and there. I am amazed at the vast amount of erudition displayed in them and the great interest of the topics on which they treat. Moreover, your command of all the refinements of our language is such that you need not fear criticism on that score. Your book will open up to many spiritualists a whole world of new ideas, and cannot fail to be of the greatest value in the enquiry which is now being so earnestly carried on.
> I beg you to accept my carte de visite, which I regret is not a better one, and remain,
> Dear Madam,
> Yours with sincere respect,
> (Sd.) ALFRED R. WALLACE.[259]

This letter was reprinted as an article in the April 1906 edition of *The Theosophist*, but was preceded by the following caption: 'Mr. Wallace...wrote her the following appreciative letter, which doubtless he would not wish to change to any serious extent after the lapse of the intervening thirty years.'[260] The recorder of this letter attempted to make an argument from silence; however, a letter of Wallace sent nine years later suggested that Wallace had changed his mind or that Wallace did not even write the earlier letter and that it was a clever forgery to give Blavatsky undeserved prestige. Wallace's actual sentiments toward Theosophy are articulated in the following letter to Mrs. Fisher written from Parkstone, Dorset on 9 April 1897:

> I have tried several Reincarnation and Theosophical books, but *cannot* read them or take any interest in them. They are so purely imaginative, and do not seem to me rational. Many people are captivated by it—I think most people who like a grand, strange, complex theory of man and nature, given with authority—people who if religious would be Roman Catholics.[261]

If Wallace did write the first letter reprinted in the April 1905 edition of *The Theosophist*, he may have been politely acknowledging her gift of *Isis Unveiled*; however, Wallace's later admission that 'Theosophical books…are so purely imaginative, and do not seem to me rational', seemed contrary to his earlier compliment that a 'vast amount of erudition displayed in them' and makes Wallace's membership in the Theosophical Society suspect.

There is a small piece of evidence that suggests that the Wallace letter reprinted in *The Theosophist* April 1906 could have been forged. This 'evidence' appeared in a footnote in *The Secret Doctrine* volume two:

> Mr. A. R. Wallace shows in his Geographical Distribution of Animals and Island Life, that the hypothesis of such a land is quite uncalled for on the alleged zoological grounds. But he admits that a much closer proximity of India and Australia did certainly exist and at a time so very remote that it was 'certainly pre-tertiary,' *and he adds in a private letter that* 'no name has been given to this supposed land.' Yet the land did exist, and as of course pre-tertiary, for 'Lemuria' (accepting this name for the third Continent) had perished before Atlantis had fully developed… (emphasis added)

Curiously, no proof of this letter exists and given Blavatsky's use of sources and the above tone of the letter written by Wallace it is plausible that Blavatsky also invented this letter to prove her theory for the existence of Lemuria.[262] Though nothing can be proved at this late date barring new manuscript discoveries, the burden of evidence appears to be against Blavatsky, given her tendency of misquoting Wallace and continuously taking his theories out of context to prove her points.

Wallace did engage in some brief communication with the co-founder of the Theosophical Society, Colonel Henry Olcott having written a letter to him on 2 May 1875 from Grays, Essex. Olcott had dedicated his book *People From the Other World* (1875) to both Alfred Wallace and William Crookes (spiritualist/chemist) 'to mark his admiration of the moral courage they have recently displayed, in the investigation of the phenomena called spiritual.'[263] Upon reading this dedication, Wallace responded by writing a letter to Olcott thanking him for his kind words. Wallace went on to express his pleasure of reading 'the interesting record' of Olcott's investigations and 'only wished it could have as large a circulation in this country as it deserves.'[264] This remark implied that Olcott's work was not well marketed in the country of England during this time period. In this letter Wallace also commented that *People From the Other World* would 'greatly aid in that reaction of modern thought against modern mate-

rialism which is becoming every day more evident.' Wallace suggested that the phenomena witnessed at the Eddy brothers' farmhouse
was unique in that he had himself 'seen nothing half so wonderful or
perhaps half so convincing as you have seen' even if the Eddy's were
eventually proven to be imposters. Though no relationship between
Olcott and Wallace was defined in this letter, it would seem from the
formal manner employed by Wallace that these two men had little to
no communications before this initial correspondence.

Wallace participated in some later correspondence with Annie Besant, the second president of the Theosophical Society. Besant had
asked Wallace to answer some questions in an effort to publicize the
common ground that existed between the Theosophists and Spiritualists. She sent him a letter which had also been forwarded to William Stainton-Moses, Sir. William Crookes, Florence Marryat, 'Mr.'
Theobald (whether this was F. J. or Morell was not specified), Countess Wachtmeister, Emily Kislingbury, Herbert Burrows and G. R. S.
Mead. The letter stated that:

> It is proposed to hold a symposium in *Lucifer* of a few representa-
> tive Spiritualists and Theosophists, with a view of clearly defining
> the points of agreement and difference in the two schools, with
> regard to superphysical phenomena....I very cordially invite your
> assistance in the carrying out of this plan, which may help to clear
> away some regrettable misunderstandings....[265]

This was followed by a list of questions including a request for
each participant to define 'spirit' and to explain their position on the
nature of spirit and mind. These questions were suceeded by a list of
phenomena (including direct writing, automatic writing, inspiration
speaking, etc.) and the question was asked: 'to what agency do you
attribute these phenomena?' Further questions included: do you believe a spirit can communicate with the living, and what do you believe concerning the constitution of the soul among others. This
above survey illustrated that even in 1892 (one year after Blavatsky's
death) the line between Spiritualism and Theosophy was not clearly
defined.

Wallace replied to Besant from Parkstone, Dorset, on 31 March
1892:

> Dear Mrs. Besant,- I could very easily answer the questions you
> send, but I do not see what purpose it would serve. Opinions are
> of no value without stating the evidence on which they are found-

ed. Again, the questions seem altogether one-sided, as none of them touch on the special teaching of Theosophy…lastly, arrangements should be made to have the whole discussion published in *Light* as well as in *Lucifer*- Your very faithfully, Alfred R. Wallace.[266]

Wallace's reluctant response to the above survey seemed typical of other Spiritualists. In the 15 May 1892 issue of *Lucifer* an article appeared which explained the results of this survey: the 'attempt to bring about an intelligible explanation of some of the phenomena of Spiritualism does not seem likely to succeed. Only one of the invited guests came to the banquet, while various Spiritualists that I have talked with agree only in repudiating each other as representative.'[267]

Wallace respectfully declined the invitation of Annie Besant to engage him in a written conversation about the relationship between Spiritualism and Theosophy and implied something that has tremendous bearing on this study- Wallace believed that 'the questions seem altogether one-sided, as none of them touch on the special teaching of Theosophy.' In other words, Wallace believed that these specific questions would receive similar answers by practitioners of both organizations. Now this likely stemmed from Wallace's ignorance of Theosophy; however, it further illustrated that even a prominent Spiritualist such as Wallace viewed little disagreement between Spiritualism and Theosophy on the issue concerning the spirit and its ability to communicate with the living.

Wallace likely understood that no matter what he said it would make little difference in reconciling these two movements. The actual justifications behind his response must remain speculative; however, it seemed entirely plausible that Wallace ascertained that the differences were minimal compared to the similarities, or perhaps he did not wish to have his name associated with Theosophy. It seemed evident that no matter what his reasoning may have been, Wallace saw little value in engaging in such a conversation.

Also, in this letter Wallace made no mention or acknowledgment of any previous affiliation with the Theosophical Society. Though this 'argument of silence' cannot prove that Wallace was never a member of the Society, based upon the above information his membership seems questionable. It is curious that out of the multiple Wallace biographies used in compiling this section, none of them associated Wallace with the Theosophical Society but some did note his belief in the irrationality of Theosophy.[268] Furthermore, Wallace's autobiography never mentioned any affiliation with the Society. Again this is an argument from silence, but based upon his known opinion of Theosophy and Theosophical books, it is certainly plausible that Wallace was never affiliated with the Theosophical Society.

Wallace was commended in the scientific world for being a co-founder of natural selection. Wallace adapted his theory of natural selection that made provision for the unique mental development of humanity which placed human beings outside of the laws of natural selection. Furthermore, Wallace was an active Spiritualist and appeared to use Spiritualism to explain concepts that science could not. Also, it has been shown that Blavatsky held a deep admiration for Alfred Wallace. She would continuously take his scientific theories and bring them into a new context based upon her speculation; thereby, using Wallace to defend her own prefabricated belief structure. Furthermore, for many years Wallace was believed to have been a member of the Theosophical Society though this is questionable given his own silence and that of his biographer's in this matter and in his letter to Mrs. Fisher in 1897 concerning the 'purely imaginative' Theosophical Society. It was also noted that Blavatsky never criticized any of Wallace's doctrines in *Isis Unveiled* showing her alliance with his ideologies. Thus, Wallace's influence on the early Theosophical Society cannot be denied even if Wallace himself was never fully unaware of the longstanding effect of his writings. For the purpose of this study the mere fact that Wallace would not later engage in a discussion between the similarities of Spiritualism and Theosophy remains perplexing

Notes

[1] *Who's Who, 1905: An Annual Biographical Dictionary*, ed. Henry Robert Addison (London: Adam and Charles Black, 1905), p. 967.
[2] As one reviewer of his novel *The King of Topsy-Turvy* (1870) said 'it is a small volume, in which the author works hard to be amusing. We are sorry that we cannot congratulate him on his success.' 'New Year Gift Books' in *Daily News*, 3 January 1871. His other work *Puppet's Dallying* was reviewed by *The Graphic*: 'Mr. Arthur Lillie is a clever man, and has written a clever book, which, though it is by no means as good as it ought to have been, and in some respects signally fails, yet contains elements of success enough to make us feel interested in the author and his future. 'New Novels', *The Graphic*, 5 October 1872. This is assuming that the 'Arthur Lillie' who wrote these works is the same 'Arthur Lillie' who confronted Blavatsky.

[3] Lillie was referred to as a soldier in the British army in the book *The Literary World: A Fortnightly Review of Current Literature*, Vol. 24 (Boston: E. H. Hames and Company, 1893), p. 223. Lillie was called 'Major' in London Gossip, *Birmingham Daily Post* (Birmingham, England), 15 May 1891. and a 'Captain' in London Gossip, *Birmingham Daily Post*, 8 August 1884.

[4] Arthur Lillie, *Buddhism in Christendom: Or, Jesus the Essene* (London: Kegan Paul. 1887), pp. 76, 305.

[5] Addison, *Who's Who*, p. 967.

[6] Dipesh Chakrabarty, *Provincializing Europe: Postcolonial Though and Historical Difference* (Princeton, NJ: Princeton University Press, 2000), p. 102.

[7] Ranajit Guha and Gayatri Chakrvorty Spivak, *Select Subaltern Studies* (Oxford: Oxford University Press, 1988), p. 80.

[8] Ranajit Guha, *Elementary Aspects of Peasant Insurgency in Colonial India* (Duke University Press, 1999), pp. 248-249.

[9] Arthur Lillie, *The Influence of Buddhism on Primitive Christianity*, (London: Swan Sonnenschein & Co., 1893), p. 17.

[10] For more information on the Great Indian Rebellion of 1857 see Kim A. Wagner, *The Great Fear of 1857: Rumours, Conspiracies, and the Making of the Indian Uprising* (Witney, Oxfordshire: International Academic Publishers, 2010)., Saul David, *The Indian Mutiny: 1857* (London: Penguin Books, 2003)., Biswamoy Pati, *The Great Rebellion of 1857 in India: Exploring Transgressions, Contests and Diversities* (London: Routledge, 2009)., and Rosie Llewellyn-Jones, *The Great Uprising in India 1857-58: Untold Stories, Indian and British* (Rochester, NY: The Boydell Press, 2007).

[11] Randeep Ramesh, 'India's Secret History: A Holocaust, One Where Millions Disappeared', *The Guardian*, (24 August 2007) <www.guardian.co.uk/world/2007/aug/24/india.randeepramesh> [accessed 14 August 2011] (para. 1 of 17)

[12] Michael Gomes, 'Interview with Madame Blavatsky', *Canadian Theosophist*, 5: 67 (November - December 1986), 98 – 102 (p. 101).

[13] Arthur Lillie, *The Cobra Diamond*, 3 vols. (London: Ward and Downey, 1890), I, pp. 34, 44.

[14] In some advertisements Lillie's name was written with the letters M.A. after it presuming that he had earned a Masters degree. 'Literary Notes and Gossip of the Week', *Glasgow Herald*, 8 September 1900. and 'Literature', *The Leeds Mercury*, 22 December 1900. It is more likely that this was an error that came from a careless reading of his postnominals MRAS (Member of the Royal Asiatic Society) since it was admitted that he was not a 'trained scholar.' Unknown, *The Literary World*, p. 223. The level of Lillie's scholarship was often questioned; however, noting that he lectured in seminars with the great scholars listed above evidenced that at the very least his theories were taken seriously. 'New Books' in *Birmingham Daily Post*, 2 April 1890.

[15] 'Captain Lillie's pamphlet and its defenders are fain to have recourse to the defence usually adopted by the advocates of every weak cause-personal abuse and assertion without proof... Captain Lillie has rendered the greatest service to reason and common sense by the publication of his pamphlet, which crushes Koot Hoomi Lal Singh's power of evil through Madame Blavatsky by the revelations of plagiarism contained in the Esoteric Buddhism, and the contradictions exhibited in its theory.' 'London Gossip', *Birmingham Daily Post*, 8 August 1884.

[16] Henry Kiddle, 'Esoteric Buddhism', *Light* (1 September 1883), p. 392.

[17] A.P. Sinnett, *The Occult World: Fifth American from the Fourth English Edition* (Boston: Houghton, Mifflin and Company, 1888), p. 212.

[18] Darrell Erixson, 'Plagiarism and the *Secret Doctrine*', *Theosophical History*, 12 (2006), 19-34 (pp. 21, 26).

[19] Erixson, 'Plagiarism and the *Secret Doctrine*,' pp. 24, 27.

[20] Blavatsky's last article written on 27 April 1891 was entitled 'My Books' and was written to deal with the accusations of plagiarism (and she specifically hints towards Coleman). One of her complaints was that 'It has been said at various times by my ever active opponents that Isis Unveiled was simply a rehash of Éliphas Lévi and a few old alchemists.' Here, it is evident that the concept of plagiarism was an important issue and Blavatsky endeavors to defend her academic integrity by justifying her reliance on secondary sources. The point of this note is to observe that during this time period plagiarism was a valid accusation that Blavatsky evidently took seriously. See Helena Blavatsky, *Collected Writings: 1890-1891*, comp. Boris De Zirkoff, 15 vols. (Pasadena: CA: Theosophical Publishing House, 1966), XIII, pp. 191-202.

[21] 'Mr. Sinnett's Reply to Mr. Kiddle', *Light*, 3:142 (22 September 1883), 424.

[22] Blavatsky's second guess was correct in noting that this article was published in August. Norman Pearson, 'After Death' in *Nineteenth Century: A Monthly Review*, ed. James Knowles (August 1883), p. 262.

[23] Letter No. XXVII in *The Letters of HP Blavatsky to A. P. Sinnett*, ed. A. T. Barker (Pasadena, CA: Theosophical University Press, 1973), p. 60.

[24] Barker, *The Mahatma Letters*, p. 24. Blavatsky refers to Plato's theory of forms to prove that an idea is the essence of any earthly subject (or object).

[25] Blavatsky does mention Norman Pearson again in the appendix of *Isis Unveiled* (reprinted from *The Path*, 1:8 (November 1886), 239f.n.) in relation to her views on reincarnation. She notes that in Pearson's article 'theosophical ideas and teachings are speculated upon without acknowledgment or the smallest reference to theosophy, and among others, we see with regard to the author's theories on the *Ego*.'Blavatsky incorrectly cites this article as appearing in the August issue when it was actually printed in the September issue. The article to which she refers is Norman Pearson, 'Before Birth,' in *Nineteenth Century: A Monthly Review*, ed. James Knowles (September 1886), pp. 340-363.

[26] Barker, *The Mahatma Letters*, p. 122.

[27] Blavatsky was certainly aware of Harris as she makes reference to him in her collected writings, but it is hard to overlook the fact that this exact poem is found in Kiddle's work which chronologically predates this particular Mahatma letter. Henry Kiddle, *Spiritual Communications Presenting a Revelation of the Future Life and Illustrating and Confirming the Fundamental Doctrines of the Christian Faith* (New York: The Authors Publishing Company, 1879), p. 64.

[28] Blavatsky's last article written on 27 April 1891 was entitled 'My Books' and was written to deal with the accusations of plagiarism (and she specifically hints towards Coleman). One of her complaints was that 'It has been said at various times by my ever active opponents that *Isis Unveiled* was simply a rehash of Éliphas Lévi and a few old alchemists.' Here, it is evident that the concept of plagiarism was an important issue and Blavatsky endeavors to defend her academic integrity by justifying her reliance on secondary sources. The point of this note is to observe that during this time period plagiarism was a valid accusation that Blavatsky evidently took seriously. See Helena Blavatsky, *Collected Writings: 1890-1891*, comp. Boris De Zirkoff, 15 vols. (Pasadena: CA: Theosophical Publishing House, 1966), XIII, pp. 191-202.

[29] Lilly, *Koot Hoomi Unveiled*, p. 3.

[30] Christopher McIntosh, *Eliphas Levi and the French Occult Revival* (Albany: State University of New York Press, 2011), pp. 144-145.

[31] H. P. Blavatsky, 'The Secret Doctrine', *Light*, 8: 416 (22 December 1888), p. 634. reprinted in Blavatsky, *Collected Writings*, X, p. 243.

[32] Vsevolod Sergyeevich Solovyoff, *Modern Priestess of Isis* (London: Longmans, Green, and Company, 1895), p. 257.f.n.

[33] Coleman, 'The Sources of Madame Blavatsky's Writings', p. 357.

[34] To see how Blavatsky assimilates Lévi see Appendix I in *The Letters of HP Blavatsky to AP Sinnett*. A copy of the article 'Death' by Eliphas Lévi is reprinted alongside notes written in blue pencil by Koot Hoomi. *The Letters of HP Blavatsky to A. P. Sinnett*, p. 369-375. Also, Blavatsky supplied a translation of Lévi's chapter on the magical evocation of Apollonius of Tyana in London to the *Spiritual Scientist* (Boston) as early as November 1875. Reprinted in H. P. Blavatsky, *Collected Writings*, ed. Boris de Zirkoff, 15 vols, (Wheaton, Theosophical Publishing House, 1988), third ed. 1988, I, pp. 144-150. For a discussion of Blavatsky's debt to Lévi, see Nicholas Goodrick-Clarke, *Helena Blavatsky* (Berkeley: North Atlantic Books, 2004), pp. 91-102, 148-159.

[35] Eliphas Lévi, *Transcendental Magic*, p. 262.

[36] Lillie, *Madame Blavatsky and Her 'Theosophy'*, p. 182.

[37] Arthur Lillie, 'Madame Blavatsky and Her Theosophy', *Light* (9 March 1895), 116-117 (p. 117).

[38] Arthur Lillie, *Buddhism in Christendom; or, Jesus, The Essene* (London: Kegan Paul, Trench & Co., 1887), p. 358.

[39] Arthur Lillie, *Modern Mystics and Modern Magic: Containing a Full Biography of the Rev. William Stainton Moses* (London: Swan Sonnenschein & Co., 1894), p. 115.

[40] Lillie, *Modern Mystics and Modern Magic*, pp. 115-116.

[41] Arthur Lillie, *Koot Hoomi Unveiled; or, Tibetan "Buddhists" versus the Buddhists of Tibet* (London: The Psychological Press Association, 1884), p. 13.

[42] Lillie, *Koot Hoomi Unveiled*, p. 13.

[43] This tendency was noted on page 69: She took spiritualism from Home, the Brothers of Luxor from Colonel Olcott, the notion of controlling 'Elementals' from Mr. Felt. And hearing for the first time about these Mahatmas from Dayananda Sarasvati she promptly assimilated them likewise. Elsewhere he noted that Blavatsky was attempting to erase her background in Spiritualism. Arthur Lillie, *Madame Blavatsky and her 'Theosophy': A Study Buddhism in Christendom*, (London: Swan Sonnenschein &. Co., 1895), pp. 18, 37, 43, 48, 53-54.

[44] Lillie, *Modern Mystics and Modern Magic* p. 123.

[45] Lillie, *Buddha and Early Buddhism*, pp. vii-x.

[46] *Anacalypsis* suggested that the earliest antediluvian races possessed a true understanding of religion. This religion consisted of several attributes. Some of these included: 1) an emanationist origin of the world; 2) the immortality of the soul; 3) a belief in the trinity; 4) the androgynous character of God; 5) metempsychosis; 6) reabsorption into the one deity; and 7) the periodical renewal of the world. According to Higgins, these concepts have been reconceptualized by various religions over time and have become 'clothed with bodies and converted into living creatures' yet these tenets comprised the doctrine of the universal religion. Godfrey Higgins, *Anacalypsis: An Attempt To Draw Aside the Veil of The Saitic Isis*, 2 vols (London: Longman, Rees, Orme, Brown, Green, and Logman, 1846), I, pp. 33, 36-38, 223. Also, in *The World's Sixteen Crucified Savior* there was the pervading belief in a universal analogy of all religions. Kersey Graves *The World's Sixteen Crucified Saviors, or, Christianity Before Christ* (New York: Peter Eckler Publishing Company, 1919), p. 373. Higgins became interested in travel and longed to conduct a journey to the Eastern oriental lands. Based upon his later reflection noted in his Preface of *Anacalypsis* (1833) this trip never occurred: 'I am now turned sixty...yet I have not entirely given up the hope of going as far as Egypt: but what I have finished of my work must first be printed.' Higgins, *Anacalypsis*, I, p. viii.

[47] Lillie, *Buddha and Early Buddhism*, p. 253.

[48] Lillie, *Buddhism in Christendom*, p. vi.

[49] Lillie, *Influence of Buddhism on Primitive Christianity*, pp. vii-viii.

[50] Lillie, *Modern Mystics and Modern Magic*, p. 125.

[51] Lillie, *Buddhism in Christendom*, p. 405.

[52] William Emmette Coleman, 'The Sources of Madame Blavatsky's Writings', in Vsevolod Solovyoff, *Modern Priestess of Isis* (London: Longmans, Green, and Company, 1895), 353-366 (p. 353).
[53] Coleman, 'The Sources of Madame Blavatsky's Writings', pp. 354-357.
[54] Coleman, 'The Sources of Madame Blavatsky's Writings', p. 355.
[55] The claim that Blavatsky had plagiarized from Randolph's *Pre-Adamite Man* has recently been disputed by John Deveney. Deveney noted that 'Madame Blavatsky does cover much of the same ground as Randolph has and she discusses "Pre-Adamite" spirits and the likes and cites ("for what it's worth") a statement from Randolph's book (*Isis Unveiled* 1:127), but it is difficult to discern any extensive pattern of plagiarism of Randolph's work generally... Randolph, who had been dead for more than two years when *Isis* was published, can scarcely have been considered useful to her.' John Patrick Deveney, *Paschal Beverly Randolph: A Nineteenth-Century Black American Spiritualist, Rosicrucian, and Sex Magician* (Albany: State University of New York, 1997), p. 544.
[56] Coleman, 'The Sources of Madame Blavatsky's Writings', p. 357.
[57] Goodrick-Clarke, *Helena Blavatsky*, p. 52.
[58] Coleman, 'The Sources of Madame Blavatsky's Writings', p. 363.
[59] Nicholas Goodrick-Clarke, *Hitler's Priestess: Savitri Devi, the Hindu-Aryan Myth, and Neo-Nazism* (New York: New York University Press, 1998), p. 34.; Also, see Mahatma Letter No. X in Barker, *The Mahatma Letters*, p. 104.
[60] William Emmette Coleman, 'Madame Blavatsky and Theosophy A Reply to my Critics: Part Two', *The Religio-Philosophical Journal* (22 September 1888), 2.
[61] Wouter J. Hanegraaff, *New Age Religion and Western Culture: Esotericism in the Mirror of Secular Thought* (Albany: State University of New York Press, 1998), p. 455.
[62] Coleman, 'The Sources of Madame Blavatsky's', p. 358.
[63] Some of these 'accusations' were proven by the author when writing this work. Coleman accused Blavatsky of directly plagiarizing 'in vol. ii., pp. 599-603. Nearly the whole of four pages was copied from Oliver's *Pythagorean Triangle*, while only a few lines were credited to that work.' This was proven by the author who compared *The Secret Doctrine* volume II (*SD* II) with the 1875 version of George Oliver's *Pythagorean Triangle* (*PT*) confirming the following instances where this occurred: *SD* II:599 - *PT*:104- 'The tetrad...extremes.'; *SD* II:599 - *PT*:112-'The Pythagorean world...mixed bodies.'; *SD* II:599 - *PT*:104- 'This number four...tetragon.'; *SD* II:601 - *PT*:114- 'Moreover, according to Theon...fourth.'; *SD* II: 601 - *PT*:115-'The 4 was called by the Pythagoreans the Key-Keeper of Nature.'; *SD* II:601 - *PT*:171- the Moon, for this planet is forced ...seven days.'; *SD* II:601 -*PT*:172/3- 'the distance of the Moon from the Earth...diapason harmony.'; *SD* II: 601 - *PT*: 106- 'the Achaean Greeks regarded the tetrad...the elements.'; *SD* II:601 - *PT*:107/8- 'The figure of the Cross...good

and evil.'; *SD* II:601 - *PT*:112/3- 'The intelligible world…quaternity' [Blavatsky takes Reuchlin's quote from Oliver and quotes it as her own- secondary quotation without giving credit]; *SD* II:603 - *PT*:175- 'The use of number seven…Homer.' [It is curious that Blavatsky omitted a negative reference to the Indian from Oliver's original work 'the seven *bobun* of perfection exhibited in the religious code of the Hindoos; with the defective geographical knowledge if the same people…'] See George Oliver, *The Pythagorean Triangle; or, The Science of Numbers* (London: John Hogg & Co., 1875), p. 175.

[64] Coleman, 'Madame Blavatsky and Theosophy A Reply to my Critics', p. 2.

[65] Coleman, 'The Sources of Madame Blavatsky's Writings', p. 364).

[66] Coleman, 'The Sources of Madame Blavatsky's', p. 364.

[67] 'On the Watch Tower', *Lucifer*, 16:93 (15 May 1895), 177-184 (p. 180).

[68] This is merely one instance out of multiple others. Robert Spence Hardy, *Eastern Monachism: An Account of the Origin, Laws, Discipline, Sacred Writings, Mysterious Rites, Religious Ceremonies, and Present Circumstances of the Order of Mendicants Founded by Gotama Budha* (London: Partridge and Oakey, 1850).

[69] Sylvia Cranston, *HPB: The Extraordinary Life and Influence of Helena Blavatsky, Founder of the Modern Theosophical Movement* (Santa Barbara, CA: Path Publishing House, 1993), p. 379. Michael Gomes, *Dawning of the Theosophical Movement*, (Wheaton, IL: The Theosophical Publishing House, 1987), p. 147.

[70] Gomes, *Dawning of the Theosophical Movement*, p. 147.

[71] Gomes, *Dawning of the Theosophical Movement*, p. 147.

[72] Cranston, *HPB*, pp. 381-382.

[73] Cranston, *HPB*, pp. 382-383.

[74] Campbell, *Ancient Wisdom*, p. 34.

[75] Michael Gomes, *Dawning of the Theosophical Movement*, p. 152.

[76] For example Coleman noted that 'In Isis, i., 353,354, et seq., she professed to quote from a work in her possession, whereas all that she quoted was copied from *Demonologia*, pp. 224-259.' It has now been confirmed that Coleman's simple notation was an understatement. In fact, page 354 in *Isis Unveiled* I was taken verbatim from *Demonologia* pages 227-228. Page 355 in *Isis Unveiled*, I, was taken nearly word for word from *Demonologia* pages 228, 232, and 234. No citations to *Demonologia* are listed on these pages. See J. S. Forsyth, *Demonologia: Or, Natural Knowledge Revealed* (London: John Bumpus, 1827).

[77] For example the final paragraph on page 353 in *Isis Unveiled* I was derived from *Demonologia* pages 209, 210 f. n., 224, and 226. Though still a questionable example, Blavatsky appeared to have altered Forsyth's work sufficiently.

[78] William E. Coleman, 'Theosophy and Spiritualism', *The Religio-Philosophical Journal*, (6 August 1881), p. 2.

[79] Coleman, 'The Sources of Madame Blavatsky's Writings', p. 365.

[80] Michael Gomes, 'Studies in Early American Theosophical History: H.P.B.'s American Correspondence', *The Canadian Theosophist*, 71:5 (Nov. – Dec. 1990), 101- 106 (pp. 106).

[81] Elliott Coues, 'Blavatsky Unveiled! The Tarta Termagant Tamed by a Smithsonian Scientist', *New York Sun* (20 July 1890), 17.

[82] William Emmette Coleman, 'The Conflict Between Spiritualism and Theosophy', *The Two Worlds*, 4:170 (13 February 1891), 158-159 (p. 158).

[83] Coleman, 'The Conflict Between Spiritualism and Theosophy', pp. 158-159.

[84] A. T. Baird, *Richard Hodgson: The Story of a Psychical Researcher and His Times* (London: Psychic Press, 1949), p. 3.

[85] *Essays in Psychical Research*, ed. William James, (Cambridge, MA: President and Fellows of Harvard College, 1986), p. 426.

[86] Baird, *Richard Hodgson*, p. 2.

[87] F. B. Smith, 'Hodgson, Richard (1855 - 1905)', *Australian Dictionary of Biography*, 4 (Melbourne University Press, 1972), pp. 406-407.

[88] J. J. Morse, 'Health in Relation to Mediumship, *Light* 1:20 (21 May 1881), 153-155. T. L. Nichols, 'The Question of Purity', *Light*, 1:13 (2 April 1881), 99. George Wyld, 'Clairvoyance in Relation to Medicinal Substances', *Light*, 1:9 (5 March 1881), 69. Hannah W. Wolff, and Psychic Effects of Hasheesh', *The Two Worlds*, 3:114 (17 January 1890), p. 112. In 'Madame Blavatsky: To The editor of "The Better Way' *Two Worlds*, 4:213 (December 1891), 671-672 (p. 672). Blavatsky was noted as endorsing the use of mind altering substances. These represent only a few of the articles in relation to the topic of drug use and Spiritualism.

[89] *1897 Sears Roebuck & Co. Catalogue* (New York: Skyhorse Publishing, 2007), p. 30. In 1805, a pain killer was discovered by the scientist Friedrich Serturner that produced a euphoric, dream-like state for the user- this drug was named Morphine after Morpheus the Greek god of dreams. Gregory Busse, *Morphine* (New York: Infobase Publishing, 2006), p. 19. An organization known as the Pharmaceutical Society of Great Britain was established in England in 1841 that allowed the sale and advertisement of any drug concocted. S.W.F. Holloway, 'The Regulation of the Supply of Drugs in Britain before 1868', *Drugs and Narcotics in History* (Cambridge: Cambridge University Press, 1997), 77-96 (p. 86). The origination of this Society was followed by the Arsenic Act of 1851 which prohibited the sale of arsenic and poisons. This was followed by the discovery of the hypodermic syringe by Alexander Wood in 1853, trailed by the Pharmacy and Poisons Acts of 1868 which regulated the sale of opium to registered users and chemists in Britain. This Act made little importance as it was rarely enforced; however, it would provide a legal precedence and would be amended in 1906 when the legalization of opium was being reconsidered. In 1898 the Bayer Pharmaceutical Company of Germany synthesized heroin from opium as a morphine substitute; the development of heroin quickly led to an epidemic of

drug addiction which forced governments to place restrictions on its sale. Paul M. Wax, 'Historical Principles and Perspectives, *Goldfrank's Toxicologic Emergencies*, 8th ed. (McGraw-Hill Company, 2006), 1-17 (p. 9). In 1916, the United Kingdom passed the Defense of the Realm Act (DORA) a piece of war time legislation from World War I that attempted to restrict drug distribution. This act was followed in 1920 by the Dangerous Drugs Act which further sought to control and restrict the sale of all drugs. In the United States, the Opium Exclusion Act was passed in 1909 which prohibited the importation of opium. This was followed in 1914 by the Harrison Narcotics Act which required drug distributors to obtain a license.

[90] Richard Hodgson, 'The Possibilities of Mal-Observation and Lapse of Memory from a Practical Point of View' in *Proceedings of the Society for Psychical Research: Volume IV* (London: Trubner and Co., 1887), p. 381.

[91] Baird, *Richard Hodgson*, pp. 254-255.

[92] Baird, *Richard Hodgson*, p. 33.

[93] Michael Sage, *Mrs. Piper and the Society for Psychical Research*, trans. Noralie Robertson (New York: Scott-thaw Co, 1904), p. 9.

[94] Baird, *Richard Hodgson*, p. 235.

[95] Alan Gauld, *The Founders of Psychical Research* (New York: Schocken Books, 1968), p. 258.

[96] Richard Hodgson, 'Observations of Certain Phenomena of Trance', in *Proceedings of the Society for Psychical Research: Volume VIII* (London: Kegan Paul, 1892), 1-58 (p. 57).

[97] Richard Hodgson, 'Observations of Certain Phenomena of Trance', in *Proceedings of the Society for Psychical Research: Volume VIII* (London: Kegan Paul, 1892), 1-58 (p. 58).

[98] Richard Hodgson, 'A Further Record of Observations of Certain Phenomena of Trance', *Proceedings of the Society for Psychical Research: Volume XIII* (London: Kegan Paul, 1898), 284-582 (p. 406).

[99] Smith, 'Hodgson, Richard', p. 407.

[100] Mark Antony De Wolfe, *A Memoir of Richard Hodgson: 1855-1905* (n.p., 1906?), pp. 6-7.

[101] Gauld, *The Founders of Psychical Research*, p. 266.

[102] Brendan French, *The Theosophical Masters*, I, p. 175.

[103] Gauld, *The Founders of Psychical Research*, p. 334.

[104] Podmore, *History of Spiritualism*, I, p. v.

[105] Janet Oppenheim relied heavily upon this work in her writing of *The Other World* as did Joscelyn Godwin in his *Theosophical Enlightenment* to name a couple examples of Frank Podmore's influence on modern Western Esoteric history.

[106] Isaac K. Funk, 'Communications Purporting to Come From Dr. Richard Hodgson' in *The Psychic Riddle* (New York: Funk & Wagnalls Company, 1907), 47-84.; 'Report on Mrs. Piper's Hodgson-Control: 1909', in *Essays in*

Psychical Research, ed. William James (Cambridge, MA: President and Fellows of Harvard College, 1986), p. 253.

[107] William James, *Report on Mrs. Piper's Hodgson-Control* (London: Society for Psychical Research, 1909), pp. 2, 4, 6.

[108] Henry Sidgwick, 'President's Address: First General Meeting', *Proceedings of the Society for Psychical Research* 1882-1883 (London: Trubner and Company, 1883), II, pp. 10-11.

[109] 'Statement of Committee,' *Proceedings of the Society for Psychical Research* (London, Trubner and Co., 1885), III, pp. 202-203.

[110] 'Statement of Committee', pp. 202-203.

[111] Gauld, *The Founders of Psychical Research*, p. 203.

[112] *Journal of the Society for Psychical Research: Volume 1,1884-1885*, p. 420.

[113] H. Sidgwick, 'A Report of the General Meeting, July 10', *Journal of the Society for Psychical Research: Volume 1, 1884-1885*, 1: 18 (July 1885), 460-464 (p. 463).

[114] Sinnett, *Incidents in the Life of Madame Blavatsky*, p. 258.

[115] *Autobiography of Alfred Percy Sinnett*, p. 23. A similar concept was used by Frederick Hockley (1808-1885) to communicate with spirits using a mirror and a seer. As Joscelyn Godwin observes in the Mahatma's case, 'the process entailed a further stage of "precipitation" onto paper by the "seer", who was not a medium but an initiate in training.' Joscelyn Godwin, *The Theosophical Enlightenment*, (Albany: State University of New York Press, 1994), p. 172.

[116] Richard Hodgson, *Proceedings of the Society for Psychical Research: Volume III* (London: Trubner and Co., 1885), p. 204.

[117] Hodgson, *Proceedings of the SPR: Volume III*, p. 227.

[118] Michael Gomes, *The Coulomb Case: Occasional Papers Volume X* (Fullerton, CA: Theosophical History, 2005), p. 6.

[119] Emma Coulomb, *Some Account of My Intercourse With Madame Blavatsky From 1872 to 1884: With A Number of Additional Letters and a Full Explanation of the Most Marvellous Theosophical Phenomena* (London: Elliot Stock, 1885), p. 37.

[120] Coulomb, *Some Account of My Intercourse With Madame Blavatsky*, p. 42.

[121] Coulomb, *Some Account of My Intercourse With Madame Blavatsky*, p. 44.

[122] Coulomb, *Some Account of My Intercourse With Madame Blavatsky*, p. 45.

[123] Coulomb, *Some Account of My Intercourse With Madame Blavatsky*, p. 46.

[124] *Journal of the Society for Psychical Research: Volume 1* (Westminister: The Society's Rooms, 1884), pp. 209-210.

[125] 'The result of his investigations was one which could hardly give pleasure to any party. No one interested in psychical research could hear with satisfaction that so great a mass of apparently well-attested phenomena were in fact, referable to fraud and credulity. *Journal of the Society for Psychical Research: Volume 1* (Westminister: The Society's Rooms, 1884), p. 420.

[126] *Autobiography of Alfred Percy Sinnett*, p. 31.

[127]Janet Oppenheim, *The Other World: Spiritualism and Psychical Research in England, 1850-1914* (Cambridge, Cambridge University Press, 1985), pp. 164-165
[128] Olcott, *Old Diary Leaves*, III, p. 99. Also, an article appeared in the October 1884 edition of the Theosophist which praised the efforts of this Society though cautioning them to adopt a more deductive form of reasoning. 'Proceedings of the Society for Psychical Research', *The Theosophist*, 6:1 (October 1884), 21-22.
[129] Olcott, *Old Diary Leaves*, III, p. 102.
[130] *A Short History of The Theosophical Society*, comp. Josephine Ransom (Adyar, Madras: Theosophical Publishing House, 1938), p. 199.; 'Statement of the General Meetings in May and June, 1885', *Proceedings of the Society for Psychical Research* (London, Trubner and Co.,1885), III, p. 201.
[131] Gomes, *The Coulomb Case*, p. 4.
[132] *Autobiography of Alfred Percy Sinnett* (London: Theosophical History Centre, 1986), p. 27.
[133] *Autobiography of Alfred Percy Sinnett*, p. 27.
[134]*Autobiography of Alfred Percy Sinnett*, p. 27-28.
[135] 'General Meeting', in *Journal of the Society for Psychical Research: Volume 1* (Westminister: The Society's Rooms, 1884), 71-77 (pp. 74-75).
[136] *Journal of the Society for Psychical Research: Volume 1*, p. 50.
[137] 'SPR Archives: The First S.P.R. Man at Adyar?', *Theosophical History*, 1:4 (October 1985), 74-80 (p. 74).
[138] *Autobiography of Alfred Percy Sinnett*, p. 15.
[139] *Autobiography of Alfred Percy Sinnett*, pp. 8-9.
[140] *Autobiography of Alfred Percy Sinnett*, p. 10.
[141] 'Obituary', *Journal of the Society for Psychical Research*, 5:40 (May 1892), 263.
[142] J. Herbert Stack, 'SPR Archives: The Stack Memorandum', *Theosophical History*, 1:1 (January 1985), 4-13 (p. 7).
[143] Stack, 'SPR Archives', p. 8. Actually in 1884 the following members converted to Theosophy: David Hewavitharne, on February 2 at the age of 19, later to be known as the Anagarika Dharmapala, Bertram Keightley, with a group on April 6 that included his uncle Archibald, Mrs. Cooper-Oakley and her husband Alfred; Mabel Collins Cook, April 9, Vsevolod Soloviov, May 17; Hermann Schmiechen, June 20, (who went on that summer to paint the adepts' portraits); Elliott Coues, July 7, the Russian diplomat, Olga Novikov, August 9; Laura Cooper, November 6, a member of H.P.B.'s 1890 Inner Group, who would became the wife of G.R.S. Mead. Gomes, *The Coulomb Case*, p. 5.
[144] 'The President in Great Britain', *Supplement to The Theosophist* (November 1889), p. xvii.
[145] Annie Besant, *Annie Besant: An Autobiography* (Philadelphia: Henry Altemus, 1893), p. 343.

[146] J. D. Buck, 'To the Members of the Esoteric Section T.S. by J.D. Buck: Facsimile of October 1889 Original', *The Esoteric Papers of Madame Blavatsky*, ed.Daniel H. Caldwell (Whitefish, MT: Kessinger Publishing, 2005), p. 187.

[147] Letter No. XLI in *Letters of H.P. Blavatsky to A.P. Sinnett*, pp. 94-95.

[148] *Letters of H.P. Blavatsky to A.P. Sinnett*, p. 108.

[149] Marc Demarest, *Hypotheses on The Orphic Circle- REVISION 4- DRAFT*, (May 2009) <http://www.ehbritten.org/docs/hypotheses_on_the_orphic _circle.pdf> [accessed on 13 September 2011], pp. 7.

[150] Emma Hardinge Britten, 'Occultism Defined', *Two Worlds* (18 November 1877), 3-4 (p. 3).

[151] In 1885, an amendment was passed in England that would protect women and young girls from rape and seduction known as the Criminal Law Amendment Bill. See Susan Edwards, 'Discourses of Denial and Moral Panics: The Pornographisation of the Child in Art, the Written Word, Film and Photograph', in *Behaving Badly: Social Panic and Moral Outrage-Victorian and Modern Parallels*, eds. Judith Rowbotham and Kim Stevenson (Aldershot, Hampshire: Ashgate Publishing Company, 2003), 177-192 (pp. 179-181). In 1890s in the United States, based on pressure from the New York Committee for the Prevention of State Regulation of Vice and the National Women's Christian Temperance Union the legal age of sexual consent was pushed from 12 to 16 or 18 depending on the individual state's decision (Tennessee raised it to 21). See Carolyn Cocca, *Jailbait: The Politics of Statutory Rape Laws in the United States* (Albany: State University of New York Press, 2004), p. 14.

[152] Godwin, *The Theosophical Enlightenment*, p. 403.

[153] Mathiesen, *Emma Hardinge Britten*, pp. 6, 11.

[154] Deveney, *Astral Projection*, p. 35.

[155]Mathiesen, *Emma Hardinge Britten*, p. 14.

[156] 'Wants', *New York Daily Tribune* (2 June 1857), p. 1. from Marc Demarest, 'Emma Hardinge Britten Archive' <www.ehbritten.org> [accessed on 7 October 2011]

[157] Mathiesen, *Emma Hardinge Britten*, p. 16. and Godwin, *The Theosophical Enlightenment*, p. 205.

[158] Godwin, *The Theosophical Enlightenment*, p. 205.

[159] William Britten, *Ghost Land,, or, Researched into the Mysteries of Occultism*, trans. Emma Hardinge Britten (Boston: Emma Hardinge Britten, 1876), p. 12. There is some dispute as to whether Britten's personal home and the offices of the *Western Star* were affected by this tragic event or rather this event only affected the affairs of her financial supporters who withdrew their support having lost their personal assets in this conflagration.

[160]Emma Hardinge Britten, *The Electric Physician: or, Self Cure Through Electricity* (Boston: William Britten, 1875), p. 56.

[161] Mathiesen, *Emma Hardinge Britten*, p. 19.

[162] Emma Hardinge Britten, 'Theosophy: its Origin and Founders', *The Two Worlds*, 4:187 (12 June 1891), 359-360 (p. 359).

[163] Emma Hardinge Britten, *The Faiths, Facts and Frauds of Religious History* (Melbourne, George Robertson, 1879), p. 3.

[164] Emma Hardinge Britten, *Nineteenth century Miracles, or, Spirits and Their Work in Eve of the Earth* (London: William Britten, 1883), p. 1.

[165] Britten, *Autobiographical Sketch of the Life and Spiritual Experiences of Emma Hardinge Britten*, p. 262.

[166] James Robertson, *Noble Pioneer: The Life Story of Emma Hardinge Britten* (Manchester: Two Worlds Publishing, 190?) reprinted on p. 29. <www.eh britten.org/text/annotated/2009-01-01-2.pdf >.

[167] Olcot, *Old Diary Leaves*, I, p. 186.

[168] Marc Demarest, 'Introduction', in *Art Magic* (The Typhon Press, 2011), p. xi.

[169] Despite Olcott and Blavatsky's later insistence that Louis was not the same type of adept as her Tibetan masters (See Olcott, *Old Diary Leaves*, I, pp. 193-194.), it seemed that while writing *Isis Unveiled* Blavatsky believed Louis to be an authoritative adept in a mysterious science. See Blavatsky, *Isis Unveiled*, I, p. 367.

[170] Emma Hardinge Britten, *Art Magic, or, Mundane, Sub-Mundane and Super-Mundane Spiritism* (Chicago: Progressive Thinker Publishing House, 1909), p. 361.

[171] 'We commenced this section by affirming that is all the fragments that have been written on the history of the Sun-God and the order of the astronomical religion were gathered together, they would fill a library. Britten, *Art Magic* (1909), p. 53.

[172] Demarest, *Art Magic*, p. xxii.

[173] Demarest, *Art Magic*, p. xvi.

[174] Olcott, *Old Diary Leaves*, I, p. 189.

[175] Demarest, *Art Magic*, pp. xxix-xxx.

[176] Emma Hardinge Britten, 'Theosophy: its Origin and Founders, *The Two Worlds*, 4:187 (12 June 1891), 359-360 (p. 359).

[177] Britten, 'Theosophy: its Origin and Founders', p. 359.

[178] Britten, 'Theosophy: its Origin and Founders', p. 360.

[179] Emma Hardinge Britten, 'Theosophy, Its Origin and Founder: Third and Concluding Part', *The Two Worlds*, 4: 188 (19 June 1891), 369-370 (p. 369).

[180] Emma Hardinge Britten, 'The Impassable Lines of Demarcation Between Spiritualism and Theosophy: Abstract of two Lectures delivered by Emma Hardinge Britten at Daulby Hall, Liverpool, on Sunday, November 3rd, 1889', *Two Worlds*, 3:105 (15 November 1889), 1-3 (pp. 1-3).

[181] 'Can Spiritualists and Theosophists Unite On a Common Basis of Belief?', *Two Worlds*, 3:148 (12 September 1890), 518-520 (p. 518).

[182] 'Can Spiritualists and Theosophists Unite On a Common Basis of Belief?', p. 518.

[183] 'Can Spiritualists and Theosophists Unite On a Common Basis of Belief?', p. 519.
[184] 'Can Spiritualists and Theosophists Unite On a Common Basis of Belief?', p. 519.
[185] 'Can Spiritualists and Theosophists Unite On a Common Basis of Belief?', p. 518-519.
[186] Dear Col. Olcott, I have seen several suites of apartments, both furnished & unfurnished that might suit our fair friend, but am going again Wednesday to procure more definite information. I found that those most desirable already let since I first saw them. Now I believe this will be the fate of all researches until Madame is quite ready to enter upon possession. The city is filling fast & desirable apartments are in demand; now I could advise that when Madame is ready to return here she may consult the N.Y. Herald in which everything that is to be had is advertised - let her clearly state which advertisements she selects; state what she requires, & about what prices she would go to, & I am quite willing to go look at said places & report wherever the bids are. - Will that do? - My husband at my request carried down my crystal to your office yesterday, but the bird had flown. Very truly yours, Emma H. Britten (handwritten letter from Carl. A. Kroch Library, Cornell University).
[187] Olcott, *Old Diary Leaves*, I, pp. 188-189.
[188] See Marc Demarest, 'Emma Hardinge Britten Archive' (17 May 2011) www.ehbritten.org [accessed on 7 October 2011] Furthermore, Demarest went on to set this relationship up in his latest work:
My own feeling is that Britten was, first and foremost, a propagandist — a paid advocate — and that she viewed the field of her work, in the early 1870s, in dismay: her audience was in danger of disintegrating into feuding splinter factions, the broader culture found this infighting to be *prima facie* evidence of Spiritualism's lack of *gravitas*, and Britten's means of earning a living were threatened. I think her turn, after the demise of *The Western Star* in December of 1872, to galvanic medicine was an attempt to leave Spiritualism, and to establish an occupation for herself based on the relatively strong (as she saw it) science behind Mesmerism. Her return to Spiritualism, publicly, in late 1874 was a return to crisis (and an admission of the failure of her galvanic medical enterprise), and she met that crisis — with some assistance from Blavatsky, Olcott and others — by a turn toward the occult, to save Spiritualism from itself. Demarest, *Art Magic*, p. xlix.
[189] 'Is Spiritualism a Failure?', *Boston Daily Advertiser* (14 April 1873).
[190] Demarest, *Art Magic*, p. ix.
[191] It was in 1873 that a rivalry broke out between Mrs. Guppy, Florence Cook, and the Holmeses. In January 1873, Guppy called on the Holmes to assist her in throwing vitrial [sulphuric acid] into the face of the popular medium Florence Crook who was much prettier and more successful than Mrs. Guppy. Holmes refused to participate in this assault and ended up

being ousted out of Holmes' house where she was presently residing. Gup-py then turned against the Holmeses employing a confederate to sit for a séance and to light a match in the middle of some phenomena concerning levtitating instruments, thus revealing the strings attached to perform this illusion. This led to retaliation by Mr. Holmes who threatened to expose Guppy in a letter written to D. D. Home on 16 September 1876 and noted that 'If necessary, I can give you the details of the infamous transactions of Mrs. Guppy with Miss Emily Berry, 1 Hyde Park Place, also why Mrs. Guppy used her pretended mediumship for base purposes, and gave séanc-es solely for assignation meetings to better certain disreputable parties to further carry out their lewd propensities.' Ronald Pearsall, *The Table-Rappers* (New York: St. Martin's Press, 1972), pp. 49-50, 245. Soon thereafter the Holmeses were exposed by William Crookes around 1875 and the Theo-sophical Historian Michael Gomes noted that after which time 'coverage would be focused mainly on recurring exposures' instead of the phenome-na. Thus, at a minimum mainstream culture's acceptance of Spiritualism shifted from embracing to exposing during this time period. Gomes, *The Dawning of the Theosophical Movement*, p. 61. Also, *The Spiritualist* published a report in 1873 titled 'Spirit Forms' which explained an 'elaborate system of testing; had been developed that would protect mediums from the 'odium of being supposed to do the manifestations themselves,' and armed with this rational sitters began to search mediums prior to the séance and to bind them securely once were in the cabinet. Owen, *The Darkened Room*, p. 68.

[192] See Frank Podmore, *The Newer Spiritualism* (New York: Henry Holt and Company, 1911), p. 9. and Frank Podmore, *Modern Spiritualism: A History and a Criticism* (Methuen & Co., 1902), p. xiii.

[193] 'A Decline in Spiritualism', *The New York Times*, 23 February 1875.

[194] Helena Blavatsky, 'My Books,' in *H. P. Blavatsky: Collected Writings: 1890-1891*, comp. Boris De Zirkoff, 15 vols (Pasadena: CA: Theosophical Publishing House, 1966), XIII, 191-193 (p. 197).

[195] Henry Steel Olcott, 'The First Leaf of T. S. History', *The Theosophist*, 12:2 (November 1890), 65-70 (p. 68).

[196] Patrick Deveney *Astral Projection or Liberation of the Double and the Work of the Early Theosophical Society*, ed. James Santucci (Fullerton, CA: Theosophical History, 1997), p. 3.

[197] Deveney, *Astral Projection*, pp. 4-5.

[198] Deveney, *Astral Projection*, pp. 16-20.

[199] Demarest, *Art Magic*, p. x.

[200] Most of this article originally appeared in *Banner of Light* magazine though it was reprinted in the *Spiritual Scientist*. Emma Hardinge Britten, 'The Slan-derers of Art Magic', *The Spiritual Scientist*, 3:16 (23 December 1875), p. 183.

[201] Emma Hardinge Britten, 'Another Book on "Art Magic.'", *Spiritual Scien-tist*, 5:1 (6 September 1876), 8-9 (p. 8). The whole 'obligation of secrecy,'

was generally an unpopular shift in the early Theosophical Society proposed on 19 January 1876 and passed on 16 February. In an official letter sent out by the Theosophical Society on 30 March 1877 it was officially disseminated that the Society was now a 'secret organization.' Along with this declaration was included a list of Theosophical officer; it is curious to observe that when this list was reprinted in the April edition of the London *Spiritualist* Britten's name was replaced by C. C. Massey. Thus, Britten's resignation from the Society coincided with this secrecy shift though it seemed likely that her leaving probably had more to do with Blavatsky than secrecy. Michael Gomes, 'Studies in Early American Theosophical History', *The Canadian Theosophist*, 70: 4 (Sept.-Oct., 1989), 76-81 (pp. 79, 81). Gomes reprinted the actual 'Pledge of Secrecy' signed on 19 January in his *Dawning of the Theosophical Movement*, p. 91.

²⁰² Mathiesen, *Emma Hardinge Britten*, p. 41.

²⁰³ Marc Demarest, *Revising Mathiesen: Updating Richard Mathiesen's Work on Emma Hardinge Britten- REVISION 3- DRAFT*, (October 2009) <http://www.ehbritten.org/papers/revising_mathiesen.pdf> [accessed on 6 September 2011], p. 5.

²⁰⁴ *The Life and Letters of Charles Darwin*, 2 vols. ed. Francis Darwin (New York: D. Appleton and Company, 1887), I, p. 473.

²⁰⁵ Alfred R. Wallace,'The Origin of Human Races and the Antiquity of Man Deduced from the Theory of "Natural Selection"', *Journal of the Anthropological Society of London*, 2 (1864), clviii-clxxxvii (p. clix).

²⁰⁶ Wallace, 'The Origin of Human Races', p. clxiv.

²⁰⁷ Originally published by Alfred R. Wallace, 'The Origin of Human Races and the Antiquity of Man Deduced from the Theory of "Natural Selection"', *Journal of the Anthropological Society of London*, 2 (1864), clviii-clxxxvii (p. cixvi). though reprinted with this addition in Alfred Russel Wallace, *Contributions to the Theory of Natural Selection: A Series of Essays* (London: Macmillan and Co., 1875), pp. 325-326.

²⁰⁸ Wallace, *Contributions to the Theory of Natural Selection*, pp. 325-326.

²⁰⁹ Malcom Jay Kottler, 'Alfred Russel Wallace, the Origin of Man, and Spiritualism', *Isis*, 65: 2 (1974), 144-192 (p .147).

²¹⁰ Wallace, *Contributions to the Theory of Natural Selection*, p. 360.

²¹¹ Darwin's new focus on sexual selection was obvious in the title for this work: Charles Darwin, *The Descent of Man And Selection in Relation To Sex*, 2 vols. (New York: D, Appleton and Company, 1871), I, pp. 245- 409; Charles Darwin, *On The Origin of Species by Means of Natural Selection* (New York: D. Appleton and Company, 1869), pp. 83-85.

²¹² Janet Oppenheim, *The Other World: Spiritualism and Psychical Research in England- 1850-1914*, (Cambridge: University of Cambridge Press, 1985), p. 302.

²¹³ Wallace, *The Origin of Human Races*, p. clxviii.; Alfred R. Wallace, 'Mr. Wallace on Natural Selection Applied to Anthropology', *Anthropological Review*, 5:16 (1867), pp. 103-105 (p. 105).

[214] See Percival Lowell, *Mars and Its Canals* (London: The Macmillan Company, 1906).

[215] Alfred Wallace, *The World of Life: A Manifestation of Creative Power, Direct Mind And Ultimate Purpose* (New York: Moffat, Yard, and Company, 1916), pp. 380-381.

[216] 'Owing to the highly complex nature of the adjustments required to render the world habitable and to restrain its habitability during the aeons of time requisite for life-development, it is in the highest degree improbable that the required conditions and adaptations should have occurred in any other planets of any other suns, which might occupy an equally favourable positions as our won, and which were of the requisite size and heat-giving power.' Alfred R. Wallace, *Man's Place in the Universe: A Study of the Results of Scientific Research in Relation to the Unity of Plurality of Worlds* (New York: McClure, Phillips & Co., 1904), pp. 306, 318-319.

[217] Marchant, *Alfred Russel Wallace*, p. 67.

[218] A 'loo table' is a table with a round top used to play the popular Victorian card game 'Loo'. This game is typically played with five cards (though there was version that used three cards) that were dealt out to each player. Another card is turned up for the trump; the jack of clubs generally is the high card and it is called 'Pam.' Then the ace of trumps is the next highest card and then the rest in succession (similar to whist) [and poker]. Each player is allowed to change their cards in from the rest of the pack or of throwing up their hand 'in order to escape being looed. Those who play their cards either with or without changing, and do not gain a trick, are looed; as likewise is the case with all who have stood the game, if a flush occurs, which obliges each, except a player holding Pam, or an interior flush, to deposit a stake, to be divided among the winners at the ensuing deal, according to the tricks which may then be made. For instance, if everyone at dealing should take half-a-crown, the tricks are entitled to sixpence apiece, and whoever is looed must put down half-a-crown, exclusive of the deal: sometimes it is settled that each person looed shall pay a sum equal to what happens to be on the table at the time. Five card of a suit, or four with Pam, compose a flush, which sweeps the board, and yields only to a superior flush, or an equal one in the elder hand. When the ace of trumps is led, it is usual to say, "Pam, be civil;" the holder of Pam is then expected to let the ace pass.' Edmond, Hoyle, *Hoyle's Games: Improved and Enlarged by New and Practical Treatises* (London: Longman and Co., 1847), pp. 73-74.

[219] *Infinite Tropics: An Alfred Russel Wallace Anthology*, ed. Andrew Berry (New York: Verso, 2003), p. 233.

[220] Malcolm Jay Kottler, 'Alfred Russel Wallace, the Origin of Man and Spiritualist', *Isis*, 65:2 (June, 1974) 144-192 (p. 163).

[221] Alfred Russel Wallace, *Miracles and Modern Spiritualism: Three Essays* (London: James Burns, 1875), p. 128.

[222] Wallace, *Miracles and Modern Spiritualism*, p. 129.

[223] Wallace, *Miracles and Modern Spiritualism*, p. 132.

[224] Nicholas Goodrick-Clarke, *The Western Esoteric Traditions*, p. 174.

[225] Alan Gauld, *A History of Hypnotism*, p. 5.

[226] Gauld, *A History of Hypnotism*, pp. 205-206.

[227] Joel S. Schwartz, 'Darwin, Wallace, and the Descent of Man', *Journal of the History of Biology*, 17:2 (1984), 271-289 (p. 283).

[228] James Marchant, *Alfred Russel Wallace: Letters and Reminiscences* (New York: Harper & Brothers Publishers, 1916), p. 432.

[229] Richard Hodgson, 'Account of Personal Investigations in India, and Discussion of the Authorship of the Koot Hoomi Letters', *Proceedings of the Society for Psychical Research* (London: Trubner and Co., 1885), pp. 201-400.

[230] Wallace, *Miracles and Modern Spiritualism*, p. 101.

[231] Alfred Russel Wallace, *The World of Life: A Manifestation of Creative Power, Directive Mind and Ultimate Purpose* (NewYork: Moffat, Yard and Company, 1916), pp. 428-429.

[232] 'But there is for all an eternal progress, a progress solely dependent on the power of will in the development of spirit nature.' Wallace, *Miracles and Modern Spiritualism*, p. 109.

[233] Wallace, *On Miracles and Modern Spiritualism*, p. 116. The idea that the spirits do not know of any God are further illustrated in William Stainton Moses, *Higher Aspects of Spiritualism* (London: E. W. Allen & Co., 1880), p. 82.

[234] James Marchant, *Alfred Russel Wallace: Letters and Reminiscences* (New York: Harper & Brothers Publishers, 1916), p. 436.

[235] Martin Fichman, *An Elusive Victorian: The Evolution of Alfred Russel Wallace* (University of Chicago Press, 2004), p. 286.

[236] Alfred Russel Wallace, *The World of Life: A Manifestation of Creative Power, Directive Mind and Ultimate Purpose* (New York: Moffat, Yard, and Company, 1916), p. 431.

[237] Wallace, *On Miracles and Modern Spiritualism*, p. 116.

[238] Alfred Russel Wallace, *Studies Scientific & Social*, 2 Vols. (New York: Macmillan and Co., 1900), II, pp. 378-379.

[239] Wallace, *The World of Life*, pp. 423-424.

[240] Wallace wrote to the noted biologist Thomas H. Huxley (1825 – 1895) about his newfound beliefs in Spiritualism. Huxley (who was known as Darwin's bulldog for his strong Darwinian beliefs) responded in a letter dated November 1866: 'It may be all true, for anything I know to the contrary, but really I cannot get up any interest in the subject. I never cared for gossip in my life, and disembodied gossip, such as these worthy ghosts supply their friends with, is not more interesting to me than any other. As for investigating the matter, I have half-a-dozen investigations of infinitely greater interest to me to which any spare time I may have will be devoted. I give it up for the same reason I abstain from chess—it's too amusing to be fair work, and too hard work to be amusing.' Marchant, *Alfred Russel Wallace*, p. 418.

[241] Marchant, *Alfred Russel Wallace*, p. 417.

[242] Alfred W. Wallace, *A Defence of Modern Spiritualism* (Boston: Colby and Rich, 1874), p. 62.

[243] Goodrick-Clarke, *The Western Esoteric Traditions*, p. 216.

[244] Blavatsky, *Isis Unveiled*, I, 155, referencing Alfred R. Wallace, *The Geographical Distribution of Animals* (London, MacMillan and Co., 1876), pp. 6-7.

[245] Wallace, *The Geographical Distribution of Animals*, pp. 6-7.

[246] Wallace, *The World of Life*, pp. 423-424. 'At the birth of the future man, the monad, radiating with all the glory of its immortal parent which watches it from the seventh sphere [this is Kabbalistic terminology]...' Blavatsky, *Isis Unveiled*, I, p. 303.

[247] Blavatsky, *Isis Unveiled*, I, p. 296.

[248] Edward Bulwer-Lytton, *The Coming Race* (Edinburgh: William Blackwood and Sons, 1871), p. 48.

[249] Bulwer-Lytton, *The Coming Race*, pp. 16-17.

[250] It is interesting that Blavatsky never criticized the theories of Wallace in *Isis Unveiled*, but rather spoke of him with the greatest of admiration. All of the following passage were taken from Volume I: 'Science': p. 38: Blavatsky described Wallace as 'an eminent mind.'; p. 42: Blavatsky noted that Wallace was a superior man who was brave, loyal and highly commendable.; p. 55: Blavatsky called Wallace a great anthropologist.; p. 177: Wallace was called an esteemed and illustrious scientist.; p. 195: Blavatsky described Wallace's defense of psychic phenomena.; p. 293: Blavatsky made a comparison of Wallace's and Darwin natural selection.; p. 294: Blavatsky noted his belief in mental progression in natural selection.; p. 295: Wallace's pre-historic biology was mentioned.; p. 326: Wallace was noted for his theory noting the similarity between the brains of animals and savages.; p. 331: Blavatsky noted Wallace's theories concerning brain size.; p. 407: Wallace's generalization 'that there is no consensus on the nature and origin of man' was quoted by Blavatsky.; pp. 421-422: Wallace's definition of a miracle was noted as 'any act or event necessarily implying the existence and agency of superhuman intelligences.'; p. 428: Blavatsky simply noted that Wallace was an anthropologist and ex-materialist.

[251] Blavatsky, *Isis Unveiled*, I, p. 294.

[252] Oppenheim, *The Other World*, p. 470.

[253] Alfred Russel Wallace, 'Have We Lived on Earth Before? Shall We Live on Earth Again?', *The London*, 13:76, ed. Charles H. Smith (November 1904), 401-403 (p. 401).

[254] This was a widespread belief among the early Theosophical Society though it seems to have been largely based upon Madame Coulomb's (a detractor of the Theosophical Society) recollection of statement made by Blavatsky who claimed that 'Mr. Wallace and other Fellow's of the Royal Society' had joined the Theosophical Society. Emma Coulomb, *Some Accounts of my Intercourse with Madame Blavatsky from 1872-1884* (London: Eliot

Stock, 1885), p. 7. Also, this was also noted by 'ATS' in 'Theosophy in America', *The Theosophist*, 6:1 (October 1884), p. 25. Wallace's membership into the Theosophical Society was also confirmed in Emmett A. Greenwalt, *The Point Loma Community in California 1897-1942: A Theosophical Experiment* (Berkeley: University of California Press, 1955), p. 4. C. Jinarajadasa claimed Wallace's membership began in 1877 in his *Golden Book of the Theosophical Society* (Pasadena, CA: Theosophical Publishing House, 1925), p. 29. This connection was more recently purported by Bruce Campbell, *Ancient Wisdom Revived*, p. 87. These are just a few of the sources that admit Wallace's membership in the Theosophical Society without referring to any specific source material.

²⁵⁵ Henry S. Olcott, 'Spiritualism and Theosophy', *The Theosophist*, 2:3 (December 1880), 49-52 (p. 52).

²⁵⁶ Oppenheim, *The Other World*, p. 470.

²⁵⁷ H.P. Blavatsky, *The Letters of H.P. Blavatsky Volume 1: 1861-1879* (Wheaton, IL: Theosophical Publishing House, 2003), p. 362.

²⁵⁸ This appears to align with Wallace's personal chronology having lived at Rose Hill, Dorking, Surrey from July 1876–March 1878. George Beccaloni, 'Home Sweet Homes: A Biographical Tour of Wallace's Many Places of Residence', *Natural Selection and Beyond: The Intellectual Legacy of Alfred Russel Wallace*, ed. Charles H. Smith and George Beccaloni (Oxford: Oxford University Press, 2008), p. 33.

²⁵⁹ 'Cutting and Comments: Wallace to Blavatsky- 1 January 1878', in *The Theosophist*, 7:27 (April 1906), 559.

²⁶⁰ 'Wallace to Blavatsky', p. 559.

²⁶¹ Marchant, *Alfred Russel Wallace*, pp. 432-433.

²⁶² This is the conclusion of Sumathi Ramaswamy, *The Lost Land of Lemuria: Fabulous Geographies, Catastrophic Histories* (Berkeley: University of California Press, 2004), p. 253.

²⁶³ Henry S. Olcott, *People from the Other World* (Hartford: American Publishing Company, 1875).

²⁶⁴ 'Alfred Russell (sic) Wallace to H. S. Olcott: 1875', 53:11 (August, 1932), p. 494.

²⁶⁵ 'Theosophy and Spiritualism: Have they Common Ground?', *The Review of Reviews*, ed. W. T. Stead. 5 vols (London: The Review of Reviews, 1892), V, p. 479.

²⁶⁶ 'Theosophy and Spiritualism: Have they Common Ground?', V, p. 479.

²⁶⁷ 'On the Watch Tower', *Lucifer*, 10:57 (15 May 1892), 177-184 (p. 177).

²⁶⁸ 'Wallace wrote very little about Blavatsky, but he must have found Coué's brand of theosophy more congenial than hers, for the two men became good friends.' Ross A. Slotten, *The Heretic in Darwin's Court: The Life of Alfred Wallace* (New York: Columbia University Press, 2004), p. 388; 'Wallace regarded theosophy as bordering on the irrational.' Martin Fichman, *An Elusive Victorian: The Evolution of Alfred Wallace* (Chicago: University of Chi-

cago Press, 2004), p. 186. James Marchant in *Alfred Russel Wallace.*, Peter Raby in Alfred *Russel Wallace: A Life*, and Michael Shermer in *In Darwin's Shadow* all make mention of Wallace's membership into the Society of Psychical Research, but mention nothing concerning his membership in the Theosophical Society. No reference to the Society is found in: Lancelot Thomas Hogben, *Alfred Russel Wallace: The Story of a Great Discoverer* (London: Society for Promoting Christian Knowledge, 1918), pp. 64., Amabel Williams-Ellis, *Darwin's Moon: A Biography of Alfred Wallace* (London: Blackie, 1966), pp. 261., Harry Clement, *Alfred Russel Wallace: Biologist and Social Reformer* (London: Hutchinson, 1983), pp. 215.

Part VII.

CONCLUSION

7.1 The Final Word: Concluding an Inconclusive Study

Multiple biographies of various individuals have been introduced in this work for the purpose of understanding the complex relationship between Theosophy and Spiritualism in the late nineteenth-century. After completing this study, it should seem evident to the reader that this relationship was much more complex than a simplistic dualist 'yes' or 'no' answer could provide; rather, the lines separating these two movements were never clearly defined and this relationship varied based on who was describing this relationship and during what time period. This conclusion is perhaps best exemplified in one of the primary co-founders of the Theosophical Society- the life of Madame Blavatsky.

As Alvin Kuhn noted in his chapter 'From Spiritualism to Theosophy' in his *Theosophy*: 'Nothing seems more certain than that Madame Blavatsky had no definitive idea of what the finished product was to be when she gave the initial impulse to the movement. She knew the general direction in which it would have to seek." That direction appeared to be Spiritualism. Blavatsky's feelings towards Spiritualism were continuously shifting though in her early days it remains indisputable that she identified with Spiritualism through her zealous conversion (whether under D. D. Home or not) and in her establishment of the Société Spirite in Egypt. Furthermore, Blavatsky went on to establish the Theosophical Society along with a dozen other individuals in 1875 which was founded as a reformative and philosophically advanced Spiritualist organization. From its inception, the Theosophical Society appeared to adopt a Western Esoteric view of Spiritualism as evidenced through both Blavatsky and Olcott's articles in the *Spiritualist Scientist*, but also in Olcott's first presidential address.

Blavatsky viewed her role in this new movement as a reformer bent on establishing a philosophically sound statement of belief and systematizing an order which would provide safeguards for its practitioners. In a period which saw the exposures of many respected mediums, Blavatsky responded by establishing her 'theory of elementals' which justified the widespread fraudulency of such mediums by blaming their actions on manipulating and deceitful spirits; however, her views did not receive the type of reception that she had hoped. After the inception of the Theosophical Society in 1875, Blavatsky seemingly abandoned the early Society in favor of composing her work *Isis Unveiled* which was published in 1877. In 1879, Blavatsky relocated the Theosophical headquarters to India aligning her organization with the Hindu fundamentalist group the Arya Samaj. Regardless of this later Oriental emphasis and the relocation of the Theosophical Society to India in 1879, Blavatsky still made provision for the basic tenet of Spiritualism throughout her later writings.

In 1874, Blavatsky teamed up with the credulous Colonel Olcott whom she had met while attending a séance at the Eddy Brothers farm in Chittenden, Vermont. Olcott had already established his own vehicle to disseminate his personal opinions through his employment as a reporter for the New York *Daily Graphic*. Through Olcott Blavatsky had opened an avenue for promulgating her ideology to the Western world, especially through their alliance with Gerry Brown and the *Spiritual Scientist* whose article's evidenced the strong influence of both Western Esotericism (occultism) and Spiritualism on these two founding figures. Blavatsky's belief in 'Theosophy' was shown to be directly connected to her idea of an ancient wisdom tradition (*prisca theologia*) explained in her *Isis Unveiled* and *Secret Doctrine.*

Olcott had similarly emerged out of a Spiritualist background influenced by his uncles, through his involvement with an all male Spiritualist circle in Ohio and his early communications with Andrew Jackson Davis. Furthermore, although Olcott's philosophy appeared 'Eastern' it contained many basic Western elements apparent through the implementation of mesmeric healings on his third tour of Ceylon in 1882, the setting up of Sunday Buddhist schools similar to the Sunday Lyceum, and through his heavy Presbyterian influence as noted by Stephen Prothero. The influence of Spiritualism on Olcott's form of Theosophy was recognized by the contemporary Indian religious leader Swami Vivekananda who categorized Olcott's teachings as an 'Indian grafting of American Spiritualism;' thus, evidencing a Spiritualist continuity to the Theosophical belief system.

The mere fact that Olcott was able to maintain 'life-long' and 'intimate' relationships with two of the main representatives and advocates of Spiritualism in the Victorian era illustrate that the alleged issues separating Theosophy from Spiritualism were really not all that divisive. Olcott's later expeditions in Ceylon and his writing of *Bud-*

dhist Catechisms reveal a clear 'Oriental shift' in his philosophy though his healings that he began practicing on his third missionary journey were derivative from his mesmeric practices from the West. Through his experience in the East, Olcott implemented an extremely inclusive ideology in the Theosophical Society which centered upon the concept of brotherhood. Inside this inclusivity the door seemingly remained opened for Spiritualists who were allowed access into this eclectic movement. Thus, Olcott could be accused of being eclectic though he did not seem hostile towards Spiritualists.

The history of Spiritualism remains a fascinating and incomplete study in its own right with numerous practitioners who have been neglected by modern history. Despite this gap in the historical record, the parallels that existed between Spiritualism and Theosophy include the 'precipitated' writings of the Davenport Boys and their creation of a Spirit being named 'John King' who went on to become the sole invisible friend reconceptualized by Madame Blavatsky. John King provides a definitive and continual link between Blavatsky and Spiritualism. Though King eventually became the servant to the Brotherhood of Luxor he soon vanished out of the pages of Theosophical literature only to become replaced (or reconceptualized) as Blavatsky's Tibetan masters.

Also connecting these two movements were certain common philosophical elements and traits. An examination of Andrew Jackson Davis brought forth many similar conceptualizations including his move away from the séance driven Spiritualism towards a philosophically ordered branch, his belief in harmonial philosophy which focused upon the brotherhood of humanity, his communication with a spiritually-evolved being, and his translation of an unknown language. Additionally, it seems probable that Blavatsky's development of her 'elementals' was inspired by Davis' belief in *diakkas*.

Despite the enormous influence of American Spiritualism on Blavatsky it remained apparent that the Theosophical Society was also in no small way impacted by the teachings of Allan Kardec and his Spiritist movement of nineteenth century France. Kardec's views of innumerable spheres, reincarnation, the progression of the soul from matter to spirit, and his view of infinite time aligned with Blavatsky's conceptualizations found in her philosophy. Furthermore, Blavatsky could be directly connected to the Spiritist movement because in 1871 she established the Société Spirite in Cairo to teach Kardec's philosophy. It was also put forth that Blavatsky had mentioned the 'fluidic perisprit' (sic) as the astral soul in *The Secret Doctrine* and Blavatsky's view of 'fohat' seemed to resemble this philosophy in her later writings. This direct connection between Spiritism and Theosophy was also noticed by those contemporary with Blavatsky most notably by W. F. Kirby a reporter for *Time Magazine* who noted that 'Among the various American and European systems of spiritualists philosophy which there are several, Spiritism...is most closely allied to Theosophy.'

Using Janet Oppenheim's brilliant (though sometimes disputed) comparison of Spiritualism and Theosophy some of the similar basic beliefs adhered to by both organizations prompted her to observe that 'on a wide range of other issues, however, Theosophical convictions were scarcely distinguishable from spiritualist arguments.' These issues included a shared desire to combat materialism which entailed understanding that spirit existed independently of matter, the promotion of a universal brotherhood through shared religious beliefs, the development of human faculties for their profound capabilities, and an attempt to attach meaning to life and death in a materialist age and culture. Also, of note was the fact that in the nineteenth century it was not uncommon for an individual to identify themselves as both a Theosophist and a Spiritualist (as seen in C. C. Massey, William Stainton Moses, and Emily Kislingbury) evidencing that these two belief structures remained reconcilable at least by certain members.

The following section dealt briefly with the role of newspapers in understanding the relationship of Spiritualism and Theosophy though this relationship remained ambiguous even in examining these diverse articles. Despite discovering a wide range of differing views on the nature of this relationship; nonetheless, it was not uncommon for writers to define 'Theosophy' as a Spiritualist movement, thus, solidifying the thesis of this work. The intriguing section on the *Medium and Daybreak* has revealed that Blavatsky was viewed by her contemporaries as a mundane medium that simply relocated to an Eastern setting. This idea was evident first in the quote made by Scrutator Junior: 'we have heard of Madame Blavatsky, we conclude that she is just an ordinary physical medium;' and, secondly, by both James Burns and William Henry Harrison who agreed that Blavatsky (even in her later years) was an advanced Spiritualist medium possessing advanced psychical abilities whose phenomena remained commonplace, similar to those produced by D. D. Home and Mrs. Guppy. Thus, according to these Spiritualist writers Blavatsky's production of phenomena was nothing incredible. This very belief that

Blavatsky remained a Spiritualist medium in the eyes of contemporaneous Spiritualists lends authority to the general thesis of this work.

Blavatsky theatrically employed a 'hypnotic' writing formula for her texts which appeared similar to the automatic writings of Spiritualism; it was also shown that her discovery of precipitated messages had historical precedence in the séances of the Davenport brothers. An examination of Blavatsky's major works yielded important affinities with Spiritualism; however, it also illustrated some of the distinctions between these two groups as Blavatsky's thought process evolved to include ideas of root races, annihilation, and the belief that Nimranayakas (i.e. adepts and masters) could control mediums. These ideas evidenced Blavatsky's 'Oriental shift' (which was much more apparent that actual) and her assimilation of various religious philosophies into her Theosophy. Blavatsky's assimilation of Eastern influences combined with her belief in Western Esotericism made her branch of Spiritualism more unique (though not unlike Freemasonry and the Rosicrucianism). The very fact that Blavatsky kept the Theosophical Society open to Spiritualists seemed implied in the inclusive title of her monthly periodical: *The Theosophist: A Monthly Journal devoted to Oriental Philosophy, Art, Literature and Occultism:* **Embracing** *Mesmerism,* **Spiritualism,** *and Other Secret Sciences.*

Throughout her major works the evolution of Blavatsky's belief in the basic tenet of Spiritualism continuously changed. In *Isis Unveiled* (1877) the major determining factor for spirit communications concerned the relationship of the medium to the deceased; other instances of communications with the spirit world were related to the 'will' of the medium and adepts though the end result was that the basic tenet of Spiritualism found sympathy in this earlier work. In the Mahatma letters the medium's connection with the discarnate soul remained accessible with those souls who were either the products of suicide or other violent and/or accidental deaths. These same sentiments are echoed in *Esoteric Buddhism* (1883); however, in *The Secret Doctrine* (1888) it seemed that mediums had lost any ability to communicate with departed spirits. This belief would be counteracted in *The Key to Theosophy* (1889) which claimed that the medium could communicate with the departed soul only in the rarest of circumstances which included the two following exceptions: 1) the soul was in a unique pre-devachanic state or they 2) could communicate through a mahatma.

It is curious that all of Blavatsky's major works allowed a provision for the basic doctrine of Spiritualism except for *The Secret Doctrine*. It is here that William Stainton Moses' 'alliance' with Blavatsky remains crucial towards understanding her opinion of Spiritualists during this time period. An alleged 'alliance' was suggested between these two prominent figures that each of them would attempt to influence their organizations to become more sympathetic to one another. Though this 'alliance' was not embraced by the Spiritualist public at large; nonetheless, the very fact that Blavatsky consciously attempted to make her Society more inclusive of Spiritualists and their beliefs reveals the close doctrinal beliefs between these two organizations. Thus, Blavatsky and her Theosophical Society's acceptance of Spiritualism remained evident throughout her major writings and their history.

A series in the monthly periodical the *Theosophist* titled 'Fragments of Occult Truth' provided Blavatsky with an opportunity to make a distinct break away from Spiritualism; however, she followed these articles (originally published and compiled by A. O. Hume based on the Mahatma Letters he had received) with a follow up column in January 1882 called 'It is Idle to Argue Further.' The 'Fragments of Occult Truth' apparently caused dissent among Spiritualist Theosophists which led Blavatsky to print this follow-up article which was apologetic in nature and stated that this misunderstanding which had arisen as a result of these articles was simply an issue of semantics and that 'as for the rest, we are at one with the Spiritualists with but slight variances, more of form than of substance' (it is curious that reading this series of articles 'Fragments of Occult Truth' motivated the French Spiritists to break away from the Society disgruntled at the septenary constitution and annihilation of the soul had they of translated this article they could have observed Blavatsky's shifting attitude).

Blavatsky's critics provided an alternative image of Blavatsky and the Theosophical Society during this time period. It is curious that while some of her critics argued to prove that Blavatsky was simply a Spiritualist medium, others (such as Emma Hardinge Britten) attempted to disassociate Blavatsky from the Spiritualist movement altogether- two opposing approaches with the same goal. One such critic of the first camp was the British war veteran Arthur Lillie. Lillie's arguments were not unique and his 'conspiracy-theory' style of accusations seemed harsh; however, he identified some valid points especially related to Blavatsky's Spiritualist practices. His final conclusions were that *Esoteric Buddhism* represented a perverted form of American Spiritualism and that Blavatsky was nothing more than a

Spiritualist medium that moved to the East. A similar argument was raised by one of Blavatsky's most well known critics the Spiritualist William Emmette Coleman.

Coleman criticized Blavatsky for her use of sources and her blatant plagiarisms. Though he seemingly approached his investigation of Theosophy with an open-mind towards the possible benefit that it could have exerted on the cause of Spiritualism, Coleman eventually came to the conclusion that Blavatsky was a fraud. Arriving at this initial conclusion, Coleman (in keeping with Lillie) attempted to paint Blavatsky as a rogue medium who was a self-centered and confused Spiritualist. Coleman's final conclusion of Theosophy appeared to be that it was a perversion of Spiritualism and was based upon the eclectic and continuously shifting opinions of Madame Blavatsky. He believed that a more appropriate name for Theosophy was 'Blavatskyism' as all of the doctrines of this movement were the product of Blavatsky's creative imagination. This 'Blavatskyism' was a philosophically eclectic belief that remained connected to Spiritualism in some of its ideologies and its phenomena as evidenced through the connection which Coleman observed.

Of course, Richard Hodgson's work and his report for the Society for Psychical Research (1884/5) remained a crucial aspect of this study though not for the reason that many other biographers have mentioned. Hodgson's work illustrated that Blavatsky never received the confirmation and validation that she so desperately desired to receive from Western Spiritualism. Blavatsky's willingness to become subjective to the investigations of this Western pseudo-scientific research organization could be used to argue that she strongly desired to be vindicated and validated by Western Spiritualism especially from the Kiddle incident that resulted in negative news coverage for the Theosophical Society. Hodgson's report indicated that many of the unique manifestations that occurred in India were based on cultural issues such as the primitiveness of the indigenous natives and the fact that their roofs were not made of plaster which made them conducive to letters falling. Emma Coulomb the infamous Theosophical detractor echoed these sentiments in her work noting that the mango trees and their branches provided an ideal frame for dropping letters on unsuspecting individuals giving the illusion that these letters had fallen out of the sky. Hodgson's subsequent conversion to Spiritualism seems important though it is curious that he never recanted his report on the Theosophical Society. Though many aspects of Hodgson's report remain disputable; nonetheless, it is important in its comparison of Blavatsky's phenomena with Western Spiritualism and the analogies and correspondences that are implied in the early reports in the S. P.R. journals

Another Spiritualist, Emma Hardinge Britten maintained an unusual relationship with the early Theosophical Society. She went from being a faithful member (even allowing the Society to meet in her house) to being one if its chief adversaries during Blavatsky's final years. Britten and Blavatsky shared a similar Type A personality and a desire to reinstitutionalize Spiritualism in order to earn a living. It seemed that Britten's belief that both Spiritualism and Theosophy could not be reconciled stemmed from her personal experience with Blavatsky and may have concerned a personal issue between these two dynamic personalities (rather than the philosophical alignment of Theosophy and Spiritualism). Britten ardently campaigned against Theosophy and after hearing about the demise of Blavatsky went on to publish a series of articles in the *Two Worlds* describing the history of the Theosophical Society from her own perspective (skewed as it may have been). The irony is that Britten's continual and hostile treatment of Theosophy in the *Two Worlds* revealed something that it seemed Britten was hoping to hide: the very fact that Britten continually attempted to demarcate the lines between Theosophy and Spiritualism evidenced that these lines were probably not very distinguishable. If these two organizations were clearly defined there would have been little need to publish articles like the ones Britten had in her periodical; rather, the differences would have been obvious. Yet, Britten herself admitted that she received countless letters explaining that these two organizations were aligned philosophically and should therefore partner together. Thus, it seemed that even though Britten saw a clear philosophical distinction between these two movements these differences were not as apparent to many of her contemporaries.

The final character studied was Alfred Russel Wallace who proved an integral part of this research though not so much for his actions and writings, but for how Blavatsky used him and his writings in her own work. Blavatsky claimed that Wallace was a member of the Theosophical Society even though this seemed extremely unlikely given the evidence explored in this section. Furthermore, Blavatsky took his work and applied it to particular situations that Wallace had never intended. In the end, Wallace was known for his involvement in Spiritualism and was requested by Annie Besant in 1892 to fill out a survey form in order to publicize the common ground between these two movements. This implied that the lines between Theosophical Society and Spiritualism were not clearly defined at this time in 1892 and his excuse for not participating was that he did not see a clear difference in questions related to the spirit and its ability to communicate; thus, illustrating that it was not uncommon for prominent Spiritualists in the nineteenth century to view Theosophy as aligning with the Spiritualist view of spirit communications.

Each of the above facts presented in this study, illustrate that the lines between the Theosophical Society and Spiritualism were never clearly defined even as late as 1892 one year after Blavatsky's death. These facts exhibit a continual connection between the Theosophical Society and Spiritualism both in philosophy and methodology, but also in shared membership. Some type of connection did exist between the Theosophical Society and Spiritualism though to what degree remains inconclusive as this relationship varied and continuously shifted; however, the author feels completely justified in claiming that the Theosophical Society remained completely inclusive and accessible to Spiritualists from the years 1875-1891 and could in fact have been considered a Spiritualist organization during this time period.

****

In this work I have tried to clearly present many of the facts related to this ever changing relationship between the Theosophical Society and Spiritualism. After embarking on this historical journey I feel it is appropriate for me to take these facts and lay out my own opinion on how these two organizations interacted during this time period. I believe that there is sufficient ground to prove that Blavatsky intentionally kept the Theosophical Society accessible to Spiritualists in order to gain prestige and fund her own movement. It seemed around the years 1887-1888 that Blavatsky began to re-shape her philosophy to exclude Spiritualists until her recorded alliance in 1888 with William Stainton Moses through which she would again accept the basic tenet of Spiritualism (to some degree) up until her death in 1891.

Blavatsky's 'double-faced attitude toward Spiritualism' and her desire to convert Spiritualists to Theosophy seemed to be not so much an attempt to change Spiritualist belief systems, but to institutionalize (and to some degree capitalize) upon this belief system and extract annual dues, sell magazine subscriptions, and to add to the prestige of the Society.² Furthermore, despite my reluctance to advocate this idea, I believe that Lillie's postulation of the opportune Blavatsky demands serious attention in future studies. Also, it seems apparent that Blavatsky blatantly staged phenomena in order to gain an audience for her reformed philosophy which was continually shifting. Blavatsky changed her doctrines in order to benefit herself though not primarily for monetary gain. Rather, it remains perfectly plausible that Blavatsky genuinely believed in Western Esotericism (occult) and that this was connected to the universal religion which manifested itself in Spiritualism and was the basis of all world religions; however, she also maintained a controlling and dominating personality doing whatever was necessary to instill herself with a sense of meaning and purpose by proving that she was unique and that she alone possessed the ability to reveal the hidden knowledge through her works which humanity needed in order to evolve to the next stage in their spiritual evolution. For this reason, the Theosophical Society remained an embracing organization for Spiritualist members.

In closing, it seems appropriate to end with a quote from one of Blavatsky's faithful followers - Alfred Percy Sinnett. Sinnett while writing apologetically on the relationship between Spiritualism and the Theosophical Society attempted to prove that Blavatsky had continually maintained an inclusive attitude towards Spiritualism even in her later years. When the 1913 version of *Incidents in the Life of Madame Blavatsky* was published Sinnett added the following notes on page 140 (some may take this excerpt to evidence that Sinnett had his own brand/version of Theosophy; however, given Blavatsky's shifting attitude toward Spiritualism this 'story' seems entirely plausible).

This addendum was covertly placed in the body of the text directly following Blavatsky's statement concerning the Arya Samaj and Spiritualism in Blavatsky's new Hermetic flavor: 'we mean to fight the prejudices of the Sceptics… and to show certain fallacies of the Spiritists. If we are anything, we are *Spiritualists*, only not on the modern American fashion, but on that of ancient Alexandria, with its Theodadiktoi, Hypatias, and Porphyries.' Sinnett followed this bold declaration with the following 'addendum' concerning Spiritualism; it concludes by noting again the wavering attitude that Blavatsky exhibited towards the open doctrine of Spiritualism and her desire to amend it:

> For the new edition of this book I must here interpolate a note warning the reader against too submissive an acceptance of the

views set forth in the letter quoted above. I do not think Mme. Blavatsky would have endorsed them at a later stage of her occult education. However frequently it may happen that communication from the astral world may be confused and corrupted by the unconscious influence of imperfectly developed mediums, it does not by any means follow that in all cases the 'spirits' of the séance room are 'empty materialized shadows' or 'simulacra of men and women made up of terrestrial passions and vices, etc.' It was not till long after the date of the letter quoted that Mme. Blavatsky shared with myself in India the fuller teaching concerning life on the astral and higher planes of consciousness which put an intelligible face on the variegated and often bewildering experiences of spiritualism. That great movement was as definitely designed by higher wisdom for the illumination of civilized mankind, as the far greater movement that has since put us in touch with the mysteries of the higher occultism- that it was simply designed to break down the materialistic drift of thinking that was prevalent in the middle of the last century. It was designed simply to show us that there was another life for human beings after the death of the physical body. Those who had passed on, and were living on the astral plane, were furnished with a means of making their continued existence known to friends still in incarnation. Of course these opportunities were available for great numbers of astral entities surviving from the ignoble varieties of mankind, and many of these may have flocked in during Mme. Blavatsky's investigations of current spiritualism, confirming impressions she had acquired concerning the characteristics of the astral plane life; but multitudes of spiritualists knew perfectly well that they often had touch with departed friends still maintaining the personalities of the earth life, and in this way it unfortunately happened that Mme. Blavatsky's sweeping condemnation of all spiritualism as delusive and unwholesome alienated large numbers of people who ought to have been the most ardent sympathizers with the Theosophical movement. All later students of occultism know now that the astral plane plays a much more important part in the future life of most people 'passing on' than the misleading old 'shell' theory led us to suppose in the beginning.[3]

Notes

[1] Alvin Boyd Kuhn, *Theosophy: A Modern Revival of Ancient Wisdom* (New York: Henry Holt and Company, 1930), p. 89.

[2] Kuhn, *Theosophy*, p. 94.

³ *Incidents in the Life of Madame Blavatsky*, ed. A. P. Sinnett (London: The Theosophical Publishing House, 1913), p .140.

Index

A

Adepts (see 'masters'), 2, 22, 29, 31,
33, 46, 49, 50-56, 60-62, 66-68, 75,
80, 83, 85, 89-90, 93, 95, 97, 101,
108, 123, 134, 154, 172, 175-178,
181, 193, 200, 202, 212, 215, 222,
239, 247, 252, 264, 270, 282-283,
287, 298, 304, 311, 335, 342, 344,
346, 357, 359
Aksakoff, Alexandr Nikolayevich,
39-40, 127-128
Art Magic, 46, 92, 176, 295, 297-301,
307-308, 312-313, 346-348
Arya Samaj, 31-32, 75, 90, 141, 356,
364
ascent/descent theory, 146, 184, 218-
219

B

Banner of Light, 3, 23, 59, 88, 118, 312,
348
Besant, Annie, 35, 68-70, 94, 97, 147,
228, 293, 332-333, 344, 362
Bettanelly, Michael, 23, 307
Blavatsky, Helena Petrovna, 1-3, 5,
7-11, 13-26, 28-56, 59-60, 62-64,
66-72, 74-76, 78, 80-98, 101, 107-
108, 112-114, 117, 120, 123-130,
133-148, 150, 152-173, 175-199,
201-210, 212-226, 228-232, 237-
248, 251-275, 278, 281-290, 292-
294, 297-302, 304-315, 317, 322,
325-332, 334-341, 343, 345-349,
352-353, 355-366
Britten, Emma Hardinge, 14, 26, 46-
47, 50, 60, 75, 92-93, 105-107, 112,
116-117, 129, 145, 158, 160-161,

168, 176, 180, 188, 242, 263, 292,
294, 297, 307, 311, 313, 315, 345-
349, 360, 362
Britten, William, 168, 176, 242, 296-
297, 313, 345-346
Brotherhood of Luxor, 25, 29, 49,
52-54, 56, 94, 97, 357
Brown, Eldridge Gerry, 25-26, 88,
91, 159, 338, 356
Burns, James, 152-156, 160, 164, 166,
168, 350, 358
Burr, William, 43, 270
Bush, George, 115

C

Chevalier, Louis, 176
Coleman, William Emmette, 30, 55,
89, 92, 156, 182-183, 192, 195,
202, 214, 228, 242, 254, 257, 262-
267, 269-274, 336-337, 339-341,
361
Corson, Hiram, 39, 44, 48, 134-135,
178-180, 307
Coulomb, Emma, 87, 202, 212, 214,
246, 282-285, 343-344, 352, 361
Countess of Caithness, Marie, 91,
141, 143, 145
Countess Wachtmeister, 97, 215-217,
239, 246, 332

D

Darwin, Charles, 99, 146, 166, 181,
184, 220, 315-317, 325, 349, 351-
353
Davenport Brothers- Ira Erastus and
William Henry, 50, 100-108, 157-
159, 175, 223, 357, 359
Davids, Thomas William Rhys, 70,
192, 195, 243, 264-265, 268
Davis, Andrew Jackson, 3-4, 57, 60,
85, 95, 108-109, 111, 121, 124-126,
128-130, 134, 144, 159-163, 168,

P-307 APB married Michael Bettanelly
in 1875 until May-25-1878 in
Either NY or Peoro Philladelphia.

CPSIA information can be obtained at www.ICGtesting.com
Printed in the USA
LVOW121011260212

270478LV00002B/42/P

9 781612 335537